THE SIMPLE ABUNDANCE PRESS

SCRIBNER

Also by Sarah Ban Breathnach

Simple Abundance:
A Yearbook of Comfort and Joy

The Simple Abundance Journal of Gratitude

Something More: Excavating Your Authentic Self

The Illustrated Discovery Journal:
Creating a Visual Autobiography of Your Authentic Self

The Simple Abundance Companion

A Man's Journey to Simple Abundance

Sarah Ban Breathnach's Mrs. Sharp's Traditions:
Reviving Victorian Family Celebrations

The Victorian Nursery Companion

ROMANCING
THE
ORDINARY

A Year of Simple Splendor

Sarah Ban Breathnach

THE SIMPLE ABUNDANCE PRESS

SCRIBNER

New York   London   Toronto   Sydney   Singapore

1230 Avenue of the Americas
New York, NY 10020

Permissions start on p. 558

SCRIBNER and design are trademarks of Macmillan Library Reference USA, Inc.,
used under license by Simon & Schuster, the publisher of this work.

For information regarding special discounts for bulk purchases
please contact Simon & Schuster Special Sales at 1-800-456-6798
or business@simonandschuster.com

DESIGNED BY ERICH HOBBING

Text set in Granjon

Manufactured in the United States of America

1   3   5   7   9   10   8   6   4   2

Library of Congress Cataloging-in-Publication Data

Ban Breathnach, Sarah.
Romancing the ordinary: a year of simple splendor/Sarah Ban Breathnach.
p. cm.
1. Women—Conduct of life. 2. Spirituality. 3. Simplicity.
4. Self-actualization (Psychology) I. Title.

BJ1610 .B36 2002
158.1—dc21
2002026653

ISBN 0-7432-1877-9

There is only one romance—the Soul's.

— W. B. YEATS

To my Sirs with love
and
Anne Windsor
with boundless gratitude

From Heaven to Earth, from Heart to Reader,
Past shoals to safe harbor
on her good watch.

Contents

Upon Reading This Book

January

February

March

April

May

June

July

August

September

xiv

And did you get what
you wanted from this life, even so?
I did.
And what did you want?
To call myself beloved, to feel myself
beloved on the earth.

—Raymond Carver
"Late Fragment"

Upon Reading
This Book

Use your eyes as if tomorrow you would be stricken blind. . . . Hear the music of voices, the song of the bird, the mighty strains of an orchestra, as if you would be stricken deaf tomorrow. Touch each object as if tomorrow your tactile sense would fail. Smell the perfume of the flowers, taste with relish each morsel, as if tomorrow you could never smell and taste again. Make the most of every sense; glory in all the facets of pleasure and beauty which the world reveals to you.

—Helen Keller

Dear Reader,

Welcome. If you're a new acquaintance, I hope that by the end of our year together you'll think of me as a good friend. And if you're a cherished chum, welcome back. How wonderful to be in your dear company again! However, no matter the depth of our affinity, I think that you're in for as much of a treat reading this book as I had in living and writing it. In fact, at times *Romancing the Ordinary* was the happiest writing I have ever done, which I find odd because it was conceived during a dark season of my life, when I had lost all hope that I would ever be happy again.

During the mid-1980s, while eating out, I discovered that

1

Chicken Little knew what she was talking about: the sky *could* fall suddenly, and it landed on my head by way of a large ceiling panel, knocking me onto the table. No one else in the restaurant was hit.

Although I never lost consciousness, I sustained a head injury that left me bedridden, confused, and disoriented for months, and partially disabled for a year and a half. During the first few months of recuperation, my senses were all skewed. Without warning, the unimaginable scenario Helen Keller challenges us to contemplate became very real for me. My eyesight was blurry and I was extremely sensitive to light, so the shades in my bedroom had to be pulled down at all times. Even seeing the different patterns on the quilt on my bed jarred my equilibrium, so much so that it had to be turned over to the plain muslin backing.

I couldn't listen to music because it made me dizzy; I couldn't carry on telephone conversations because, without visual clues such as reading lips, I couldn't process the sounds coming through my ears and rearrange them into meaningful patterns in my brain.

I couldn't taste my food or smell the luscious fragrance of my baby daughter's hair after it was washed. There were days when the slightest touch was painful; something as light as a sheet on my bare legs became unbearably heavy. Pulling a sweater on over my elbows caused the same kind of jolt that you get hearing fingernails scratching down a chalkboard.

Other senses I had taken for granted my entire life became strangers and I sorely missed them. Like a cat who's had her whiskers trimmed, I lost my *sense of balance,* as well as my perception of depth and distance. Because of the accident I was denied the consolation of my keenest companions—the written and spoken word—not to mention my livelihood, and my *sense of belonging* as a journalist writing regularly for one of the most prestigious newspapers in the country. Having to spend my days in bed and not in the company of my family, unable to care for my daughter, I lost my *sense of identity;* if I wasn't a wife, mother, writer, who was I? In one freak moment, my *sense of humor, sense of place, sense of purpose, sense of safety,* and, most important, *sense of peace* were erased.

These unsettling side effects lasted for a few months and had an impact on my life in ways I could scarcely have imagined. Because I was unable to speak articulately or read with comprehension, I was overcome with a *sense of shame;* and when I was no longer confined to bed, I felt so embarrassed that I didn't venture farther than my own backyard. Naturally this reluctance even to visit friends contributed to my growing *sense of isolation.* All that filled my days was an enormous feeling of loss, only to be replaced during the nights by a terrifying dread about my unknown future.

Reliving those difficult days with you now on the page brings tears to my eyes. However, as the poet Robert Frost confessed, "No tears in the writer, no tears in the reader. No laughter in the writer, no laughter in the reader." Gratefully, my story has a wonderful, almost fairy-tale ending. But eighteen years ago, if you had told me that I would not only recover remarkably but go on to become a bestselling author, publisher, and speaker, I would have thought you cruel and sent you packing.

During this senseless period, I also tried to send Spirit packing with my bitter "why me, why this, why now?" litany, because my bizarre accident made no sense. Why had God singled me out for this misery? Of course, now I know that the accident wasn't an act of God, but a head-on collision between circumstance, fate, karma or planetary alignments, and human error—the fact that the panel hadn't been completely screwed back in place after a repair to an air-conditioning duct. But Spirit uses each event in our lives to draw closer to us. I believe, with every fiber of my being, that when we are struck down by adversity, God weeps with us and, then, because we are so loved, heals us in ways we can never expect or even imagine. My downtime was a perfect opportunity for Heaven to get my complete attention. There were priceless spiritual lessons to be discerned. I was about to become an apprentice to the supreme Alchemist—and learn the secret of the ages: how to turn our hours of lead into days of gold. If you're game, I'd like to share this secret with you on these pages.

Chief among your discoveries: that *Surprise* is another one of Spirit's concealed names and Divinity is to be found where and when you least expect it. Moses found his God in a burning bush. I found mine in a pot of homemade spaghetti sauce. I'm hoping you will discover that God is present in the exquisite warmth of a soft blanket on a chilly night, the soothing sips of chamomile tea when you're weary, the fragrance of homegrown roses.

After my accident, the spaghetti sauce was the first thing that I had been able to smell distinctly in months. As the aroma of a friend's kind gift simmering on the stove wafted upstairs to my bedroom, I could scarcely believe my nose. Euphoric, I followed the strange but familiar fragrance of garlic, onions, plum tomatoes, peppers, and oregano down the stairs and into the kitchen. I was beside myself with delight. Instinctively, I was moved to take off my shoes. I knew I was standing on holy ground in my own house. I had discovered the miracle of the sacred in the ordinary and my life would forever be changed.

Taking a spoon, I dipped it into the source of my delirium and brought it to my lips. Although smell and taste are the two most closely related senses, I still wasn't able to taste the sauce, just distinguish temperature and texture. It didn't matter. I was so grateful to inhale the glorious scent of ordinary life, I needed nothing more. I went up to the bathroom and got out a jar of Vicks VapoRub. Yes! Eucalyptus! Next, the soiled laundry on the basement floor, which smelled, marvelously, like rank, dirty clothes. I was so invigorated by my sudden turn for the better that I was inspired to do the wash. After a few months of not participating in the details of daily life, I found that this most mundane household task took on a mystical quality. When I buried my face in the warm laundry and deeply inhaled the fragrance of a fresh shirt, I was enfolded in the palpable loving presence of Spirit.

And so it went. For the next few happy weeks I rediscovered Life with the audible sniffs of an inquisitive bloodhound and the same exuberant sense of wonder as my little girl. Taste came next, followed by hearing, sight, and touch. Each sensory restoration became a spiritual revelation in the truest sense of the expression, for each revealed not only a strange new world but a strange new woman embracing her own astonishment. Like any rapprochement after a long and painful estrangement, each sensory reunion was accompanied by unexpected rapture and sudden tears. I cried eating a ripe, juicy peach. I cried at the dazzling sight of bright sunlight streaming through a newly washed window. Listening to music made me weep. So did being able to wear my favorite sweater.

I was stunned and ashamed at my appalling lack of appreciation for what had been right under my nose. Whether it's a cliché or not, we don't know how blessed each of us is until misfortune strikes. No more. I swore I would never, ever forget. My near-life experience was over. My new life as a passionate sensuist was about to begin.

Sensuist? Don't be shocked. Before you stop reading for fear that I'm about to lead you down the slippery slope of sin, stay with me for a few more paragraphs. A *sensuist* is a person who revels in life's sensory experiences. One of the greatest sensuists of all time was not the Queen of Sheba, Mata Hari, or Marilyn Monroe but a blind, deaf, and mute woman. However, Helen Keller's remaining senses were so robust that she exulted in life's textures, tastes, and aromas and was constantly urging others to do the same. Every ordinary day was another ecstatic experience for her. With the grace of God, it can be for us as well.

Organized as a saunter through the year, *Romancing the Ordinary* celebrates the spirituality of the senses. It's my belief that women are endowed with not just five but seven senses, and each month we'll explore their pleasures. Just as my personal sensory reawakening took place gradually, over the course of a year, so will yours. Besides rediscovering sight, sound, scent, taste, and touch, you will also come to cherish your sense of "knowing"—a woman's intuitive sense—and "wonder," your sense of rapture and reverence. Throughout the book you'll find seasonal indulgences intended to help you come to your senses by restoring your weary soul (as they did mine) with the things we both love—recipes, rituals, decorating, fashion, and gardening simplicities.

One last thought before we begin. In *Simple Abundance* I frequently referred to the people with whom you share your daily life—husband, children, partner, parents, siblings, friends, and colleagues. As much as possible, I've tried to avoid that in this book. Why? Certainly not because I've forgotten how many different directions we're pulled in every day; I am a woman who juggles work deadlines and helping with a child's homework assignment in the same hour, just like you. But because I know all too well how much we care about the people we love, I also know how hard it is to care for ourselves. In *Romancing the Ordinary* I'm putting you first—for mere minutes a day—to help you gently learn the sacred soulcraft of self-nurture. At times this approach might seem startling, even blasphemous. Yes, my recommendations for sensory pleasures are suggested for you alone, even if you're constantly surrounded by a crowd. *This is intentional.* It has been said that the only time men are referred to as husbands and fathers is at their own funerals. But as far as I can tell, a woman's relationship status always precedes her. Not in this book.

But more important, I see my role here as matchmaker. In the living and writing of this book, I have finally been reunited with my soul's mate—the lover I was created for—and I want you to know this thrill as well. Through *Romancing the Ordinary* I have passionately fallen in love with Life—despite all of its complexities, compromises, and contradictions—and Life has passionately revealed how much I'm loved, in spite of mine. Believe me, you will never find a lover who will adore, desire, caress, embrace, and delight you more than Life. So give me a few minutes a day to chat Life up on your behalf. You have nothing to lose but your discontent, discouragement, and, whether married or single, a secret loneliness so deep and so profound you can't even bring yourself to acknowledge it.

And to gain? Nothing less than the discovery of Heaven on earth and one heck of a sensuous romp all the way to Paradise.

Sarah Ban Breathnach
Newton's Chapel
Lincolnshire, England
June 2002

January

And what does January hold? Clean account books.
Bare diaries. Three hundred and sixty-five new days,
neatly parceled into weeks, months, seasons. A
chunk of time, of life . . . those few first notes like
an orchestra tuning up before the play begins.

—Phyllis Nicholson
Country Bouquet (1947)

*D*ark past breakfast. Dusk before supper. Down flits the
snow. Fragrant wood fires, fresh air, rosy cheeks, flickering candlelight. Hunt and gather January's joys—a playful snow walk, a seductive read, a luscious cup of cocoa, a soothing soak. Then, behind closed doors and frosted windowpanes, peek at the opalescent moon as bare-branched beauties, wrapped in luxurious white cloaks and icy diamanté, dazzle for your private pleasure. So burrow in. Snuggle deep. A winter idyll of simple splendor awaits.

Truth or Dare

Now let us welcome the New Year,
Full of things that have never been.

—Rainer Maria Rilke

One year ends, another begins. The German poet Rainer Maria Rilke's invocation to us to be open to *receiving* the New Year's bountiful blessings challenges me to look deep within— not only in anticipation of all the wonderful new things that have never been before, but in wistfulness for the simple abundance overlooked. Splendid gifts overlooked because they were hiding beneath Life's plain brown paper wrappers.

Before *Simple Abundance,* I obsessed on the perfection of my days rather than on their lush possibility. Consequently, I didn't welcome the New Year with as much joy and good cheer as I do now. Instead, I greeted January with steely will, dogged determination, and a list of resolutions so demanding and daunting I was doomed to fail from the start. "This year I'll earn a hundred thousand dollars, write a bestseller, study sculpture, stop smoking, lose thirty pounds, learn to lambada, become fluent in French, build a barn, raise rare sheep, conquer clutter, redecorate the kitchen, hike the Himalayas, and master the stock market," I used to promise myself.

Was I out of my mind? In a word: yes. Naturally, by the end of the first week of January I was emotionally exhausted by my unrealistic expectations. And so, year after year, no matter how hard I tried, my impossible ambitions made me feel like a complete failure, privately and publicly. Who could live up to that woman's hallucinations, and who'd want to anyway?

One New Year's Eve, as I reviewed a decade's worth of personal diaries recording a litany of unfulfilled longings, I realized that I had woven a subtle but strong pattern of self-defeating behavior

10

into my life. By always taking on too much at once—and yearning for instant transformation—I was unconsciously engaging in self-sabotage. What's more, I realized that my unrealistic annual resolutions were designed less to improve the quality of my life than to lift me out of the banality of my "ordinary" existence as a wife, mother, and journeyman writer.

Truth or dare: How many times have you prayed for a life "less ordinary" than the one you're living? If you're being honest, you'll say, "Often." Can I challenge you to a dare? Today, stop praying for anything other than the life you have! Join me as we tear up that list of resolutions. You don't need them anymore. All you have is all you need. But more than that, *all you have is all you could possibly want.* If you don't believe it, stick close by me this year and I'll prove it.

So before we begin the year, with a sense of adventure, give thanks for your most "ordinary" life. This is how the miracle begins, as we embark with a sense of adventure seeking the splendid in the simple gift of the everyday.

The Second Time Around

*What happiness there is when I awake to
find near me the gift of a Morning!*

—Abbie Graham

There is something so splendid, so abundant about Life's "second chances" that arrive each morning. Perhaps it's because second chances (or third, fourth, and fifth!) are the golden opportunities we thought too good to be true the first time around. Now we know better.

Let your New Year begin with a ritual of reverence and reconnection I call Tabula Rasa—a clean slate—which is an evening dedicated to dreaming about the weeks and months to come and how you'd like to savor them. Revel in them. Appreciate them. A sweet New Year's ritual is to be "at home" to the Future. Curl up in your favorite chair, listen to some soothing music, sip something festive and bubbly, and slowly light twelve votive candles— one for each new month. As you light the first candle, ask the month of January, are there any old desires you need to relinquish in order to move on? Ask February, what new-to-you "ordinary" ritual can you begin integrating into your daily round or week that will be self-nurturing? Perhaps it's *leave your desktop clear of clutter at the end of each day,* but it could just as well be *take a nap on Sunday.* Ask March, what new dream is seeding itself in your imagination? Be fanciful, curious with your questions. When you ask each month its question, whatever answer pops up, be it whimsical or practical, act upon the suggestion and notice how you feel later. Keep a record of your experiment in a journal.

Pretend you've never been given the gift of a new year before. Dame Good Fortune has swept in with her arms full of presents just for you. In a little book that I cherish, *Ceremonials of Common Days,* written by Abbie Graham in 1928, she describes her annual visit this way: "I open the door. The gorgeous guest from afar sweeps in. In her hands are her gifts—the gift of hours and farseeing moments, the gift of mornings and evenings, the gift of spring and summer, the gift of autumn and winter. She must have searched the heavens for boons so rare."

Sense Speak

Better to be without logic than without feeling.

—Charlotte Brontë

*W*omen were created to experience, interpret, revel in, and unravel the mysteries of Life through their senses. Our senses speak the secret language of the soul—longing. If there is anything every woman understands—whether she is single or married, eighteen or eighty—it is the dialect of desire.

Emotion is the feminine mother tongue. Think of how often the senses are evoked in our casual conversation to convey a woman's inner life: "I was so *touched* . . ." "I *heard* that . . ." "I *see* your point." "I *felt* misunderstood." "I could *taste* it, I wanted it so badly." "I had a *hunch* you'd call."

And yet how often in the course of one day do you deny your feelings' validity? How often do you turn away from their urgings or suppress the unruly things? Could it be that we don't trust our feelings because we haven't ever given ourselves permission to live as we are meant to? Luckily, most of us are born fully sentient beings, able "to perceive the world with all its gushing beauty and terror, right on our pulses," as the poet and naturalist Diane Ackerman tells us in her exquisite evocation *A Natural History of the Senses.* And yet we continually shut ourselves down, condemn ourselves to misery by rendering ourselves blind, deaf, and mute.

Think back to the three best moments of your life. Slowly summon them to return. Watch them ride a wave of rediscovery on your sense memories as you bring back the setting and mood and power of those moments.

Call back a moment of exhilaration and engagement. What were you doing? What were you looking at, holding, or hearing?

Call back a moment of clarity and commitment. What private prompt of your intuitive heart did you act upon?

Call back a moment of transcendence and transformation. What wonder was hidden in the tastes and textures of your everyday life?

Today revisit those moments when your soul soared and yet you were completely connected to earth. And then, throughout the day, echo James Joyce's heroine Molly Bloom's exquisite moment of surrender by offering it to Heaven as a private psalm: *And yes I said yes I will Yes!*

A Spirituality of the Senses

Nothing can cure the soul but the senses,
just as nothing can cure the senses but the soul.

—Oscar Wilde

*A*ncient spiritual traditions—from the Egyptian to the Celtic—have recognized the sacredness of sensuality and have honored the senses as spiritual messengers. "To be sensual or sensuous is to be in the presence of your own soul," the Irish poet and scholar John O'Donohue reminds us in his glorious exploration of Celtic spiritual wisdom, *Anam Cara*. "Your senses link you intimately with the divine within you and around you."

While this spiritual truth should trigger a sense of exultation, unfortunately, for many women, it's the complete opposite. That's because we intellectually associate our senses with pleasure, which, in turn, is immediately associated with shame and guilt.

No wonder. From the moment your little hand got slapped as you reached for another cookie, gratifying your pleasure has been something "nice" and "good" little girls don't do.

Listen, a lifetime pattern of self- and soul-denial isn't going to be erased overnight. But a good place for us to start is with a frank little chat between us babes about the birds and the bees.

And I am not referring to sex. We'll muse about sex another day. Today I want you to ponder the real sensual pleasures of the birds and the bees. Can you distinguish between the song of the starling, the wren, and the robin? It's hard because the starling amuses herself in winter by imitating the other birds' songs. Do you know that the little song thrush spends January "whispering" and that her full music comes only when she "feels" the pleasure of spring in the air? Or that the hedge thrush finds the perfect spot for her nest by singing? If she experiences pleasure in the sound of her own song in a particular spot, that's where she'll lay her eggs.

How many different types of honey have you ever tasted? You say you don't like honey. That's what I thought until I discovered that over three hundred types of honey are made in this country alone. The flavor of honey comes from the nectar the all-female worker bees collect as they flirt and flit among the blossoms. Oddly enough, your front lawn clover isn't the first choice for these ladies. What flavor sounds too good to be true? There's lavender, sage, avocado, wild blueberry, and pumpkin-blossom honey awaiting your sampling.

So this afternoon, along with your tea and toast, go ahead and just do it. Slather a little sensory pleasure on your dry crust of habit. And if the ancient punitive sound of one hand slapping haunts you, try tuning it out just long enough to hear Heaven's applause.

For if Spirit endowed the birds and bees with sensual joys, can you imagine what's waiting for you?

Reawakening
Your Essensual Self

There is no way in which to understand the world without first detecting it through the radar-net of our senses.

—Diane Ackerman

"*We* think because we have words, not the other way around," Madeleine L'Engle muses in her inspiring memoir *Walking on the Water.* "The more words we have, the better able we are to think conceptually."

Occasionally, however, writers come up short when they can't find the precise word or phrase to help them impart a new concept or resurrect an ancient one. In that case, illumination by association helps. So here are two words—one new, one old—that can bring more romance into your daily round.

Dear Reader, meet your *essensual self.* Get to know this babe and your ordinary won't be the same-old anymore.

The word *essensual* can't be found in a dictionary, but you will find *essence* and *sensual.* The *essence* of something is its soul, spirit, or substance. To be *sensual* is to perceive the world through your senses rather than logic or reason.

Your *essensual self* is your original self. Nothing is more essensual than a newborn baby deciphering the overwhelming mystery surrounding her through the radar-net of her senses. "A creamy blur of succulent blue sound smells like week-old strawberries dropped onto a tin sieve as mother approaches in a halo of color, chatter, and a perfume like thick golden butterscotch" is how Diane Ackerman describes an infant's fantasia in *A Natural History of the Senses.* Not a bad way to kick-start a gray January morning.

Because a baby's essence is sensory, she engages the world through curiosity and instinct. Guiding her is the essensual self, using sight, sound, scent, taste, touch, knowing, and wonder to nudge her in the direction of pleasure and safety. Unfortunately, all too quickly baby's "cozy blur in the nursery vanishes into the rigorous categories of common sense."

You grow up. You are told in no uncertain terms that you must wear boots to school instead of your hot-pink flip-flops. Why? Because it's five below outside. You cry, you rant, you rage. Mother is rigid in her vigilance and not much of a play pal. However, your essenusal self knows it would only take a few steps off the front stoop before those frozen feet would be clamoring to get into dry boots. Enough fuss. Enough fights. You've come to your senses.

From this day forward, when and where you decide to show off your tootsies is your choice. But knowing the essensual self, if it's today, she's probably got a pair of soft, warm socks waiting. Ready, whenever you are.

Come to Your Senses

Sole Mates

*S*ocks—the simple and splendid—will be where we begin our experiment with essensual living, for not all socks are created equal. Terry-cloth slipper socks, gray cashmere socks, new-term yellow kneesocks, thick white cotton socks with reassuring ribbed cuffs—each pair has a personality all its own. Are socks practical or passionate? A plain pair will tell you one thing, plaid or polka-dot, quite another. But like a sensuous woman, can't they be both? Just ask a pair of purple-heather, tweed socks with cream crochet tops meant to peek out of sturdy leather walking boots their opinion. Better yet, slip a pair on and find out for yourself.

This week let your frazzled and frozen feet get you to a sock emporium, so you can stock up on the affordable luxury of seven new pairs—one for each day of the week, each new sense.

How about a leopard-print pair that makes you smile just looking at them . . . a pair so soft and padded you can't *hear* your own steps as you cross the floor . . . a pair of thick, white cotton socks to wear after a rose-oil-scented foot massage . . . a comfy lamb's wool pair you ceremoniously don before snuggling down with something *tasty* . . . a pair you *intuitively* put on when you want to meditate on the deeper meaning hidden beneath the pleasure of ordinary things (try wearing bubblegum-pink angora socks to bed for inspiration).

And a pair chosen just to provoke *wonder*. Can these outrageous flirts waiting to flash your ankles be considered part of the feral sock family at all? Wild, slinky, silky, fishnet, and black-seamed?

You're the only woman I know who wears seamed fishnet stockings under pants, a friend once observed with as much astonishment as approval.

Not anymore.

Actually, they were a bodacious pair of *ain't she misbehaving* bootees masquerading as socks.

But essensual women don't touch and tell. . . . Whatever would the trousers think?

The Essence of Sight

One eye sees, the other feels.

—Paul Klee

*T*he thirteenth-century German mystic Meister Eckhart once observed, "The eye with which I see God is the same eye with which God sees me." At first, the point of his comment seems obvious, but if you stay with it for a moment, then the mystery it slowly reveals is overwhelming. And highly personalized. What's obvious to you might very well be oblivious to me.

When that happens, it's usually because I'm overwhelmed by the glut of daily demands, dilemmas, or decisions; no time to see clearly or even look where I'm going. Forget glasses, contact lens, or even laser surgery. The extreme myopia many women suffer from renders sightless even those with twenty-twenty vision.

Ancient Chinese belief in yin and yang—the complementary opposite female and male energies inherent in the universe—tells us that there are two extremes to everything. The pattern is in plain sight: dark and light, cold and heat, sorrow and joy, career and home, intimacy and solitude, earth and Heaven. So, too, are there two aspects for each of our seven senses. The two facets of sight are *looking* and *seeing*. One is practical, the other passionate. One aspect is used for navigation, the other for connection. One eye makes an instant judgment, the other eye contemplates. The duality of what we're missing in every minute can be so distressing, it's no wonder we're cross-eyed with confusion. But the spiritual alchemy of your essensuality is what brings the practical and passionate together in mystical union.

The gift of vision was so important that when the world was created, Love's first command was for there to be Light in order for us to see. In his gently thought-provoking art primer, *The Zen of Seeing: Seeing/Drawing as Meditation,* the artist Frederick Franck invites us to experience each ordinary moment as if we were seeing something for the very first time. "Everyone thinks he knows what a lettuce looks like. But start to draw one and you realize the anomaly of having lived with lettuces all your life but never having seen one, never having seen the semitranslucent leaves curling in their own lettuce way, never having noticed what makes a lettuce a lettuce rather than a curly kale."

Franck does it with a pencil. You can do it with a pause. The next time you're making a salad, take another look at a head of lettuce. What do you see? Look closely, look with reverence, look with gratitude, and what you'll see will be more than meets your eyes.

The Essence of Sound

Make passionate my sense of hearing.

—William Shakespeare

*H*earing and *listening* are the practical and passionate aspects of our sense of sound. The word *sound* is an enormous catchall referring to the cacophony of life's audible vibrations traveling rapidly through the air and relentlessly toward your eardrums. Just as with looking, hearing is a navigational tool, an interior sonar device enabling your brain to distinguish between the soft purring of a cat and the shrill shriek of the alarm clock. However, *listening* is Spirit's accomplice in the romantic seduction of our souls. When Shakespeare asked to have his sense of hearing made passionate, he was imploring Heaven for the gift of being able to "listen." And his simple prayer was abundantly answered, blessing us all.

Each day listening offers us an invisible path to pleasure laid out in notes, measures, tempo, and tone—whether it's the music of the spheres or the sound track of our own thoughts. There are three ways in which we listen: perceptive listening, emotional listening, and sensuous listening.

Perceptive listening is when we deliberately move from hearing to listening. When we consciously shut out the distraction of background noise to focus our complete audible attention on something. Let's say you're at the stove sautéing some onions and a radio's playing in the background. You also happen to be on the phone. Suddenly your daughter rushes in. You can see from her face that she needs to talk to you urgently. Something's happened. But what? As you concentrate on her face, body language, and emotions, looking for inaudible clues, you have begun to listen to your daughter through the sonar of your perception. Now you say good-bye to your friend, turn down the stove, turn off the radio, and turn to her. Tuning out the rest of the world to listen to what your daughter has to say is perceptive listening.

Emotional listening is what happens when a particular sound bite instantly transports you to another dimension of time and space: the realm of memory. Perhaps it's the haunting song on the radio that recalls all you've tried to forget, or the lilt of a loved one's laugh, or nature's rustling that reveals Spirit's presence as you take a long, solitary walk in the country.

Sensuous listening invites us to experience life through our senses. The music that makes your happy feet start tapping, the soothing pattern of the rain lulling you into a much needed nap, or the heartfelt conversation that makes you want to reach out to hold a hand or offer an embrace.

The English poet Samuel Taylor Coleridge believed "no sound is dissonant which tells of life." But being able to distinguish between the world's sound and fury and life's major and minor chords of contentment is how you come to your senses. Today try asking Heaven to *make passionate your sense of hearing* and prick up your ears.

The Essence of Scent

Smell is the sense of memory and desire.

—Jean-Jacques Rousseau

"*S*mells spur memories, but they also rouse our dozy senses, pamper and indulge us, help define our self-image, stir the cauldron of our seductiveness, warn us of danger, lead us into temptation, fan our religious fervor, accompany us to heaven, wed us to fashion, steep us in luxury," Diane Ackerman tells us. Considering how powerful scent can be, swaying our behavior or enhancing our moods, it's amazing that over time smell has come to be regarded as the least necessary of our senses.

22

Or so you might think, until you're suddenly struck down with *anosmia,* the inability to smell, which affects over 2 million people in this country. You know how narrow and unpleasant the world seems when your head's stuffed up with a cold or sinus infection. Without the internal sextant of scent, you're bereft of two of life's great pleasures—appetite and infatuation. The last thing a woman heavy with cold wants is a swank dinner date, no matter how many months it took Rhett Butler to get the reservation. But more than that, you've also lost the ability to protect yourself, from tainted food to predators. The smell of fear is real. You know when you walk into a room and instantly don't like someone? You're picking up hostile (to you) pheromones. The same is true with love at first sight, or, rather, first scent. It's your sense of smell that informs your brain about a person's attractiveness, not your eyes.

The nuances of how scent works are more mysterious and subtle than those of our other senses. At the front of your brain two olfactory bulbs dangle nerves down into the top of your nose, where they will receive aroma molecules triggering either a memory message to the brain or one of arousal. However, while the two aspects of the sense of smell—memory and desire—are past- and future-tense prompts, the soul of scent is only truly discovered when we delight in its myriad pleasures every day. Scent is at its heady best, like life, in the present moment.

Walk through your front door and smell "home": lemon-scented furniture polish, cat dander, damp dogs, wet boots and mittens mingling with this morning's coffee, tonight's cheese casserole, and tomorrow's ripening fruit. As you climb the stairs, your nose is sniffing and sorting the familiar from the strange: soapsuds in the bathroom; rumpled sheets in the bedrooms; the laundry in the hamper. Downstairs that bouquet of flowers desperately needs fresh water, but its wizened scent blends in with the dried potpourri, burning logs in the fireplace, and newsprint scattered on the living room floor.

Of all our senses, scent is the one most frequently associated with Spirit. So sacred was the power of scent to God that Moses was commanded to build an altar of fragrance and burn sweet incense before he prayed. Although spiritual practices and traditions around the world differ greatly, Valerie Ann Worwood tells us in her book *The Fragrant Heavens: The Spiritual Dimension of*

Fragrance and Aromatherapy that fragrance is the spiritual thread connecting souls on the earth together. From the smoldering resins of frankincense and myrrh in Catholic and Eastern Orthodox rituals, to the sweet-smelling rosewater Muslims use in their mosques, from burning incense sticks at Chinese Buddhist shrines, to the Sabbath blessing for light and fragrance in Jewish homes, scent is the winged messenger carrying our devotions to Spirit and bringing in return a whiff of Heaven on earth.

The Essence of Taste

Taste is the feminine of genius.

—Edward Fitzgerald

*T*he word *taste,* which comes down to us from the Old English word *tasten*—to touch and test—has always had a double meaning. This year we'll be delving into both interpretations as we explore and celebrate the simple splendor of this intensely personal sense.

The primary definition of *taste* describes the sensory faculty that enables us to distinguish substances dissolved in the mouth as sweet, sour, bitter, or salty. It doesn't matter if you're eating in a diner or dining in a five-star restaurant, every cook has only four basic flavors to play with. But that's actually where the fun or taste of adventure begins.

The second definition of *taste* describes the mental faculty by which we discern or appreciate things for the pleasure they bring us. It's hard to describe accurately what is "good taste," although there are hoards of professional arbiters in the media whose sole job is to tell us how to decorate our homes or adorn our bodies.

Most of us have had the delightful experience of walking into someone's house and feeling immediately comfortable. The decor is pleasing to our eyes and soothing to our souls. We praise our hostess on her "good taste," but really we're complimenting ourselves as well, for noticing and appreciating our surroundings.

Or we've had the unpleasant experience of having a saleswoman in a swank boutique ask, "Isn't this to your taste, madam?" as we take an exorbitantly priced scarf from around our neck and hand it back to her. Usually, when reeling from sticker shock, we just mumble something unintelligible under our breath and slink away. We will have become truly evolved and enlightened when we can just look her in the eye and say in our most ingratiating manner, "No, I'm afraid it just won't do."

Good taste doesn't require money, either in the grocery aisle or department store. All you need for a sense of good taste is a heightened awareness of your own particular pleasure, whether it comes on a plate or on a hanger. A sense of humor also helps. The famous fashion editor Diana Vreeland believed what was truly essential for good taste was a little bit of bad. "A little bit of bad taste is like a nice splash of paprika. We all need a splash of bad taste—it's hearty, it's healthy, it's physical. I think we could use *more* of it. No taste is what I'm against."

The Essence of Touch

*Touch is the landscape
of what is possible.*

—Kate Green

*A*s strange hands pull you from the dark, cozy realm of the soul into the cold, harsh light of day, your sense of touch guides your first few conscious moments. After the security and warmth of the womb, frigid air assaults your fragile, naked body. No wonder you let out a big wail. Life seems terrifying. Only after you're cradled safely in your mother's arms does your sense of touch provide a glimpse of its essensual purpose—bliss.

Touch is usually the last sense we experience as we depart this world, hopefully the squeeze of a loved one's hands. Sight, sound, scent, and taste have gone before us. "The first sense to ignite, touch is often the last to burn out," the science writer Frederich Sachs tells us, "long after our eyes betray us, our hands remain faithful to the world."

Unfortunately first impressions are lasting, especially primal ones, which goes a long way toward explaining the reason many women get uncomfortable when they think about touchy matters, whether the topic is their skin or what's gotten under it. Perhaps this is why the word *touch* is such a popular metaphor—only at a distance does this most intimate sense feel safe.

We describe our mood swings as "feelings," and when something strikes a deep, sentimental chord in us, we say that we've been "touched." When we are scattered, alienated, and adrift we describe our isolation as "losing touch with reality." Bumper stickers ask, "Did you hug your child today?" What I want to know is, when was the last time *you* were hugged? Because we all need to be hugged and touched. Tiny, premature babies need touch therapy if they're going to survive. Fully grown women need to delight in their sense of touch if they want to thrive—and there are as many ways to do that as weeks in a year. From the feel of freshly laundered sheets against your bare skin to a warm, fragrant foot-soak after you come in from the cold, each day holds its own sensory secrets waiting to be discovered.

Do you remember AT&T's popular "reach out and touch someone" advertising campaign? During the next year we're going to get reacquainted with this powerful, spiritual gift, so often disregarded and mistrusted because it's misunderstood. "We are forever in the dark about what touch means to another," the writer Jessamyn West confided in her memoir, *Love Is Not What You Think,* written in 1959. We must accept that we can't always know the effect of our touch on another. But to be numb to your own sense of touch is "unfeeling" in the true sense of the word.

The Essence of Knowing

I don't believe. I know.

—Carl Jung

*I*ntuition—the capacity to know something without rational evidence that proves it to be so—is commonly called our "sixth" sense. The English writer D. H. Lawrence, who spent his entire life writing about women in love, was convinced that the intelligence arising "out of sex and beauty" was intuition. And he was right. Women *are* more intuitive when we're in the throes of romance. Why? Because when we are in love with another, we are in love with Life. Our sensory perceptions soar. We suspend disbelief. Nothing's too good to be true. Suddenly we don't think our way through the days of our lives, we feel our way. We feel alive. We become the woman William Wordsworth described as "one in whom persuasion and belief / Had ripened into faith, and faith became / A passionate intuition."

Or a passionate intuitive. One who honors, trusts, and revels in her subliminal sense. The writer Florence Scovel Shinn tells us that "intuition is a spiritual faculty, and does not explain, but simply points the way." The logical explanations will come later, with hindsight. But only after you've taken a leap of faith and followed that hunch.

The best way that I've come to understand, describe, and use intuition in my own life is as an inner knowing. I call it soul knowledge. *Knowing* that you need to cut a trip short suddenly because you just *have* to get home. Don't be silly, you're told, everything's fine. No, it's not and you *know* it. You arrive a few hours before your child needs an emergency appendectomy. Or *knowing* a risk will pay off, even when all the odds are stacked against you, even when your back is against the wall, and especially when they say it's never been done before. After the "miracle" happens, they'll call you a seer. Today, before the miracle, you need to call yourself a *know-it-all,* especially about your own life.

Intuition sends us Morse code messages in inventive ways, but always through the senses. This year we'll explore the many different ways—from visions to voices, from whispers to shouts. Call it inspiration, impulse, instinct. Call it weird, wacky, whimsical. Call it freaky-deaky, neeny-neeny. But call on it. And then you'll be able to call yourself blessed.

The Essence of Wonder

Wonder is the promise of restoration:
as deeply as you dive, so may you rise.

–Christina Baldwin

*T*oward the end of her life, the great environmentalist Rachel Carson confessed that if she could bestow a birth gift on every child, it would be "a sense of wonder so indestructible that it would last throughout life, as an unfailing antidote against the boredom and disenchantments of later years" and the inevitable "alienation from the sources of our strength."

Actually the sense of wonder is already a birthright, but it's probably been so long since you've played or prayed with it, you've forgotten you ever had it. And while spiritual gifts are indestructible, that doesn't mean they're not extinguishable. What snuffs out our sense of wonder is adult ennui. When we're little, a parental litany of "Not now" to perfectly plausible questions, such as *Why is each snowflake different? Why doesn't the ocean freeze in the winter?* or *Why can't cats ice-skate?* stifles the spiritual growth hormone of curiosity, a crucial component of wonder. Sooner than can scarcely be imagined, innate wonder is replaced by indifference. Do you know how many jaded seven-year-olds there are today? Don't blame it entirely on television, the Internet, or movies (although they certainly are co-conspirators). Perhaps kids grow up so fast because they find childhood in our company so dull. Who could blame them? We're so caught up in the drudgery of our daily rounds, we're not much fun to be around and apathy at any age is contagious.

Wonder is that extravagant state of bliss induced by something new—the strange, astonishing, mysterious, and the unexpected. Yesterday. Today. Tomorrow, if we're lucky enough to have one. Nothing in particular and everything that surrounds us. Open your eyes, perk up your ears—suddenly you'll find wondrous things in the most surprising places. The fascinating conversation about alpacas you'll start with a stranger in the supermarket checkout line. The plumber who actually shows up on time and doesn't wipe out your retirement fund. Realizing that you're not out of breath after twenty minutes on the treadmill, *finally*. Staring at the full moon and contemplating for one whole minute why it doesn't fall out of the sky.

All women lead lives of intrigue, mystery, and wonderment, including you. And yet, how often do we approach each day as if it were an exhilarating adventure instead of another chain in a life sentence without parole? Not often enough. If you've ever wondered why life is doled out to us in only twenty-four-hour increments, it's because we can barely handle even that.

Lily Tomlin believes that if we want to be happy, we need to exercise our "awe-aerobics." Hopefully, this year you'll discover why. Each glorious day should begin and end in the reverence and rapture of wonder. In *Simple Abundance* I challenged you to transform your life by finding five things each day for which to be grateful. This time I dare you to discover five reasons each day to say, "This is wonderful." Keep track of your wonders in your Gratitude Journal. Being thankful for all the wonderful things in our lives—the simply splendid we discover each ordinary day—is how we keep our romance with Life alive.

Will wonders ever cease?

No, thank Heavens.

Eyes Wide Shut

*We should live each day with a gentleness,
a vigor, and a keenness of appreciation which
are often lost when time stretches before us
in the constant panorama of more days and
months and years to come.*

–Helen Keller

*I*f you found out today that you had only three more days to
see, what visual memories would you start gathering? Helen
Keller posed that provocative question in an article titled
"Three Days to See," published in the January 1933 issue of
Atlantic Monthly. Coming at the start of another uncertain year
when America was gripped by the economic and emotional terror of the Depression, Miss Keller's poignant plea urged readers
to realize that despite their hardships, they were overlooking
priceless blessings—their senses. "Those who have never suffered impairment of sight or hearing seldom make the fullest
use of these blessed faculties. Their eyes and ears take in all
sights and sounds hazily, without concentration and with little
appreciation. . . . I have often thought it would be a blessing if
each human being were stricken blind and deaf for a few days at
some time during his early adult life. Darkness would make him
more appreciative of sight; silence would teach him the joys of
sound."

Ouch. There's unvarnished, unforgiving, unrelenting truth,
and it's chilling to the soul. Most of us have been given a miraculous gift—the ability to see—but we barely use our eyes more
than to glance around and avoid bumping into the furniture.

A few years ago a dear friend of mine had serious trouble with
her eyesight and had to undergo several nerve-racking surgeries.
As she expressed her worries about becoming blind, I felt help-

less to offer comfort. It wasn't Life's big vistas she mourned, but every day's miraculous minutiae: being able to drive her children to the dentist, do her grocery shopping, put on her makeup, feed the cats, walk the dog, read the newspaper, experiment with new recipes, tend to her plants, see the faces of those she loves. Infinitesimal, precious moments that make up the days of our lives. Gradually and gratefully, my friend regained her eyesight, but the lesson was well learned. Her favorite expression these days is "Look at this . . ." It should be ours as well.

Helen Keller told her readers that on the morning of the first day of sight, she'd like "to see the people whose kindness and gentleness and companionship have made my life worth living." Who would be on your list? In the afternoon she would "take a long walk in the woods and intoxicate my eyes on the beauties of the world of Nature, trying desperately to absorb the vast splendor which is constantly unfolding itself to those who can see." Where would you take a nature walk?

On the second day of sight, Helen Keller wanted to "arise with the dawn and see the thrilling miracle by which night is transformed into day." When was the last time you saw the sunrise?

On her last day of sight, Helen Keller confessed that she would realize how much magic remained in the world just waiting to be seen. But she would be filled with gratitude rather than regret.

Would we? What if today we were called up short with our eyes wide shut? "You would use your eyes as never before. Everything you saw would become dear to you. Your eyes would touch and embrace every object that came within your range of vision. Then, at last, you would really see, and a new world of beauty would open itself before you."

The Scent of a Woman

God is the best perfumer there is.

—Tanya Sarne

Not long ago I was searching in a used-book shop for out-of-print books on the senses. The owner, a man I'd guess to be in his forties, was curious about why I was interested in this subject. I told him I was writing a book on the spirituality of the senses—that I believed the senses are our portals to the Divine.

"And the dead," he said softly. A look of incredible sadness came over him. He told me his wife had died suddenly the year before; they didn't have any children. "We were soul mates. We traveled the world together—life was a wonderful adventure with her." One of their favorite places was the garden at the Palace of Versailles near Paris, which they'd first visited on their honeymoon. After his wife's death he made a pilgrimage there.

"It was January. The ground was frozen, the trees were bare, nothing was blooming. It was bleak. I sat down on a bench and started to cry. We'd been inseparable for twenty years. I couldn't believe she'd abandon me so completely, even in death. I was so angry, I screamed at her, the sky, and at God. It was a good thing no one else was there or they would have dragged me away, not that I cared. Eventually I quieted down and began to slowly walk back to the front gate. Suddenly, I was surrounded by her scent. No woman ever smelled as good as my wife, or even like her. She smelled of lilacs, spring . . . and baking. My wife loved to bake. She smelled vibrant and happy. And all around me were fragrant wisps of *her*."

The image of this devastated man standing alone in a winter's garden, enveloped in a scent cloud of his dead wife's love, brought me to tears.

"You probably think I'm crazy but I knew she was there . . . with me." I assured him he was not crazy—he was lucky. He told me that this fragrant visitation lasted for about fifteen minutes and then she was gone. Sadly, he's not "sensed" his wife again. But the sense memory of that mystical encounter will last beyond this lifetime.

Every woman has her own scent, and I'm not talking about a favorite perfume. A woman's scent is a deeply personal bouquet of diet, heredity, hormones, hygiene, and health; an aromatic as distinctive as her DNA. Napoleon sent a dispatch to his wife, the Empress Josephine, asking her not to bathe before he arrived home the next day. He adored her natural aroma. When my daughter was little and I went away on business trips, she would sleep on my pillow and underneath my down-filled comforter because they "smell like you, Mommy."

Many women shun even the thought of their natural scent; we spend a small fortune trying to mask our essensuality. Are we secretly afraid that we will offend? We think we "stink" at so many things we do, why would our *eau naturelle* be any different? But one of the miracles that occurs when we fall for Life is we begin to see ourselves through the lens of unconditional Love. We relax into the Real. We stop hiding behind artifice.

The "hot" new luxury these days is a one-of-a-kind, personalized perfume. The English writer Susan Irvine, an expert on fragrances, writes about them in her book *The Perfume Guide*: "It's strange, the moment you first inhale your own scent."

She is, of course, referring to a fragrance custom-made *for* you.

But the custom fragrance that comes *through* you—the essensual scent—is an equally pleasant surprise. However, this subtle aromatic is difficult to discern, because we mask natural fragrance with chemicals and synthetic cologne. This week, try an experiment: use pure soap and unscented deodorant. Start in small steps to come back to your essensual self.

Did you know some of the most exquisite scents in the world—gardenia, lily, lilac, orchid, lily of the valley—can't be naturally captured in a bottle? They can only be replicated in a lab. I think that's a wonderful thought to meditate on today.

Since Egyptian times, the feminine art of fragrance has been revered. Finding a perfume that complements and enhances your sense of well-being is a spiritual gift and sensuous pleasure. However, the crucial first step is discovering your own "base note" before the layering of other fragrances. The true "scent of a woman" begins with you.

Mornings
of Imperishable Bliss

*D*id you know that in the beginning oranges blossomed only in the perfumed palace gardens of Far Eastern potentates? But even Chinese empresses, Arabian princes, and Indian maharajas reserved this rare, prized fruit for special occasions: love offerings.

The history of the orange is the stuff of great romance.

After gifts of gold, silk, and fragrance failed him, King Solomon seduced the Queen of Sheba with oranges. Queen Isabella gave royal orange tree cuttings to Columbus—a bonus for discovering a new world. The great seventeenth-century Spanish writer Miguel de Cervantes found inspiration sampling them as he wrote his bittersweet romantic fantasy *Don Quixote*. And the nineteenth-century French painter Paul Cézanne was so besotted with oranges, he couldn't stop painting them.

A queen's ransom probably sits on your kitchen counter right now. But when was the last time you contemplated the sweet, succulent mysteries of the navel? Or a Valencia? January is when the not-so-ordinary orange is at the peak of her glory—bringing color, taste, and dreams of warmer climes to our wintry days. In fact, oranges possess so much variety, flavor, and allure, the English food writer Brian Glover rightly observes, "One could almost imagine that if oranges were indeed the only fruit, the hardship wouldn't be too bad."

Next time you can visit a large supermarket with a good produce section (organic grocery stores are my choice), wander the fruit aisle slowly. You're on a field trip in search of the marvelous in the mundane. Look for as many different citrus fruits of the orange family as you can find (leave lemons and limes for later). You know how good wineshops and gourmet markets hold wine and cheese tastings? Well, you're invited to a citrus tasting.

Spend a glorious half hour just exploring their individual mysteries of flavor and fragrance: mild mandarin oranges (from China), tangerines (from Tangier), clementines, satsumas, mineolas, pomelos, and blood oranges. Even kumquats are distant citrus cousins. Have you ever tasted a kumquat? Now's your chance.

To spiritually induce sunny sensations on even the gloomiest morning, slowly sip a glass of freshly squeezed blood-orange juice; it won't be just the antioxidants that have you coming back for more.

So consider the orange anew. What about Roast Chicken with Orange, Lemon, and Ginger for dinner tonight? Or Orange-and-Fennel-Poached Sole? A fabulous winter salad is roasted beets, blood oranges, Belgian endive, and asparagus, but a simple combination of red onion, orange segments, and mint leaves is scrumptious. For dessert, please move quickly past packaged sherbet to Chocolate-Orange Cheesecake with Orange-Tangerine Glaze, Orange Caramel Soufflé, or, if you're woman enough for it, Carrot Marmalade Torte Paradiso, an exquisite reminder, dear Reader, that your own moments of imperishable bliss are only bites away.

Carrot Marmalade Torte Paradiso

There are two parts to this recipe—the carrot marmalade cake and the marmalade cream filling.

You will need:

For the Cake:

4 egg yolks
⅝ cup sugar
1 cup finely ground hazelnuts
1 cup finely shredded carrots
2 tablespoons all-purpose flour
2 tablespoons orange marmalade
5 egg whites
Pinch of salt

For the Cream Filling:

1½ cups heavy cream
⅓ cup orange marmalade
for garnish, thin orange slices and (if you can believe it) even more whipped cream. Relax, it's January, we don't put the bathing suit on for another six months.

Preheat oven to 300° F. Butter and flour 2 springform pans (6½ x 3 inches). In a small bowl, beat egg yolks and sugar at high speed until pale yellow (about 5 minutes). Stir in ground hazelnuts, shredded carrots, flour, and marmalade. Mix well and set aside.

Wash and dry the beaters. In a large bowl, beat egg whites and salt at high speed until stiff but not dry. Gradually fold egg whites into batter. Pour batter into pans. Bake for 45 minutes until browned and cakes just begin to pull away from sides. Let them cool for about a half hour. (Don't worry if the cakes shrink and fall slightly; they all do, even on television cooking shows.) After the cakes are cool enough to touch, loosen the edges with a knife. Remove from the pans carefully. Slice each cake in 2 layers horizontally. The layers will be fragile; a wide rubber spatula helps to move them. Set aside.

Wash those beaters again. Whip the heavy cream until it forms peaks. Fold in the marmalade. Spread one-quarter of the whipped cream mixture on each cake layer, including the top. Garnish with fresh orange slices. Pipe additional whipped cream atop the cake for decoration. Take a picture and serve promptly (at least within a half hour, or it will cave in). Brew a fresh pot of orange spice tea and revel in your cleverness.

They Can't Take That Away

Shunning the upstart shower
The cold and cursory scrub
I celebrate the power
That lies within the Tub.

—Phyllis McGinley

Your hand grasps the chrome tap, and with one quick turn a waterfall of delight gushes into the porcelain tub. With only the slightest forethought or effort you have performed a divine conjuring act. In an instant, the elixir of life. Even today, incredulous millions around the world shake their heads with wonder at such a sight.

It is time that certain things were said. It is time to save the Bath.

The once royal beauty treatment of Cleopatra and other discerning women like ourselves is greatly threatened. We may have done it behind closed doors, but, toots, our secret is out. Our private pleasure has become public domain. And I don't like it.

The Bath must be ransomed from the plots of the women's magazines and the clutches of the cosmetics and toiletries cabal, for they know and feed on our feminine weakness for frolicking naked in the water at night. If we don't act quickly to restore Bath's luster, protect her reputation, promote her virtue as the last refuge of an ordinary woman's sanity, her very name will become an object of ridicule, relegated to the catechism of cliché where scented candles and "living in the present moment" now wither. If the redeeming qualities of meditation and aromatherapy can be snuffed out by the banality of the self-enhancement poseurs, can our beloved Bath be far behind?

But perhaps I am too late. Half-used bottles of salts, powders, bubbles, and potions litter every nook and cranny of your bathroom cabinet, bearing silent witness to the truth: The thrill is gone from your pampering routine. Perhaps it seems that beginning your day with a quick shower is more convenient than ending it in a soulful soak at eventide. However, the truth is, my dear, familiarity and mass marketing have bred ennui.

What distresses me most is the bait-and-switch tactics used. Picture this: A woman we all know, a woman who earns $30,000 with a couple of kids in day care, is weary, worn to a raveling after a long day. She can't wait to take a bath. While the water is running, she flips the pages of a slick and sophisticated magazine glorifying the joys of the simple life. She comes to an article on turning her bathroom into a spa, her very own home oasis. Start with furniture you'd only find on a movie set, such as a $450 apothecary cabinet to hold washcloths. A $250 lamp invitingly sheds the soft glow of a twenty-watt bulb, providing a relaxing ambience. The supplies for exfoliating, buffing, and cleansing are at the ready on a light-weight tray ($75) or in an imported porcelain bowl ($72). And then there are all the bath potions available, lined up like so many fragrant soldiers, ranging in price from $18 to $60. For that much money, the bubbles had better be Moët & Chandon Brut.

So instead of feeling uplifted and inspired she shuts off the tap and turns away— bored, angry, diminished, and perplexed. Bored because nothing new is suggested. Angry because instead of a home spa to relax in she's got a bathroom the size of a hall closet. And diminished because on one page she's exhorted to take care of herself, and on the very next are pictured the tools necessary for the job, and she can't afford them. Empowerment, diminishment. Empowerment, diminishment. The subliminal message is crushing and cruel.

The best editors, photographers, art directors, and creative directors in the magazine business perpetuate the perfect, airbrushed version of what simplicity looks like if you have extraordinary taste, an income of $150,000 a year, and probably no children. This is the reader of their dreams, the one who *buys buys buys,* putting money into the coffers of their advertisers. But is that you? Is that your best friend or sister or neighbor?

So let's seize this opportunity to Just Say No. Let them become the laughingstocks, not our Beloved Bath, which continues to bring solace and warmth and delicious scents to the ends of our harrowing days.

For what could be more miraculous than what you can gain tonight from the simple twist of your wrist? They can't take that away!

Come to Your Senses

What Goes On Behind Closed Doors

*Feeling a bit touchy tonight? Then let us consider restoration to your charming, agreeable self through the sense of touch. Let us, weary Reader, reconsider the mystical properties of the Bath.

After a day of having all your senses assaulted with too much information, worrisome newscasts, disagreeable demands, rushing around, and inclement weather that chills to the marrow of your bones, your soul yearns for hot, steamy nights.

For the last several years I've been collecting ancient beauty rituals for hair, face, and body from around the world—amazing concoctions that manage to provide pleasure in their perusal, vicarious rapture in their contemplation, and whiffs of exotic adventure and forbidden romance in their practice.

Join me. You have nothing to lose but your boredom and dry skin. Making our baths even more enticing is that all of the inexpensive ingredients necessary can probably be found in your kitchen, and if not there, then easily at the supermarket, health food store, or ethnic grocery shop. As Michelle Dominique Leigh discovered when she was compiling her wonderful book *The Japanese Way of Beauty,* for the cultures that valued inner as well as outer beauty, "the realms of food, medicine, beauty, and even ancient religion and magic overlapped." What's more, since all of these ancient beauty rituals have been handed down orally from one generation of women to another, it stands to reason that they live up to their reputations. An added enticement for trying them is that if one doesn't work for you, there's no collection of expensively packaged, half-empty reminders cluttering your counters.

Tonight's bath is based on two ancient Japanese winter baths— rice wine and citrus. (I'm assuming that at this point in your life you know how sensitive your skin is; both alcohol and citrus juices are astringent, and if you are sensitive, you'll want to forgo this one.) Although this marvelous bath eases tired, sore muscles, eliminates toxins, warms and stimulates circulation, and induces sleep (afterward, not during), the rice wine bath is revered most for its skin-softening properties. Skin is so smoothed and pampered by the *sakeburo* that in Japan a special bath sake is sold for this purpose, known as the *tama no hada sake,* or "the skin-like-a-gleaming-jewel sake." I've not yet discovered this particular sake here, but any rice wine has worked well, even the most inexpensive.

However, because the rice wine bath has too faint a scent for my liking, I was inspired to combine it with sweet-smelling tangerines.

This is the manner of it. Fill the bathtub with hot water. When it's nearly full, add a cup of sake. Break apart three tangerines and place the segments along with broken-up peel in a piece of gauze or cheesecloth, securing it with a cord. You can either dangle the gauze bath bag over the faucet as the water is running or let it soak in the tub.

Before you get in, prepare a pot of herbal tangerine spice tea for sipping as you soak. Add a few whole tangerines to float in the tub for your amusement. I must confess, while lying back and playing footsie with them, I have wondered what sake-infused tangerines might taste like, but since this bath does eliminate toxins (you'll be amazed at how murky the water gets), so far I've resisted nibbling and would recommend that you do the same. This sake and citrus bath is delightful, aromatic, and incredibly self-indulgent in the best possible way.

The evening bath is sacrosanct for Japanese woman, a delicious, languorous, sensual time of centering, soothing, and recovering a sense of well-being. It can be for you as well.

Between the Lines

Tangerine Dreams

"Over the past few hundred years our culture has looked upon sensuality with apprehension and guilt. The pleasures and pains of the physical life have been so separated from the life of the soul that we have all but forgotten how heaven and hell are nowhere if not on earth, not only in our hearts and minds, but also in the way we taste and touch, hear and see and smell," the English philosopher Roger Housden reminds us in his exquisite and provocative book *Soul and Sensuality: Returning the Erotic to Everyday Life.*

In this meditation entitled "Tangerine Dream," he describes how the simply splendid tangerine sensuously reveals the sacred hidden in between ordinary life's lines.

I once dreamed I was sitting under a rock in the desert, surrounded by red sand that stretched to a glittering haze on the horizon. I had a goatskin which was still half-full of water, but I had just run out of my last tin of food the night before. I was aware that my situation did not appear promising, but I was not, for some reason, especially concerned. . . . As I was looking out over the desert, I was astounded to see a little out of arm's reach, over to my left, a bright tangerine perched on the sand. I had brought no tangerines into the desert. No one else could have passed this way recently. . . . Yet there it was, all by itself, a bulging tangerine, perfectly round, a meal for one in an orange suit. I leaned over and picked it up. It smelled fresh and bright, as tangerines do. I felt its soft mandarin skin and cracked it open like a ripe pod to reveal the fruit and its protection of sinewy latticework. It released a cool mist of delicious odour into the desert air and over my hot face.

With my index finger I slowly pulled one of the segments away and brought it, trailing a rubbery white frond, to the edge of my lips. Holding it for a moment between my teeth, I eventually split the tight skin and a shower of fine juices sprayed into my mouth. Slowly, I chewed the flesh out of the segment, reduced it to pulp, and let it slip effortlessly down my throat with barely the reflex of swallowing. I savoured its energy, and felt it clear my head. Then I tore off another segment, full to bursting, felt its body billowing between my fingers, and sent it the same way as its absent neighbour. A third and fourth segment followed, then another, and another; the cool shock of their tang traveled right through me until, with the last one, I awoke to a cool autumn morning in England.

—Roger Housden,
Soul and Sensuality: Returning the Erotic to Everyday Life

On Keeping Winter

Winter is come in earnest and the snow
In dazzling splendour. . . . Spreads a white world
All calm . . . Fancy's pliant eye delighted sees a
vast romance displayed.

—John Clare

*L*ast night it snowed. I suspected as much when I turned over in the dark and glimpsed dazzling beams of light streaming through the window. When I looked outside, a hushed white world was bathed in moon glow. Mother Nature had pulled a soft, muffling comforter up to the countryside's chin and tucked us in for a brief winter's reverie. Gratefully, I slipped back down under the covers and felt the relief of a reprieve. There would be no early-morning trip to town or DHL delivery later in the day. No places to go or urgent pages to revise. Nothing to do but rest. And so I did.

I love the eighteenth-century English expression of "keeping" a season, which refers to the traditional ways people in the country restored their bodies and nurtured their souls by honoring, in their daily rounds, the rhythm of the natural world. Sowing, reaping, sitting still.

After a lifetime of dreaming of stone walls and oak beams, I have a cottage built of both, nestled deep in rural England. When it snows, there are no plows to dig us out or trucks to salt the narrow, icy lanes. In the winter, in the country, when it snows, you "keep" in one place, which for me is in front of the fireplace with a pot of tea and a large stack of books. In a few days when the sun shines and the temperature climbs above freezing, the snow will melt—your hint that the hiatus is over. Refreshed and invigorated in a way that no planned vacation ever provides, you pick up whatever was set down. Once again, happy with your lot in life, you dispatch your obligations with good humor, efficiency, even contentment. What is this unusual state of grace? You have "kept" winter, and winter has "kept" you from losing your mind.

However, once this little country mouse rejoins her city and suburban mice cousins, even the first twaddle about snow sets off an anxious frenzy, both physical and psychic: stocking the larder, raiding the video store, and making futile calls to other desperate women who have their own child-care problems. In the city and the suburbs we do not "keep" to anything but obligations and schedules, even if it means tugging cranky kids (who'd rather be sledding) with us. Should we be forced indoors by blizzard conditions, as long as the electricity is on, we're wired, on top of it, performing. And doing a pretty lousy job.

If you can't even remember the last time the very thought of snow brought a twinge of pleasure, take yourself to the children's section of the library (preferably without a child, so that you can dawdle). Ask the nice lady behind the desk to point you in the direction of the winter picture books. Take a few or as many as you can carry. Sit in a little chair and slowly peruse the pages as if you're discovering winter for the first time as an adult.

You are.

"Look at winter / with winter eyes," the painter and poet Douglas Florian urges us in his charming book *Winter Eyes*. For if we take the time to savor a few stolen seasonal moments—to keep Winter company—we'll learn a priceless secret:

> *The "dead" of winter*
> *Or so they say.*
> *But winter lives*
> *In her own way.*

Come to Your Senses

Sip, Sup, Savor, Sigh

*A*dd to that list of winter's sublime seductions hot, milky drinks. The fun here is that there are so many variations. Think back to your childhood. Open the kitchen cupboard of nostalgia. What will you reach for to pour into your "white" milk—Hershey's syrup, Ovaltine, or a jar of Horlick's chocolate malted milk—before Mom heats it on the stove?

But now that you're all grown-up, you can and should indulge in the affordable luxury of real hot cocoa.

A winter comfort beloved by the sublime essayist M.F.K. Fisher is hot chocolate soup for supper. Layer pieces of hot buttered toast, cut into square inches, in the bottom of a soup bowl (about ten to twelve pieces). Sprinkle with a heaping handful of fresh mini marshmallows and slowly ladle the real hot cocoa over the toast. Savor with soupspoons. After all the toasty bits are gone, you can continue with animal crackers!

Grown-Up Girl's Hot Cocoa

YOU WILL NEED:

⅓ cup well-chilled heavy cream
1 tablespoon sugar
4 ounces fine-quality bittersweet chocolate (not unsweetened)
2 cups milk (your choice of whole or semiwhole, but what difference does it make at this point? Whole will be richer-tasting).

In a bowl with an electric mixer, beat cream with sugar until it just holds stiff peaks. Chop chocolate and reserve 2 teaspoons. In a small saucepan, heat milk with remaining chocolate over moderate heat, stirring, until it just comes to a simmer. Pour hot chocolate into large mug and top with whipped cream and reserved chocolate. Two servings.

Sensing Simple Splendors

Grace growest best in winter.

—Samuel Rytherford

I'm always on the lookout for new ways to experience the grace and power of gratitude. One way is to be specific. If you're wrestling with an emotionally charged issue in your life, such as money, health, or a relationship, concentrate on that issue in your Gratitude Journal. Let's say you're worried about money. Unfortunately, the more you focus on what's missing from your life, what you can't have or afford, the emptier you'll feel. Instead, anytime you sense abundance unexpectedly (a friend springs for lunch, the repair bill is less than you imagined, you find $20 in the pocket of a coat you haven't worn for a while, you're thrilled with a thrift-store find) make a note of it. You'll be amazed at how many times during each day all you have is more than enough.

Rethinking romance is our focus this year. Just as a lover woos with one sweet gesture at a time, so does Life. That's why we're going to be grateful for the *unexpected ordinary,* moments or pleasures that bestow a genuine sense of contentment and well-being. Here's a peek at the unexpected ordinaries that popped up in my Gratitude Journal this month:

A fireplace, a cord of dry wood, fire starters that really work, long matches, frozen lakes, ice-skating without breaking any bones, Sonja Henie movies, slowly simmering Crock-Pot stews, the perfect snow-scraper, great winter boots, having the walk shoveled by someone else, Welsh rarebit on toast, feeding the birds, not losing one of my favorite gloves before the month is over, having two pairs of my favorite gloves in case I do, getting the electricity back on, the reassuring sound and scent of heat coming through the old radiator, a winter hat I look good in, getting home before the snow starts . . .

Now, what are yours?

February

Pleasures newly found are sweet
When they lie about our feet:
February . . . Praise of which I nothing know.

—William Wordsworth

Cold, gray, wet, muddy mornings make the shortest month seem the longest. But lingering afternoons and pink sunsets hold out promise. Like matters of the heart, February is full of surprise, contradiction, and the spell of the sensuous. Cherish your romantic impulses. Succumb to cabin fever. Become your own courtesan. Light your own fire. Have a clandestine affair with contentment. Play with your food, hide under the covers. Indulge in armchair adventures—unusual sleuths, film noir. Try on fantasies. Reconsider red—lips, nails, shoes, walls. Slip on bangles or slip into silk. Trade the treadmill for the tango. Curl your hair, cinch your waist. Chocolate becomes you, so show off your curves. Remember flirting is good for the soul. Make peace with your past. Lose your heart to Life.

The Great Romance

*A love affair between the senses and the great suitor
Life – an intimate relationship with living – awaits
every woman who in her wisdom chooses to fill
her heart with the multitude of wonders unfolding
in the stillness of a moment.*

–Elizabeth Millar

*D*id you know that making love is the only endeavor to simultaneously engage and excite all seven of woman's senses: sight, sound, scent, taste, touch, knowing, and wonder? That's because love makes all things new. When we are in the throes of a great romance, our sensory perceptions soar. "The flesh of a peach, the luminosity of early morning, the sound of distant church bells—the pleasure the lover takes in all the small experiences is heightened by love, suffused with special meaning," Ethel S. Person tells us in her fascinating exploration of romantic passion, *Dreams of Love and Fateful Encounters.* We become magnets drawn ineluctably into the meaning of Life because love initiates us "into the divine mysteries."

Like many women I was raised to believe that the good things in life—the peach, the sunrise, the church bells—are meant to be shared. However, into the span of every woman's life comes a solitary season through choice, change, or circumstance. But in July the peach grows heady in its sweetness and hypnotic in its fragrance, whether or not we walk through the orchard with a partner, lover, or husband. For three lonely summers after my long-standing marriage ended, I found myself too "busy" to continue the tradition of visiting a local farm to collect peaches. If there wasn't someone to share this pleasure with, why bother? If no one was going to praise my pie, why bake it? Without realizing it, I transformed the arbor into another ark, to be entered into two by two, or not at all.

Women often confuse love and romance. God knows I did. While both are frequently in each other's company, they're not the same. Think of love as emotion. Romance is its evocative expression. Romance reveals the depth and breath of a lover's feelings in a particular way. Romance is the flourish, embellishment, poetic gesture. Love can be conveyed in an e-mail, but when a woman receives a handwritten letter, she's being romanced. The time it took, the glimpse of her name in his handwriting—these are the things that make her heart beat faster.

If love is dessert, romance is a pear tart with apricot sauce and muscat-raisin ice cream. If love is a dance, romance is a tango. If love is a trip, romance is a journey on the *Orient Express* or a ride through the park on a bicycle built for two.

A woman can be loved truly, madly, deeply, but if the only way your suitor can express it is to mumble "Ditto" after you reveal your feelings, you might have love, doll, but you definitely don't have romance.

Women want and need love but our constant craving is for romance. So what are we supposed to do? Spend the rest of our days experiencing romance vicariously through films, soap operas, and pulp fiction? I don't think so. Most of the make-believe doesn't even come close to the Real Thing.

So we do what we've always done: take care of it ourselves. We stop wishing that one of these days he'll do it better. He won't. And if we're alone, we stop waiting for him to come along. He might, but then again, he might not.

However, if you think not having a partner is stopping me from living my romantic dreams, think again. And it doesn't have to stop you. Married or single, for the rest of this glorious year, we're going to woo ourselves. Seduce our souls by romancing the ordinary. We're going to come to our senses and let Life sweep us off our feet. "What if," the novelist Willa Cather wondered, "what if Life's the sweetheart?"

Hold that thought.

Beginning to See the Light

If Candlemas Day be fair and bright
Winter will have another flight
If on Candlemas Day it be shower and rain
Winter is gone and will not come again.

—Old English proverb

Since the Middle Ages, February 2 has been known as Candlemas, an old feast day when candles were blessed and sent home with parishioners so that Divine Light could direct their earthly steps. Candlemas was also considered the midpoint in winter; dark winter mornings required candlelight. It became customary for women to make an inventory of their candle supply on this day and replenish the household's reserve.

There's a good chance another storm or two is headed your way, whether it's rain, sleet, or snow. Where there are storms, there are power outages. When we were in our wonder years, if the electricity was lost during a storm, it was more magical than inconvenient. Everything was transformed by candlelight, and everyone gathered together in one room—a special conviviality for a special occasion. We slowed down, edged our way through the darkness, and used all our senses to rediscover the familiar.

I love observing Candlemas for both poetic and practical reasons. I've never known a room or woman who didn't grow more beautiful by the glow of candlelight. So, tonight, why not gather as many candles as you can and take a look at your own supply? Toss out all the ones burned down to their nibs; if the wick's buried in wax, even knives, tweezers, or ice picks won't pry it loose, so don't bother to try. Do you have the right candles for the different sizes and shapes of your holders? Do you have enough matches? These are rhetorical questions, but not ridiculous ones, as only a woman who has stood cursing in the darkness knows.

Now turn off all the lights for an entire evening. Granted, this is easier if the decision is yours alone, but it's not completely out of the question if you have a family. When my daughter was small, she loved celebrating Candlemas because she was able to pick out a special candle of her own; when it burned down, it was time for bed. (Tiny tea-lights are very handy!) To get the candles to reflect more light, place them in groups before a mirror. Make sure you don't place them near curtains or leave candles burning alone.

Notice how you feel by candlelight; how differently you choose what to do and how you do it. If you live with others, notice how your interaction changes; do you talk more or less? How does the conversation differ? Is it quieter, more intimate? It's interesting how our body language changes, too. With candlelight, we're like moths to the flame, moving closer to one another.

The eighteenth-century English essayist Charles Lamb described candlelight as "the kindliest luminary" and "everybody's sun and moon." Golden orbs in our ordinary; peculiar "household planet" deserving of respect and thanksgiving. Blessings be to match, wax, flame. Gratitudes to the Kindler on this our Candlemas Day.

Paradise Found

If there is a paradise on the face of the earth,
It is this, oh! It is this, oh! It is this.

—Mogul inscription in
the Red Fort at Delhi (1640)

In 1926, the English author D. H. Lawrence wrote a story that was a new version of the Resurrection. In it Jesus decides he doesn't want to take on the divine mission of saving the world and so he "cuts out" and disappears. As he rediscovers everyday life on his own, he "begins to find what an astonishing place the phenomenal world is, far more marvelous than any salvation or heaven," and he thanks his stars that he doesn't have to feel guilty about thinking about putting his own happiness before that of humankind. All of us have what we need on earth to save our own souls.

Is it any wonder that our souls seek God in earthly pleasures? There should be no surprise (or guilt) here, because in the beginning, earthly pleasures were created by Spirit to romance us.

What the world's been so quick to call sin was originally "in"— eat all you want and still not worry about frolicking naked. So let's travel back to the proverbial source of all pleasure. Let's return to Eden. Remember the enchanted garden? Adam, Eve, and the serpent lived there briefly, until they were thrown out for not appreciating how good they had it.

But forget Adam. There's no Adam to complicate things this time around. Just Spirit and you—together again, at long last. In Eden. On earth. And lots of luscious surprises await. "The strongest, surest way to the soul is through the flesh," the writer Mabel Dodge Luhan observed in 1932. This is precisely why Divinity's interested in what specifically inspires *you*. What makes the blood rush to your head? *The fragrance wafting out the doorway of a chocolatier? Discovering your favorite singer in the musical selections on a plane's headset? Watching a virtuoso instrumentalist play a passage at the speed of light? Riding in a fast car on a sunny day with the top down? Opening a box of old clothes and being enveloped with the perfume your mother used to wear on special occasions?*

What makes your heart skip a beat or knees shake with anticipation? *The silky squeak of a taffeta slip? The buttery softness of a new pair of leather gloves? Biting into a liqueur-filled chocolate? Your cat licking your face? The first sight of forsythias in the spring? Discovering a new-to-you book by your favorite author?* Do you know? Can you remember? Nothing's off-limits this time, so please look, listen, smell, touch, and taste to your heart's delight.

This is nuts, you're thinking. Get real. My daily bump and grind ain't no Paradise.

I beg to differ, dear Reader. Perhaps if you'd start behaving as an eager participant instead of a jaded critic, Life would surprise you. Of course, that means you'll have to:

1. Suspend your skepticism.
2. Follow the private prompts of your intuitive heart as if they were invitations to sacred sensory adventures.
3. Indulge the inquisitive urgings of your gutsy, lusty imagination instead of dismissing them as frivolous.

For, daughter of Eve, if desire is what got women thrown out of Eden, then surely desire can help us return.

What's in a Name?

God, I can push the grass apart
And lay my finger on Thy heart.

—Edna St. Vincent Millay
Renascence (1917)

*E*mily Dickinson believed *Home* was another name for God. Helen Keller described God as the "Light in my darkness, the Voice in my silence." The thirteenth-century mystic Julian of Norwich told her novitiates, "God is our clothing that wraps, clasps, and encloses us." Every time I slip into my beloved comfy robe at the end of a long, harrowing day, I know how right she was.

In the Hebrew tradition, so holy and hidden is the Almighty's identity that the proper name of God cannot be pronounced. But in English it is written as *YHWH*—four sacred letters representing the past, present, and future tense of the verb *to be*. God told Moses to call on the great "I AM," and when Moses did, the seas parted and his people were fed daily while wandering in the wilderness for forty years. Many of them probably looked up to the sky calling God *Manna,* the name of the heavenly sustenance that kept them alive.

When it's been raining for two weeks, I address Spirit as the *Sun.* As a winter storm rages, my name of praise for the Sacred is

Heat. If you've ever been terrified or traumatized, your name for God might be *Safety.*

Every woman who believes in God calls the Holy One by a particular name; just as those who have no faith or experience one different from yours or mine will choose another word to ·describe God. In my books I often use the word *Spirit* for God, because I do not want to impose on my readers my own view of Divinity, which is always expanding, thank Heaven. As Caitlin Matthews tells us in her luminous *Celtic Devotional: Daily Prayers and Blessings,* Celtic spirituality has many exquisite and descriptive names for Divinity, all of which honor the sacred in the ordinary: *Source of All Mystery, Gate of Gladness, Mother of Memory, Piercer of Doubt, Kindler of Hope, Keeper of Good Cheer, Ever Present Provider, Compassionate Listener, Guardian of the Hearth, Holy Source, Ancient Dream, Glad Giver, Weaver of Wonder, Revelation of Evening, Teller of Tales,* and *Queen of Quietness.*

"Mystics and poets of all eras and spiritualities have called upon the Divine according to the needs of their heart: as rock, door, tree, ground of knowledge; as mother, father, sister, brother, friend, beloved; as keeper, creator, watcher, restorer, and giver of hope," Matthews tells us. "Mystics are poets of the spirit who speak with the metaphor of delight. But every living person is also a potential mystic with an immediate and spontaneous response to the wonder of the universe."

Whom will you call on today?

Come to Your Senses

Name Thy God

*I*n the early stages of a romance I once cherished, I told my new sweetheart that my relationship to God was the most passionate in my life. I conveyed this information quite matter-of-factly, the way I'd also told him I was the mother of a fabulous nineteen-year-old girl whom I adored. My daughter's existence and prominent place in my life and heart caused not a ripple of reaction, but the God bit did. Because I was falling in love with this man, I heard myself start to qualify the declaration, but then I stopped abruptly. This was ridiculous. God was here first, and if the other guy didn't like it, now was the time to find out, because if we didn't share a spiritual connection, we could share nothing.

Later I realized that one of my greatest blessings is my conception of God as so expansive that not many people, especially men, get it or me in the beginning. That's okay. If they stick around, they begin to see a voluptuous and delicious side of Divinity. The artist and writer Julia Cameron, who gave the world the brilliant *The Artist's Way,* believes in a festive and creative God and I agree.

"After all, Somebody had an awfully good time making hibiscus blossoms, red clay cliffs, rivers, starfish, pinecones, coral snakes, and stars," she points out in *The Vein of Gold: A Journey to Your Creative Heart.* "In our culture, God is so often thought of in terms of Calvinist austerity and renunciation that we forget there was clearly a godly glee in creative excess, an artist in love with the materials themselves." For those who are uncomfortable with the concept of a loving, expansive, abundant Divinity, she suggests thinking of God as "good, orderly direction," which is a great way to reimagine Spirit. But "ultimately we all get the God we believe in," which is why "it behooves us to be very conscious of which god we believe in and invoke."

As you read this book, please be open to the vastness of the Divine and the limits of language, for I shall use many different ways to express the concept of Spirit, and some of them may surprise you. In the course of a day I may invoke several. When I'm writing, I ask the Great Creator to inspire me; if I'm hurting, I invoke the help of the Gentle Healer; if the unexpected blessing of a boisterous guffaw pierces through my earnestness, I have Milady of the Laugh to thank; when I'm fretful and worn to a raveling, I turn my exhaustion over to the beloved Sower of Sleep.

Here's a hint: If you come across a word beginning with a capital letter, I am trying to describe, however feebly, an aspect of Divinity that has comforted, sustained, and delighted me. "I understand why one wants to know the names of what [she] loves," the writer Jessamyn West explains. "Naming is a kind of possessing, of caressing and fondling."

It is a winter's day. A sky of lead hangs ominously over New York City, where I live part of the time. The prophets of doom are predicting a fierce blizzard. Outside the air feels sharp, frigid, icy, stinging. I can smell the flakes before they fall. Looking into the grim faces of the people sharing the grocery checkout line with me, I sense their apprehension, as they must sense mine. But tonight all will be well. Let the darkness close in. I'll bask in the spiritual solace of a supper that nourishes both body and soul. Spirit, thy name is Fettuccine. And if you think I'm blaspheming, then you must have my recipe.

Divine Fettuccine

You will need:

½ pound spinach fettuccine (large, flat ribbon noodles)
½ stick unsalted butter
½ cup light cream
½ cup low-fat milk
2 egg yolks
Coarse kosher salt
Freshly grated black pepper
Grated Parmesan cheese

Bring salted water to a boil and add fettuccine. Cook according to pasta instructions. If the instructions read 8 minutes, don't boil it for 15. You don't want it to turn to glue. At the proper time, drain and then pour back into the pot.

In a skillet, melt the butter. Add the cream and milk and heat just until boiling. Beat the egg yolks together and slowly add to the cream/butter mixture, a little at a time, whisking until completely blended. Simmer on low heat for a couple of minutes. (Don't walk away!)

Now pour the sauce over the drained fettuccine, mix well, and slowly warm the pasta over low heat for a minute or so. Lather it into a big bowl, and season with as much salt, pepper, and Parmesan cheese as you desire.

Light the candles. Pour the wine. Say grace. Take a bite. Give thanks. Savor! (This is supposed to serve two and it does: me and me again.)

The Soulcraft of Pampering

Self-nurture is not about being selfish.
It is about self-care.

—Alice D. Domar, Ph.D.

*M*ost women think that pampering is self-indulgent. Actually, pampering is a sacred soulcraft because pampering is self-preservation. Have you ever noticed how you feel on the fourth day of a vacation? You wake up well rested and your aches have disappeared or diminished. You realize that your emotional equilibrium is back—once again a glass of spilt milk is just that; something to be wiped up, not screamed about. You break into a grin more easily, have more energy, and are as spontaneous as the weather. If it's rainy, you'll read; if it's sunny, you'll play outside. Doesn't matter. You're back in touch with a warm, witty, wonderful woman who is fun to be around all the time, and it feels like a happy reunion.

Unfortunately, everybody's favorite gal is only around when she's been pampered—charmed, cajoled, and coaxed out of hiding. But it doesn't have to be two weeks at an expensive spa. A few days of tuning out the wants of the world and a little attention is all a blissful babe asks. It's not much.

Oh yes, it is. But stay with me. Most women think of pampering as recuperative, after they've crashed and burned. I know I did. In reality, pampering is every day's most urgent need and the best preventive medicine. "Losing touch with ourselves is easy to do these days. We are conditioned to ignore the warning signs that protect us from becoming ill," Barbara Close reminds us in her soothing guide to sensory self-care, *Well-Being: Rejuvenating Recipes for Body and Soul.* "Instead we push ahead to meet deadlines and live up to our responsibilities and commitments until fatigue or sickness overwhelms us and forces us to stop." As a

practicing aromatherapist, herbalist, and founder of Naturo-
pathica (a line of natural therapies and botanical skin-care products), Barbara believes in simple, restorative rituals that engage
all our senses. Pampering from the inside out helps us "reestablish a sense of connection to ourselves."

One of her winter therapies is "midnight massage oil," a rescue remedy for those nights of endless tossing and turning.
While the calming scent of sandalwood induces yawns, using the
oil to massage your temples, ears, and back of neck is what makes
this ritual feel so good. Perhaps it's because you are "making it all
better" for yourself.

In the beginning, introducing small moments of pampering into
your daily round is going to feel strange, unnatural, and forbidden.
But persevere, one small, kind gesture at a time. Pampering is
really Life's most natural remedy for whatever ails us physically
and psychically. So when those guilt feelings start to creep close,
remember that pampering is not selfish or frivolous. Pampering is
soulful. Pampering is how you reach out and touch your essensual
self. Pampering is the spiritual secret to becoming self-possessed.

Come to Your Senses

Let the Night Retire

Midnight Massage Ritual

*O*nce upon a time, the expression *midnight* meant waking up in the middle of a good night's sleep. Now midnight is the normal bedtime of a lot of women, who then wonder why they're so cranky in the morning. An old adage tells us that an hour of sleep before midnight is worth two hours after. So stop tiring the night in toil with a "midnight massage oil." Here's an adaptation of Barbara Close's nurturing night self-massage to help you drift off sooner rather than later.

You will need:

1-ounce glass bottle with dropper
1 ounce carrier oil
12 drops sandalwood essential oil. (A carrier oil is a cold-pressed vegetable, nut, or seed oil that reduces the possibility of irritation

when the mixture is applied to the body. Never apply an essential oil directly to the skin. Sweet almond oil is best for massage blends.)

Squeeze one dropper of oil on your hands and gently rub together. Place them over your nose and closed eyes and breathe deeply 3 times. Now slowly massage oil into your temples and rub firmly over the outer ear. Next, massage the back of your neck and shoulders using a circular motion with your fingertips. Massage your cheeks and jawline. Take another deep breath. Sigh. Turn off light and lay head on pillow. Close eyes again. Do not open until morning.

The Way You Look Today

Accustom yourself to continually make
Many acts of love for they enkindle and melt the soul.

—Saint Teresa of Avila

*A*n approving glance, a warm smile, an unexpected compliment—every day in many ways Life flirts with us. Few things in life feel as good as being the object of someone's undivided attention, even if it's fleeting. The writer Marya Mannes tells us that flirtation is "a small impermanent spark between one human being and another," but Spirit is the flint.

Flirting is a trifle, a notion entertained briefly. Flirting is the art of the possible. Flirting invites, cajoles, charms, and delights both the giver and the receiver. However, the real intent of flirting has been bludgeoned by the heavy-handed cliché of seduction. Flirting is making connection; seduction is about commandeering. If it's obvious, it's not flirting. Flirting should leave its recipient with a bit of curiosity, a touch of intrigue, and not entirely certain that what just happened was real or perceived or even intended for her (or him).

Some of the happiest women and men I know are outrageous flirts. While flirting seems to be more natural to some than others, in reality flirting is an acquired skill. Flirting has nothing to do with looks, age, or your weight. Flirting has everything to do with your attitude and your sense of adventure.

This week is devoted entirely to becoming reacquainted with the spiritual gift of flirting. Flirting is the oldest form of play and the youngest. Babies instinctually know how to flirt. Have your eyes ever met with a baby's in a restaurant? Big, inquisitive beacons give you the stare. When you engage her eyes, baby looks up, then down, then away, then back to meet your gaze. She's irresistible; you're captivated. You smile. Baby returns the smile, and a disarming game ensues until one of you departs. Although brief, your lighthearted interlude leaves a lingering good feeling for both of you. That's flirting.

On the surface flirting appears to require loads of confidence, but really what it takes is a sense of generosity and unself-consciousness. As one of the shyest people in the world, I know that reaching toward someone new can be paralyzing; nothing is more miserable than being in a room full of strangers and not knowing what to say. However, when we concentrate on making other people feel fabulous instead of impressing them, guess what? They're impressed by how fabulous we are and want to know us better. Works like a charm every time.

The most pleasant way to learn how to flirt is to allow your seven senses to lead you. So let's start by making eye contact. The eyes may be the windows to our soul, but too many of us go through life with the curtains closed. So draw them open. Begin by looking kindly and directly at everyone you meet, whether you know them or not. "Flirt for fun and leave it at that. Flirt with the man at the diner, the woman in the video store, the couple looking at the gardening tools," the writer Rachel Synder suggests. "Let them ask quizzically, *Is she flirting with us?* Laugh in a lilting kind of flirty way, toss out a little panache, a bit of *je ne sais quoi.*

Flirt until the flirting is done, then flit away, leaving a flirtatious air behind you and not one iota more."

Today throw out a few happy glances and see what comes back.

Extra Scentual Perception

Perfume is like a parenthesis. . . . Perfume follows you, it chases you and lingers behind you. It's a reference mark. Perfume makes silence talk.

—Sonia Rykiel

O ne of the most charming men I've ever known began our friendship with a flirtatious aside. A half hour earlier, we'd been complete strangers. Now we were sitting next to each other around a large conference table with ten other people. As something that I'm sure was crucial was being discussed at the far end, the man leaned in toward my ear as if he were about to convey a top secret. Instead, he whispered, "You smell so good!" I didn't know whether to laugh, scream, or swat him, I was so shocked. Actually I wanted to do all three. Instead, I behaved as if I'd just been given the statistics I'd requested. Even now, years later, recalling his outrageous behavior makes me blush. Needless to say, he made quite an impression and it was delightful.

There are many similarities between flirting and fragrance. Both are more effective when they surprise and are handled lightly. Both speak volumes but are silent languages. Both make people feel good about themselves. Both are gently provocative, nudging us past our comfort zone. Both flirting and fragrance enhance a woman's femininity, allowing her to be spontaneous and sensual. Just as flirting reveals your secret vivacious self, so does fragrance. Both are fleeting, but can be unforgettable.

"Fragrance has the instantaneous and invisible power to penetrate consciousness with pure pleasure. Scent reaches us in ways that elude sight and sound but conjure imagination in all its sensuality, unsealing hidden worlds," Mandy Aftel observes in her wonderful book *Essence and Alchemy*. "As potent as it can be, however, smell is the most neglected of our senses. We search for visual beauty in art and in nature, and take care to arrange our homes in a way that pleases the eye. We seek out new music and musicians to add to our CD collections . . . We spend time and money on sampling new and exotic cuisines, even learn to cook them. We pamper our sense of touch with cashmere sweaters, silk pajamas, and crisp linen shirts . . . Yet most of us take our sense of smell for granted, leaving it to its own devises . . . We never think about its cultivation or enrichment, even though some of life's most exquisite pleasures consequently elude us."

In Latin countries, when a woman walks down the street bestowing momentary whiffs of her scent on passersby, they turn around and inhale deeply as a compliment. But then, in Latin countries, flirting is the national sport. If you don't want to sit on Life's sidelines anymore, there are many ways that you can begin to flirt with fragrance. Spray a linen handkerchief with cologne and leave it in your favorite evening purse. Find a sprig of a scented herb that you love, such as rosemary or geranium, and press it into a cookbook, poetry volume, or your address book. Don't just apply perfume behind your ears, but also behind your knees. Indulge in a fragrant liquid soap, so that every time you wash your hands you enjoy their scent. Line your desk drawers with scented paper, tuck lavender sachets in with your gym socks, as well as your lingerie.

Like flirting, Mandy Aftel tells us, "Scent has always provided a direct path to the soul, and no one who becomes immersed in it can fail to be pleasurably changed by the experience."

Live and Let Love

*It is the loving, not the loved, woman
who feels lovable.*

—Jessamyn West

*T*his year, for a refreshing change, I thought we'd celebrate the
feast day of Saint Agabus, the patron saint of fortune-tellers,
instead of Saint Valentine, the patron saint of disappointment. For
who among us does not secretly want to know what the future
holds, especially concerning matters of the heart?

When I was in my mid-twenties, I became incredibly curious
about the world of spirits. Not God, mind you, but the lower
spiritual realm—divination—which is seeking to know the future
or hidden things through supernatural powers.

What I wanted to know: *When was I going to find true love?* So
I regularly visited crystal-ball gazers, astrologers, psychics, and
mediums. While a psychic can be a medium and vice versa, by
definition a medium is someone through whom the spirits of the
dead are said to communicate to the living. Remember Whoopi
Goldberg in the movie *Ghost?* She was a medium. A psychic, on
the other hand, has extraordinary intuitive sensibilities that allow
her to "see" the future or communicate telepathically, from mind
to mind.

After months of waiting, I was able to get a "reading" with a
famous psychic, who told me that I would spend the next twenty
years searching for my affinity, but once I found my soul mate, I
would discover it wasn't necessary to search for anything else ever
again. *Twenty years?* I was aghast. "But He must be a very important man," the psychic tried to reassure me. "Because I sense the
word *Him* is written with a capital and I see the word *abundance*
surrounding you in many languages."

Twenty years? Good Lord, if this guy was right, I'd be forty-five before true love found me. Well, what do psychics know anyway? Naturally, to resist crawling out on the nearest ledge, I had to put my own positive spin on this devastating news. A couple of glasses of wine convinced me that the prediction meant I'd marry the Aga Khan or an international financier, and at the very least, I'd spend my dotage in luxurious comfort.

Wrong again. No marriage to an international financier. No Far Eastern potentate on bended knee. But how freaky-deaky that two decades after that prediction, I wrote a book entitled *Simple Abundance,* which to date has been translated into thirty languages.

And *Him?* Well, the Him I found wasn't at all whom or what I'd expected. But then the Real Thing always comes as a surprise. "For me, nothing is so exciting as to imagine that *life* is my lover—and is *always* courting me," Julie Henderson confides in *The Lover Within.* "To relate to life in that way is a challenge and a surrender that invites me deeper into being alive in every moment that I can manage it."

I finally stopped seeking psychic advice once I came to the awareness that spiritual time and earthly time are not the same. I'm thankful that many of the predictions made in my twenties came true decades later in rather astonishing ways. But what I'm really grateful for is the realization that when we wait for a future others have foretold, we return to sender the gift waiting for us today: the present.

These days I continue to wish upon a star, open fortune cookies, and occasionally delve into bibliomancy. One of the oldest forms of divination, bibliomancy is forecasting events by opening the Bible and seeing what message is waiting for you. Saint Agabus was a contemporary of Jesus', and I suspect that he may have contributed toward bringing divination back to the realm where it belongs and should stay: Divine Knowledge. For when you seek and follow the wants and whispers of Spirit, your good fortune in Life and Love is assured, here and now.

Lost and Found

One knows what one has lost, but
not what one may find.

—George Sand

Should you ever find yourself footloose in Paris, take a walk near the artists' district of Montmartre to No. 16 rue Chaptal. In this lovely house and quiet garden is the Museum of Romantic Life, a small jewel of remembrance dedicated to the life and loves of the nineteenth-century French writer George Sand, who frequently went over the top in her pursuit of passion. I wish that I could tell you that I discovered this sensory delight while roaming the streets of Paris arm in arm with a lover, but alas, I can't. Like most of my romantic encounters during these last five years, it was a solitary sensation.

One of my favorite writers is the "life coach" Martha Beck, who has the extraordinary gift of making you laugh while she dismantles your hard-held illusions, such as the fantasy that romantic fulfillment only comes from sharing our lives with the perfect partner. Years ago Martha also found herself alone in Paris, but instead of feeling isolated, she almost swooned with enchantment. "Walking the streets of Paris in a thin spring rain, breathing the smell of apple blossoms and coffee, I realized that you don't have to wait around for the perfect companion to have a richly romantic life. There are people who have relationships but no romance, and there are those whose lives are full of romance even when they're not paired up."

The most delicious midlife secret for a woman is that while the tango requires two, living a deeply rewarding romantic life requires only one. You. "When you're living from the heart, every moment brings another chance to fall in love," Martha Beck reminds us this Valentine's Day. "The only thing you must do to live a deeply romantic life is to base every decision you make on love: self-love; love of others; love of ideas, activities, and places; love of smells, tastes, sights, sounds, and textures. Living this way brings romance into the smallest, most ordinary moments and leads to a lot of large and extraordinary ones."

Come to Your Senses

Falling in Love with Love

*F*alling in love with love, always wanted to. What's a babe to do? Can't help it. Love's always been my thrill. How about you? Simple reason. It feels *so* good. Have you ever noticed the way your everyday life changes when you are falling, or have fallen, in love?

Every woman has her own secret agenda of bodily pleasures, even if they aren't being shared with the new object of her affection: buying a new perfume or, perhaps, if she has stopped wearing one, beginning again . . . making sure that every speck of unwanted hair is removed from her legs and underarms . . . moisturizing her entire surface, not just her hands and face . . . having her hair done in a fancier way or a new tint . . . painting her toenails . . . donning pretty underwear, sheerer stockings, sexier clothes . . . buying herself new accessories, jewelry, lingerie . . .

Which do *you* do? And just think of how much pleasure these acts give you in private as you perform them and carry yourself afterward: feeling soft and smooth and beautiful, looking and smelling delicious . . . loving *yourself* as you make yourself lovable.

Now, think about your other behavior, as you excitedly wait for—or daydream about the last time you saw—your beloved. Or think of him while you must be apart. Do you imagine gloriously romantic scenarios unfolding between you, even if they might not even remotely happen? Read poetry? Look at works of art that depict lovers? Listen to love songs? Seek out novels and movies and lyrics that reflect your feelings about this person, your hopes for the relationship, how you see yourself during such a magical jumble of anticipation and memory and happiness? How much do you read into such works, at such times? How much do you draw *out of* them?

When you're in love, do you take particular care to clean your home, primp your bedroom, make your bathroom enticing? Do you prepare or buy delectable meals or tidbits for your lover? Together, do you seek out candlelit, intimate restaurants . . . or go as a couple to "in" spots, the theater, other memorable events?

Do you find yourself humming as you go about your day, smiling at strangers, doing extra good deeds or being kinder, because you just feel so *good* that you want everyone else to feel that way, too?

Wait a minute. If all this feels so wonderful, why do you give yourself permission to feel it only if another person is involved? Can you see how much you are actually doing for *yourself* when you are in love?

Love wakes us up to the wonders of the world, and also to the wonders of our own selves. It is so easy to neglect our senses when we secretly feel they'd just be *wasted* on only us. Pursuing pleasure on our own seems too decadent. Narcissistic. Self-indulgent. We need to get over that, quick. If you can't please yourself, when you know better than anyone else how to do it, who else is gonna do it for you? What they say about a woman knowing how to let her lover please her extends way beyond sex.

Get yourself in the mood by remembering how giddily inspiring it felt to be in love. Remember how you believed yourself capable of anything, how you wished you could gobble up life itself? Read old letters, the lyrics or fiction that made your heart sing, recall all the good parts of the love affairs that went wrong (no one can take those memories away, not even lovers who turned out to be disappointments). Feel your pulse race, look at how your face glows.

If you've been in love even just once, you can feel loved however and whenever you wish. By yourself. You don't have to wait for a man of flesh and blood to come along to release the good feelings of being an attractive, fascinating, capable woman.

So, bathe and make yourself delicious. Outfit yourself with trinkets and clothing that give you pleasure. Prepare the kind of meal or dessert you'd make for company, or take yourself out to a restaurant with a good book for company. Go to a show, a sporting event, whatever it is that you find exhilarating when you're out on a date. Light those candles for yourself, and bask in how beautiful you now look in the light. Become the most sparkling, confident company you have ever known and you'll be alone only as long as you want to.

Strive to develop a conscious awareness of what an intoxicating creature you *automatically* become when you are in love with someone else . . . and learn how to re-create this, how to turn it on at will for your own delight *especially* when you are alone. Your ideal human lover may not be around at the moment, but the glories of your own self and your world eagerly await your attentions.

Game, Set, Match, Love

*Falling in love consists merely in uncorking
the imagination and bottling the common-sense.*

—Helen Rowland

"*L*ife coaches" such as Martha Beck help their clients learn how to rearrange their priorities so that their daily choices support their deepest passions. Unlike therapy, life coaching doesn't focus on the past, but on the present. When the clock is running out, a football coach doesn't ask the quarterback to rethink where he went wrong in the first half. "My objective with all my life-design clients is to find out what makes them feel passionate, mesmerized, sensually stimulated, and carried away by desire and fulfillment," Martha explains.

In other words, what turns them on. What motivates them to get off the bench or their butt and start moving toward the life and love that's waiting for them. Romance is not a spectator sport.

"I've watched dozens of people approach their true life's work the same way they approached their true love: first a timid, tentative flirtation, then an electric connection, then an overwhelming sense of coming home, and finally a lifelong relationship full of hard work and deep contentment. You can fall in love with anything that feels like part of your destiny: a new baby, the house you decorated yourself, long-distance running, the monthly discussions at your book club."

For me, it's rare sheep. As they say, when you least expect it and aren't looking, zing goes the strings of your heart. Two years ago a friend asked if I'd like to go to a British livestock show of rare breeds—cattle, sheep, goats, pigs, and poultry. It sounded like a pleasant outing, so I agreed. The morning of the show I awoke with what can only be described as first-date jitters. I changed my boots three times. For some unfathomable reason I was nervous. It wasn't anxiety, mind you, but the delicious frisson of anticipation. When we reached the fairgrounds, the earth beneath my feet began to rumble. By the time we got to the barn with the rare sheep, my heart was pounding. Ms. Practical broke into a sweat, but my soul was soaring.

I took one look at all the different kinds of sheep, beautiful breeds whose lineage stretched back to biblical times, and felt as if I were on Noah's Ark. Then, I took one look at her—a little Balwen Welsh Mountain lass—and fell head over Wellingtons in love. She was a small black ewe (the feminine, pronounced "you") with a white face, four little white "socks," and the most soulful eyes I've ever looked into. I know you'll find this as hard to believe as I did, but I swear it seemed as if she smiled back at me. It was the look I'd always expected to exchange with my soul mate, and in the truest sense of instant/ancient recognition, it was. Now, over the years I've learned to surrender a lot of expectations about love's packaging, but the tail *was* a surprise.

Of course, now my life has changed in wondrous ways, and so have my dreams, priorities, and choices. I also understand why it was necessary for me to have been "singled out" by Spirit for a few solitary years. My true love—Life—needed a little matchmaking help. But I won't kid you, it would be fabulous if someday the shepherdess and her little flock found a shepherd with a great Border collie. In the meantime, she reads and studies *Small-Scale Sheep Keeping* with a passion.

Your soul mate will most likely be wearing more than a sheepskin when you lock gazes. Maybe your true love will be a man, but maybe it will be a painting, a gourmet vegetable garden, or the view from the first mountain you ever climb. What's important is to realize how much we shortchange our chances for real happiness when we insist on how "it" has to be. All that's required is that we stop observing life from the sidelines. Or as Martha Beck puts it, "Make your life a romantic adventure and love will find you."

Come to Your Senses

Table for One

*D*ining alone on the most romantic day of the year need not be depressing. It's an opportunity for you to treat yourself to an assembly of petite delicacies that (alas!) many men would find too dainty for dinner. For you, consider it a very celebration of your femininity.

Prepare your table: Bring forth your best lace or damask table-cloth, your "good" china and glassware, a real cloth napkin. Dim the lights in favor of tall, flickering tapers. Buy yourself a full-blown red rose—no, not for a bud vase: take down your prettiest fruit or salad bowl (ideally crystal or faceted glass, to catch that candlelight) and fill it with water. Float the petals on top. This will be your centerpiece and, later, your finger bowl. If you enjoy wine, reserve a nice rosé for the occasion.

Set the mood with a selection of dreamy music: violin concerti or Chopin nocturnes; Tchaikovsky's ballet music; the love songs of Kern, Porter, Berlin; operatic love duets . . .

Lay out a dressy dress, your party shoes, and sparkly jewelry; do your hair and makeup as if you were going out.

Start dessert the morning or evening before, so that it will be chilled in time for your St. Valentine's Day dinner: a luscious chocolate mousse.

Not Meant to Share Mousse

You will need:

2 ounces (2 squares) semisweet baking chocolate
2 teaspoons unsalted butter
1 tablespoon Kahlúa or prepared coffee
1 egg, separated
Pinch of salt

1. In a small double boiler over hot but not boiling water, melt the chocolate and butter, stirring with a whisk until smooth. Whisk in the liqueur or coffee, and the egg yolk. Remove from flame.
2. In a small bowl, beat the egg white until soft peaks form, sprinkle on the salt, and continue beating until stiff but not dry. Fold, a spoonful at a time, into the chocolate mixture.
3. Evenly distribute the mousse between two teacups or wineglasses. Cover with plastic wrap and refrigerate.

For your romantic entrée, stop by a gourmet grocery for small quantities of perfect, sweet, *tiny* vegetables: finger-size zucchini or two-bite pattypan squash, baby carrots, snow peas, miniature artichokes, and the like. Pick up as well a Rock Cornish hen, one-quarter pound of fresh mushrooms (shiitake or straw are more flavorful than button), and tricolor orzo (rice-shaped pasta) for:

Spiced Rock Cornish Hen Platter

You will need:

2 tablespoons olive oil
¼ pound mushrooms, cleaned and sliced

¼ teaspoon salt, plus an extra pinch
¼ teaspoon cinnamon
¼ teaspoon cardamom
Pinch each of cumin and turmeric
1 Rock Cornish hen, washed and wiped dry
Various small vegetables, rinsed and left whole
½ cup (dry) tricolor orzo
1 pat of butter

1. Heat 1 tablespoon of the olive oil in a small skillet and sauté the mushrooms over medium heat for 5 minutes. Sprinkle with a pinch of salt once cooked.
2. Preheat oven to 375°, and have ready a baking pan with a rack.
3. Combine the spices and the remaining salt. Sprinkle one-quarter teaspoon of the mixed spices inside the hen, then stuff with the mushrooms (sew closed or secure with skewer). Rub remaining tablespoon of the olive oil on the bird, and sprinkle on the remaining spice mixture. Place the stuffed hen breast down on the rack in the baking pan.
4. Roast at 375° for 30 minutes. Remove hen from the oven, turn it over, and baste it with pan juices. Continue to roast at 375° for another 40 minutes, basting every 10 minutes with pan juices.
5. During the final 15 minutes as the hen roasts, prepare the orzo according to package directions, and steam the vegetables whole.
6. Spread the cooked pasta on a serving platter and dot with butter, top with the roasted hen, and surround the bird with the colorful, steamed vegetables.

Light those candles, start the music . . . and appreciate how beautiful your table looks, how inviting and fragrant that dish. What a *shame* it would be to share it with another person who wouldn't appreciate it. Approach your meal as if an invisible butler had just set it down before you, as if you are attending an exclusive dinner party at which you are the single guest of an unseen, unknown admirer who has spared no effort to please you.

Eat voluptuously. Once you have cut into the hen, pick up the parts with your fingers . . . and eat the vegetables with your fingers, too. Swirl forkfuls of orzo to soak up the succulent drippings. Restore pristine splendor to your delicate hands by dabbling your fingertips in your rose-topped centerpiece. And now, more lady-like, reach for dessert . . . nibble it in the smallest possible spoonfuls, to make it last.

At bedtime, slip into your prettiest nightie and leave yourself a bedside note: to treat yourself to that *second* portion of mousse for breakfast when you awaken. Oh, what decadence! What a senses-gratifying evening . . . and morning after.

Becoming Your Own Courtesan

We are ourselves our happiness.

—Letitia Elizabeth Landon (1825)

Since antiquity, and until this last century, women have basically had two lifestyle choices: lives of "worth" (in the home or church) or wantonness (on the stage or in brothels). However, down through the ages, certain intrepid females have shunned both paths, preferring to take their lives and fortunes into their own hands as courtesans.

"The true courtesan was traditionally more than a beautiful prostitute," Megan Tressider explains in her stunning book *The Secret Language of Love.* "Many of the most successful courtesans in history were cultured and sophisticated, enjoying considerable power and prestige." Courtesans were accomplished women of great beauty, wit, and intelligence. Highly sought companions of royalty, prime ministers, and wealthy gentlemen, they were expertly skilled in the elegant arts, which, besides lovemaking, included conversing (debate, tête-à-tête, riposte), flirtation, entertaining, music, poetry, art, sports, politics, and intrigue. "The courtesan might seem at first to represent the antithesis of love, but in many ways her history is spectacularly romantic. . . . These women often commanded intense love and prompted great works of art, from the tragic heroine of Verdi's opera *La Traviata* to Manet's fascinating portrait of the haughty, naughty French cocotte whom he named Olympia."

As with other specialty trades—Spanish bullfighting, Venetian gondoliering, and vaudeville—learning the subtle nuances of courtesanship was mostly a family affair. In the delightful 1958 film *Gigi,* based on a short story by the French writer Colette, a young girl is being groomed as a courtesan by her grandmother, and her training includes everything from table manners ("Bad table manners, my dear Gigi, have broken up more households than infidelity") to the art of entering a room. Allure is attainable.

There's much to be said for the revival of courtesan grooming for women of all ages. Not to woo the world, mind you, but to seduce yourself. Here's how to start. Say aloud, *I am the most fascinating woman in the world because I can . . .* Then fill in the blanks. *I can prepare the perfect lobster risotto. I can speak Italian fluently. I can play billiards or poker, or chess.* What have you always wanted to do or understand? The difference between a bull and a bear market? How to remember that *The Iliad* is about war and *The Odyssey* about love? Make a list. What social situations do you avoid because you feel awkward? From learning how to hold a fish fork or hold up your end of a conversation, make up your mind that you're going to dismantle your fear with information. We can all use a little finishing-school polish—whether it's through lessons, lectures, books, or asking Jeeves questions on the Internet. So become a secret know-it-all. Do you have any idea how thrilling it is to actually enjoy your own company? It's like having a numbered account in Switzerland. Something you can always bank on. Begin to think of this year as your cosmic charm course.

"*What* a desire! . . . To live in peace with that word: Myself," the English writer Sylvia Ashton confessed in her memoir. Become your own courtesan and watch the world begin to court you.

Awaiting Love

Love charms are temporary things if your mojo ain't total.

—Toni Cade Bambara

*N*othing is more mysterious, mystical, or magical than falling in love, except perhaps preparing for its arrival. "The quest for love is at the heart of much of our striving, yet it is not striving that invokes it. Although there are no absolute strategies for making love happen and no surefire oracles for predicting the time and place of its arrival, there are ways in which one can prepare for it," Nancy Bauch and Michelle Lizieri remind us in their tiny jewel of a book, *Awaiting a Lover.* First, one must cultivate "the conditions of being that will not only invite love but also encourage it to thrive."

The women are talking about reviving "the lost arts of love," and we'll get there in a little bit. But first, inspired by the sight of my own romantic setting, I'm curious about what surrounds your being today. If Love unexpectedly knocks on your door, would you be too embarrassed by the household chaos engulfing you to answer? Could you ask Love to make himself comfortable or would you have to dig out the chair from underneath the clothes, videos, stray shoe? Could you open your refrigerator door and whip up something tempting or do you not even want to go there? When Love wants to wash off the dust from the long journey to your side, do you think the sink scum will enchant? What about the week's worth of newspapers strewn about the living room floor? Is it enough tinder to light Love's fire? Sometimes love charms, potions, and spells are not what we need to get us in the mood, toots.

So here's a practical magic spell for drawing romance toward you. If you open it, close it. If you take it out, put it back. If you throw it down, pick it up. If you take it off, hang it up.

Gotta go change the sheets.

The Lost Arts of Love

*For believe me, the more one is, the richer
is all one experiences. And whoever wants
to have deep love in his life must collect and
save for it and gather honey.*

—Rainer Maria Rilke

*B*elieve it or not, the art of arranging beds (of which changing
the sheets is a crucial step) was one of the sixty-four romantic skills mentioned in the *Kama Sutra* as essential when preparing
for Love's arrival.

Like the Bible, the *Kama Sutra* seems to be one of those books
that everybody has strong opinions about, especially if one has
never read it. Written in India during the second century B.C. by a
nobleman named Vaysyayana, the *Kama Sutra* is one of the world's
most ancient and revered texts of sexual wisdom. During the
"swinging" decades of the 1960s and 1970s, excerpted portions of
the *Kama Sutra* became notorious for their detailing of myriad sexual positions. However, far from being a dirty book that espouses
"free love" or sex without strings, the *Kama Sutra* is the opposite—
a guidebook devoted to the care of a lover's body *and* soul—written to draw a man and a woman closer together through mutual
pleasure and respect for each other's desires and needs.

As for the rather athletic sexual positions that gave the *Kama
Sutra* its bawdy reputation, they don't appear to be as peculiar or
perverted as the catechism of cliché would have you believe, once
you understand that Eastern philosophies do not separate sex
from its spiritual nature: The suggested techniques incorporate
yoga positions.

But it's the lost romantic arts of the *Kama Sutra* that hold our
interest today. Here is the Love curriculum we've never been
taught in school, broken down by categories.

81

The Arts of Performing—Singing, playing musical instruments; dancing—expressive movements with hands and body to convey emotions and feeling; drawing—skill at using different art mediums with charm and feeling.

The Arts of Handicrafts—Cutouts (making stencils for decorating the body); mosaics; bookbinding; needlework; lace-making; basket-weaving; woodwork and carpentry.

The Floral Arts—Making custom carpets out of blossoms; garlands for the body and bed hangings; bouquet arranging; floral crowns; and head ornaments.

The Art of Pleasing Appearance—Makeup, including preparation of color dyes for the body and the teeth; the art of manicure; the art of massage; the art of care for the hair—grooming and decorative.

The Art of the Glance and Facial Expressions

The Art of Jewelry—Making of ivory and mother-of-pearl ear ornaments; detailed knowledge of stones and gems.

The Art of Decorating and Furnishing Houses—the art of arranging beds; the art of dining; the art of resting areas.

The Art of the Bath

The Art of Entertaining—Preparing meals that bring sensory pleasure—via sight, aroma, taste; the art of unusual cuisine intended to surprise and delight; the art of preparing drinks; the art of service; the art of aphrodisiacs.

The Art of Conjuring—Knowledge of love charms, potions, and magic utterances for greater sexual prowess and to enhance beauty (but not black magic, which is forbidden); the art interpreting omens and consulting oracles.

The Art of Wordplay—Knowledge of dramatic storytelling; recitation of quotations and classical texts; solving riddles, puns, and conundrums; knowledge of the dictionary and poetic meter; the art of composition—the verse, the love letter, the invitation; knowledge of enhancing memory.

The Art of Games—Children's games; holiday games; dice; chess; games of chance and sport.

The Arts of Arboriculture—Gardening; knowledge of stock breeding and care of animals.

The Art of Speaking—Knowledge of foreign languages and regional dialects; knowledge of sign language.

The Art of Behavior—*Knowledge of good manners; knowledge of
rules of success; knowledge of the art of approach and withdrawal; the art of persuasion.*
And last, but certainly not least, my favorite, which defies a
category:
The Art of Teaching Parrots to Recite Poetry.

I don't know about you, but to me the *Kama Sutra*'s curriculum
sounds like a wonderful prerequisite for Life, not just romance.
Because any man or woman who is this accomplished, intelli-
gent, and savvy is going to be an irresistible magnet to others.
When analyzing the deeper meaning behind the purpose of the lost
arts of love, what becomes clear is that Heaven has always intended
for us to become wonderfully whole and complete within ourselves
before seeking the company of another.

Which art do you want to start perfecting? I'm already familiar
with several, but many I'm not, and a few sound so irresistible
that they must be considered, especially teaching a parrot poetry.
Imagine for a moment inviting the object of your desire to your
home and, after he crosses the threshold, having a beautiful bird
recite Rumi:

*Since the beginning of her life, she has been looking for your
face and today she has found it. Welcome . . .*

Adult education, indeed.

Come to Your Senses

The Food of Love

When she turned fifty, the Peruvian writer Isabel Allende realized that her biggest source of sighs—both of pleasure and remorse—were associated with the senses. And so, repenting of her diets ("the delicious dishes rejected out of vanity"), as much as lamenting "the opportunities for making love that I let go by because of pressing tasks or puritanical virtue," she set forth on a "mapless journey through the regions of sensual memory" with pen and spoon. The result became *Aphrodite: A Memoir of the Senses,* a luscious, charming, and saucy exploration of the sensual arts of food and love.

Here is a cookbook meant to be savored in bed as much as in the kitchen, for it's a glorious celebration of the aphrodisiac power of the imagination, and of the bewildering array of substances and practices from different cultures around the world believed to arouse passion and desire before Viagra. But getting past the taboo of even the word *aphrodisiac,* named in honor of the Greek goddess of love, is an enormous feat for many women. If it makes you uncomfortable, take a deep breath—you're not alone. What comes to mind? Half-told high school tales of "Spanish fly" or ghastly concoctions of crocodile semen and powdered rhinoceros horn? Why not think about violets, chocolate, coffee, asparagus, honey, basil, peaches, or pears? Down through the centuries, these natural wonders have also been coveted and condemned because of their abilities to kindle romantic urgings. If that's the criteria, why not add Cole Porter and a chilled glass of champagne to the list of the forbidden? Better yet, let's not. I'll just pop the cork and instead of facing the music, let's listen to it and shake off a tabootie or two.

For at the end of the day or the end of a life, "the only truly infallible aphrodisiac is love," Isabel Allende reminds us. "When love exists, nothing else matters, not life's predicaments, not the fury of the years, not a physical winding down or scarcity of opportunity." And Love comes, bidden or not, in many guises.

In that spirit, here's another "ordinary" aphrodisiac—figs—that certainly brings my soul and body together in mutual pleasure. And that's a good thing! Cooking in the nude is optional, but do be careful of splattering oil. That's a bad, bad thing.

Kama Sausages with Fig Sauce

Served on a bed of rice.

You will need:

½ cup sugar
½ cup red wine vinegar
1 stick cinnamon
½ teaspoon ground cloves
1 teaspoon nutmeg
2 slices lemon
1 pound fresh or canned figs (drained)
¾ pound sweet Italian sausage
2 tablespoons white wine
2 teaspoons olive oil
Salt and pepper to taste

For the fig sauce, combine the sugar, vinegar, cinnamon, cloves, nutmeg, and lemon in a saucepan. Bring to a boil. Reduce heat and simmer for 5 minutes. Add the figs. If you're using fresh figs, cook on low heat for 20 minutes; only 5 minutes for canned figs.

Cool the fig sauce in the refrigerator. The next day, cook the sausage in the wine and olive oil in a skillet until thoroughly cooked and the wine has evaporated. Serve the sausage on a bed of rice and top with warmed fig sauce and add salt and pepper to taste.

Sin and Sensibility

Chocolate is no ordinary food. It is not something you can take or leave, something you like only moderately. You don't like chocolate. You don't even love chocolate. Chocolate is something you have an affair with.

—Geneen Roth

Chocolate and sex share a clandestine allure. Perhaps that's because chocolate is one of the earliest recorded aphrodisiacs. Both carnal pleasures are powerful conduits of intense sensation, capable of triggering a crescendo of emotions—from elation to guilt. Both arouse comfort as well, which is why, in the absence of love, chocolate and sex are often used as sensory surrogates.

"The Aztecs and Mayans were the first to recognize the potency of chocolate, celebrating the harvest of the cacao bean with festivals of wild orgies," Martha Hopkins and Randall Lockridge tell us in their delightful *InterCourses: An Aphrodisiac Cookbook*. Because the Aztecs believed that drinking chocolate endowed them with higher powers—wisdom, enlightenment, and sexual prowess—it was consumed only by men of the ruling or religious classes. Reportedly, the Aztec leader Montezuma drank fifty goblets of chocolate each day to better serve his harem of six hundred women. This historical footnote explains why he was caught with his guard down when the Spanish conquistador Hernán Cortés arrived in Mexico in 1519. The following year, after Cortés crushed the Aztec empire, he brought back not only gold and jewels, but also the Aztec's methods for extracting the undiluted, unsweetened mystical liquor from fermented cacao beans.

When the Spanish royals first tasted chocolate, they may very well have called it Montezuma's revenge; his brew was bitter and unpalatable to their refined palates, so they sweetened their chocolate drinks with honey and sugar. But again, chocolate's amorous thrills were reserved for only the nobility and remained a closely guarded state secret for almost a century. However, in 1615 when a Spanish princess married French king Louis XIII, chocolate traveled from the boudoir to the dining table. Chocolate's sensuous spell spread like wildfire throughout Europe, as specialty purveyors began to concoct all manner of chocolate aphrodisiacs: cakes, candies, and liquors. When Spanish women became so addicted to chocolate that they began to sip it from flasks during long church services, the French gourmet Jean-Anthelme Brillat-Savarin observed, "This sensuality . . . brought down upon them the wrath of their bishops." Chocolate was deemed a lustful weakness of the flesh, thereby giving to yet another pleasure the patina of sinful irresistibility.

Aztec women were forbidden to drink chocolate because Montezuma feared it would unleash feminine magical powers even more terrifying than extinction by the conquistadores. One could argue that the Aztec civilization would still be thriving today had women been given their just desserts.

In her luminous novel *Like Water for Chocolate*, an enchanting fable of love, sex, war, cooking, and Mexican history as seen through the eyes of women, the writer and kitchen mystic Laura Esquivel reminds us that whether "to the table or to bed, you must come when you are bid."

Remember that. Go now, my good woman, and sin some more.

So here's a heavenly love potion to take to table or bed. It's the signature drink of New York's restaurant Serendipity 3.

Frozen White Hot Chocolate

You will need:

½ cup heavy cream
6 ounces white chocolate, preferably 2 ounces each
    of different quality brands, such as Lindt, Valrhona,
    Callebaut, Nestlé Premier, or Ghirardelli
¾ cup milk
6 fresh mint leaves, plus 2 sprigs for garnish
Maraschino cherries for garnish,
Dark chocolate sprinkles for garnish

Whip the cream and refrigerate. Chill two 12-ounce glass goblets. Break up the chocolate, place in a heavy saucepan over low heat, and stir until melted. Remove from heat and whisk in half of the milk until well blended.

Place the remaining milk in a blender with the white chocolate mixture, 6 mint leaves, and 2 cups of ice. Blend at high speed until smooth, frothy, and the ice is pulverized. Pour into goblets, top with whipped cream, mint sprigs, cherries, and chocolate sprinkles.

Makes 2 servings. This sin may be shared. However, in memory of the chocolate deprivation suffered by the women of Montezuma's harem, this seduction is all the company you need on a long winter's evening.

Come to Your Senses

Divine Decadence

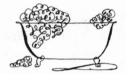

*I*s there a woman alive who has not attempted to drown her romantic woes in a tub of chocolate? Well, now you can save the frosting for the cake. Celebrate February with a chocolate milk bath known as Divine Decadence. Mix together well: 2 cups of powdered milk, 3 tablespoons of powdered cocoa, and one-quarter cup of cornstarch. Pour one-quarter cup of the mixture underneath the tap while the bathwater is running. (Be sure to store the remaining milk bath in an airtight glass container.) This bath is heaven-sent: the frothy fragrance goes to your head and not your hips. One caveat: as you would after an illicit rendezvous, you'll have to cover your tracks. This dunking does leave a telltale bathtub ring.

How to resist drinking the water? Concentrate on another sense—listening. How about a private serenade by Michael Feinstein, who croons the romantic hits of the thirties, forties, and fifties, the way Jerome Kern, Ira Gershwin, Cole Porter, and Rodgers and Hart wrote them to be sung. His CD *Michael Fein-*

stein: Romance on Film, Romance on Broadway is the perfect way to bring romance to the bathtub.

Chocolate Becomes You

Much serious thought has been devoted to the subject of chocolate: What does chocolate mean? Is the pursuit of chocolate a right or a privilege? Does the notion of chocolate preclude the concept of free will?

—Sandra Boynton

*I*t should come as no surprise that women crave chocolate more than men do. However, what is a pleasant discovery is that our passionate codependency has meaning and purpose.

In a word: psychopharmacology. Both chocolate and romance are opiates of choice for the fabulous, fully functioning female brain because they trigger production of Mother Nature's mood-elevating brain chemical phenylethylamine, or PEA (pronounced *fen-nel-ethel-uh-mean*). From the first flush of lust to the last luscious bite of a brownie, that amphetamine-like rush that goes to our heads makes sense. What's more, your well-being depends on it.

Unfortunately, because chocolate so powerfully replicates the heady sensations of infatuation, it's the most emotionally charged food imaginable. When the romance ends, or a woman's depressed for "no reason" (other than being sad, scared, lonely, jilted, worried, or hormonal), her craving for PEA intensifies. If she honors that craving, a little chocolate goes a long way. And if she doesn't? Eventually, she'll binge. The next morning, when she's surrounded by empty ice cream containers, pleasure becomes punitive, gratification becomes guilt, and she stays trapped in an endless cycle of deprivation/overindulgence. Do you want to continue living that way? Well, she doesn't, and I don't blame her.

This year it would be wonderful to restore chocolate to its lofty origins, as the Divine gift it was intended to be. But to do that you must stop denying and dismissing your cravings and start listening to your body. "If you understand the way your female body functions, it will empower you to take care of yourself and respond to your body's food needs every day—even when your body is telling you that it needs chocolate. Yes, chocolate," nutritionist Debra Waterhouse reassuringly explains in *Why Women Need Chocolate: Eat What You Crave to Look and Feel Great*. "Food cravings are Mother Nature's way of informing us that we need to eat a specific food in order to look and feel great . . . food cravings are not a problem to be treated, but a blessing to be encouraged."

I know the very thought of trusting your body to tell you what it needs is threatening enough to make you devour an entire bag of Oreo cookies in the supermarket aisle. But wait a minute. Instead, why not put four on a pretty plate and pour yourself a nice glass of milk. Now as you dunk and savor, consider this: Isn't trust the greatest gift we can offer to a lover? Savoring your perfectly plausible pleasures every day just *might* be the beginning of a great romance.

Has anyone told you lately that chocolate becomes you?

Between the Lines

Sense-Drenched Spirituality

*M*any people spend their entire lives struggling with the mistaken idea that to live a sensual life means you cannot be spiritual. Should these thoughts cross your mind, it's reassuring to go back to the Good Book—the Bible—and rediscover through your own understanding, rather than through someone else's interpretations or opinions, Spirit's view on the senses. Begin in Genesis with the creation story, and you'll discover the first Divine imperative was *Let there be light.*

In her stunning book *A Natural History of the Senses,* poet and naturalist Diane Ackerman points out that essensuality is there for all to seek and find in between the lines of one of the Bible's most revered passages, thought to have been penned by King Solomon.

The most scent-drenched poem of all time, "The Song of Solomon," avoids talk of body or even natural odors, and yet weaves a luscious love story around perfumes and unguents. In the story's arid lands, where water was rare, people perfumed themselves often and well, and this betrothed couple, whose marriage day approaches, in the meantime converse amorously in poetry, sweetly dueling with compliments lavish and ingenious. When he dines at her table he is a "bundle of myrrh" . . . or muscular and sleek as "a young gazelle." To him, her robust virginity is a secret "garden . . . a spring shut up, a fountain sealed." Her lips "drop as the honeycomb: honey and milk are under thy tongue; and the smell of thy garments is like the smell of Lebanon." He tells her that on their wedding night he will enter her garden, and he catalogues all the fruits and spices he knows he'll find there: frankincense, myrrh, saffron, camphire, pomegranates, aloes, cinnamon, calamus and other treasures. She will weave a fabric of love around him, and fill his senses until they brim with oceanic extravagance. So stirred is she by this loving tribute and so wild with desire that she replies yes, she will throw open the gates of her garden to him: "Awake, O north wind; and come, thou south; blow upon my garden, that the spices thereof may flow out. Let my beloved come into his garden, and eat his pleasant fruits."

—Diane Ackerman
A Natural History of the Senses

March

A light exists in spring
Not present on the year
At any other period –
When March is scarcely here.

–Emily Dickinson

*L*ike a restless heart looking for love, the frozen earth yearns for spring. But to rush a season or romance is to miss Life's subtle nuances. March is our go-between. So change your mind about change. It's here today, gone tomorrow. Lighten up. Luxuriate in the fullness of waiting. Stop juggling until you find your balance. Celebrate new rites of passage. Let Mother Nature nurture. Cultivate sacred space. Find the "inscentive" to make a clean sweep. Get lucky. Weed your closet. Send ghosts packing. Play around with alternative remedies—the color of daffodils, the fragrance of lavendered linen. Take a deep breath, have a good cry, puddle-jump over problems. Stand still, so you can spring forward to a fresh start.

Between the Dreaming
and the Coming True

Waiting is one of the great arts.

—Margery Allingham

*U*ntil recently, I've shared T. S. Eliot's approach to waiting: "Hurry up please it's time." But it never *is* time for the waiting to be over, until it's time. No matter how much wringing of the hands, crying, begging, or bargaining we do, the waiting will continue until it's damn good and ready, which is rarely soon enough.

It's been my excruciating experience—over and over—that the torture of waiting only ceases after you're no longer consciously aware that you're waiting. You stop jumping every time the phone rings, stop checking your e-mail every half hour, stop pacing up and down until the post arrives. Exhausted, you loosen your grip on the situation. Why? Because you've given up, that's why. Lost hope. Let go. Licked your wounds and moved on. Call it what you will, you've detached yourself from the final outcome, as the enlightened would say. But what malarkey that sounds like when you're driven half-mad with desire.

How I wait.

First week: Hopeful. Confident. Cheery.

Second week: Optimistic. Philosophical. Edgy.

Third week: Discouraged. Depressed. Snarly.

Fourth week: *Have mercy! Hurry up please it's time!!!! I don't care what happens, just let the torment be over!*

Fifth week: I don't want to talk about it. Don't you *dare* tell me the Universe knows best.

Indeterminable time in the future: Oh, my God. You're kidding! Really? You wouldn't joke about this, would you? I don't believe it! *Thankyouthankyouthankyou!!!!*

Well, now, that wasn't *so* bad.

The only good thing to be said about waiting, and I hate to be the one to say it, is that it works. Waiting is the soul of the Divine Scheme of Things, whether it suits our plans or not. Heaven and earth may pass away but waiting won't, so we'd better learn to deal.

What waiting is not: Waiting is not punishment, bad karma, or lousy luck, although at any wretched moment while you're waiting it feels that way.

The truth is that waiting is when the magic happens. Waiting is the mystical space between the dreaming and its coming true. What we need to do is remember all the times that waiting felt full, rather than empty. When a woman is pregnant, planning a wedding, a dream vacation, or long-desired renovations, waiting feels like a state of grace. She's willing to wait because she's fairly certain she knows what the outcome will be. It's when we haven't a clue as to what's going to happen that we go crazy. So let's realize that uncertainty, not waiting, is the enemy. And I can't help you with that this morning, any more than I can help myself. I guess we'll just have to wait it out.

I know a woman who waits with such infinite grace, she makes waiting look like fun. "How do you do it? What is your secret?" I asked her. Get busy, she told me. Distract yourself, as you would a small child. Become self-indulgent. Do the unexpected. Plan on treating yourself to something so wildly extravagant that if the Universe doesn't deliver the goods, you will. This way, you *can* detach yourself from the outcome. Finally, remember, as Carrie Fisher tells us, "Waiting, done at really high speeds, will frequently look like something else."

Come to Your Senses

The Waiting Game

SELF-INDULGENT DISTRACTIONS WHEN BORED WAITING

- Reread beloved childhood classics, as if a parent soothing a small child. *Little Women . . . The Little Prince . . . Goodnight Moon . . .*

- Transport yourself to another time and/or place by immersing yourself in a lavishly illustrated travel or decor book, or brochures for madly expensive cruises.

- Play Wishbook with mail-order catalogs, the more luxurious the merchandise, the better.

- If at home, play dress-up as a little girl might: try on all your evening clothes and shoes and jewelry, experiment with fanciful hairdos. Strike silly, sultry poses at yourself in the glass.

- Pretend you're a child on a long car trip. Count out-of-town license plates . . . walk without stepping on any cracks . . . pick a color and see how many things you can find of that shade. *Be* where you are, have some fun with it, as long as you have to be there at all.

- If indoors, play alphabet search: look about and find one thing beginning with each letter. Try to remember them in alphabetical order as you proceed. Or, if the setting isn't sufficiently inspirational, try to think of foods, articles of clothing, or items of some other general topic, in alphabetical order. Even if you can't control your life right now, you can still think orderly thoughts. During a stressful time some years ago, I bought myself a portable Scrabble game and played, for points, against myself. Having to concentrate on words and numbers was wonderfully calming.

- Wherever you are, think about all the songs you loved when a child. Can you remember the words, the music? Go back to the very earliest you can recall. What did you sing to your child when she was small? Like comfort food, the lullabies and the music of our youth can be as great a stress reliever to an adult as to a child.

Wildly Extravagant Treats for the Very Patient

- Enter a parenthetical time zone away from everyday place and thought, until you're ready to step back into your life. Arrange to give yourself over to a professional facial, a massage or hot herbal wrap, a half day at a spa.

- Check yourself in at a pretty, pampering bed-and-breakfast for just one night, even if in your own city or town. Take no emotional baggage along, just a pretty nightie, a box of bonbons, and some pleasure reading to tickle the hours until bedtime.

•Call a good restaurant and see if you can get a gourmet treat delivered. Eat in bed by yourself.

Wild Thing

Spring, which germinated in the earth, moved also, with a strange restlessness, in the hearts of . . . women. As the weeks passed, inextinguishable hope, which mounts with the rising sap, looked from their faces.

—Ellen Glasgow

*G*radually winter's cold begins its retreat, letting go of its grip upon our imagination and inclinations. All things seem to be stirring, including you. Suddenly you have a desire to walk on the wild side. So what's up? Well, your earth-born body is responding to something primal—your essensual nature—and energy is engaging all your senses. For centuries, this heady sensation has been known as spring fever, but really it's the return of hope. We often think of hope as quiet and reserved, but like the month of March it can also be surprisingly wild and erratic.

"Just as sap in the dormant trees moves upward stimulating the burst of colorful blossoms and green leaves, so does March's energy rise within us. We, too, have been 'dormant,' or turned inward, for the months of January and February," Francis Bernstein reminds us in her marvelous book *Classical Living: Reconnecting with the Rituals of Ancient Rome,* a compendium of rites, celebrations, and home-centered traditions Roman women cherished throughout the year. "This is the month to let out our strong feelings, those that sometimes overwhelm us, those that have been bottled up inside of us all the dark, cold winter. March is the time to laugh, play, make love, and create. Look around at the natural world. March is not the month to be shy or keep desires and thoughts hidden inside."

So often the emotion we shy away from or try to stifle is hope. But hope does spring eternal. And as the writer Barbara Kingsolver tells us, "The very least you can do in your life is to figure out what you hope for. And the most you can do is live inside that hope."

Come to Your Senses

Wild Things to Do
While Waiting

*I*t's the little moments that are so maddening. The ones we aren't even supposed to notice we're wasting.

Waiting for nails to dry and trying not to move so that you don't mess them . . .

Waiting to be called into a doctor's appointment (three-month-old magazines to flip through) . . .

Waiting for a recorded message to connect you to a live person ... or waiting for an important call ...

Waiting for the post or a delivery, or a repairman ...

Waiting in line for something pleasant, like a movie or dinner at a restaurant ... waiting in line for something mundane: to mail a package, make a deposit at the bank, or check out at the grocery store.

Waiting for a bus or train or plane, or to meet someone arriving by one ...

Waiting for traffic to move ...

Not enough time, in any of these waiting zones, to really *do* anything! So, what to do, to feel you're not just wasting precious time?

The trick to transforming waiting into life's extra recess opportunities is to prearrange activities that can be accomplished or enjoyed in short takes ... things that, in fact, you might not even think to do had you *more* time at your disposal.

Consider the investment of a small cassette player with an earphone, if you don't already have one. Don't play familiar favorites, but use the device to explore new sounds that you will truly attend to: audiotapes of poetry; lively, fun, and new-to-you music (Calypso, folk songs, thirties jazz); soothing Gregorian chants or Elizabethan lute songs. Or how about the sound track to your favorite movie; "screen" the scenes in your inner eye wherever you are.

Carry a small artist's sketchbook and slender, pocket-size color markers and draw yourself a diary of your thoughts, feelings, surroundings. No artist would go out of the house without one because inspiration is everywhere. Remember women are artists of the everyday, so what ordinary wonders beg to be set down today?

Take up a portable, easily stop-and-start craft such as tatting or crocheting. In the several days you might be stuck in jury duty, for instance, you could create a fine lace edging for lingerie, a T-shirt, or a pillowcase, with simply a ball of cotton string.

Organize what has probably been *wasting* your time for too long: fill in a new address book that has spaces for all those e-mail addresses, fax numbers, and office versus home numbers ... and transfer into it all those marginal, scribbled updates from your old book, one section at a time. You might even go over the top and include the names of spouses or significant others, children, pets, birthdays. You'd never take the time to do this, so take advantage of the opportunity. (You'll be so proud of yourself when it's done, you'll want to show it off!)

Too early for an appointment? Stop into a card store and read the funny greeting cards. Anticipate upcoming occasions: instead of buying those cards in a rush when the dates are upon you, look for just the right images and messages and get them *now*. Add a "stickie" to each card purchased, to remind you of the intended recipient, and clip them to your calendar when you get home.

For sit-down waiting interludes, teach yourself origami, via a pack of paper and a softcover instruction book. Offer the other people in your waiting area your finished figures with a smile. (Wouldn't it be *magical* to see the entire roomful of people become absorbed in folding a paper menagerie . . . like a scene out of a French film . . . all the more enchanting if it's a room full of grown-ups!)

Discover the joy of short stories and essay compilations—each so absorbing, so satisfying, and complete in but a few pages. Go for the exotic—cultures that aren't your own—and erotic classics, such as Sir Richard Burton's grown-up, unexpurgated *A Thousand and One Nights* (they weren't written for the kids!) or Anaïs Nin's *Delta of Venus*. You can be assured everyone else will wonder why you're smiling in line, but I'll never give away the gleam in your eye. . . .

For Laundromat reading take along some offbeat classic, say *The Scarlet Pimpernel,* or Samuel Beckett's play *Waiting for Godot.* And try on for size being an intellectual. Carry a book of truly evocative poetry that sets you pondering while you're pausing: Yeats, Whitman, Neruda, Tagore, Dickinson, Eluard. Allow yourself to be transported, a single poem at a time, into the mysterious cavern of your own longings. Then memorize a verse and enjoy spicing up staid dinner-party conversation when it just rolls so effortlessly off your tongue. *As Yeats knew* . . . Oscar Wilde's observations are great fun to commit to memory as well. The whole point is to polish up your showing-off skills.

Learn to play solitaire—no, not the computer game, but the real thing, with cards. Little surprise that the British name for this old game is Patience.

Pretend you're a famous person, incognito. Keep a pair of outrageous dark sunglasses or ones with wild vintage frames in your purse for just such boring moments. Feel mysterious, inscrutable. See if, without actually doing anything, you can *will* others to look at you wonderingly, wondrously. See if you can set them thinking: How come *she* looks so calm, so contented? What's her secret?

Probably because she knows how to cool her heels with panache. Now, so do you. And trust me, all these minute diversions work like a charm. I should know; I thought them up while waiting, of course.

Letting Mother Nature Nurture

*The beautiful rain falls . . . [but] whose tears
run in the gutter, melting where the
stationary cars wait for departure . . .*

—Kathleen Raine

*I*t's widely believed that there is a direct link between our emotions and the weather. I know several women who become depressed during the winter because there is less light. As spring arrives and the sun begins to shine once more, their dark moods disappear as suddenly as they descended.

But are we happy because the sun shines or does the sun smile because we're happy? I don't know about you, but before my senses set me straight, I allowed my moods be affected by the Weather Channel's forecasts. Now I know that there is, indeed, a correlation between the weather and feminine energy, but it's the weather mirroring our feminine emotions, not vice versa. Another mystical way that Mother Nature nurtures.

This revelation came during a long, sad trip to the airport after a much anticipated reunion (which I'd been dreaming about for twenty years) did not end in Happily Ever After. I wanted to be alone and take a taxi, but a kind friend insisted on driving me. For two hours I wept. Unable to get control of myself, I apologized with embarrassment. My friend said softly that he felt privileged to "bear witness" to my vulnerability and would only become cross if I continued to say how sorry I was. "One does not apologize for tears," he gently admonished me. "Tears are the antifreeze of the soul." For the rest of the trip he said little. What a blessing it was to cry uncensored and in silence.

Halfway through our journey, the bright blue sky darkened, much like a woman's face when she discovers someone has hurt her child. Piercing the foreboding blackness were deafening roars of thunder (her screams of protest?) and then crackling bolts of lightning (her rage?). Next, the Heavens ripped open as if a mystical heart had been torn asunder, and a deluge of tears fell to earth. My friend said, "Mother Nature is furious at the way you've been hurt. The angels are weeping with you."

The torrential downpour continued outside the car for quite a while, but the inner storm softly subsided to an occasional sniffle and shudder. In the warm, moist, foggy myopia of the car, my swollen eyes could neither see where I had come from nor where I was headed, but I knew I wasn't alone. I was comforted beyond expression by Mother Nature's empathy. The next best thing to a friend letting you cry in silence is having one cry with you. At that moment I realized how truly loved I was. Although it was very different from the way I had expected to be loved that day, it was exactly the kind of love I needed.

"Nature is the common, universal language, understood by all," the Scottish poet Kathleen Raine reminds us. "Meanings, moods, the whole scale of our inner experience, finds in nature the 'correspondences' through which we may know our boundless selves."

Rain Rapture

*Rain is grace; rain is the sky condescending
to the Earth; without rain there would be no
life.*

–John Updike

*B*uried beneath waiting's layers of ennui and resignation are inviting interludes in which to reassess our unconscious attitudes and assumptions. Take rain, for example. From Noah's ark to the weather forecaster's apologies, rain has been held in ill repute. That's because we think of rain as restrictive rather than redemptive. However, unless you've been flooded out of your home, the charms of rainy days beg for reconsideration.

Living in the English countryside has deepened my appreciation for rain's many pleasures. This is a good thing because, in England, fair weather consists of "some sunny spells" or days that are "mostly dry with the odd wet patch." Because the timing of English rain is unpredictable (not, however, its occurrence), one learns to be flexible, prepared at any moment to adjust accordingly, especially if the sun is bright and the skies are blue. This is marvelous psychological conditioning because success and happiness in Life are largely contingent on how well we shift to plan C when we can't carry out A or B. In England, one doesn't argue with the weather. Sure you can moan, but if you've got a fetching rain hat, coat, and umbrella when you're out and about and a teapot at home, why bother?

Consider this. From the first few drops of a gentle sprinkling, to a wind-lashing deluge, rain is a permissive pal. Rain restores serenity to our daily endeavors because it slows us down, or it should. It's been my observation that when it rains, no one—from the dog to the boss—really expects much to happen or get done. This means we get to indulge in activities that would otherwise make us feel guilty—dawdling, idle conversation with coworkers, naps. "Gosh, isn't the weather dreadful," we mutter as our frazzled bodies and restless spirits downshift with a sigh of relief.

In her charming travel memoir *England for All Seasons,* Susan Allen Toth, a rain devotee, points out that there are different kinds of rain. "The best kind of rain, of course, is a cozy rain." This is the "rain that falls on a day when you'd just as soon stay in bed a little longer, write letters or read a good book by the fire, take early tea with hot scones and jam, and look out the streaked window with complacency." Convenient rains also give us much to be grateful for. "This rain occurs on a day when you have reluctantly agreed to an expedition you really don't want to undertake." Now you don't have to, *hee, hee, hee.*

Rediscovering the splendors of rain through your senses is a wonderful way to make an attitude adjustment. Watching a storm from a couch, window seat, or bed, especially as it grows dark, can be thrilling; looking through the prism of raindrops when the sun is shining induces smiles as wondrous as the arc of red, orange, and indigo in the sky. Cracking the window so that you can hear rain's melody—patters on a windowpane, drips through leaves, drizzle down drainpipes—is so soothing, the sounds are prescribed for insomniacs; and falling asleep to rain pelting the roof is sublime, especially in the middle of the afternoon. When you get caught in a rainstorm, do you just get wet, or do you allow yourself to feel the rain upon your skin? Breathe in the fragrance of rain before you shut the door behind you. Rain smells different on pavement or in the garden than it does on your woolen sleeve. A spring rain smells fresh and earthy; the fragrance of a summer shower is spicy, like incense. One of the most sensory delights is coming into the house drenched to the bone, stripping your clothes off, jumping into a hot shower, then toweling off and dressing in warm pajamas and comfy slippers. The memory of it sends shivers of bliss up my spine.

Waiting often forces us to pay attention to life's present tense no matter what the weather, or whether we like it or not. Rainy days are powerful personal prompts sent to remind us that in our desire to accomplish so much each day, we cherish ordinary time-outs too little.

Come to Your Senses

Saving for a Rainy Day

*B*eing in charge of your own amusement can often seem more daunting than entertaining the hordes who might live under your roof. But "millions long for immortality who do not know what to do with themselves on a rainy Sunday afternoon," the writer Susan Ertz observes.

Of course, she's *not* referring to us.

While it's true that we become adept at whatever skill we use on a regular basis—such as plotting and planning pleasure for others, particularly our children—it's also true that the talents, inclinations, passions, and senses we ignore will diminish with disuse until they disappear. "If you atrophy one sense you also atrophy all the others, a sensuous and physical connection with nature, with art, with food, with other human beings," Anaïs Nin observed in 1935. When we atrophy our sense of spontaneity, should a solitary rainy Sunday afternoon arrive, our sources of private delight seem limited to videos or naps.

Now, I am an aficionado of both these esteemed pastimes, but sometimes at the end of a tough week, I'm too frazzled and restless to sleep in the middle of the day and there's nothing on the video shelves I want to rent. What to do besides whine? How about going to the Rainy Day Cupboard and seeing what surprises await the inner babe?

Rainy Day Cupboards were the saving grace of Victorian mothers. In these treasure troves of inspiration were neat, clearly marked boxes of arts and crafts supplies, games and novelties that were enjoyed *only* on rainy days. (If you have small children and this ritual cupboard isn't part of your repertoire, make creating one a priority.)

Same clever concept—a simply splendid assortment of neat, clearly marked projects for you to enjoy only on a rainy day— adapted to capture the interest of tired, jaded women who have outgrown the pleasures of macaroni necklaces and painted seashells.

Do you have a comfort drawer at home? Actually I hope you already swear by this *Simple Abundance* home remedy; there's nothing like it for those nights when all you want to do is pull the covers over your head. But comfort drawers are intended to do just that: provide comfort. Rainy Day Cupboards are meant to convince you that there's plenty that's fun and fascinating to help you while away a few luxuriously idle hours.

Two caveats ensure the success of this tradition: novelty and preparation. These shouldn't be among the arts and handicraft projects you work on regularly—and they should engage your sense of touch as well as your vision (that's why I don't include reading books in mine). Like physical exercise, working with your hands becomes another avenue to release stress.

For those of you who think you're not the "crafty" type, think again and think beyond the familiar ones such as needlecraft (knitting, crocheting, embroidery, needlepoint, tatting, cross-stitching, crewel, and quilting). Take a creative excursion to a well-stocked arts and crafts shop and cruise the aisles. See what catches your interest. Why not basketry, bead craft, leather craft, rug hooking, pottery, stained glass, ribbon craft, paper craft (decoupage, collage, marbling, paper cutting), bookbinding, framing, and carpentry? These days you can find complete kits available for single projects. Get a couple of different ones to experiment with. Several years ago a friend of mine ordered a catalog of do-it-yourself Shaker reproduction kits and began with hanging shelves. She now has a waiting list of friends eager to buy her beautiful furniture.

Let me tell you what projects wait in my Rainy Day Cupboard: a button box containing fabulous buttons found at flea markets and antiques shops to make bracelets and broaches; another box holding an old beloved black jacket I cannot bring myself to part with and a set of divine black and Bakelite buttons from the thirties waiting to give it a new lease on life; a couple of lampshade projects—fashioning two small lampshade "slipcovers" out of a set of embroidered vintage linens; another pair of small, white silk lampshades and dried rosebuds waiting to be glued to their edges; a crimson accent pillow waiting for a tapestry insert and some stunning silk braid also found on a flea market jaunt.

But my definition of handicrafts also extends to culinary crafts, so there's a baking pan filled with all the ingredients (except perishables) including the recipe to make an English Bakewell tart. This idea came from preparing just such a package as a hostess gift for a friend, and I was dazzled by its clever adaptability for the Rainy Day Cupboard. You see, when you open the cupboard, everything you need is supposed to be in there. It's been my experience that spontaneous fun has about three minutes to grab hold of my interest before I sigh and slink back into a chair. But if I can just pull out a fun box to slink into the chair with, I'm set.

There's also a big yellow mixing bowl filled with all the ingredients for the finest rainy day treat—gingerbread. This recipe came from one of my favorite writers and cooks, the late Laurie Colwin, and its secret is the molasses, Steen's Pure Ribbon cane syrup, which has to be specially ordered from Louisiana. Now why isn't the can of Steen's syrup in my kitchen cupboard? Because I won't see it behind the other cans and bottles, and if I do, it will be gone before I get to make the gingerbread. But every time I open the Rainy Day Cupboard, I start grinning. For nestled inside the big baking tin are also my daughter's tiny baking tart tins. She's forgotten I even have them, but I haven't. I'm just saving them for my next solo rainy day play date.

Drat, the sun's shining.

Laurie Colwin's Gingerbread

1 stick sweet butter
½ cup sugar, light or dark brown
½ cup molasses
2 eggs
1½ cups flour
½ tsp. baking soda
1 tbsp. ground ginger
1 tsp. cinnamon
¼ tsp. ground cloves
¼ tsp. ground allspice
2 tsps. lemon brandy, or plain vanilla extract
½ cup buttermilk

1. Cream butter with sugar. Beat until fluffy and add molasses.
2. Beat in eggs.
3. Add flour, baking soda, and ground ginger (this can be adjusted to taste, but I like it very gingery). Add cinnamon, ground cloves, and ground allspice.
4. Add lemon brandy. If you don't have any, use plain vanilla extract. *Lemon extract will not do.* Then add buttermilk (or milk with a little yogurt beaten into it) and turn batter into a buttered tin.
5. Bake at 350° for 20 to 30 minutes (check after 20 minutes have passed). Test with a broom straw, and cool on a rack.

Lady Luck

I've always thought you've got to believe in luck to get it.

—Victoria Holt

"It's hard to tell our bad luck from our good luck sometimes. Hard to tell sometimes for many years to come," writer Merle Shain gently reminds us. "And most of us have wept copious tears over someone or something when if we'd understood the situation better, we might have celebrated our good fortune instead."

That's advice well worth remembering because we've all had experiences that seemed to be the worst sort of luck while they were happening, but later, with hindsight, were a cause for humble thanksgiving. As the country singer Garth Brooks puts it, "Some of God's greatest gifts are unanswered prayers."

In March comes St. Patrick's Day, which has me musing on the role that luck plays in our lives, for better or worse. But I don't feel particularly lucky right now because I'm stranded in the copious-tears stage of a confounding romantic situation that has me waiting for my prayers to be answered (the way *I'd* like them to be, thanks very much). I'm waiting for a miracle. Waiting for my luck to change.

But what do you think the chances of that happening are? If I were a betting woman, I'd say nil.

Because even as I wait, I'm expecting the worst and making contingency plans. I'm expecting the worst because when it comes to matters of the heart, I always believe I'm unlucky. And while miracles do circumvent the laws of earth, Spirit's laws are immutable. As you believe, so shall you receive.

This isn't to say that I believe I'm an unlucky woman. On the contrary, most days I feel like destiny's darling. As far as my health, career, finances, creativity, child, and circle of women friends are concerned, I'm bountifully blessed and incredibly grateful. But I've been sick, unpublished, poor, childless, and lonely. When I look back, I see that my reversals of bad luck only came about as I believed my good fortune into being with prayer, patience, persistence, and pluck. It was only when I decided I was going to change my luck by deliberately changing my perceptions and taking risks that I started believing Lady Luck was looking out for me.

Now, you may be lucky in love, but feel unlucky in finances or career breaks. It doesn't matter. What matters is that you take a look at the one area of your life where you're wanting and waiting for your luck to change and nothing seems to be happening. Luck is equal parts grace and gumption, and both of these things require your active participation.

"Creating luck is a cocreative process with God," Azriela Jaffe writes in *Create Your Own Luck: 8 Principles of Attracting Good Fortune in Life, Love and Work*. Changing your luck means consciously "ridding yourself of the obstacles you place in your own path—'luck busters' and 'luck blockers' such as your own thinking, which is the foundation for your belief system."

Because when you change your beliefs, you change your behavior. Change your behavior, change how you make choices. Change your choices, get more chances. Get more chances, take more risks. Take more risks, find more four-leaf clovers. The seemingly random pattern of luck seems quite undeniable. "How can you say luck and chance are the same thing?" asks Amy Tan. "Chance is the first step you take, luck is what comes afterwards."

Every Breath You Take

I burned my life, that I might find
A passion wholly of the mind,
Thought divorced from eye and bone,
Ecstasy comes to breath alone.

—Louise Bogan

*A*s much as I revel in solitary delights, occasionally loneliness creeps in like a sudden fog and usually at the most inconvenient times. Every woman experiences these isolated interludes, even in relationships. So the next time one occurs, take a slow, deep breath and then remember that Spirit's first love offering to each of us was the breath of Life. And with the exception of our first and last breath, this gift comes to us in pairs—in inhales and exhales—so that we might never feel alone.

There are many pleasures you can enjoy with a partner. However, exploring the sensuality of breathing—surprise, surprise—isn't one of them. That's because, short of CPR, no one can breathe for you. How *do* you breathe, by the way? If you're like me, probably not as well as you should or could. Unfortunately, unless we're consciously paying attention to our breathing through meditating or in an exercise, yoga, or Lamaze class, our breathing is too shallow and too quick for our own good.

Because breathing is the first thing we begin to do after birth, we assume it's natural and doesn't require practice or discipline. If this were true, opera singers wouldn't spend most of their training learning how to breathe rather than how to carry a tune. Day in, day out, when I'm anxious, agitated, excited, nervous, or tense, I habitually hold my breath, and I'll bet you do, too, which is exactly the opposite of what we should be doing. So don't save your breath anymore.

There are two reasons we breathe—inhaling and exhaling.

The first reason, inhaling, is to supply our bodies and brains with oxygen; the second reason, exhaling, is to rid our bodies of poisonous gases; both are crucial to our survival. We can live without food for a few weeks and without water for a few days, but without oxygen—life's most vital nutrient—we'll die within a few minutes.

When I began exercising regularly, one of the genuine surprises was that I actually started to feel better almost immediately. Why? Because I started *breathing*. "There must be something to this oxygen-to-the-brain thing," I'd joke. But it was true. Most of the time when we explode in anger or tears, we think it's our emotions or hormones run amok, when actually it's an internal toxic buildup expulsion. Breathing is how we are supposed to eliminate the body's gaseous waste by-products, but because women are always waiting to exhale for one reason or another, we end up having regular *Thar she blows* episodes.

Go ahead, laugh. That's another way we get rid of excess toxins, and certainly giggling feels more fun than screaming harangues do. But we're supposed to be expelling negativity about 23,040 times a day through our gift of breath. Yes, we're tired, cranky, stressed to the max, but two of the reasons could be that we're all oxygen-starved and self-polluting.

Perhaps a short breather might be in order. "For some reason, in our culture, there is a lot more emphasis on inhaling than exhaling. While we associate taking in oxygen with doing something useful and good for ourselves, we expel carbon dioxide surreptitiously, almost as if we were taking out the garbage—in a rush, nose pinched, mouth open. Always on the uptake, we derive almost no pleasure from relaxing our chests, clearing our airways. . . . To breathe deeply and effortlessly, don't wait to exhale. Think of breathing as giving, not taking. Just tell yourself that you are going to fill up your lungs *in order to* expel as much air as possible. Don't scrimp," the marvelous French writer Veronique Vienne observes in her charming book of essays *The Art of Doing Nothing*.

"Before you know it, your chest swells, your thoracic cage enlarges, and your shoulders relax. Precisely at the moment when you would expect your pulmonary chamber to be filled to capacity, the lobes in the back of your lungs open up like tiny parachutes. It is the most effortless high you've experienced in a long time—but it's nothing compared with the delicious sinking feeling that's yours when you exhale. Few things in life are as satisfying as this long, gentle dive into serenity."

So stop for a moment and take a deep breath. Now let it out slowly, as a sigh of self-contained pleasure. "When you breathe a sigh a relief, it's your body smiling," Veronique Vienne reminds us. "A measure of happiness is how often we sigh with ease."

Phantom of Delight

And now I see with eye serene
The very pulse of the machine;
A being breathing thoughtful breath;
A traveller betwixt life and death.

—William Wordsworth

Think of the word *meditation* and two clichés immediately come to mind: being uncomfortable and breathing calisthenics. So let's do the reverse this morning—get comfortable and then start considering breath's true nature—as Wordsworth calls it, a phantom of delight.

"Breath is sensuous, rhythmic, and always with us, as long as we are alive. Also, breath is a gift to us from the larger world . . . an intimate exchange with the entire cosmos in which we live and move and have our being," Camille Maurine and Lorin Roche remind us in *Meditation Secrets for Women: Discovering Your Passion, Pleasure and Inner Peace.* "Breath is intrinsically full of grace."

So is their wonderful book, which is the first one to honor and celebrate the truth that women's meditation needs differ radically from those of men. "For thousands of years monks have been the primary custodians of the knowledge of meditation and the creators of its techniques, so naturally it has been designed to meet their needs. Consequently, most teachings on meditation

116

are still shaped by attitudes that worked in the distant past, in the Far East, for reclusive and celibate males," Camille Maurine points out. "Most teachings just do not comprehend the female body and psyche."

Because I refuse to sit cross-legged in a lotus position, back aching, mind racing, and hyperventilating, I've always had the problem of answering the question "Do you meditate?" But I do luxuriate in my senses, indulge my yearnings, rejoice in my desires, long for the Divine, and pray each day to be delivered to my passion. "This is meditation—luxuriating in the sensory world, resting in the simplicity of your own being, enjoying yourself shamelessly," Camille Maurine reassures us. "Nature designed us to blossom in the bodily state of pleasure," and "your meditation time is the perfect place to cultivate this natural connection. It may seem like an indulgence, a luxury, but such connection is a vital necessity. . . . No denial of the body, of the instincts, of emotion. . . . With pleasure at its foundation, your meditation is a coming to your senses."

Using our senses to regularly rediscover the joy of breathing is a way to stretch our capacity for pleasure. Now, you may ask, what delights are waiting to be found in something as ordinary as breathing? (This question would never cross your lips if you've just recovered from a bout of bronchitis.) "How luscious can you let it be?" asks Maurine. Today when you're outside, take a deep breath and feel the frostiness; tonight after a steaming bath using fragrant oil, inhale the moisture of warm air. Crack open a window in the room where you're sleeping for some fresh ventilation; place a fragrant lavender sachet under your pillow; softly blow on the inside of your arm or thigh and tickle yourself. As you drift off to sleep, ride the gentle wave of inhaling and exhaling until the sound of your breath becomes a sigh of grateful contentment.

Inspired Breathing

Thoughts that breathe,
Words that burn.

–Thomas Gray (1767)

*L*et's muse a moment on the connection between breathing and inspiration. The word *inspiration* literally means to breathe "in Spirit," which any artist will tell you is exactly what it feels like to have an inspired flash. Perhaps this is why we call them "Aha" moments—we literally catch our breath, surprised at the exaltation of a "second wind."

When was the last time you felt inspired to make a change or choice? If you feel that it's been too long, remember that after we inhale, we're expected to exhale, which is why when I'm creatively blocked, I look around to see if there is someone nearby who needs the gift of an inspired thought to breathe more easily on her own. Or an encouraging word to rekindle the passion of a dream that is so delayed it feels dead.

"Do something very courageous, very bold, very exhilarating, and pass the energy along. Be infectious. Lower your voice and lean in to tell [someone] how awesome it is to move halfway across the country with no money, no job, no place to live. Breathe in, breathe out, breathe into another. Tell another woman how you left a suffocating job—so she knows she can do it. Tell a young woman about the thrill of traveling around the world alone, so she knows she can try it. Be as healthy, as vibrant, as beautiful, as authentic as you possibly can be, in a way that speaks silently to others, *You can be this, too,*" Rachel Synder encourages us in her illuminating book of meditations, *365 Words of Well-Being for Women.* "Smile at other women's dreams and their hopes, and reassure them that they'll survive whatever black hole they're currently navigating."

Today some woman around you is bound to need a little inspirational CPR, so don't stop breathing. Your own life may depend on it.

The Breathing Home

There are homes you run from, and homes you run to.

—Laura Cunningham

*L*ife feeling a bit stale? Well, even if it's not, your surroundings probably are. The thing about stale air or stagnant lives is that we rarely notice until we've had a breather apart from either the routine or the rooms we inhabit.

"Our home is an extension of ourselves and, like us, needs to breathe. Fresh air and natural light must flow freely through the home if the occupants are to enjoy bountiful energy and good health," Suzy Chiazzari tells us in *The Healing Home.* "If you want to make the most of the protection and love your home can offer, you must allow it to breathe."

Imagine for a moment living in a petri dish that's been sealed up most of the year. Not very appealing, is it? Well, rooms that have been shut off from light and air for months are often the reason we constantly feel sick and tired at the tail end of winter. There are a lot of reasons you can't shake off that cold; what you can't see is hurting you.

Actually, it's a good thing we can't see what's swirling around us in the air at home, because we'd be running for our lives. For starters there's gas or smoke fumes, aerosol and spray emissions, chemicals emitted by synthetic carpets, curtains, and furniture, bacteria in the sink scum, and last month's flu virus, still airborne. Although we may not associate feeling bad with our surroundings, just because we can't see mold growing up the walls doesn't mean we can assume that the air we're breathing in our homes is unpolluted. Our Victorian great-grandmothers knew this was the month to take down the heavy draperies, turn over the mattresses, beat the rugs, and throw open the windows. Placing new plants throughout all the rooms of your home also helps both the house and yourself breathe easier. Suzy Chiazzari points out, "Formaldehyde is the most commonly found toxin in indoor air and can be found in resins, paper towels, tissues, floor coverings, fabrics, garbage bags, chipboard and plywood." That's right—the same preservative we kept dead frogs in during Biology 101. Thankfully, Mother Nature once again comes to our rescue with lilies, gerbera daisies, moth orchids, English ivy, and philodendron plants, which have all been found to be excellent at removing toxins from the air and are easily available in plant stores this month.

It is absolutely miraculous what a little shift of perception can do. Beginning to think of our homes as living, breathing entities requiring a loving, reciprocal relationship with their tenants is one of them. "When we look back at the places where we have lived during our life, we remember some with nostalgia and love while others we remember as places connected to unhappiness and pain. We often assume that the ups and downs of life are associated with the place where certain events in our life occurred," Suzy Chiazzari points out. "Most people leave it at that, never considering that the house and buildings themselves may have contributed to their feelings of discontentment or well-being. Buildings are essentially alive."

Come to Your Senses

Why Scent Your Surroundings?

*T*hink of the immediate jolt we experience when encountering a whiff of baby power, garlic, chlorine bleach, a freshly peeled orange.

Now take a sniff as you enter your front door. What's your first impression? Furniture polish, ammonia, a flowery carpet cleaner? Your pets? What you last cooked, even if it was last night? How appetizing does your kitchen smell between meals? How refreshing is your bathroom scent? Your bedroom? Your laundry room? Your linen closet? How many uncoordinated perfumes, candles, and cleansers are masking each other's effects or producing an unintended, collective shout? Does your home smell like *you,* or (cigarette smoke drifting in, perhaps, or their frying chicken) like your neighbors'?

As far back as ancient times, people sought to sweeten their surroundings, as often for medicinal as for aesthetic purposes. Greeks and Romans used fragrant woods for storage cabinets, scented clothing and bedding with herbs and flowers, and perfumed the air of homes and temples with aromatic candles. Floors were strewn with herbs and grasses (the strewing of palms before Jesus is the source of the observance of Palm Sunday). Until the turn of the twentieth century people carried pomanders (not the clove-studded orange of today, but decorative, pierced carriers of metal or ceramic for herbs and flowers) and wore cloth "sweet bags" into public places, to ward off germs and shield sensitive nostrils from the stench of unwashed neighbors. Even the Bible contains (Exodus 30:23–24) a recipe for a "holy anointing oil" of spices mixed with olive oil—with precise measurements, as dictated by God to Moses!—along with instructions on how to apply it throughout the house of worship, to purify virtually every surface.

Many modern products attempt to imitate what our ancestors used to scent their homes. Lemon- and pine-scented cleansers and polishes, for example, trace back to past centuries when the *real* substances were put to such uses. Floral carpet powders harken back, and yet bear little resemblance to, the fragrant aftermath of sweeping a carpet with a sprinkling of dried lavender (which still works beautifully today). And let's not even get into the nasty pungency of commercially made insect repellents . . . especially as compared with age-old and effective rosemary or thyme. Who exactly are you trying to get rid of, anyway?

There are so many wonderful ways to spread the good smells around: fresh fruits, live or dried herbs, essential oils, fragrant woods, ground spices. A few drops of essential oils can be simmered in water, carefully warmed over a burner, dropped onto a lightbulb before turning it on, or rubbed on our temples. Simply cutting into the skin and flesh of fresh fruits, crumbling some green herbs, lightly tossing dried potpourri, is all that's needed to release gorgeous, *good for your peace of mind and pleasure* scents.

Studies have shown that certain odors can indeed induce calm or sleep, ease feelings of depression, and help us to concentrate, even reduce pain. You needn't be an aromatherapy expert to benefit from the powerful qualities of nature's own secret remedies—scents—to enhance your daily round. You just have to be curious.

Relaxing scents include vanilla and warm "apple pie" spices (cinnamon, allspice, cloves, nutmeg). It's not surprising that these fragrances bring with them happy associations of baking, holidays, coziness—they are the "comfort food" of the nose and don't add an ounce to the hips.

Mind-focusing, reviving scents, on the other hand, include, besides citrus, such florals as jasmine and rose; basil, ginger, rosemary, and mint. Although it's usually associated with Christmas, I write year-round inhaling the glorious resinous scent of frankincense.

You might know that eucalyptus and lavender can make you feel better when groggy with colds or flu (in a warm bath, or through a humidifier, even if you can't smell it). Their oils (as well as the pungent tea tree oil and genuine pine oil) can also disinfect surfaces, such as telephone receivers and counters. But did you know the scent of green apples has been found to ease headaches, while the fragrance of spiced apples jump-starts the creative process? The eighteenth-century poet Johann Friedrich von Schiller, who wrote the opera *Wilhem Tell,* used to keep rotting apples in a desk drawer, sniffing them deeply and often when he was suffering from writer's block. Now medical researchers have confirmed Schiller's instinct; spiced-apple scent can subdue panic attacks—which is exactly what happens when a writer struggles for the right word. As Schiller observed, no doubt after a heady whiff, *There's no such thing as chance / And what to us seems merest accident / Springs from the deepest source of destiny.* Or the right scent!

But as far as sensual healing goes, let's think first about how you might remove or lessen those odors you *don't* want surrounding you.

Smoke, distasteful cooking vapors, and pet smells can be reduced by an electronic ionizer, or simply by opening a window or turning on a fan (yes, an obvious solution, but how often do we do it during the colder months?). Rid your shelves of all aerosol sprays (including body deodorants and hairsprays) and nose-wrinkling cleansers. Freshen air the old-fashioned way, by leaving out some pure, white *ordinary* vinegar in a bowl—an excellent banisher of cigarette smoke. Get rid of jarring new-paint smells by leaving out bowls of salt and skinned, halved onions. If a room has been closed up, clear the air with a bowl of fresh orange and lemon peel set on top of a radiator. Wash the hard surfaces and floors of your bathroom and kitchen with only baking soda and water, not harsh, odoriferous detergents.

Now, you're ready to think about how you'd like your home to smell so that the air enveloping you might, as Shakespeare knew, "nimbly and sweetly recommend itself unto our gentle senses."

Coming into Balance

I dream of an art of balance, purity, tranquillity, devoid of disturbing or disquieting subject matter . . . something akin to a good armchair.

—Henri Matisse

*A*s I write, I'm recovering from an hour spent falling down and then picking myself up, just to fall down again. I'm bruised, out of breath, still wobbly (even though I'm sitting down), and exhausted. Exactly the way I'm supposed to be, according to my fencing instructor, who placed me in the center of a core board and expected me to stay standing as I lunged my way to humiliation. Although I work out regularly, I'm flummoxed to discover how unequal the right and left sides of my body are with regard to balance and strength. But I'm told, in sports and life, you can't find your balance until you completely lose it.

"All too often when we think of living in balance, we approach balance in the same frantic, rushing way that we approach the rest of our lives," Anne Wilson Schaef reminds us in *Meditations for Living in Balance,* which is the sequel to her groundbreaking *Meditations for Women Who Do Too Much.* "We want to balance work and home. We want to balance relationships. We want to work out and exercise and eat good food. We want to stay healthy so that we can do more. We want to fill everything up, our selves, our time, our activities, our relationships, and our lives. If we are not careful, we will add balancing our lives to our already long list of doing too much."

Today is the first day of spring, the vernal equinox, when light and darkness find equal balance in the natural world. It's also a perfect day for us to consider how we balance the many aspects of our busy lives. For most of us, doing too much feels normal. In any twenty-four-hour period, we're constantly pulled in at least a dozen different directions—work, children, personal relationships, chores, errands, friends, family, finances, promises to others, health concerns, deadlines, and our own unfulfilled dreams and desires—which leaves little time for Reflection, Renewal, and Recreation, the holy trinity of balance. Start thinking of them as rites of passage to contentment.

So get off the teeter-totter of your to-do list and find an armchair. One of the more delightful ways to find balance is to realize that not everything that needs to be done has to be done today. "Many tasks and issues in our lives will take care of themselves if we will but let them," Anne Wilson Schaef recommends. "The 'impossible' task that *had* to be accomplished immediately looks very different tomorrow or next week. Often, I have found that when others are pushing something as *urgent* . . . my best response is just to slow down."

Or as the Zen koan reminds us: *Sitting quietly, doing nothing, spring comes, and the grass grows by itself.*

Who Could Ask
for Anything More?

Transient luster, beauteous clay,
Smiling wonder of a day.

—Mehetabel Wright (1733)

*D*id you ever wonder what heartbeats, breaths, pulses, planets, clocks, monks, menstrual cycles, credit card bills, and dripping faucets have in common?

A regular pattern of reoccurrence.

Rhythm. The steady, reassuring course of the natural world: the ebb and flow of the tides, the recurring sequence of the four seasons, the monthly phases of the moon, and the daily progression from day into night.

Rhythm. The ancient antidote to the uncharted terror we face every day.

Rhythm. Something familiar you can count on and look forward to. Regular mealtimes, bedtimes, quiet times, haircuts (without having to pretend they're doctor's appointments). Monthly book club gatherings. One day off a week set aside to get in touch with your sacred *sense of wonder.*

But what would sophisticated, savvy, successful women of the world, such as ourselves, know about syncopated sanity? We don't know rhythm from a flea's foot.

On the other hand, we sure do know how to sing the blues. This is the time of the year when many women fall into a deep funk. We call it stress. We call it hormones. We call it the lack of seasonal light. Or sleep. We call it everything but what it is. Not taking care of ourselves.

In case you've been wondering, the appalling psychic imbalance most of us call real life is a hallucinogenic joke conjured up for convenience. Lurching from one task to another like zombies, cramming yesterday's exhaustion into tomorrow's obligations, is not ordinary life, it's lunacy. There's much to be said about living each day as if it were your last on earth, but the point of that wisdom is to *enjoy* your last day here, not to try to get "caught up" before you check out.

A woman's seventh sense is wonder. The wonder of *It All.* Life—why we're here. Not the wonder of how we've lasted this long. (Although that thought does inspire a pause.) Introducing a sense of rhythm into your daily round—a regular pattern of sleep, work, exercise, rest, and play—is the first step to restoring your wonder years.

Rhythm, reverence, reflection, repose. Say those words aloud slowly. Even their cadence brings relief. Because when you've got rhythm, sweetie, you've got *your* life. And you won't want or need to ask for anything more.

Savoring Your Day

How we spend our days is, of course, how we spend our lives.

—Annie Dillard

For thousands of years Chinese physicians have treated patients based on the premise that our sensory perceptions and emotions fluctuate not only seasonally, but also throughout the day, much like the high and low tides of the ocean. In India, medical practitioners, known as Vedic sages, took into consideration not only the time of day the symptoms of their patients intensified, but also their work habits, sleep patterns, and diet. Only after they had the entire vision of a person's day were "holistic" remedies prescribed, intended to bring the body's "dis-ease" into harmony with the soul.

127

To our rational, "prove-it" Western minds, these ageless teachings, now touted in "New Age" magazines and books, seem arcane and confusing. However, after you've made the connection between what ails you and when it occurs, taking control of your well-being becomes as "simplicity itself," as Sir Arthur Conan Doyle described Sherlock Holmes's thought process.

In her insightful book *Savoring the Day: Recipes and Remedies to Enhance Your Natural Rhythms,* food and health authority Judith Benn Hurley seamlessly blends ancient wisdom with cutting-edge science and great culinary taste, inviting us to rearrange our daily habits to suit our natural rhythms with ease and pleasure. The results of following her advice have triggered many exciting *Eureka!* moments for me.

According to Ms. Hurley, who combines both Chinese and Ayuvedic (meaning "knowledge of life") practices in her recommendations, each day can be broken down into six different time periods: early morning, midmorning, noon, midafternoon, evening, and night. Follow your own body's daily ebb and flow and see if this doesn't make sublime sense.

For example, the early morning is the best time of the day to eat in order to lose weight because activity throughout the day helps to burn off food as fuel. Exercising in the morning, even if it means getting up an hour earlier, raises your metabolism and increases your energy throughout the day. I spent practically my entire adult life not eating breakfast in order to control my weight, until a wild "what the heck" moment with a bowl of cereal revealed how much easier it is to work with my body instead of fighting it.

If you can avoid meetings, you probably get more work done during midmorning because you're more alert (especially if you eat breakfast!). But did you know that between 10 A.M. and noon is also the best time for a photograph because your skin is at its most radiant?

The Chinese refer to noon as the time of joy and laughter. "Interestingly, this timing corresponds with the natural surge from our brains through our bodies of what twentieth century researchers call serotonin, the good-time hormone," Ms. Hurley explains. "Chinese doctors of long ago could never have known of serotonin, but they nonetheless made the same connection. Despite the sophisticated world we have created, it seems our natural rhythms have changed little in thousands of years."

A woman's sense of knowing is always pointing her in the direction of her highest good. Sometimes it comes one book or bowl of cereal at a time. Today let your essensual self guide you toward the rejuvenating sense of well-being you crave. Be willing to experiment, but start slowly. Just observe your own natural rhythms throughout the next week. Trust me, once you discover that a root canal is easier to endure in the midafternoon because your mouth is less sensitive, you'll think you've discovered the wisdom of the ages. And, babe, you have.

Come to Your Senses

Stewing in Your Own Juices

*M*arinades make it possible for you to treat yourself to a fabulous feast that celebrates, at the very least, the intention of living life in balance.

Someday, surely. Actually, tomorrow. That's because one of waiting's wondrous secrets is learning to enjoy stewing in your own juices: creatively and culinary. I'm just mad about marinades, in theory and in practice. In theory I marinate ideas all the time. I've learned that if an idea is promising, it will be brilliant after I've slept on it. Same principle applies to supper.

The earliest known cookbook, published in Venice in 1475, was Plantina's *De honesta voluptate* ("Concerning Honest Pleasure"), which celebrated all life's sensual pleasures. It paid homage to ancient gods and goddesses, particularly Aphrodite, the Greek goddess of love, who knew a thing or two about the pleasure of delayed gratification, which is a marinade's "come hither."

The word *marinade* comes from the Latin *marinara,* meaning "of the sea," because in Roman times seawater (that is, salt water) was used as a brine to preserve fish. As the Roman army marched throughout Europe, the soldiers transported their food with them, and it needed to be cured, brined, or marinated for preservation. Eventually as the Roman empire expanded, so did their menus, including marinades. Can't you hear them in Gaul as they're discovering French tarragon and chardonnay grapes? "I've got a little substitute for the brine I want to try."

Experimentation is what makes marinades so much fun once you understand that every marinade is made up of three equally important parts: acid, oil, and aromatics. The first ingredient, acid, such as wine, vinegar, lemon (or even yogurt), acts as a softening agent for the meat or fish. Softening speeds up cooking, but since moisture is lost, oil is the second ingredient. Finally, aromatics give the marinade flavor, fragrance, and unique character. They can include anything from fresh or dried spices and vegetables to liqueurs.

For those nights when you're worn to a raveling, and a rave or two would be appreciated, here's a secret recipe meant to be shared. In a large Ziploc bag, place 1 crushed or chopped garlic clove, one-half cup of soy sauce, and 2 tablespoons of dark sesame oil. Add 1 pound of meat (chicken, beef, pork), salmon, or even tofu. Close the bag and squeeze it to distribute the marinade evenly. Now put it in the refrigerator and forget about it for however long you have. You can marinate meat or tofu for a day or overnight (which is best), but with fish, only marinate for a half hour. Cook the meat or fish as you would normally—bake, broil, add to a stew.

By far my favorite marinated food is the scrumptious Peruvian

Roasted Chicken from the sadly missed El Pollo Restaurant in New York City. If you're trying to learn the virtues of patience, this meal will convince you.

Peruvian Roasted Chicken

You will need:

2½ tablespoons garlic powder or 2 tablespoons freshly minced garlic
1 tablespoon ground cumin
4 tablespoons white vinegar
2½ tablespoons paprika
2 teaspoons ground black pepper
¾ teaspoon sea salt
3 tablespoons white wine
3 tablespoons soya or canola oil
1 lemon

Mix all the ingredients in a medium bowl. Wash a plump roasting chicken thoroughly with the juice of 1 lemon mixed with 1 quart cold water. Remove excess fat from inside the chicken. Dry off with paper towels. With a knife poke deep holes all over the chicken, including under the wings. Place the chicken in a large Ziploc bag and pour the marinade over the chicken, squishing the bag to make sure the chicken is evenly coated. Place the chicken in the refrigerator for a minimum of 2 hours, but 24 hours is preferable.

When you're ready to prepare your meal, remove the chicken from the bag and dilute the marinade with 1 tablespoon water. Place the chicken on a rack in a roasting pan, and cook for 1 hour at 375°, basting with the marinade every 10 minutes. When I serve this with the simplest green salad and couscous, I'm told I've missed my calling. So try it, and expect applause. A modest smile and an enthusiastic "Thank you, you're *too* kind" is a response always in good taste!

Come to Your Senses

Yummy Kitchen

*W*e all eat, we all drink; many of us cook and bake with regularity. And yet, do we truly seize control of the scents of our kitchens? So many lovely fragrances whisk by without due appreciation; so many others intermingle to form lingering symphonies that say "pumpkin pie was baked here" or "chicken soup was cooked from scratch," all over the house—yet cannot be captured without the painstakingly complete act that created them. But many other ordinary herbs and spices sit at the ready, trapped in jars, while other fragrances abound in foods stored in the refrigerator.

It's so easy to pleasure your senses in that most scent-sensory of rooms. Set your coffeemaker with a timer to awaken you with the delicious fragrance of a fresh brew. Morning is a wonderful time to mix yourself a tasty palate of pleasant odors as well as flavors (in fact, it's often hard to separate taste from scent). Squeeze your own fruit juices. Cook some hot cereal or pancakes with maple syrup, or make yourself cinnamon toast (butter the bread, then top with a spoonful of sugar and cinnamon, mixed well; broil for a few minutes, till the bread is golden). Within moments the room will smell of warm, comforting foods. When you make herbal or fruit teas, don't be in such a hurry to discard the leaves: in an extra cup, let them steep their sweet scent into the room, till cool.

Wean yourself from that microwave! Learn to make, from scratch, long-simmered pilafs, casseroles, and stews that call for herbs or spices. They do take more actual *preparation* time than processed items, which produce nearly scent-free reheating—but the payoff is the glorious scent of undisturbed *cooking*. A simple Middle Eastern–style rice dish, for example, in which spices and the rice itself are stir-fried before the addition of broth, creates an exotic aroma that can make your home smell like a romantic Casbah for *hours*. Slow-roasting a chicken, basting it with rosemary crumbled into butter or oil, is as satisfying an aroma to anticipate and savor as the chicken is to eat. Many "quick" breads, such as molasses-and-spice-based ones, bake in around half an hour, yet can leave your house deliciously scented right through to the next morning . . . and let's not get started on the heady fragrance of yeast breads! Mmmm.

Once preparation is done, dilute pine, citrus, or tea-tree oil with water, to clean out trash bins or wipe down countertops. They are natural disinfectants and leave no traces of harmful chemicals, as do many store-bought cleansers you'd prefer to keep away from foods. And, if you don't want them near your food, why would you want them near you?

Don't forget the freshening powers of genuine lemon. Pressing your fingertips to a lemon slice, kept close by a smelly task (boning fish, slicing onions), will cleanse and deodorize your hands far better than soap. A drop of real lemon juice, blended into a paste with baking soda, will freshen baking pans and pots far better than any commercial washing agent. In fact, baking soda, neat, with water, will make all your glassware and metal shine, scent-free—wash the items with hot water, and finish with cold for the most remarkable gleam you've ever seen.

The kitchen is the ideal place for an herb garden on a sunny sill, enabling you to tear off (don't snip) just a spoonful of thyme or basil as you need it. And every time you water the plants, they release a bounty of grateful scent into the room. Buy fresh, stemmed herbs, tie together, and hang them upside down from curtain rods. Hang an herbal wreath or garland near your stove or favorite food-preparation surface: string upon a florist's frame (available at craft stores) various fresh herbs, colorful chilies, aromatic dried fruits and peels, cinnamon sticks, and whole nutmegs. Keep within reach, so you can pluck these items to use as you cook or bake. A far scent from sterile jars of browning greenery, yes?

Allow fresh food itself to perfume the room: a ripe pineapple or melon, a single quince, a bowl of apples or clementines, even just ripe bananas. Prepare for yourself a still life of scented fruits and pause to admire each separate element with your nose as well as your eyes.

Whatever the season, and with little effort, your kitchen can be as headily fragrant as groves, orchards, gardens . . . bakeries, brasseries, coffeehouses, and tearooms. If you view food and beverages as simply substances to be eaten and drunk quickly, you're missing more pleasure than you could imagine.

Ghost of a Chance

Does one ever see any ghost that is not oneself?

—Joseph Shearing

*P*erhaps it's because human beings have such a hard time letting go that we love ghost stories. Bring up the topic of ghosts at any dinner party and most of the guests will be able to contribute an anecdote—a sighting or a haunting—usually set in old houses.

But "objects have ghostly emanations, too, that attach themselves to their solidity," the writer Dominique Browning tells us. "Things with drawers—chests, armoires, night tables—trunks—seem to be the most populated pieces of furniture."

I don't know about you, but I've never been as haunted by other people's ghosts as I have been by my own, especially when I open my unconscious catchalls. But when we begin the task of spiritual housekeeping, one of its crucial functions is exorcism. What stuff do you have squirreled away in the scary space euphemistically known as "storage"? No doubt, like me, talismans of all sorts, from the sublime to the ridiculous; touchstones that trigger every emotion: drawers of letters, photographs, bank statements, mismatched earrings, locks of hair, one baby shoe, menus, ticket stubs, orphaned keys. In the bedroom closet, more clothes that you don't wear than you do: clothes that make you feel uncomfortable, fat, or sad. You say you can't get rid of them because they were expensive? Unfortunately, toots, our mistakes are often costly. But we don't have to keep repeating them or looking at them every day.

An energy surrounds and attaches itself to every object in our homes, transforming them into palpable memories, both good and bad. Often when we feel depressed but can't identify the source of our distress, it's because we're looking for something we've hid too well. I've begun to realize that anxiety attacks that I thought were free-floating were actually anchored in the stultifying clutter of my home or office. I kid you not. What's ailing us is what lies beneath the psychic surface of our lives. The things stuffed in the back of your closet or the kitchen junk drawer—the past—cry out to be buried once and for all, or given another incarnation with a friend or thrift shop.

"I have tried to give away some of the things in my house that have ghosts; I think they would be better off somewhere else, and I want to be rid of certain memories," Dominique Browning confesses. "The armoire that was part of a marriage, the carpet that was part of a love affair, the photograph that was part of hope, the bedcovers that were part of too many sleepless nights. Begone."

Begone and good riddance, because if not, we don't have a ghost of a chance of living the life that's waiting for us. Doesn't matter whether you're looking for the perfect person or pair of shoes; if there's no room in your life, neither soul nor sole mates are likely to find you.

Weeding Out

No one wears velvet in July.

—Anna Johnson

Is there a woman alive with as much storage space as she really needs, or as many closets as she truly wants? Of course not. Which is why the sanest women I know are ruthless about seasonal closet purging, approaching their tasks like gardeners pulling weeds. They also know and respect the need to pace themselves—one closet a week in order of how much it's driving them crazy. Too much of a good thing, too quickly, even enthusiasm, is exhausting and can burn out resolve as well as romance.

"There is nothing like fixing up closets to give you a feeling of complete satisfaction," Henrietta Ripperger wrote in *A Home of*

Your Own and How to Run It, published in 1940. Likewise, few things are as frustrating as searching for something you know should be in there and not finding it because it shares a hanger with something else. "The real waste in clothing comes not in the buying, but in not using it," Mrs. Ripperger reminds us, and we know she speaks the truth.

Realistically it takes about three hours to completely clean and reorganize one closet, which I've come to view as a sixty-minute investment each for mind, body, and spirit.

Cleaning out closets sounds simple, but unless you want to end up just "straightening" the confusion, you have to come prepared with determination to sort, sift, and say farewell, so you'll need lots of large trash bags. Start by taking everything out of the closet and sorting it all into two piles—the immediately wearable and the torn. Let's look at the second pile first. You'll be amazed at how many pieces aren't being worn because they're irrevocably torn, stained, or zipperless. Now unless something has such sentimental value that you'd grab it in case of fire, toss it. (If it were that important, you would have had it repaired years ago.) I once kept a green satin evening suit from the forties that was two sizes too small and zipperless. I'd held on to it for over a decade because it represented both a memory and a fantasy—the babe I'd been in my twenties when I'd lived and written about fashion in Europe, and the spirit of the woman I wanted to become again. As soon as I made the connection, I gave it away to a friend who could wear it as soon as she replaced the zipper, which she did in about a week.

Now evaluate the importance of the wearable clothing by asking each piece these four questions:

When were you last used or worn?
Did I feel beautiful or comfortable in you?
When and how could you be used or worn in the future?
If I were moving instead of cleaning, would I take you with me?

This last question in particular elicits your true feelings.

There are bound to be items of clothing that you've not worn because they don't fit anymore (and don't fool yourself into thinking that losing a few extra inches or pounds will make a difference!). But do the clothes hanging in your closet fit your lifestyle, or has it changed without your closet catching up with you? Do the clothes you reach for every day fit your daily round? Or the becoming reflection you'd like to see in the mirror? Perhaps you traded in working in an office and now work from home. Or hiking has become you new passion instead of golf. If the shoe continues to fit, wear it, but if not, recycle.

Ralph Waldo Emerson believed that a weed was "a plant whose virtues have not yet been discovered." If you can say the same thing for some of the clothing and accessories clamoring for closet space, it's time to begin weeding so that you'll find them when you want them. Serenity is very becoming in a garden and on a woman's face.

Come to Your Senses

Going into the Closet

*S*torage and scent go together as hand in glove, for perfumes, oils, and potpourris love the cool dark.

We can take advantage of this natural affinity.

Let's start with your dressers and chests. It's not too hard to scent paper liners so they coordinate with the scent you use on your body. Get new paper (inexpensive paper, not vinyl or vinyl-coated—wallpaper is an excellent substance for this, a virtual sponge for scent), then measure out and cut to fit the drawers. Take a large, lidded plastic container—an inexpensive underbed chest would be perfect—and place into it several paper envelopes into which you have tucked cotton sprinkled with your favorite scent or dry potpourri. Put the drawer liners into the box, close the lid tightly, leave the papers undisturbed for two weeks to absorb the fragrance. Then line your drawers. The scenting box may be reused over and over to perfume other things, including writing papers, handkerchiefs and lingerie, or bed linens.

Now for your closets. There are so many natural alternatives to keep moths away. Traditionally cedar has been an excellent insect repellent, but it can become ineffective through overexposure to air. Did you know that you can revive cedar by lightly sanding it to expose a new surface? Another way to keep moths at bay is to rub cedar oil onto wood surfaces where clothing or bedding will not come into contact with it. This can be done in any kind of wood-composition dressers and armoires, by rubbing the oil onto the undersides of drawers and shelves.

Other natural insect repellents include lavender, rosemary, or even a sweet blend of pipe tobacco. An especially lovely moth repellent is a blend of four tablespoons each of lavender and cloves, plus two tablespoons each of dried lemon verbena and orrisroot powder. Place in fabric casings and suspend from hangers used for woolens, or scent and pad wooden hangers by slip-covering them with tubes of cloth joined at the center and filled with a hearty sprinkling of the moth-chasing herbs.

A lovely way to perfume your clothing with the same scent as your perfume is to buy a box of coordinating soaps and plant each soap in a different storage spot to scent all around it. Don't discard the scented box the soaps came in: use it for small items such as handkerchiefs or hair ribbons. (A box from quality chocolates is also a wonderfully fragrant cache for small things, too . . . but *don't* get carried away and plant individual chocolates about your shelves and drawers. It will attract the bugs you're trying to repel.)

If your storage areas smell musty or mildewy, you might have a problem with excess humidity. Small dishes of borax or even clay cat litter will absorb both damp and odors from surrounding air;

also, check hardware or closet stores and catalogs for silica-gel crystals, which can be suspended in closets in cloth bags (don't place against clothing, as the crystals may become damp as they work) or set out in open-topped jars inside drawers and on shelves. You can also make little shoe fresheners by sewing sacks of silica gel to tuck into the toes. Silica can be spread on a baking sheet and aired to dry out and used again, unlike litter or borax.

As you go about the practical applications of introducing new scents in your home, keep in mind that your aim is to accomplish two things: to stop using pungent artificial scents while introducing natural ones that it is a pleasure to catch a whiff of, but more important to delight in the simple splendor of the overlooked ordinary!

The Threads That Bind

Let go of the people who cause constant pain; let go of the negativity that colors a room more darkly than any coat of paint. Keep close the people you love, the ones who stay engaged and open to life, who bring joy and peace to the house and garden.

—Dominique Browning

*W*e think that it's dresses, skirts, and pants hanging in our closets, but really it's our past, for most items of clothing are associated, for good or ill, with people, places, and periods in our lives. I can't even look at the cover of a Laura Ashley catalog without "seeing" the wife and daughter of a small-town mayor, identically dressed in white sailor dresses, red-ribbon straw boaters and parasols for the Independence Day parade; it doesn't matter how far removed either Laura Ashley or I have become from cottage sprig—we're embalmed in an emotional memory.

And while it's true that the past asks only to be remembered, that doesn't mean you need to entomb your regrets. I once fell in love with a black lace cocktail dress that cost me more than I ever thought I'd earn, but I envisioned wearing it for a special, hopefully romantic, occasion and I was willing to pay the price for both fantasies. I may have looked gorgeous in the dress, but that didn't alleviate the distress that accompanied the evening, foreshadowing what turned out to be a romantic disaster. Long after I parted from the man, the dress remained on its hanger. Every time I cleaned the closet I convinced myself that it had cost too much money to give away. But what was really so hard to abandon was all the pent-up emotion, frustration, disappointment, and anger that hadn't been expressed those many years ago. Finally, last spring I'd reached a point in my life when I truly wanted to move on, but the fancy threads were binding me to a part of my past best left behind. So I decided to create a ritual romantic exorcism. Once again I got all dolled up in the dress, poured myself a glass of champagne, and sat down at the dining room table for a little uncensored conversation with the greatest love I never had. It was very therapeutic. Now a good friend of mine looks terrific in my former misery; in fact, it's become her "lucky in love" outfit. (Go figure, although I did bless it and have it dry-cleaned before passing it on!)

It's easy for us to get rid of clothes we've physically outgrown. But severing the emotional threads that bind us, whether they're silk, wool, or gossamer, requires unconditional commitment to our future happiness, and sometimes that desire takes longer than we think it should to make its way down to the soul level.

A great way to help move the process along is to throw an annual party and invite your friends to "shop" from your closet. Do this either on your own or invite them to bring their wearable memories to your house. Set it up like an exclusive boutique in your living room, have plenty to eat and drink, and listen to "you go, girl" type of music (Gloria Gaynor, Sheryl Crow, Annie Lennox, Melissa Etheridge). You'll have so much fun, it will become a spring ritual, both literally and fashionably!

Not long ago, I was sorting in the attic and came across the box that contained my daughter's and my former Fourth of July costumes. The thought crossed my mind, "I'll just keep those for Kate and her little girl," and then I thought again and asked her if she wanted me to keep them.

"No. I don't remember us as being very happy in them. Why would I want to pass on bad vibes to my kid?"

Of course she was right, which is why several of the sweetest mother-and-daughter outfits are waiting in a thrift shop to be discovered by a new mother-and-daughter duo.

However, I do have a wonderful picture of us in the outfits that I cherish, and recently Kate and I looked at the photo together.

"Now, you have to admit, we do look adorable," I told her.

"That I'll admit," she said, smiling. "So let's hold on to that memory."

She lifted her eyebrow and kissed me on the forehead before she grabbed the car keys and headed out the door.

As I said, the past only asks to be remembered, and when you do, it will happily let go and let you go on.

Between the Lines

Sacred Duality

What does the physical have to do with the emotional or the spiritual? Everything. We are as much beings of the Earth as we are beings of the stars . . . our senses and connection to our bodies are just as integral to our physical, emotional and spiritual well-being as is our connection to our higher selves.

The old doctrines, which regard the physical as inferior to the spiritual, may have made sense for the medieval belief that the Sun orbited the Earth; those beliefs have been supplanted by more enlightened ones. *Fortunately. Because it is impossible to truly feel that we* belong *in the universe, just as much as the ground we walk on and the air we breathe, until we entirely accept our own natures as physical and spiritual creatures.*

—Nancy Conger
Sensuous Living:
Expand Your Sensory Awareness

143

April

That enchantment that I lightly took
out of the lovely April is for ever.

—Leonie Adams

*E*nchanted April beguiles with a shy coquette's knowing blush, casting a spell over our jaded senses. So shake off winter's doldrums by entertaining heady possibilities. This month Mother Nature offers a thrilling tutorial in feminine wiles. Think basic-instinct refresher course. Hold that gaze, flash a smile, cross your heart, and hope to start living. Remember what red shoes did for blue-checked gingham but realize that you've always possessed the power to get wherever you want to go. Become the sorceress's apprentice with a bewitching role model: Glenda the Good, Samantha, Veronica Lake, Kim Novak. Create a stir with springtime saucery. Pick a potent love potion from the herb patch. Imagine loving yourself until attitude turns to pulchritude. Unleash the power of spoken declarations, rhyming chants, prophetic prayers. Every little thing a woman does *is* supposed to be magic. This month discover that a charmed life is *intentional,* not accidental.

Enchanted April

*The unendurable is the beginning of the
curve to joy.*

—Djuna Barnes

*H*appiness is much more difficult to write about than sorrow,
just as the longing for love is easier to describe than its fulfillment. Still, I suspect that many writers secretly wish they could
write from a deep well of happiness, at least once, just to know
what it feels like. I know that I do, although I'm not sure why. For
the reality is, when a writer's happy, the last thing she wants to do
is examine it, turn the emotion over, upside down, inside out, and
dissect the ephemeral; she wants to exult in the euphoria, not
explain the phenomenon. And while I revealed earlier in the year
that this book has given me my happiest writing experience, what
I really meant was that on many days the moments lost in writing
were far more pleasurable than the ones I was facing the rest of the
time. But that's not how I want to continue living, nor should you.
What pulled me from the brink was coming, once again, back to
my senses.

Often writers cast their words out prophetically, as a sorceress
might cast a spell, and many times when the words return to you,
enclosed between covers, your phantom is so fully fleshed out in its
own persona, you don't recognize your own creation. Mind you,
Mary Shelley did not know she was creating Frankenstein in 1818
when she wrote, "Thus strangely are our souls constructed and by
such slight ligaments are we bound to prosperity or ruin." The
woman started off writing a love story.

"Magic is the craft of shaping, the craft of the wise, exhilarating,
dangerous—the ultimate adventure," Starhawk, the writer on
feminine spirituality, tells us. "The power of magic should not be
underestimated. It works, often in ways that are unexpected and

146

difficult to control." Nowhere is this more evident than in writing or reading, where imagination is the bridge between self-disclosure and self-discovery.

The Australian writer Elizabeth von Arnim wanted to write a happy book when she sat down at her desk overlooking the Mediterranean Sea in April 1921. Well, actually she needed to. She'd just turned in a dark but cathartic novel based on her notoriously turbulent marriage to an English nobleman. While her publishers were relieved to finally have her long-delayed manuscript in their hands, there was a slight problem. Everyone had been expecting a frothy comedy. It was just after the end of World War I and the British reading public wanted to feel good again. Hopeful. She was quickly ordered to serve up something lighter—an omelette without breaking any eggs—*the happy book*.

Like most authors, Elizabeth drew upon personal experience in all her writing, but at this moment the inspirational bank account was overdrawn; she was physically and emotionally exhausted, spiritually spent. However, she was also suddenly a single mother who needed to support herself and her children. Lack of money can't always focus the attention creatively, but it can certainly engage the will.

Thinking that perhaps a bucolic setting might inspire her, Elizabeth rented a medieval *castello* overlooking the Italian Riviera, a marked change from cold, dark, rainy London. She was optimistic with *one good day* behind her (probably a couple of pages), but by the following morning she'd come to a complete halt. Her diary of April 3, 1921, notes: "Staring open-mouthed all a.m." Although hope was blossoming outside her window, it was beyond her reach as a writer, just as love had been for her.

The fragrance, feel, taste, sound, and sight of hope was dazzling and intoxicating. "So wildly, ridiculously, divinely beautiful" was the only way she could first describe it.

All the radiance of April in Italy lay gathered together at her feet. The sun poured in on her. The sea lay asleep in it, hardly stirring. Across the bay the lovely mountains, exquisitely different in color, were asleep too in the light; and underneath her window, at the bottom of the flower-starred grass slope from which the wall of the castle rose up, was a great cypress, cutting through the delicate blues and violets and rose-colours of the mountain and the sea like a great black sword.

But Elizabeth didn't want to be writing about happiness, she wanted to be experiencing it! Anyway, how does one describe the first stirrings of redemption? Word by word. Sense by sense. She persevered, sticking her head out the window every so often to inhale the fragrance of wisteria, then returning sullenly to her desk to capture the scent on the page. She'd stop to savor a few relaxing sips of fennel tea, then cup it in her hands so that its warmth could radiate through her body. It's always the first sip or two that stirs the soul. Why is that? Then, a nibble of a cloud-light, almond-flavored ladyfinger. Luscious. Each sense indulged yielded one more sentence. She had a setting; she needed a plot. Could the senses be her characters—spiritual graces as earthly agents provocateurs? No, that might be too far-fetched. But sight, sound, smell, taste, touch, knowing, and especially wonder would be the book's supporting players.

She stared. Such beauty; and she there to see it. Such beauty; and she alive to feel it. Her face was bathed in light. Lovely scents came up to the window and caressed her. A tiny breeze gently lifted her hair. . . . How beautiful, how beautiful. Not to have died before this . . . to have been allowed to see, breathe, feel this. . . . She stared, her lips parted. Happy? Poor, ordinary, everyday word. But what could one say, how could one describe it?

Luckily for the rest of us, the result of Elizabeth von Arnim's struggle to describe happiness became *The Enchanted April,* a sweet, sumptuous, and sensual story about four very different women, each miserable in her own way, who are wooed back to Life through the magic, enchantment, and romance of the ordinary. But knowing how she gave birth to it, through racking sobs, makes me appreciate the gift and its message so much more. Thank you, Elizabeth.

Finding What You Never Lost

*Faced with unmeasurables, people steer their way
by magic.*

—Denise Scott Brown

*A*fter it was published in 1922, *The Enchanted April* was
hailed as a "delicious confection" capable of working "its
magic on all." No one was more surprised than its author. For she
would fall under the novel's spell as deeply as any of her characters
or readers.

*It was as though she could hardly stay inside herself, it was as
though she were too small to hold so much of joy, it was as
though she were washed through with light. And how astonishing
to feel this sheer bliss, for here she was, not doing and not going to
do a single unselfish thing, not going to do a thing she didn't want
to do.*

Of course, Elizabeth would be the first to acknowledge that the
novel was a far-fetched feminine fantasy. A heartaching, heart-
awakening, heart-aligning, heart-wrenching hallucination. Certainly she couldn't remember the last time she'd been able to have
a day to herself, and she suspected that neither could her readers.
What would be the most radical act the novel's heroine, Lottie
Wilkins—dowdy, middle-aged, childless—could commit? What
about deciding once and for all to stop being a martyr for goodness? What about just doing it? Now *there* would be a riveting plot.
Cast Lottie as a feminine saboteur, about to hide anarchy in
between the puffs of meringue.

*According to everybody she had ever come across she ought at
least to have twinges.* She had not one twinge. *Something was*

149

wrong somewhere. . . . [Impossible] that at home she should have been so good, so terribly good, and merely felt tormented. Twinges of every sort had there been her portion; aches, hurts, discouragements, and she the whole time being steadily unselfish. Now she had taken off all her goodness and left it behind her like a heap of rain-sodden clothes, and she only felt joy. She was naked of goodness, and was rejoicing in being naked. She was stripped, and exulting.

Stripped of her sackcloth of self-sacrifice, Lottie becomes a subversive force for dynamic and divine change in the lives of others, as well. In one of the most moving passages for me, agent provocateur Lottie Wilkins convinces another woman whom she has just met to join her in running away to Italy for a vacation without their husbands. As the women start dreaming of one blissful month on their own—the first in their entire lives—they immediately begin to have second thoughts.

> *"It only shows . . . how immaculately good we've been all our lives. The very first time we do anything our husbands don't know about we feel guilty."*
> *"I'm afraid I can't say I've been immaculately good . . ."*
> *"Oh, but I'm sure you have—I see you being good—and that's why you're not happy. . . ."*
> *". . . I'm sure you don't mean really that goodness, if one could attain it, makes one unhappy."*
> *"Yes, I do," said Mrs. Wilkins. "Our sort of goodness does. We have attained it, and we are unhappy. There are miserable sorts of goodness and happy sorts—the sort we'll have at the mediae-val castle, for instance, is the happy sort."*

The Very Pink of Perfection

I was shown round Tutankhamen's tomb in the 1920s.
I saw all this wonderful pink on the walls and the artifacts.
I was so impressed that I vowed to wear it for the rest of
my life.

—Barbara Cartland

*B*ecause *The Enchanted April* seems to say, better than any other way I know, that no life is beyond the redemptive love of one good woman, especially her own, reading Elizabeth von Arnim's novel and seeing the film (on videotape) is always a reassuring and restorative springtime ritual for me. But here's something curious. The first time I saw the film, I was married, and I responded to its message like a plant leaning toward the light. Five years later, when I was no longer married, watching the movie was difficult going and I had to view it over a couple of days. Why? Well, I realized that although my domestic arrangements had changed, my pattern of overloading other people's needs onto my back had continued. I identified with Lottie much more as a single woman. As the writer Amy Lindgren puts it, "Women run on expectations, the way a car is fueled by gas. And it doesn't matter whose: unspoken assignments from parents, bosses, clients, children, and lovers crowd our calendars' borders, in ink only we can see."

Usually by April, the rest of our world is also coming out of hibernation alongside us, and with it come requests, demands, and obligations that might not be addressed to us but, nonetheless, still manage to arrive on our doorstep. Don't blame it on the mail.

You might not be able to run away to a medieval castle this month. Neither can I. But we can remember that the first day of April is set aside for celebrating foolish notions—such as discovering what can make you, day in and day out, essensually happy. Here's a hint. Try looking for something pink. And when you find it, keep looking until you find another. There's something about the color pink that inevitably makes you smile. By the time you have five pink things to list in your Gratitude Journal, you'll feel as if you've just had a magic wand waved over your consciousness. It shouldn't take long.

"How funny . . ."
"What is funny?"
"We are. This is. Everything. It's all so wonderful. It's so funny and so adorable that we should be in it. I daresay when we finally reach heaven—the one they talk about so much—we shan't find it a bit more beautiful."

"Let's go and look at that tree close," said Mrs. Wilkins. "I don't believe it can only be a tree."

And arm in arm they went along the hall, and their husbands would not have known them their faces were so young with eagerness, and together they stood at the open window . . . and their eyes . . . feasted on the marvelous pink thing . . ."

Come to Your Senses

Transcendent Flavors

"*A*n exquisite pleasure had invaded my senses. . . . When could it have come to me, this all-powerful joy?" Marcel Proust wondered in *Remembrance of Things Past,* as he bit into that sublime French confection the madeleine.

A cousin of other featherlight "génoise" (in the style of Genoa) pastries such as ladyfingers, which rely on eggs alone for their leavening, and related as well to the rather more ascetic (bereft of shortening) sponge cake, the madeleine is a two-bite treat that reawakens a jaded palate to the sheer *goodness* of the most basic of baking ingredients. Perhaps you won't be flown back on memory's wings to your aunt's parlor, as Proust's narrator was, but at the first taste you'll forge an unforgettable experience of sensuality, one that might make more complex pastries appear positively overdressed.

Although it is not clear where or when madeleines were invented (in fact, famed French chef Escoffier did not deign to mention them in his seminal cookbook), their traditional scalloped shape, buttery-golden color, and gossamer texture have been appreciated for centuries.

Yes, such variations as chocolate-flavored madeleines exist, and they are also sold iced, dipped in coconut, and so on. But experiencing the madeleine in its purest state is a revelation to nearly every one of the senses. If you have never had the pleasure . . . discover now how simple it is to tap into the same ecstasy Proust found to be nearly beyond words.

Shell-shaped pans (available from baking shops) would be an authentic touch, but even small tartlet tins or a miniature muffin pan would do—whatever could contain two tablespoons of batter at a time, with room for rising. The essential elements are probably already at hand in your kitchen.

Madeleines

You will need:

1 egg
½ cup sugar
½ cup cake flour (not self-rising), sifted
6 tablespoons (¾ stick) butter, melted and cooled
1 teaspoon pure vanilla extract
Confectioners' sugar (optional)

1. Preheat oven to 450°.
2. Grease your tins with butter and lightly dust with flour.
3. In a double boiler, heat the egg and sugar until warm but not bubbling, stirring constantly, then remove the upper pan from the heat. Use a whisk or electric mixer to beat the mixture until thick and light—at least 3 minutes.
4. Add the cake flour in small amounts at a time, continuing to beat the mixture, and finally beat in the melted butter and vanilla.
5. Immediate pour into the prepared tins, filling each only with a few spoonfuls of batter (no more than halfway).
6. Bake at 450° for around 15 minutes, or until just golden. Do not overbake.

7. Use a fork or the tip of a knife to ease the cakes out of the pan and cool on a rack before eating.
8. Sprinkle with sifted confectioners' sugar (optional)

Like Proust, you might want to dip these lovelies into tea to induce their heavenly sensory lift of sweet scent, delicate flavor, tender texture, and unique lightness. Madeleines are not just cakes to *remember,* but a transcendent flavor to prepare and enjoy again and again. This afternoon might be perfect for discovering why.

Losing What You Never Had

As truly as God is our Father, so truly is God our Mother.

—Julian of Norwich (1373)

"To what degree do we hurl ourselves and to what degree are we hurled through life, by our personal histories, our childhoods, the things that came before?" wonders Rebecca Miller. Or the things that didn't.

A few days before my mother died, she began telling me astonishing stories from her past. They were colorful tales of passion, betrayal, risk, sacrifice, but above all romance—the kind I imagine the Danish writer Isak Dinesen might have told to entertain her soul mate, Denys Finch Hatton, around an African safari campfire. I found them so impossible to reconcile with *my* mother that I seriously wondered if she wasn't delusional rather than remembering with an uncharacteristic candor and vividness.

Although I knew my mother had been an army nurse during World War II, stationed in England, I was now hearing recollections of courage and adventure, two qualities I had never associated with the woman who raised me—from driving makeshift ambulances in a night convoy during a bombing raid (I never saw her drive our car out of the driveway), to stowing away on a reconnaissance mission from England to France, so that she could be with her RAF pilot lover.

"Good Lord, Mother," I admonished her. "You could have been killed or court-martialed. What were you thinking?"

"I wasn't thinking," she said matter-of-factly. "I was feeling my way through life in those days."

Because the woman I had known for more than four decades discounted, dismissed, or even denied her feelings (and taught her daughters to do the same), she suffered a crippling depression and refused to take therapy or medication. Untreated, her despair eventually turned on her and her family, until she became the incredible shrinking woman whose world was reduced to a reclining chair in her living room.

This did not mean that on the surface of her daily round my mother's life seemed empty, at least in the years when her family was young. She was one of the most creative women I've ever known, and when we were growing up, our warm, cozy, inviting home was a magnet for her husband, children, and friends. Mother was a consummate decorator, wonderful cook, and marvelous hostess. She excelled at many handicrafts, from sewing to woodworking; her Halloween costumes were legendary, and living up to the birthday parties she orchestrated for her children daunts me even now. From my mother I first learned how a woman unconsciously performs practical magic, turning lack into abundance with moxie and gratitude. She taught me how to spin straw into gold, what do to do with a few loaves and fishes, and how rising to any occasion was a feminine art form.

Despite her inherent ability to create everyday enchantment, there was a boundary that Mother never crossed physically, emotionally, or psychically, and I, too, was taught not to cross it. A well-padded perimeter surrounded what was possible in life and what was permissible even to dream of, and this dark kingdom of diminished expectations was guarded by the harpies of fear and intimidation.

Who among us hasn't felt at some time in our life so out of

sync and disconnected with our blood family that we didn't wonder if the nurses had switched babies at the hospital? That's how
I felt after hearing my mother's deathbed stories.

After she died, my sorrow eventually turned to relief, for truly
the last years of her life without my father (who had died five years
before) were such torture, it was agony for her children to watch
her, and easier than I had expected to let her go. But the woman I
continued to mourn and search for in various ways was my Mystery Mother, the woman who felt her way through life rather
than feared it. The woman I hoped I most resembled. Like the poet
Adrienne Rich I grieved that

> The woman
> I needed to call my mother
> Was silenced before I was born.

And I was right.

Feeling Like
a Motherless Child

*Remember that imagination is the faculty of the soul and that
when it suggests new pathways to us we are being invited
to explore the territory of the soul in ways that will certainly
change and reenchant us.*

—Caitlin Matthews

The woman that many of us have wandered through life
unable to call upon is the Great Mother. That's because She,
too, was silenced before we were born, and knowledge of her
existence was kept hidden. For if the spiritual tradition of your
childhood was Jewish, Christian, or Islamic, you learned to wor-

ship a masculine God. "God has traditionally been viewed and presented as masculine—some of the words to describe Him are king, lord and master. The feminine has been suppressed except in our carefully controlled female saints and mystics. Even Mary, the most powerful feminine figure in Christianity, is robbed of her power and made a 'handmaid of the Lord,'" Galen Gillotte explains in her beautiful collection of meditations, *Book of Hours: Prayers to the Goddess.* "This is not to say that she and other female saints have not imparted a sense of the sacred; it is just that they are overshadowed by the patriarchal god of power and might."

Whether we have maintained the religion of our childhood or not, the images of Spirit introduced in the cradle are usually the ones we carry to the grave, unless we consciously try to move beyond these impressions to find our own. Can you remember how you pictured God while you were sitting in religious instruction as a child, or when you were home with your parents?

Being born into an Irish Catholic family certainly meant that I was taught to worship a masculine Divinity—the Father, the Son, and the Holy Ghost. When the expressions of Spirit made known to you are exclusively male, then your experience of God is male, too, and it's easiest to define that God through your personal impressions. If your earthly father is distant, demanding, and undemonstrative, the likelihood is great that your Father in Heaven might seem that way, as well. If you had to strive to "earn" your earthly father's expressions of affection, chances are you'll feel that way about Spirit.

One of my closest friends faced this dilemma when, at forty, she desperately wanted to reconnect with Spirit after a lifetime of "divine estrangement," as she called it. Eventually she realized she was transferring the family dynamics she had learned from her overly critical parents—who had shunned her when they disapproved of her behavior—to her relationship with God. When we talked about it, I was struck by what an epiphany this was. If we grew up feeling that love was a prize that had to be won, or that our mistakes made us unlovable, we'll find it difficult to believe there is a Source of unconditional love and support available to us when we begin to seek it.

"The urge to follow a spiritual pathway comes in a variety of ways," Caitlin Matthews, the respected authority on the Celtic spiritual tradition, tells us, "but in every case, the soul puts out its exploratory shoots in the context of personal devotion, testing the ground, discovering how Spirit responds, learning how true communion with the Divine can be brought about."

If you've never consciously thought of the dual nature of Divinity—the feminine as well as masculine—could you be open to viewing ancient truth with fresh eyes? Some of you already feel comfortable acknowledging the Goddess in your life. Perhaps you feel like writer Jane O'Reilly, who confides, "I learned to think of God as a woman and by that simple experience I discovered I could begin to think of God."

For other readers, thinking of God as a woman might be an insurmountable barrier. It certainly was for me. Trying to break through the godly gender barrier triggered the resurrection of childhood feelings of guilt, betrayal, and fear—visions of fallen women, scarlet harlots, Eve tumbling in the fall from grace, the taste of the apple still lingering on her breath.

So don't force yourself. Spirit is greater than gender and the ineffable is, quite frankly, meant to be Unknowable. What gave me a sense of peace in my searching was not choosing between them but praying to both the Lord and Lady of Life, the Great Father and Mother, the God and Goddess or God/dess. Each aspect of Divinity is an equal partner in a healthy, happy, holy mystical marriage. Both Forces watch over the world and each of us, no matter what we may call them or how we envision them. Springtime is the most beautiful season to gently explore your idea of the Great Mother because She's also known as Mother Nature. How can you take a walk outside and see the world come alive again in a riot of color, hear birds sing, swoon over the taste of fresh asparagus or the scent of lilacs, and not be at least open to the possibility of Divinity's feminine nature!

Fear is the most common devil in our search for happiness and fulfillment, whether it be through spiritual connection, love, or vocation. I have come to trust that if the next step scares me, it is probably a soul-directed act. For, as I'm always reminding myself, transpose the *a* and the *c* in the word *scared* and you will find the word *sacred*.

Gradually and gratefully I came to the awareness that until I allowed myself to seek and be found by the Great Mother, I would always feel like a spiritually motherless child, raised by a loving Father but without the knowledge of my true nature, and of the feminine Mysteries that continue to shape my life because I was born a woman.

It is such a beautiful April afternoon in the English countryside. I take a break from writing to stroll down the lane to the field where the newborn lambs are frolicking with their mothers. Have you ever seen with your own eyes the *gamboling* of lambs—a gorgeous word that means a playful frolic? It looks like leapfrog, as they jubilantly jump into the air, all four tiny legs spread out sideways like wings. They leap over Mama, quietly resting on the grass; they leap over each other in flight. They leap fearlessly because their mother is nearby. It's such a riot to watch, better than the circus, and yet it always induces a mystical reverie in me. Of course, I wonder, "How do they do that?" But even more important, I begin to wonder, "Can I learn to do that in my life? Take a leap of faith toward the new with exuberance?" Walking back home, the fragrance of hope is so fresh and green. I start off with a skip and a jump. "There is no other closeness in human life like the closeness between a mother and her baby," Susan Cheevers reminds us in *A Woman's Life*. "Chronologically, physically, and spiritually they are just a few heartbeats away from being the same person."

160

Come to Your Senses

Springtime Spa

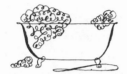

O h, how good that *warm* breeze feels on your skin! . . . the first day that you can fling open a window and leave it up . . . the first day you dare to wear your coat unbuttoned, or short sleeves, or leave the hat and gloves at home.

After being smothered beneath stuffy fabrics for months, your skin is as hungry and thirsty as a bear waking from hibernation! It's time to give that sadly overlooked layered membrane that embraces us every moment the tender, loving care it deserves.

"Our skin is what stands between us and the world. If you think about it, no other part of us makes contact with something not us but the skin. It imprisons us, but it also gives us individual shape, protects us from invaders, cools us down or heats us up as need be, produces vitamin D, holds in our body fluids. Most amazing, perhaps, is that it can mend itself when necessary, and it is constantly renewing itself," Diane Ackerman writes in *A Natural History of the Senses*. "But, most of all, it harbors the sense of touch."

Look around you—the very bounty of spring holds the answer of how to thoughtfully indulge this closest life companion. Just as in nature creatures cast off their winter sluggishness to seek out fresh-thawed water and the new birth of fruits and berries, so will your own body benefit from these age-old cleansing and astringent remedies.

Have you been drinking your eight glasses of water per day? Uh-huh, thought so. Make that your first priority. Your skin will thank you for it; and if pollen or other allergens rub you wrong with the changing of the seasons, your entire system will feel much better as such irritants are literally flushed away. Mix the water with fruit juices for an extra burst of natural goodness. And, by all means, drink lots of undiluted fruit juice, too!

If you blindly reach for the same juice bottle in the store, be bold—explore other flavors that you've perhaps never tasted even as whole fruit. Go where your taste buds have already led you . . . and then go further. If you like cranberry juice, for example, try blueberry or raspberry juice. If you like orange or grapefruit juice, what about tangerine juice, or a sweetened key lime beverage? Test the differences between Concord, white, and red grape juices, pretending they are wine. And what about those exotic fruit flavors: mango, papaya, kiwi? Play chemist. How do any of the above taste mixed with just a quick fizz of sparkling water or seltzer? Prepare flavored waters yourself, using real juices, for economical and much more healthy combinations than the premixed in the store.

Spring is the time to adopt a new regimen: set aside an hour or so per week—if not per day—to unwind, sip something healthy and colorful, and give your skin a smoothing, soothing, springtime treat at the same time. Be sure to cleanse your face of all traces of makeup before you begin. "Young ladies are delicate plants," Jane Austen reminds us, sweetie. "They should take care of themselves and their complexion."

So bring two quarts of water to a boil and pour carefully into a large bowl. Add a few drops of your favorite essential oil or a kitchen extract (almond or peppermint are nice), and allow the water to cool slightly. Put on a piece of soothing music that will last around ten minutes, then lean down over the bowl, draping a towel over your head and neck. Let your thoughts drift with the flow of the music, as the steam opens and cleanses your pores. When the music ends, you know your ten minutes have passed; pat your face dry.

Next, use your electric blender to combine three whole strawberries, a tablespoon of olive oil, and two tablespoons of witch hazel. Use this naturally astringent cleanser and moisturizer all-in-one immediately, to feed the skin of your face and throat with vitamins A and C. Apply any extra to dry or rough skin on elbows, hands, etc.

Sit or lie back and continue to sip your drink slowly, as you imagine your body communing inside and out with the renewed grace of the sweet forces of Mother Nature.

Do You Believe in Magic?

I am sure there is Magic in everything, only we have not sense enough to get hold of it and make it do things for us.

—Frances Hodgson Burnett

*D*o you believe in magic? What about miracles? Probably more women feel comfortable admitting to a belief in miracles than in magic.

One reason for this could be that down through history miracles have been religiously sanctioned (usually by men). Think of Moses parting the Red Sea, or Jesus turning water into wine or walking on the water.

However, once you start reading the Bible, you'll discover there's as much magic in the Good Book as there is the miraculous. Take, for example, the New Testament's revered three Wise

Men—Balthasar, Melchior, and Gaspar—as in the Christmas carol "We Three Kings of Orient Are." They weren't following a star across a long, hot desert because they were kings but because they were "magi," or magicians. Through their use of magic, astrology, and divination—the art of foretelling and the interpretation of signs and wonders—they heard and answered Heaven's call for them to go to Bethlehem. And they arrived just in time to double-cross the insane King Herod, determined to kill the child who would change the world. The true gifts of the Magi weren't gold, frankincense, and myrrh but the mystical courage and magical prowess that enabled them to lead the Holy Family to safety in Egypt.

Another marvelous example of the spiritual use of magic is how the Old Testament's Esther saved the Israelites by bewitching a despot intent on killing the Jewish people. One of the secret incantations or spells Esther used was a "glamour" that made her so beautiful in the king's eyes he could not bring himself to harm her or her people.

However, the world's first, and arguably most powerful, magician was Solomon, Israel's greatest king, who, because he prayed for Divine Wisdom rather than riches, was given both by God. Solomon's supernatural knowledge ranged from understanding the medicinal properties of herbs to the occult. One of the most wonderful Jewish legends about Solomon's use of practical magic involves the building of the First Temple. Because Jewish law strictly forbade the use of iron tools to cut altar stones, the king had a serious problem. But after being given a magical ring by an angel, he was able to subdue a demon worm that possessed the power to split rocks with his spit. "Thus, the First Temple, the holiest site in Jewish history, had a team of demonic builders— suggesting that demons are not necessarily evil," Rabbi David A. Cooper writes in his fascinating book on Jewish mysticism, *God Is a Verb*. "The point of this story is that when we have power over demonic forces, they can be put to good."

Nothing Conjured,
Nothing Gained

Where there is a woman, there is magic.

—Ntozake Shange

One of the most famous magical textbooks is *The Key of Solomon the King*. Like the quest for the Holy Grail, the search for Solomon's secret manuscript containing his spells, invocations, talismans, formulas, diagrams, and rituals has tantalized and tortured practitioners of the esoteric arts—from alchemists to mathematicians—for centuries. The thought of what he could do with Solomon's jottings kept Sir Isaac Newton up at night; nonetheless he managed to accomplish quite a bit on his own during the day. That's because Newton, considered the modern world's first and greatest scientist, was also a passionate mystic and one of the world's last and greatest magicians. "It is no exaggeration to say that almost everything we do in the modern world is based upon Sir Isaac Newton's enormous scientific achievements—but he was not the pure scientist of lore," Michael White tells us in his riveting biography, *Isaac Newton: The Last Sorcerer*. "Unknown to all but a few, Newton was a practicing alchemist who dabbled with the occult. He did not discover gravity by watching an apple fall—in reality, Newton's great theories were grasped within the charred base of the crucible and the alchemist's fire. Nor was Newton the idealistic puritan that he has always been seen as, but a tortured, obsessive character who risked his health in a ceaseless quest for an understanding of the universe through whatever means at his disposal." These means included studying the Bible for divination instead of dogma, the practice of natural magic, reliance on astrology and numerology when he conducted mathematical experiments, and, most of all, attempting to unravel the secrets of the cosmos through alchemy—considered by the Church to be the darkest and most dangerous magical practice—because this process could transform matter, for example, a base metal, such as iron, into gold. Tragically, throughout his lifetime, Newton was haunted and lived a lonely, hidden existence in his spiritual quest, fearing that if his practice of alchemy and passion for magic were discovered, it would discredit his "scientific" contributions, which included the intellectual alchemy that transformed mankind's view of the Universe and our place in it.

As unlikely as it appears on the surface, there are similarities between Newton's choice to play down his Divine Calling and his attraction to alchemy because of societal and cultural pressures and the choices of many women today. How often do you play small so that other people might not feel threatened? How often do we discount our gifts, accomplishments, and triumphs so that we'll be loved? As Marianne Williams says, "We ask ourselves, who am I to be brilliant, gorgeous, talented, fabulous? [But] actually, who are you *not* to be? You are a child of God. Your playing small does not serve the world. There is nothing enlightened about shrinking so that other people won't feel insecure around you." Like Sir Isaac Newton you "were born to make manifest the glory of God that is within you."

What Is Magic?

Magic is what happens when you have encountered the Divine. It is the life-altering experience of connecting to the divinity that dwells within yourself and in the world.

—Phyllis Curott

Can my life really be magical? you're wondering. Well, when was the last time you felt in love?

"Most people know intuitively that when you fall in love, the world is full of magic," Phyllis Curott, author of two extraordinary books on the spiritual practice of magic, reminds us. "What they don't know is that when you discover the universe is full of magic, you fall in love with the world."

According to *Chamber's Dictionary of the English Language,* miracles are events that circumvent the laws of the natural world through Divine intervention. Magic is the art of working wonders through a supernatural knowledge of the powers of nature. In other words, you don't have to circumvent the laws of earth (or pray that it be done for you) if you know how to use natural law to your benefit. Like alchemy, both miracles and magic are transformative processes and both are an expression of Divine energy. The difference is that miracles tap into Divine energy outside of ourselves and magic is a result of harnessing the Divine energy within each of us. But for miracles as well as magic to occur, imagination must merge with belief.

In her book *Notions and Potions: A Safe, Practical Guide to Creating Magic and Miracles,* Susan Bowes explains that because magic is based on knowledge of natural law—which includes the cycles of the moon and planets, the nuances of weather and the rhythm of the seasons—it has always been considered a feminine mystery. This stems "from the days when it was a woman's work to grow and harvest plants and herbs. . . . Women learned how the potency of plants responded to the phases of the moon, the time of day or night, and the seasons of the year. They also learned to create powerful and highly effective spells, perfumes, poisons, and potions to entice, destroy, manipulate, defeat, challenge, fascinate, and confuse. Or at least that is how the fragile male ego began to view it. Because she possessed enigmatic knowledge and abstruse healing powers," a certain type of woman in rural areas began to be feared. From the beginning of time, what men couldn't understand, they feared. Whatever was feared had to be hated, discounted, manipulated, or eliminated. That's why miracle workers came to be called saints, scientists couldn't be identified as shamans, and magic makers became known as witches.

Like most people, I grew up associating magic with witches. I've got to be honest with you, I despise the word *witch*. Actually, I recoil when I hear it. It just sets off a screed in my soul, especially when I'm trying to meditate upon every woman's beautiful, spiritual birthright of magic.

Phyllis Curott is the first to agree: "I have found that when I mention the word *Witch*, it often brings to people's minds images of hurly-burly hags casting spells, licentious young women consorting with the devil, and wizards commanding supernatural demons to appear," she admits candidly. "On the lighter side, they might think of the glamorous Veronica Lake in *I Married a Witch*, sexy Kim Novak in *Bell, Book and Candle*, or the adorable TV witches in *Bewitched* and *Sabrina* lending some desperately needed excitement, as well as some unexpected morality, to the American suburbs. Or perhaps they will remember with a child's delight *The Wizard of Oz* and Glinda, the Good Witch of the North, who tells young Dorothy the power to find her happiness, and way home, has been with her all along. This last image comes closest to capturing the real and unknown truth about Witchcraft."

In her moving and provocative memoir, *Book of Shadows: A Modern Woman's Journey into the Wisdom of Witchcraft and the Magic of the Goddess,* Phyllis explains that "contrary to the clichés in fairy tales and Hollywood films, Witchcraft is not a subculture of satanic rites enacted by wacky spinsters or mad demonologists. It is an ancient, elegant spirituality that revives the magic of being alive—the kind of magic that we have always longed for, but sadly assumed only came true in storybooks."

I don't believe the world *witch* soothes a woman's soul or redeems it, but magic can. So let's start thinking of magic as your basic instinct.

Your Life Is Your Magic

To believe in magic as a viable way of enhancing our quality of life does require a leap of faith. We must see life in slightly romantic terms; recognize falling in love or growing a flower or even cooking a perfect pie as a demonstration of the magic of balance, of everything coming together in just the right way.

—Titania Hardie

"*M*agic is the practice of moving natural (though little-understood) energies to effect needed change," Scott Cunningham, the well-respected expert on magic and herbalism, tells us. "Magic isn't a means for forcing nature to do your will. This is a completely erroneous idea, fostered by the belief that magic is somehow supernatural, as if anything that exists can be outside of nature. *Magic is natural.* It is a harmonious movement of energies to create needed change. If you wish to practice magic, all thoughts of it being paranormal or supernatural must be forgotten."

What also needs to be forgotten or put aside are those lurking fears that magic is evil. This won't be easy. But let's try. "For hundreds of years we have suffered under the misunderstanding that magic is demonic. And even those who don't believe in the devil fear that, just maybe, fooling around with magic can unleash supernatural powers beyond our control," admits Phyllis Curott. "As humans, we have an age-old fear of the unknown, and that's certainly what magical power seems to be: an unknown force from an unknown source. We're afraid we will lose control of ourselves, and of the world in which we live."

Actually the spiritual practice of Divine Magic is not something "we do to manipulate or control the Universe—it's about communing and cocreating, about bringing your own sacred power into fullest expression or manifestation," Phyllis reassures us. *"The only person we ever seek to control with magic is ourselves.* Magic, when done properly, brings you into alignment with the powers of the numinous Universe, so that they may assist you in giving form to your true purpose, your reason for being. *The energy with which you make magic is sacred and so how, and why, you make magic is sacred."*

Ultimately, "your life is your magic."

Still, I'm not going to be disingenuous and pretend that black magic doesn't exist. As with power, sex, and ambition, magic misdirected can be turned into something ugly. Just as love thwarted slowly turns to hate and passion turned inward morphs into obsession, the energy of magic can be abused, too. The one tenet of faith that all spiritual paths share is not to hurt others in ways that *you* would find hurtful—Divine Magic is no different.

Every Little Spell She Speaks

You are the spell the Universe has cast.

—Phyllis Curott

You've been casting spells ever since you were a little girl. Remember "star light, star bright," the first star you used to wish on at night? That was a spell.

"Casting spells is something you do already," my wise friend Barrie Dolnick tells me. As the author of the wonderful *Simple Spells* series (for Love, Success, and Hearth and Home), and the forthcoming *Instructions for Your Discontent,* Barrie has done more to demystify these ancient spiritual practices than anyone else I know. It's also been my great fortune to have her act as a loving, compassionate, and savvy guide during my own magical, mystical mystery tour. "The practice of casting spells is an unconscious ritual in our society. For instance, when you put on perfumes, you are amplifying your own energy through scent, which can make you more attractive to others. A gift of red roses is a common love spell, eliciting passionate energy between you and your loved one." If you have an important meeting, do you wear a special outfit or a favorite piece of jewelry or even try to schedule the meeting for a specific time of day? You're unconsciously casting a success spell. When you arrange a bouquet of flowers for your home's foyer, simmer cinnamon on the stove in the winter, set out bowls of intoxicating rose potpourri in the summer, or light candles at the dinner table, you are unconsciously casting spells (called atmospheres) to make your home more inviting. Do you listen to a certain CD to put you in the mood as you're doing your makeup before you go out in the evening? As Etta James's, Tori Amos's, or Aretha's vibrations steadily raise your psychic energy, you're subtly but powerfully casting an ancient sexual enchantment.

What, no need for eye of newt? Barrie rolls her eyes and gives me one of those *I expect better than that from you* looks. "No, you'll have no need for eye of newt—would you even know where to get one?—or a cauldron, spider tongues, or any other such trappings that people traditionally and mistakenly identify with spell casting." *What you will need,* she tells me, is "integrity, courage, and personal commitment, not to mention patience."

Sounds like the hallmarks of any spiritual practice.

Exactly.

But what *is* a spell?

A spell is an organized desire passionately, creatively, and personally sent out into the Universe through words and ritual—a three-dimensional prayer that engages all your senses.

After I had completed *Simple Abundance* but before I'd mailed the final portion to my editor, I felt inspired to create a sending-off ceremony to thank the Great Creator and all my Divine helpers for their assistance and to bless the book on its journey to my future readers. I could just have packed the manuscript up and shipped it off, but my heart and soul knew this special moment of accomplishment needed recognition and honoring. So I bought a beautiful box and silk ribbons and wrapped up the manuscript as a gift to the Cosmos. With loving attention to detail, I decorated the sacred space where my adventure in gratitude had begun four years earlier—my dining room table—by arranging flowers from my garden, lighting my favorite rose-scented candles, and placing my gift in the center of the table. Then I put on music that I had listened to as I wrote it and, in a spontaneous outpouring, sent *Simple Abundance* into the world, proclaiming that my book would find "her" way into the hands and hearts of every woman who needed the blessings of its powerful lessons as much as I had.

"So be it! Blessed be!" I heard myself declaring. Afterward, I joyfully danced around the house, sipped sparkling cider, and toasted and blessed everyone in the mystical chain of chance who'd helped me bring this dream into being. Wanting to share my good fortune, I served my beloved cats their favorite treat of tuna fish, took cut-up fruit and oatcakes into the garden for the birds, and had brownies waiting for my daughter when she came home from school. At the time I had no idea I was casting a magic spell—this was my naturally over-the-top idea of what a real thanksgiving prayer should be. Now that I am more in touch with my legacy as a She, I understand my soul was tapping into Something much more powerful than just wishful thinking. That ceremony marked the first time I'd ever allowed my prayers to be elevated to a powerful ritual, performed with passion and devotion for only myself and Spirit. Given how well things went for *Simple Abundance,* I guess when it comes to casting spells, I'm a natural.

So are you!

That's because a good, heartfelt, harm-free spell draws on "your heightened consciousness, creativity, spontaneity, and inspiration," Phyllis Curott explains. "Spells are forms of personal, creative, religious ritual. They are divinely inspired expressions that help you cocreate reality with the Sacred. Instead of commanding the Universe, [you] open your heart and soul to it. A spell can be used for ecstatic communion, or for very specific practical purposes. It can be a means of deepest spiritual transformation, or it can be a means of enriching your personal life."

Phyllis Curott goes on to say that spells can take many forms: "Planting flowers in your garden as a way of bringing greater fertility, beauty, and prosperity in your life; swimming beneath a full Moon to cultivate your psychic and spiritual powers; singing a chant that has come to you to help reenchant the world; or cleaning out your closet as a way of banishing the pain and disappointments of the past so they no longer influence your present."

Because the Universe is magical and because you are nothing less than Its personal expression of that magic, spells can be creative catalysts meant to shift the energetic boundaries of what's possible in your life. But to tap into the Power, you've got to stop thinking in clichés. Forget hocus-pocus, abracadabra, and kaboom and begin transforming the world's "Double, double toil and trouble" with your passionate "Blessed be!"

Come to Your Senses

The Magical Spell of Scent

French perfume ... what a sensuous, downright sexy image is evoked by pairing those two simple words!

Although floral blends have existed for centuries, chances are that the scents your grandmothers wore were associated with single flowers. At the turn of the last century, women could purchase dozens of perfumes forthrightly named Rose Geranium, Ylang-

Ylang . . . and even Musk! They would have been more familiar with the differences between such scents than we are today, when the air is so clouded with odors . . . and not all as pleasant!

As flowers begin to show their heads outdoors, it's time to take a breather. Time to go back to nature, to distinguish between the scents you may already be wearing but no longer even notice. Time to smell the lilacs, forsythia, gardenia.

Stop by the aromatherapy counter of an herbal or natural products store . . . even your local pharmacy might have a section. Sniff the individual fragrances—floral essential oils such as jasmine, tea rose, or lily of the valley might be familiar, but what about some of the others? Sample a few scents that are new to you by inhaling from their tester bottles, and dabbing them on your skin. Walk away from the counter to clear your senses, then sniff again. Never purchase a new scent without first doing this. It makes me shudder to think of the money wasted on perfume that was irresistible at the cosmetic counter and then became repulsive by the time I got home.

Which oils smell sweet, which citrusy, which green or woody or earthy? Which is a scent you would like to encounter, even subliminally, if you were standing next to yourself in an elevator?

Keep these sensations in mind when going on the next step of your fragrance journey, to a perfumery or a well-stocked scent counter of a pharmacy, gift shop, or department store. Have you been buying products based upon their packaging (a beautiful bottle, perhaps?) or designer name? Or have they caught your interest because the *scents themselves* appeal to you when they interact upon your skin with your own body's oils?

Although some famous makers rely primarily on synthetic scents bearing little relation to nature—Chanel was purportedly the first, whipping up her *Chanel No. 5* from purely chemical odors back in the twenties—most fall back upon using Grandma's old favorites.

Test perfumes a few at a time, closing your eyes and concentrating completely on their scents. Can you identify the jasmine, musk, and vanilla tones of Coty's *L'Aimant*? The jasmine, rose, camellia, and lily-of-the-valley mixture of *Arpège*? Or the intriguing citrus edge to Caron's jasmine, rose, and ylang-ylang blend, *Fleurs de Rocaille*? Other perfumes concentrate upon a single floral scent, such as *Diorissimo* (lily of the valley), *Narcisse Noir* (black narcissus), *Chloé* (tuberose), and *L'Air du Temps* (carnation). Still others—for example, the bergamot-scented *Eau de Givenchy*—have citrus scents as their "top notes"; or green scents (such as Elizabeth Arden's *Blue Grass*); earthy "chypre" scents (e.g., *Calèche,* with its floral and musk mixture); or spicy (such as Poison). Some scents are fruity: Calvin Klein's *Escape* smells like apples. Bulgari's *Eau Parfumée* smells like green tea!

When you find a fragrance that most appeals to your sensibilities, even a limited budget should be able to accommodate a vial of essential oil in a single scent, or a small bottle of quality perfume. Both (as opposed to diluted eau de cologne or toilet water) should be used sparingly, just a drop at a time, and are best purchased in small amounts for maximum freshness.

Take care that your other toiletries and cosmetics aren't fighting for attention with your chosen scent. Even if they are individually pleasant, odors from shampoos, lipsticks, and face powder, even deodorant or mouthwash, can confuse the senses. Wherever possible, switch to unscented brands that will allow your most deliberate and romantic fragrance to be the foremost scent to represent you!

Pulse points—remember those? Yes, they do truly make a difference in the application of perfumes or oils. Behind your ears, at your wrists, yes—but keep going. In her delightful book *Fatale: How French Women Do It,* Edith Kunz tells us what the key points are, echoing Coco Chanel's advice that a woman should apply perfume to "wherever she wants to be kissed."

> *Heels, arches, and between the toes*
> *The inner and outer ankle bone*
> *Behind the knees*
> *The underside of the derriere*
> *The pubic area and the navel*
> *Under each breast and between the breasts*
> *The shoulders and upper arms*
> *Inside the bend of the elbow*
> *The inner wrist*
> *The back of the hand and between the fingers*
> *The hollow at the bottom of the neck*

All around the collar bone
Under the chin
Along the jaw line
Behind the ears and on the earlobes
On the temples
Along the back of the neck to the shoulder blades
Around the hairline.

"The artful application of fragrance takes about fifteen minutes from bath to blush," ending by "tucking an aromatic cotton puff inside the bra between the lady's two tender treasures." While you're dabbing a drop or two on a cotton ball, place one in an envelope, and tuck the homemade sachet in with your lingerie, hosiery, knitwear. Keep another envelope with your writing papers, so that even from a distance your "signature fragrance" will indeed accompany your signature.

And be sure to dot on a bit of scent when going to bed. Isn't it the most toe-curlingly sensuous, sexy sensation to awaken to your own delicious fragrance, even before you open your eyes to the sun?

The Magic of Glamour

Until this century, glamour was associated with the occult.
The word denoted an attractiveness that was exciting, romantic,
fascinating — an attractiveness too powerful to be real.
Such personal power, had, therefore, to be allied with sorcery.

—Annette Tapert

*W*ho seemed the most glamorous woman imaginable when you were growing up? Your older sister or mother, an aunt, a teacher, an actress seen in films? What was so special about her? Was it her clothing, always so fashionable or perfectly pulled together or *crisp*? Her bearing, which set her apart from everyone else and made her a pleasure to watch, even as she sat or walked or stood? Her beauty, be it totally and deliberately natural, or a masterwork of cosmetic/hairdressing artistry? Her personality—her captivating or comforting effect on men, upon other women?

For many, it was the mystery of an adult relative performing a beauty regimen or fashion ritual, perhaps while bathing or dressing up to go out, which projected a kind of mesmerizing power. Something to do with an essence of womanliness and adulthood itself, something that made her into a kind of goddess, set apart from both men and girls.

For a friend, this was her aunt's everyday application of cosmetics—a treat to observe during those rare times as a child when she stayed for an overnight visit. Of course, looking back upon it all as an adult, it seems so ordinary a routine. But, to a seven-year-old . . . to see blue—blue!—mascara rubbed from a little cake moistened with saliva, applied with the tiniest imaginable brush, as her blonde and blue-eyed aunt held a magnifying mirror to catch the morning sunlight, following a few pressings of that extraordinary instrument, a golden eyelash curler—what could be more

Venus-like than that? And perhaps her aunt felt a little more glamorous for the awed audience. Who knows?

In *The Power of Glamour,* a riveting and rapturous recalling of the lives of the women of Hollywood during the 1930s, Annette Tapert reminds us that "the concept of glamour is not, in the end, reducible to fashion and cosmetics—it's about the woman herself. And in the 1930s, in particular, personality was the key ingredient in a star's glamour." Early movie stars such as Joan Crawford, Katharine Hepburn, Carole Lombard, Claudette Colbert, and Greta Garbo used their feminine wiles to "succeed against great odds in a tough industry governed completely by men who had created a system that gave them almost dictatorial power. And in the process of being exploited, these women used classic feminine arts—style, wit, guile—to outsmart the system" and become "the nation's first group of prominent career women. Their on-screen personae embodied the fantasies of modern women and fueled dreams for millions" as they became American women's first role models.

Early influences may affect us more than we realize. When you were young, did you ever deliberately incorporate into your own style elements of the behavior or appearance of those older women you thought were particularly attractive and personally magnetic? The way you'd do your hair? The way you'd sip your tea? When you adopted these traits, did you feel or look like the women you were emulating? Or did you feel foolish or awkward? Did you discover that, in trying to be like them, you were simply *not yourself?*

Are the women who influenced you as beautiful to you in retrospect? If you know them still, with the passage of time do they continue to command the same power, that mystery, in occasional glimpses, or as a whole? Have such qualities perhaps even increased as they've aged, or as you have matured . . . or some combination of both?

Or have you outgrown your belief that they were glamorous, unable now to see what had made such women seem so marvelous to you? Have you made the disappointed discovery that someone's beauty was a too falsely created illusion or too tied to its own time (for instance, a magnificent beehive hairdo that few of us would venture to wear today?). Was her personality only a calculated persona, no longer attractive to you now that you have a greater understanding of its origins or effects? What do you now think makes a woman beautiful or charming?

Perhaps you see what I'm driving at. Are you aware of and do you *enjoy* images of *yourself*—the gut-level impressions that you may give to others as a person—in the way you once looked up to other, influential women? Have you grown up to be the woman you imagined you would be, in not only physical appearance but also style, bearing, personality? Do you feel you've become the lush ripening of your girlhood dreams?

Amid the bustle of the everyday, especially when one constantly needs to satisfy others, it is easy to literally lose sight of one's own physical presence. *You owe it to yourself to feel attractive.* To take pleasure in your face, your body, how you move and dress, even in how your own voice sounds. Begin by finding moments to appreciate and perhaps create afresh feelings of graciousness and gracefulness, which are the underpinnings of genuine elegance, whatever your looks or wardrobe. Seat yourself, don't flop down. When you catch your reflection in a store window, adjust your walk to that of a person you would like to see approaching you. And smile! Modulate your voice to feel its warmth. Banish from your cosmetic bag and wardrobe what might have seemed like good buys, but don't *become you,* don't make you feel good. Cast for yourself a new, essensual you—a woman you would love to watch, to meet, to know, created in your own gorgeous, glorious, gutsy image. And every little thing you do *will* become magical.

Come to Your Senses

Springtime Saucery

*W*e think of April as the month when flowers and trees, drinking in the renowned rains of the season, erupt with newborn beauty. But, not too long ago, markets also burgeoned with the fresh bounty of spring—the Great Mother's ingredients for the most essensual of all enchantments—saucery or culinary magic.

Food technology, rapid transportation, and refrigeration have helped us to forget that for many, many centuries most of the delectables we take for granted and call ordinary could only be enjoyed in season and rarely outside the locale where they were grown. (This is why a tangerine or orange at the toe of a Christmas stocking was such a treat to anyone not living in citrus-growing regions.) Right into the early twentieth century, cookbooks still specified which foodstuffs were appropriate by month or season. Under April, we find such items as scallions (also known as spring or green onions), rhubarb, the first (nonhothouse) strawberries and cherries, asparagus, trout, and salmon.

"As we approach the Spring Equinox, we become more alive to our senses," Titania Hardie tells us in her scrumptious cookbook of magical feasts, *Witch in the Kitchen*. Any food prepared with love possesses magic. "This, then, is our journey—to celebrate the link between physical sustenance and love: between the feeding of the body, and the feeding of the soul and heart. En route, magical things may happen. . . . Food acquires magical properties both in the way that it is handled, and through one's understanding of the powerful properties that the ingredients themselves may contain, and therefore the physical effects they may have."

To test her theory, let's try springtime salmon. A classic preparation is to poach it in what the French call a court bouillon, a luscious broth made with wine and vegetables. Though we usually think of poached salmon as being a whole fish, laid out in a special long and narrow pot, it is in fact quick and easy to prepare as a single portion.

Springtime Salmon

You will need:

1 quart water, plus more as needed
½ cup dry white wine
1 carrot, sliced thinly
1 medium onion, chopped into ½-inch chunks
1 bay leaf
1 teaspoon salt
Dash freshly ground pepper
½ pound fresh salmon steak
Cucumber and lemon, thinly sliced, for garnish

Hollandaise Sauce:

1 egg yolk
1 teaspoon lemon juice
3 tablespoons butter, melted
2 teaspoons hot water
Dash salt and pepper

1. In a medium saucepan (enameled or stainless steel only) for which you have a roasting or steaming rack, com-

bine 1 quart of water with the wine, vegetables, bay leaf, and salt and pepper. Bring to a boil, lower heat, and simmer for 15 minutes.

2. Rinse salmon under cold running water, then pat dry. Wrap the fish in one layer of cheesecloth (this will allow you to lift out the tender cooked salmon in one piece) and place it into the broth upon the rack. The bouillon should cover the fish; if it does not, add enough water to cover.

3. Leaving heat low so that the broth only just simmers, cover the pot with its lid and poach the fish for 20 minutes.

4. While the fish cooks, prepare the hollandaise sauce. In a double boiler or a small bowl placed over hot but not bubbling water, whisk the egg yolk until smooth. Whisking continually, add the lemon juice and, in a slow stream, the melted butter; then, again in a fine stream, add the hot water. Sprinkle on the salt and pepper, whisk for another minute or two. Keep sauce over the hot water until fish is ready to serve.

5. Use a broad spatula to lift the cheesecloth-wrapped fish off its rack, and turn out on a plate. Garnish with fantasy fish scales, which you make by overlapping thin slices of cucumber and lemon.

Serve with new baby spring, parsleyed potatoes (leave skins on, boil, or roast), asparagus tips, and hollandaise sauce.

The Listening Walk

You are really not at home in a place until
you have made yourself familiar with how
it sounds and resounds.

—Jonathan Ree

*A*fter my head injury, I learned to read once again with children's picture books. There's still something very soothing and reassuring about rediscovering the world from a pint-size perspective. Suddenly, it all makes sense. One of my favorites is *The Listening Walk* by Paul Showers. In it a little boy recounts all the sounds he hears as he takes a walk around his neighborhood. From water sprinklers to the difference between power and push lawn mowers, the sounds surrounding him begin to come into sharp focus. Cars driving down the street sound different if you really listen, as do babies crying, boys on roller skates, girls on bicycles, and ladies in high heels.

Sometimes the little boy goes to the park to hear the difference between pigeons and ducks. Or the way a woodpecker's *tat-tat-tat* echoes through the trees when carried by the *whoosh* of the wind. When my daughter was little we'd go on listening walks, and her favorites were during spring showers. After listening to water pouring out of gutters, splashing from tires, and the *pip-plop* of drizzling leaves, we'd get to hear my favorite wet-weather sound: rain on the roof as we snuggled in bed for an afternoon nap.

The English writer Jonathan Ree tells us in *I See a Voice,* his philosophical history of deafness, language, and the senses, that listening is the homing device by which our soul directs us toward our sense of place. Nothing is more personal than how we listen. For instance, you and I might both visit the same lake at the same time, but we would "see" and remember the place differently because of our auditory acuity, or how well we listened to the lake's presence—its watery whispers, murmurs, or sputters. Through the poems of the eighteenth-century writer William Wordsworth, readers who have never traveled to England fall in love with the Lake District because his poetry resonates with its "audible seclusions," turning his cherished landscape into his readers' beloved soundscape.

Paul Showers's little boy reminds us:

> *It's fun to go on a Listening Walk. You do not have to go far. You can walk around the block and listen. You can walk around your yard and listen. You do not even have to take a walk to hear sounds. There are sounds everywhere all the time. All you have to do is to keep still and listen to them. . . .*
>
> *When you finish this page, close the book and listen. How many sounds can you hear right now? Close your book and count the sounds you can hear.*
> *RIGHT NOW.*

Can you close this book right now and go for a listening walk? If you can't, will you do so before you come back? Please try!

Between the Lines

Basic Instincts

Practical magic celebrates the belief that we are all a part of the "WEB OF LIFE," and that every independent entity is connected in the minutest ways to other entities by an imperceptible web of vibrations. When we perform a small, symbolic task, it is connected to the real object of our thought by these interlaced vibrations. Quite simply, the more we are in tune with these vibratory waves, the more we can effect changes (even if very small ones) on material events. If someone wishes us negativity, persistent positive thought returned to them will, little by little, alter their negative feelings. If someone is ill, our bold, optimistic thought can alleviate their condition to some extent. If we are out of touch with others, setting our thoughts in motion can eventually cause a chain of response. Never let negative thought, or disbelief, dissuade you!

—Titania Hardie

Enchanted: Titania's Book of White Magic

Come to Your Senses

Wake Up to Wonder

*I*t's striking how more pleasurable our daily round becomes once we stop playing the role of soi-disant sophisticate and choose instead to wander through our days as inquisitive sensualists.

I have a pair of turtledoves that nest by day in the apple tree in front of my cottage, but overnight on my chimney. And so each morning, I don't wake up to the shrill of an alarm clock but to the sound of wonder—the soft billing and cooing of a couple of love birds. This avian *He says/She says* has not only been delightful, but instructive, because once I started to distinguish between the male and female, I started to fall in love with birdsong.

"How do you know but that every bird that cleaves the aerial way is not an immense world of delight closed to your senses five?" the seventeenth-century English mystical poet William Blake asked. Mother Nature is waiting to teach us some of our sweetest lessons once we're willing to come to our senses, such as how to *listen* to Life.

Whether you live in a city or a more rural setting, birdsong is meant to be a healing balm. Since music began, man has attempted to imitate the enchanting voices of these wondrous creatures. But our ears have grown deaf to their charms. That's why before seeking out the real thing, listening to recordings that attempt to re-create such transparent, soaring, featherweight vocal effects can attune you to what you've been missing. Some composers succeed admirably—extraordinary examples of birdlike trilling exist in some arias by Handel, such as in the oratorio work *L'Allegro il Pensieroso ed il Moderato* ("Sweet bird, than shunn'st the noise of folly"), and in the high-flying soprano role of the fairy-tale bird character in Rimsky-Korsakov's *Le Coq d'Or.* Sopranos and/or flautists are often featured in bird-related classical songs, for instance in Alabiev's virtuoso "The Nightingale," one of whose finest interpreters was the appropriately named French soprano Mado Robin!

Contemporary songsmiths have also been unable to resist the temptation of birds as a subject, from the ever-cheerful "When the red, red robin comes bob, bob, bobbin' along" of 1926 to Hoagy Carmichael's all-instrumental "Skylark." How many songs can you find that take birds as their inspiration? Think on that the next time you're standing in line or waiting on hold.

Are you ready to go one-to-one with the birds themselves? What cheeping and cooing are outside your window? What birds are producing these musical tête-à-têtes? Time for a listening walk; can you spot the sources? Look for their nests, tucked into the branches of trees or porch eaves. New chicks of any breed of bird are adorable balls of the fluffiest down, and their peeping is a perennial expression of both life's vulnerability and a powerful hunger to live; not just to fly, but soar. Is there a particular time of day when you hear them? Their song at matins is very different from the concerto at vespers.

Increase the likelihood of hearing more music and catching a glimpse of the celestial creatures serenading you by putting up a bird feeder, or simply setting out seeds or crumbled crusts on a windowsill. I've gotten into the healthy habit of having an apple in the morning and a pear in the afternoon as a snack, so that I can leave a love offering of the juicy core for my Romeo and Juliet. Actually, like every living thing that's ever wandered into my vicinity, I've spoiled them rotten, indulging their preference for Chinese pears as often as I can. However, to see them share so generously with each other is to be reminded that true love exists and is worth the wait.

But you don't need turtledoves to start bird-watching. Even the much denigrated city pigeon is a marvel of iridescent coloring—with no two patterned quite the same—and an expert when it comes to warbling a soft, mezzo-soprano coo. The deceptively dull feathers of the sparrow encase a natural show-off, who prefers to wait until she can perform a solo.

Did you know that, like human babies, little birds aren't born knowing how to sing? Their parents teach them. Diane Ackerman tells us in *A Natural History of the Senses* that "if you raised some birds away from their parents and whistled a different song—the opening notes of Beethoven's Ninth, say—then they would learn your song, and the neighbors might well call them 'the Beethoven birds.' Equally fascinating is that birds have language dialects like people do, and a crow raised in New Hampshire won't be able to understand his Ozark cousin."

Come my next birthday I shall be four going on five, or maybe it's five going on four, I don't really remember; I was very young when I was born. But this I do know, that finally I'm delighting for the first time in all the natural wonders I was too blind to see or too deaf to hear, pretending to be a grown-up. Birdsong is one of them, which is why I'm giving my younger babe a dovecote for her birthday. But throw out your cliché of what a bird-watcher of a certain age looks like. Her rubber boots are leopard-patterned.

It was one of those beautiful, lengthening days,
when May was pressing back with both hands
the shades of the morning and the evening.

–Amelia E. Barr (1886)

*E*arth's crammed with Heaven this month . . . the days are lengthening and simple splendors are increasing. Are you looking for love in all the right places? Maybe not . . . so hone your homing instincts and redefine sacred space. Can a black silk slip turn housekeeping into an erotic art? Find out when you romance the chores with sensuous scrubbing. Satisfy wanderlust by getting in touch with your essensual spice girl. Offer sassy prayers of thanksgiving and reap profound pleasures . . . from far-flung fantasies to footbaths. The unadulterated Ordinary's got some unexpected smiles. Honey, you're home.

Sacred Partnerships

I gave my love to the house forever.
I will come till I cannot come, I said,
And the house said, I will know.

—Louise Townsend Nicholl

Sacred partnerships arrive in our lives in many forms. Sometimes they're of wood and stone instead of flesh and bone. *The House of Belonging* is an ancient Celtic metaphor for the body as the earthly home for our souls, as well as for the deep peace and feeling of safety, joy, and contentment found in intimate connections with people and places. My dear friend John O'Donohue, the Irish poet and scholar, exquisitely explores these beautiful themes in his book *Anam Cara: A Book of Celtic Wisdom:* "When you learn to love and to let your self be loved, you come home to the hearth of your own spirit. You are warm and sheltered. You are completely at one in the house of your own longing and belonging."

I truly believe that just as we have *anam cara,* or "soul friends," we each have a House of Belonging waiting for us. Waiting to be built, waiting to be found, waiting to be renovated, waiting to be cleaned up. Waiting for us to "dwell in possibility," as Emily Dickinson puts it. Waiting for us to be ready to fall truly, madly, deeply in love. Waiting for the real thing: a grown-up, romantic, reciprocal relationship.

Every relationship you have—with other people, with your work, with Divinity—reflects in some way your soul's intimate union with you. Nowhere is this spiritual truth more apparent than in the relationships we have with our home. All we have to do is take a good look around. Is your house tidy on the surface but hiding chaos and confusion in junk drawers? You can take it from there. But you can also take it from me: You deserve to live in a home that embraces, nurtures, delights, and inspires you and all who find shelter with you.

The emotional attachment—good or bad—that we have to our home is a daily spiritual tutorial in Love. "Many people have an *anam cara* of whom they are not truly aware. Their lack of awareness cloaks the friend's presence and causes feelings of distance and absence," John O'Donohue tells us. "It is wise to pray for the grace of recognition. Inspired by awareness, you may then discover beside you the *anam cara* of whom your longing has always dreamed."

When I glance back at the last several years of my Gratitude Journal, I am astounded at how frequently "my beautiful home" appears there. Over the last twenty years, my dream house has run the gamut from a Victorian gingerbread to a Frank Lloyd Wright manse. None of these fantasies, however, was destined to become my House of Belonging, which is an old stone cottage nestled deep in the English countryside. I've discovered that when it comes to houses, as it is with true love, outward appearances are often deceiving. It's what's inside that counts.

Changing Places

Wild and distant places speak to many who find in them opportunities to engage in the spiritual practices of wonder and gratitude.

—Frederic and Mary Ann Brussat

And *how* did I end up living in the English countryside? Probably because I'm a woman who knows laughing matters, especially when you want to cry. I'm also an incurable, hopeful romantic, who truly believes in love at first sight—despite the real risk that when you're swept off your feet, there's a good chance you'll end up on your ass. The combination of those two qualities is often called fatal attraction. Still, the more risks you take, the luckier you get in love and life.

In 1997, two years after *Simple Abundance* appeared in the United States, it was published in England. I wouldn't go so far as to say the English are a generation behind the Americans as far as the search for enlightenment goes, but at that time the British notion of a self-help book was *So You Want to Keep Sheep?* As Bette Midler puts it, "When it's three P.M. in New York, it's 1932 in England." Which is, of course, much of its great appeal for me.

British journalists are a cynical lot, especially the men, who can be as dour, argumentative, and repressed as they are charming, clever, and witty. In England, reviewing books in the inspirational genre is often viewed as an exercise in humorous writing or blood sport. Unfortunately, their razor-sharp ridicule can slash any legitimate insight.

No man treats a woman worse than the one who loves her but doesn't want to, unless it's a British hack who begrudgingly likes your book despite his best efforts to belittle it. As Oscar Wilde pointed out, a journalist is someone who insults you in public and then apologizes in private. "Bad hair, overdrafts, dirty floors— don't let them get you down, let them enrich you" was some of the derision meted out to *Simple Abundance*. As my luck certainly *did* have it, one particularly unscrupulous fellow (who had the gall to pretend he'd met and interviewed me) wrote a sentence that inadvertently not only became the banner headline for my book in Europe, but also set me on a path toward my true House of Belonging. "Sarah Ban Breathnach might be described as the Isaac Newton of the simplicity movement," he wisecracked. At a cocktail party this might have sounded hilarious; in print, it's high praise.

I roared with laughter when I read that. This unintentional compliment was not only a hoot, but a generous gift. No longer was it necessary for me to dream about winning the Nobel Prize; a magnificent obituary was guaranteed. My foreign publishers were particularly thrilled and used the line with glee in their publicity campaigns. *Sarah Ban Breathnach può essere paragonata all'Isaac Newton del "movimento della semplicità,"* my Italian publishers proudly boasted. I loved it! Too fabulous to wait for a memorial stone, the compliment now adorns a stepping-stone in my garden, a wonderful reminder every day that often happiness is outrageously achieved if you know how to step lively and when to laugh.

Naturally after this cosmic comparison, I developed a mad, passionate crush on Sir Isaac Newton and wanted to know everything about him.

"Total absence of humor renders life impossible," Colette wrote in a short story called "Chance Acquaintances." She could have been referring to Newton and me. Because six months later, while casually flipping through an English newspaper "coincidently" discarded in an airport waiting lounge, I discovered that a cottage that had previously been Sir Isaac Newton's private chapel was for sale. Good Heavens! How often did this happen? Maybe once in several lifetimes. Obviously, I had to at least request some details. A month later, the mystical chain of chance continued when a magazine unexpectedly sent me to London for an article on Princess Diana's funeral. And so, I extended my stay a couple of days and traveled to what seemed to me to be the wilds of rural England, *just* to take a look.

Just One Look

It was a love like a chord from Bach,
of such pure gravity.

—Nina Cassian

Just one look, that's all it took. Just one look, and the earth tilted on its axis. I fell truly, madly, and deeply in love with Newton's Chapel with the same intense witlessness that women do with unsuitable men—rashly, recklessly, and unreservedly—giving no thought to the life changes my love affair would trigger. I was newly separated and shaky after my long-standing marriage had ended abruptly; I didn't know a soul in England. *Why* am I doing this? I asked the "Voice" telling me to buy the cottage, then and there. *It will all be revealed in the Bye-and-Bye.*

There's more. The Chapel was nine hundred years old and only had two rooms. Recalling the exact moment my common sense went south—from the sublime to the ridiculous in a fleeting glance—only one word comes to mind: *certifiable.*

Why *do* we fall in love? Imagine someone whose face *lights up* every time he sees you coming toward him. How do you feel? Newton's Chapel seemed so alive, warm, loving, and happy *to see me.* I have always been so touched by the story of the American writer Samuel Clemens, who, in 1874, moved into his dream house—an imposing, nineteen-room, redbrick, Gothic mansion in Hartford, Connecticut—with his wife and three daughters. Over the next thirty-five years, Sam and Livy decorated, renovated, and lavished so much time, creative energy, emotion, and money on their house it forced him into bankruptcy. Luckily for us, Clemens solved his financial problems and continued to decorate by writing books under the pseudonym Mark Twain. But that building was not just a house, it was their *home*—their sacred partner—in their union with Life. In a letter to a friend in 1896 Clemens confided:

> *It had a heart and a soul, and eyes to see with; and approvals and solicitudes and deep sympathies; it was of us, and we were in its confidence and lived in its grace and in the peace of its benedictions. We never came home from an absence that its face did not light up and speak out in eloquent welcome—and we could not enter it unmoved.*

I can't explain my love for Newton's Chapel any better. From the moment I crossed the threshold an enchantment took hold. "What manner of sorcery is this?" I wondered. Of course, I would later learn about Newton's practical magic, but I didn't know about it then. What I sensed was that here he got away from the experiments he conducted in his house that was just down the lane; here he came to think, meditate, ruminate, ask questions, and, above all, *listen.* Here was where Heaven came down to Earth for private tutorials with the man who would give the world an understanding of the Cosmos. It feels incredibly intimate to admit

this, but the palpable awe that came over me—a sacred swoon—
was nothing less than a personal transfiguration. I knew I was
standing on holy ground. *I knew I had been led here, step by step.* I
knew I didn't ever want to leave. I had to know that I would be
coming back.

Remembering what Willa Cather said about how we find happiness, I made an offer on the spot to buy the cottage. "One cannot
divine nor forecast the conditions that will make happiness. One
only stumbles upon them by chance, in a lucky hour, at the world's
end somewhere, and holds fast to the days, as to fortune or fame."

Five years have passed since that first look and I'm still besotted.

Being Home

On the threshold the entire past
and the endless future
rush to meet one another.

—Gunilla Norris

"*W*hat meaning does this place have for you?"
Meaning? The woman I was long ago considered the
architect's unexpected query. Meaning? She had been anticipating
practical questions: Did she prefer built-in cupboards? What size
would she like the window over the kitchen sink to be?

Meaning. She sat at the circular oak table across from the architect, the table she had selected twenty years before with her
fiancé—soon to be her ex-husband—although she did not know
that yet. In a flash she could see them walking together among
hundreds of oak tables and ladder-back chairs at a furniture ware-
house in the Virginia countryside. She, meditating on the meaning
of their selection of a table at which friends and family would
gather; he, looking at price tags accompanied by increasing aggra-
vation. After two hours she had laid her hand upon the table at

which she sat. "We will love this table for the rest of our lives," she reassured him as he paid for it, his expression pinched and pale at what he considered an extravagance. But he resigned himself to the purchase because he loved her and they were not yet married.

Had they been married, he would have told her, in no uncertain terms, that the table and chairs were too expensive—that they must "think" about such purchases, consider, then reconsider, see if they couldn't find another set at a better price. Against his better judgment, he paid $800 for the solid, round oak table and four matching ladder-back chairs, swallowing his reluctance after realizing that $800 amortized over fifty years meant the investment was just $16 per year. And, of course, they would love this table for the rest of their lives.

Sitting next to the architect now, the woman glanced around the room and her eyes caught the open-shelved hutch heavy with the artifacts of daily life—chipped cups and mismatched saucers, cereal and soup bowls, plates and platters. But her gaze rested upon her mother's best china, the Johnson pink chintz pattern that had graced every holiday table as she was growing up, and now graced her own family's festive occasions.

This was the hutch that she had refinished with her mother-in-law on an oppressively hot summer's afternoon the day after she'd lost her first child, because, as she was told, *These things happen all the time, you aren't the first woman to have a miscarriage, it's best to be up and about and busy, not dwelling on the things that can't be changed. Probably there was something wrong with the baby—it's just nature's way. But you aren't that old and you'll have more chances to try again, God willing.* As it turned out, she was blessed with a beautiful, healthy child, but she never refinished another piece of furniture again.

Meaning? What meaning did this place have for her? "I thought this consultation was about what I wanted the new addition to look like," she told the architect.

"But you must first satisfy your needs, and then the wants will take care of themselves. What is it that *you need* this house to be and express? When you cross the threshold, what dreams wait to welcome you? How do you want to feel when you walk into this room? All of these are your basic *needs*. I always remind my clients that if they're to build a home for the soul instead of for show, the practical must never eclipse the passionate."

To her great astonishment, but not the architect's, the very thought that she *had* needs was enough to make the woman weep. One year later she would move out of the house where she no longer belonged, taking only the pink china with her.

"Inside your home, you keep mementos of your past that help or hinder your movement into the future. You keep the articles of warmth and refuge that help you weather the storms outside and within in you," Kathryn L. Robyn gently comforts us in her amazing book *Spiritual Housecleaning: Healing the Space Within by Beautifying the Space Around You.* "You should be able to expect this space to provide you with the means to cleanse and feed yourself, to rest your body and your mind, to engage in quality and intimate time with friends and loved ones, to entertain and stimulate you. You may take it for granted that you can unlock the door and receive these gifts of shelter every time you come home."

But the sad, sorry, silent truth is that many women—women just like you and me—don't receive these gifts when they cross their threshold. And so, because they can't come home to a house that shelters their own body and soul, they run away to the shelter of addictions—food, drink, shopping, smoking, sex, chat rooms, drugs and prescription painkillers, workaholism, and perfectionism—where the spiritually homeless gather.

"We move in and out of our homes as if they mean nothing to us, as if we mean nothing to them, as if that glorious feeling of *being alive* had nothing to do with living each day. Only now and then does something happen that causes us to comment with profound astonishment, 'That got me where I live,'" Kathryn Robyn admits (surely for most of us). Perhaps it's time to take another look at where you really do live, *as if you have never seen it before.*

"Whatever the size and scope of it, you doubtless have a kitchen, a bathroom, a place to sleep, and a place to sit. You may do all this living in a one-room studio or in a towering estate with dozens of rooms. You may live in a tent. The size of your house is not related to the size of your soul, but the condition of your dwelling does present a picture of the condition of your being—body, mind, and spirit. Is it chaotic, spare, colorful, an afterthought? Are you a person who needs an unstructured environment, a clear routine, reminders of joy, space to feel? Does your house reflect or provide you with your needs? Could it do this better? Do you know what those needs are? Or are you ignoring that knowledge, restricting your ability to respond to the requirements of your being? Have you followed somebody else's rules and abandoned your own before you even knew what they were?"

Don't feel bad if you can't answer these questions right now. By the end of the month, after a little spiritual housecleaning, you will.

So Nice to Come Home To

If we had a feminism that caused us to get out of the house, is there not also room for feminism that would bring us back home, so that our homes would reflect ourselves and would once more have soul?

—Ginette Paris

"The great thing to keep in mind when you think of the place you live in is that it is your refuge. You may not like it very much, you may hope to move soon. It may be shabby, too large, too small," the English writer Elizabeth Kendall wrote in *House into Home,* published in 1962. "But even if you're there only until next Friday, it is still your refuge."

Chances are most of us will be in the same place come next Friday, but will you look forward to crossing the threshold *tonight?* If not, then it's time to hone in on perfecting your homing instincts. There's one secret to making your home a haven rather than just a dwelling place: comfort. Is your home the most comfortable place you know? And when you're there, do you feel completely at peace *with yourself?* What you're aiming for is a nest so warm, cozy, and inviting that your soul begins to sigh with grateful pleasure as you turn the key, *Honey . . . we're home!*

What do you usually do as soon as you walk through the door? Glance through the mail? Listen to your phone messages? Check your e-mail? Turn on the evening news? Read the paper? Do you feel disappointed if nothing urgent is happening? Oddly, now that communications have become instantaneous, it's incredibly difficult to wean ourselves from the sensory overload of the outside world, unless we do it by indulging our physical senses.

What about creating an unwinding ceremonial for your common days? Grant yourself a half hour spent downshifting into private time? Take time as you change your clothes, put the kettle on, caress your pet, water the plants. Play some special music that induces serenity or smiles and listen to it only when you come home in the evening. Putter around the different rooms. Can you go out to the backyard and cut a small bouquet of flowers? Could you bring some flowers home with you? Enjoy arranging them. Can you hear a clock ticking? If your heart races, a sure way to calm it is the soothing rhythm of an old clock. Let the rooms you'll be living in tonight welcome you home!

How can you do all this when the hordes are waiting for your attention? Tell them with a smile that you'll be with them as soon as you can pull yourself together. Believe it or not, even children and partners will wait if they know they have to, and that they'll have your undivided attention soon. And if you're home alone, realize how many women—complete strangers—would instantly trade places with you for at least a half hour a day for that delicious solitude.

In the past, it was customary for people to "freshen up" before the evening with a shower and then a change of clothing. On those nights when you're so tired you just want to drop, a quick shower before you slip into something comfortable will give you a new boost of energy to enjoy a pleasant evening—doing whatever it is you want to do.

Now, about that something comfortable to wear. While it is tempting to change into old sweats, tatty jeans, or the nightgown you've had since high school (even if lights-out is hours away), would you want to answer the door looking like that? Don't be ashamed of your own company. Create a more positive, self-aware presence with something loose and soft—fresh knitwear, a sexy caftan, a striking kimono, a vintage dressing gown. If you're more comfortable in pants, a pair of unwrinkled khakis and a brightly colored T-shirt does make you feel better. Clothes don't make the woman, but what we wear at home alone is a subtle but telling indication of where our self-esteem is at the moment. For years I had public clothes and private threads. In public I was pulled together physically and emotionally; in private I was falling apart. I also wondered why I wasn't as spontaneous as I wanted to be; it was because I wasn't prepared for pleasant surprises.

Sad, but instructive: I'd just moved into my cottage and I hadn't met many of the neighbors. There came a rap on the door, and when I opened it, a handsome man stood on my front step, a single friend of a friend, looking for the American lady who'd bought Newton's Chapel. He was bearing gifts. A bottle of wine, a loaf of homemade bread, cheese, and fruit. I was so embarrassed by how I looked that I told him I wasn't the woman he was looking for, I was her cousin. About six months later I called and invited him over. "You do bear a resemblance to your cousin, but you're much younger and prettier," he commented before telling me he'd recently begun seeing another woman. There is a moral to this story. It doesn't have to be yours.

Now, after you've reconnected to everything living in your environment (and that does include you), get the evening meal started, and when it's under way, sort the mail (next to a wastepaper basket), tossing the junk mail into the trash without opening it. Should you be so fortunate as to have some personal letters, save them until you can give these rare pleasures the attention they deserve. And here's a radical thought: Set a time when you'll check your e-mail and another when you'll answer it, as well as a time to return phone calls (preferably tomorrow). If you only do one new thing this month, strive to make your evenings as personal as possible.

"You are discontented with the world because you just can't get the small things that suit your pleasure," George Eliot observed. Nowhere is this truth revealed more than when you're reacquainting yourself with the daily comforts of being home.

On Holy Ground

Earth's crammed with heaven,
And every common bush afire with God;
And only [she] who sees, takes off [her] shoe;
The rest sit round it and pluck blackberries.

—Elizabeth Barrett Browning

"*W*e long to be in touch with life, to touch and to be touched. Yet we are also afraid of letting anything 'get at us.' Afraid of letting life come too close, we keep it at arm's length," Benedictine monk Brother David Steindl-Rast observes in his exquisite book *A Listening Heart: The Spirituality of Sacred Sensuousness.* But "being out of touch makes one sick. Touch heals. We need not fear contact, only the lack of it."

Often when we feel as if we've lost touch with reality or ourselves, it's because we're being pulled in twenty different directions. The ancients believed that when this happened, a person needed to ground himself in order to call back the scattered parts of his soul. The best way was to stand barefoot on the earth and do a standing meditation. As the person prayed, he was to remember that the same Loving Energy that was above him in the air and beneath him in the earth was also flowing through him. When you're so frazzled that life seems like an out-of-body experience, try this standing meditation outdoors at night underneath the stars or a full moon. It really works.

A shared religious symbol throughout the world is removing one's shoes before entering a house of worship. In the Old Testament when God spoke to Moses from a burning bush, Moses was told to take off his shoes because he was standing on holy ground. From inscriptions on ancient Eygptian tombs, to the great Roman poet Virgil's epic *Aeneid,* removing shoes has always been a sign of respect and reverence. It ensures that you literally are "in touch" with the sacred. (In the English countryside, removing shoes means you don't leave muddy tracks all over the place, and man, woman, and child know to do it.)

The expression "Take off your shoes, you are standing on holy ground" is used to convey seeking and finding the sacred in the ordinary. For years I've always gone barefoot in my house. I love the feel of different textures as I walk around—the warmth of the rugs, the smoothness of wood floors, the coolness of my kitchen's terra-cotta tiles.

Taking off your shoes when you arrive home can become a homecoming ceremonial announcing that you've left the workday behind and entered the sacred space of your own sanctuary for rest and renewal.

And after you take your shoes off, Brother David suggests a footbath as a spiritual exercise: "For an experience in which our senses spontaneously spark off a grateful response, a footbath is not a bad choice. . . . Can anyone deny that this is a step in the direction of life abundant?"

Come to Your Senses

Holy Homecoming Footbath

*W*hile some day spas and mail order catalogs have foot tubs, I've found that a plastic dishpan large enough to let you stretch out your feet and deep enough to cover them with water above your ankle is sufficient. First lay down a big towel to go underneath the basin. Fill the basin with a few inches of very warm water (not boiling) and add two tablespoons of Epsom salts, and a squirt of bubble bath or bath oil. Before you soak your feet, give each of them a minimassage, pressing the soles and pads of your feet and then gently pulling the kinks out of each toe. Now soak your tired, aching feet for fifteen minutes. Relax. Sip a glass of wine, read, knit, listen to music, or just close your eyes and do nothing. If you're not watching the clock, you can take your feet out when the water cools down, or when your feet start to wrinkle. Dry off each foot and then massage them with body lotion or even Vaseline (which was the ballerina Anna Pavlova's secret to soft feet). Put on a clean pair of socks, so that you don't slip or stain the carpet as you toddle down the hall to the rest of your pleasant evening.

Good Vibrations

Why do we love certain houses, and why do they seem to love us? It is the warmth of our individual hearts reflected in our surroundings.

–T. H. Robsjohn-Gibbings

*H*ave you ever wondered why you love some homes more than others? Immediately after you cross the threshold you feel at ease and uplifted, much the way you do when in the company of a warm person who genuinely cares about you. Like a woman who exudes "that certain something," so do our homes. But money and style have little to do with this mysterious embracing of being; if it did, you can be sure that interior decorators would be selling it. I have a painter friend and she loves in a small two-room New York City apartment. I say *loves* rather than *lives* because every nook and cranny of Julia's home radiates her palpable, affectionate presence. One room is her painting studio; the other serves as a living room, dining room, and bedroom where she entertains her large circle of international friends, who covet her potluck dinners as if they were royal banquets. Indeed, to visit Julia is to feel royal, because she treats you that way; the magic of her enthusiasm for your presence envelops you in a warm energy that is irresistible. Once I heard she was going abroad for five months and I immediately dropped everything to get in a trip to New York just to eat, drink, and laugh with her before she left.

However, sometimes the vibrations we sense in a house are

unsettling. Have you ever walked into a house after a serious argument has taken place? Another friend of mine tried to keep her marital problems a secret for a long time. She, too, had a beautiful home and one that I enjoyed visiting very much. But gradually over the months, as she kept her distress to herself, I began to feel vaguely uncomfortable when visiting her. Interestingly enough, this feeling disappeared when we were out to lunch or walking in the park. Finally, she admitted that her marriage of thirty years was ending because of her husband's infidelity, and that they'd been having terrible arguments. The walls were literally eavesdropping, picking up the negative energy and enclosing it within the living spaces.

"If we can speak about rooms and structures as living, organic substances, then maybe they can turn sour on us, too. If your house does not feel peaceful and exquisite, if you do not feel *at home* in it, maybe the space itself needs to be healed," Kathryn L. Robyn tells us in *Spiritual Housecleaning*. "Just like anything else, concrete or ethereal, space can be torn asunder, wrenched, or violated. It's easy to see when there's physical damage, of course: a cracked wall, a rotting floor, broken windows, sagging ceiling. Repairs heal physical damage. But there is more to healing space than that."

Kathryn asks us to imagine a wall that becomes cracked by a "random act of accidental violence, such as backing into it while moving furniture. There remains a feeling of shock and remorse every time you see that damage until you can fix it. That feeling exists as the energy in the room; the energy then attaches to the furniture piece that bashed the wall. And to the reason for the moving [furniture]. And to the person who was holding the furniture."

Repairing the wall will clear away most of the negative energy if the damage was accidental. But if the wall was "busted open by a purposeful act of violence during a break-in, someone's fist, an object thrown in anger, or a drunken body lurching into it, then the feelings attached are more likely to linger even after the physical healing of repair." Getting rid of these negative feelings through the acts of cleaning, redecorating, and space clearing, through the combination of a scrub brush, paintbrush, prayer, or ceremony, is what is known as spiritual housecleaning.

"Cleaning creates an empty space where something new—

life—can happen, leaving a free area for a fresh approach. It creates neutral ground," Kathryn insists. "More than that, this is sacred work, creating hallowed ground—a space that is returned to its cleared wholeness."

You Can Hide
But You Cannot Run

*If you want the honest spiritual truth, my prayer is this:
Dear God, get me out of this mess.*

—Rita Mae Brown

*W*hen I was married, I lived over a basement that was as emotionally clogged as Love Canal was chemically toxic. There were so many unidentified boxes crammed with books, newspapers, clothes, knickknacks, and broken whatnots that we got to the point where we didn't even bother labeling another object before it was consigned to be lost forever in the hopelessness of that subterranean landfill. Now I sigh with as much compassion as regret when I think of that sorry basement. Although I didn't realize it at the time, it was a powerful physical metaphor for the chaos and confusion that engulfed me, as well as a profound spiritual symbol bearing silent witness to the distress my family was experiencing as my husband and I tried to hide our growing estrangement from each other.

However, during the writing of *Simple Abundance,* which took me four long years, I miraculously found the courage to tackle the basement, not just once but twice. The first time I did it as a birthday present for my husband; but within months the bedlam didn't just return, it intensified, for I didn't really throw any- thing away, I just moved the boxes around. (Just as I never inten- tionally started a conversation that might be unpleasant.) The second time I cleaned the basement I did it *for myself*, because I was attempting to live *Simple Abundance* and desired order as much as I did breathing. Like a prisoner plotting an escape, I waited for a couple of months and picked my moment: the week my husband and daughter went away to visit his family. I hired a strapping high school student to help me sift and sort, and a refuse man to haul away years of emotional despair masquerading as physical detritus and considered the payment as an investment in my sanity. It took me three days of deliberating about what should remain in my life and what I'd outgrown, but when I finished, the life energy, or chi, that was finally able to flow freely in that space felt electric. I was so in awe of my own determination and accomplishment that I celebrated: I drank wine, boogied by myself late into the evening, and enjoyed myself tremendously. I also said prayers, blessed this empty space, and welcomed a new feeling of expansiveness and expectation into my life. My concrete canyon of confusion had become a fertile field of dreams. Although I didn't realize it at the time, I was instinctually spiritually housecleaning.

"Prayer and housekeeping—they go together. They have always gone together. We simply know that our daily round *is* how we live. When we clean and order our homes, we are somehow also cleaning and ordering ourselves," Gunilla Norris tells us in her eloquent collection of prayers, *Being Home*. "How we hold the simplest of tasks speaks loudly about how we hold life itself."

For many years I could not reflect order on the outside of my life because there was no order within. Psychically exhausted and overwhelmed by the emotional and physical energy of trying to hide the unsightly in plain view, I lived reactively rather than reverently. Now whenever I feel stuck or mired in frustrating or distressing situations that I can't seem to change, I take a look at the piles surrounding me, whether it's files, newspapers waiting to be read, or cookbooks waiting to be reshelved. Then I start sifting, sorting, throwing out, and putting away. Piles of anything in your life represent the unresolved—you're only calling it dirty laundry.

"I know there is an order here but it will not show itself," Gunilla Norris writes. "Under the obvious, the real task can be hiding its radiance, its meaning and pain." The sacred work of spiritual housecleaning asks us "to be in relationship with it. It wants me to be equal to it and with it. . . . Then the order which has been waiting to emerge, which wanted me to find it, begins to show itself."

Messy Girl

It's good for the soul to have private space at home for our imagination to run messily wild.

—Lisa Freedman

I am now an orderly woman. By this I mean, I am a woman who reveres order. But I am not the neatest person. I have always been a messy girl, and not so long ago, in my effort to embrace my imperfection, I came to the awareness that I will probably always be a messy girl. Coming from the writer of *Simple Abundance,* which established Order as a life-changing principle, this might seem as surprising as it is inconsistent. It's not. Because as a messy girl I know firsthand that when there's sublime order in the house, my life changes for the better.

But a messy girl still lives in my house. I don't always make my bed. I don't always hang things up after I wear them or try them on. In fact on days when I can't figure out *what* to wear, my bedroom and closet look like natural disaster sites. In my office, where I write, I let books pile high on my desk and in the armchair, floating among loose papers and opened envelopes. My shoes can lie under the couch for days on end. Actually, until I want to wear them again. There is, however, a method to my peculiar imperfection: I always know approximately which stack to go through first when looking for something.

Being a messy girl, however, can be the continuing source of small miseries that eventually pile up. For a messy girl it might not only be her desk, bedroom, or house that she keeps untidy. Messy habits can leak into other areas of our lives. We let nasty comments go unanswered, or a relationship that could use attention sits unattended. It might be that we avoid confrontation and prefer to wade through a little mess as long as we can still go about our business. But then, as Anaïs Nin confesses, the moment comes when we "cannot bear outer pressures anymore" and so the only remedy is to put order back among our belongings. "As if unable to organize and control my life, I seek to exert this on a world of objects."

Actually, I find that putting my belongings in place helps me to find order within. For just as we can't really think clearly in clutter, when we're messy, we feel unfocused and frustrated.

I know myself well enough to realize that life is messy, and there will always be a little mess. But I also know that there is great relief in a tidy sanctuary. Whether it be a room or a relationship, sometimes we need to clean up.

Yet, if there is one thing I've learned as a messy girl—it's how to clean up. And if you're great at that, it's as much a valuable asset as it is an imperfection.

Come to Your Senses

When Mess Becomes More

*T*here *is* a danger in not confronting your messy girl. Or at least in not having a conversation with her. She will, if not addressed, become a helter-skelter habitué, or worse, a neat freak, which is simply unnatural.

I don't think that anything short of twenty-four-hour maid supervision will ever be enough to convert a messy girl totally. That's okay, but I have assembled some suggestions for those times when tidying holds great charm.

Hints from One Messy Girl to Another

Don't get sidetracked looking through old photos and letters. Stay *on task*.

Don't make too many piles, you'll only have to sort through them again later.

Don't overstuff a drawer; if something doesn't fit, put it somewhere else.

Don't put something neat away into something messy. If you have to, refold all the sweaters before you start putting others into the drawer.

Don't put something in the wrong place just to have it out of sight. *You will lose it* and then you will lose your mind trying to find it again. So make sure that everything has a place to go and everything goes in its own place.

Don't let your mess overflow into someone else's space. Keep it to yourself. I've heard that not everybody likes a mess.

Don't abandon your post for a cup of coffee or tea. If you take a longer break than five minutes, you might never come back.

Don't promise yourself you'll do it later, you won't.

Do sit back and enjoy the view of your room with something wonderful to drink when you're finished, because it's probably not going to look like that for long. Now, take out the box with the old photographs and letters. But remember to put it back again. And the dirty glass—to the kitchen.

A Home for the Soul

The ordinary arts we practice every day at home are of more importance to the soul than their simplicity might suggest.

–Thomas Moore

"In places and people, we seek that elusive feeling of being welcomed. We want our houses and apartments to be warm and nurturing and beautiful, but they are sometimes territories of

211

chaos and confusion," the architect and writer Anthony Lawlor ruminates in his luminous book *A Home for the Soul: A Guide for Dwelling with Spirit and Imagination*. "Yet, the haven the soul seeks is close at hand, within the stove and the cupboard, on the bookshelf, and in the closet. With the eyes to see it, and the hands to create it, we can recover the home that the soul desires."

In other words, reach for the broom. How we care for our homes is a subtle but significant expression of not only our self-esteem but the contentment of our soul. Soulfulness is not necessarily linked to religion. As Lawlor points out, "Someone may access soul through the prayers, rituals, and scriptures of their faith; but they can also encounter soul in a flavorful stew, the caress of a lover, or the textures of a pine floor. A chapel within a vast cathedral may be a shrine of spiritual peace, but a window seat within a living room can offer a haven of quiet renewal." Especially if you can see out of it.

By now you've probably begun to notice a theme over the last few days. Hopefully my writing and your reading are encouraging you to "see" housekeeping in a different light—as a sacred endeavor. For if creating a haven on earth for your soul is not meant to be inspired, then forgive me, for I truly have no conception of the Divine. But I also hope to show you that by bringing daily life back into balance between the sensuous and the spiritual, even the mundane tasks of cleaning will begin to feel restorative on a deep level.

"The most immediate way of deepening soulfulness in a home is through cleaning and repair. Housework, however, is denigrated in our society," Anthony Lawlor admits. But cleaning is an "act of discerning" what will benefit not only our homes but ourselves. "In the rush of modern living, cleaning can be a technique for settling down and engaging in the simple pleasures of bringing order to our personal corner of the world. . . . Cleaning blesses our houses and apartments with care," allowing homemaking to become "a pathway for soulmaking."

Chez Moi

I have no home but me.

—Anne Truitt

*W*e all do it, however neat and clean our home may be. As soon as we learn company is coming, we rush to straighten the pictures, fluff pillows, buff mirrors, sweep away cobwebs, and desperately camouflage any rumple or pile of untidiness. In other words, hide all evidence of our day-to-day existence. Suddenly we not only want to welcome our guests, but welcome them into a home that is a reflection of our inner ideal.

The French have a wonderful expression, *le foyer,* which means the pleasures of the "hearth" enjoyed with close family and friends. This is an intimate invitation to set aside formality and enjoy a generous sharing between kindred spirits, a personal and palpable exchange of warmth and welcome. But how easy it is to forget to welcome the daily company of our familiar selves with the spirit of *le foyer.*

Does the natural state of your home express your essensuality? Or is your space filled with the excess baggage of old relationships—parents, siblings, roommates, lovers or spouses, children who have moved out—or a self that you parted with long ago? Are there pieces of furniture, equipment, knickknacks, that might be stylish but don't resonate or reflect you anymore? Who is this woman who lives here? Are these things *hers?* If they're not, what are they doing in her most intimate, personal spaces?

Where exactly are you in this picture, cherie? Are you waiting for a magic wand to cause "real" furniture, a matched set of glassware, complete window treatments, to appear? Does your home look as if you just moved in? Or is it a ramshackle of "making do" until some other life comes along (perhaps with someone to share it) or until guests to impress arrive? Every day isn't just a moment in time, it's where you *live*. Please note the present tense of the verb. To live. Now. You don't have to be on the streets to be homeless, and isn't that the sad, sorry truth?

In her exquisite and moving memoir *Around the House and in the Garden: A Memoir of Heartbreak, Healing and Home Improvement,* Dominique Browning tells the story of a friend of hers who, like many of us, woke up one morning to discover that "what she wanted—what she had planned on—was to fall in love, get married, and make a home with someone. It wasn't happening, though." And although this woman "was a person of accomplishment, fortitude, and sophistication," as she entered her forties she began to feel increasingly uncomfortable in her own skin as well as in her living space. This was because the woman "was having a tough time giving herself permission to go ahead, buy a place, decorate, live well. She who never took no for an answer at work seemed paralyzed when it came to telling herself yes."

Don't feel embarrassed about committing to creating a home of your own. As Dominque Browning's friend finally learns, going ahead on your own *does not mean* you're "shutting the door on the hope of finding true love."

There is a wonderful French fable about a man who builds a house as a secret weapon for his seduction of beautiful women. He lavishes so much passion and attention on his house that women who cross his threshold swoon. This, too, can happen in your "chez moi."

Stop feeling apologetic about outfitting your home to suit your own self, and that includes breaking away from decorator-perfect room settings. If you would rather see that chair *over there* or in another room even if it's been *here* for fifteen years, move it! If your tastes have outgrown certain decorative items or fabrics, find them a new abode (even if it's in the trash). On the other hand, if unusual, even unstylish items give you pleasure, don't hide them away in favor of maintaining a home belonging to some strange *perfectionista*. Weed through the belongings that don't make you smile when you see them. Leave your toys out in the open. You owe it to yourself to derive as much pleasure as you can from your favorite things and surroundings.

If you're on a budget but need a change, soften and warm rooms with pillows, throws, and afghans using inexpensive fabric remnants that can easily adapt to other spaces or be replaced if you tire of them. If you can't repaint or repaper, change the color of your rooms' trim. If you don't need strong light to work by, ignore overhead fixtures in favor of lower-wattage lamps, for instant coziness. Use your real crystal or vintage pressed glass, fine china, or silver, not just for dining, but in the bathroom, by your desk, as bedroom accessories. I keep my makeup sorted using crystal glasses; not only is it easier to find a particular eye pencil when I need it, but the assortment of the sparkling glasses is pretty to look at. Silver toast racks hold stationery at my desk; an antique fish knife is my letter opener. So make even the most mundane tasks more pleasurable with the addition of things you genuinely enjoy holding or seeing. Display gadgets or small appliances in a bright color that you love (why not a purple stapler, an orange mixer?).

If you can't eliminate it, organize clutter—make a comfortable place for things that are a regular feature of your life, instead of treating them like intruders catching you unawares! Avoid buying any upholstered item, carpet, or other furnishings that you're afraid to use every day. Stick with the kinds of things you love seeing and using.

The contents of your home are year-round guests. Listen when objects speak to you; introduce them to each other in new and original combinations. Get a kick out of juxtaposing mismatched items. As I've said before, when Passion is your decorator, everything blends together beautifully. The love you feel for one object compliments the love you feel for another.

Becoming bored, rigid, or sloppy means you've stopped interacting with your belongings, that you've become blind to your surroundings, and by extension, to your self amid them. The more comfortable and self-expressive the home that you make for yourself, the more others will delight in it as a comfortable expansion of the genuine you. They will truly be entering your *foyer*—a place where the hearth of your heart is always blazing.

"Even if we're not flapping about with mates and chicks and all the little wormy things of life, we are still nesting," Dominque Browning reassures us. "We are giving ourselves shelter. Our work may be harder, but it is not less loving for being done alone."

Sacred Space

When we walk through our front door,
we should be able to leave the stresses
and strains of the outside world. A
home should provide us with a sanctuary
for the soul, a haven for the senses.

—Jane Alexander

For ten years Kathryn L. Robyn helped support herself by
cleaning houses while she was studying energy healing and
transformational theater. In her extraordinary book *Spiritual
Housekeeping,* she fuses her expertise in both healing and home-
caring into a passionate and practical spiritual practice that's bound
to speak to many women where they live.

"Your home is sacred space, a sacred space with your address.
Most people think of these places as mundane. Pity. If we ever
needed them to be sacred, we need it now," Kathryn tells us.
Unfortunately for us all, the expression *sacred space* is becoming as
clichéd as the use of the word *soul.*

What does the expression *sacred space* mean to you? Hallowed,
holy, blessed, sanctified? Why, yes, according to the dictionary and
common usage. But how about happy, enchanted, wondrous,
magical? Not really?

Well, let's think again. Unfortunately holier-than-thou words
"can be so loaded with religious teaching they make us think of
things saintly, moralistic, righteous, pious, devout. These words
hold pressure to be a certain kind of 'good' that scares many people away. And so they should," Kathryn believes. Instead, she
would like to expand the expression *sacred space* to mean "something much more innocent, more clean, more *possible* . . .

"*Sacred* comes from a root word meaning whole. To be your
own sacred self, wholly you, then, is to be connected to that divine

spirit—God, Mother Earth, the Universal Life Force—however you perceive it. When you say something is sacred to you, you mean it is special to you in an intrinsic way; maybe it helps you feel more whole. Depending on where you're coming from, you may discover sacred space in a church, a temple, a mountain grove, a rocky beach, an art museum, or even the historic home of Elvis, Virginia Woolf, or Jackie Robinson."

Admit it. This thought is smile provoking, so hold it today as you walk around the rooms where you live. Where are you the happiest in your home? Then that spot is sacred for you. "Sacred space feels inspiring, peaceful, comforting, or healing to body, mind, or spirit. Healing also comes from the word for whole, of sound body and mind. When that space is your own house, it is easier to feel whole and connected in your daily life."

Sensuous Scrubbing

Home, sweet, home: sweet to look at, listen to, to touch, smell and taste. The home is our emotional heartland, a place where the rhythm of events is under our control, a potential pleasure zone for our sensuous being.

—Ilse Crawford

*A*n Englishman once commented at a dinner party that the most erotic fantasy he could imagine was the sight of Annette Bening furiously vacuuming in her slip and rubber gloves in the film *American Beauty.* Hmmm . . . until I heard that I'd never quite thought about housecleaning as an erotic art, but over the last year I have discovered it *can* be a sensuous one.

For as long as there have been the sensuous being called woman and the sensuous haven called home, we've been cleaning them. "Performing the rituals of the ordinary as an act of faith," Marilynne Robinson tells us in her heartbreaking novel *Housekeeping*. And once upon a time it wasn't with artificial lemon-scented chemical cleansers and dimethyl benzyl ammonium chlorides. Instead women in the past used the rinds and juice of real lemons, lavender, herbal vinegars, linseed and flax oil, corn flour, salt, bran, honey, stout beer, cider, beeswax, the leaves of sorrel, leeks and ivy, rhubarb stems, milk, and essential oils of orange, grapefruit, and rosemary. Once upon a time our mothers, grandmothers, and their mothers before them were ancient priestesses, skilled in the sacred knowledge that the "dear ordinary heals." Perhaps on the first warm spring day as they hung their bed linens to dry, they thanked the Goddess and blessed the wind billowing the sheets for the good night's sleep they and their loved ones would know at the end of the day.

There are many reasons for us to revive traditional homemaking tips, such as using natural cleaners, as we incorporate the concept of spiritual housekeeping into our daily round. Chief among them is the security of knowing their contents. If you polish a copper kettle with salt and vinegar, you can be fairly sure that your skin and the tender membranes of your nasal passages are not at risk. I was shocked to discover that many of our modern cleaning marvels promising to kill "99.9% germs within seconds" don't even list their ingredients. My advice: If you don't know what's in a box or spray bottle, put it back on the grocery shelf.

I certainly don't wish to beat my rugs rather than use a vacuum cleaner any more than you do. But our grandmothers practiced a domestic alchemy that has become almost lost to us. Almost, but not quite. What follows is a small sampling of some of my favorite, sensuous spring-cleaning secrets, which are so good for you to use you might not even need to wear rubber gloves. But don't entirely dismiss the idea of exchanging the apron for a black silk slip until you've tried it!

Come to Your Senses

Heaven Scent

*T*he most pleasurable way I know to approach homecaring is by "playing house." Remember? Afraid your split-level doesn't exactly encourage this fantasy? Begin wherever you are by "playing" at making some of your own old-fashioned home-caring remedies, and I bet you'll change your mind.

"What Is That Heavenly Smell?"
Lavender Wood Polish

YOU WILL NEED:

8 ounces pure turpentine
2 ounces pure beeswax, grated
1 ounces pure soap, grated
3 ounces linseed oil

4 drops essential oil of lavender
2 drops essential oil of rosemary

In a large heat-proof glass jar, place the beeswax, soap, and linseed oil and then set the jar in a saucepan surrounded with a few inches of cold water (to act like a double boiler). *Gently* heat until the wax and soap are melted. Take the mixture off the heat and mix in the turpentine, then the essential oils. Stir well and allow the mixture to cool. Store in a cool place as this mixture is flammable. Shake well before use and apply to wood sparingly. Buff the wood to a glow by hand (with a lintless cloth). This works on wooden floors as well, but do not use an electric polisher for safety reasons. You use very little, so this should keep for a long time.

Sensational Soft Soap

From ancient times soap has been seen as a luxury. No Victorian woman would throw away even a sliver of soap. Instead tiny pieces would be saved until enough were gathered to make a batch of soft soap. Soft soap is so easy and pleasurable to make and even more sensuous to use for hand-washing delicate clothing.

Using a hand grater, grate about 4 ounces of soap remnants and put them in an old saucepan (one that you don't want to *ever* cook food in again!). Add 2 pints of cold water and place the saucepan over low heat. Bring it just to a boil, then lower the heat and simmer gently for 15 minutes, stirring frequently. If you want to scent the soap, now is the time to add a few drops of the essential oil of your choice, such as lavender, geranium, rosemary, lemon, or cedar. Let the mixture simmer another few minutes, stirring again. Pour the hot, liquefied "soft soap" into a heat-proof jar (such as a jam jar) with a tight-fitting lid. Let it cool completely. The soft-soap mixture will be opaque-looking and have the consistency of a gel.

Romancing the Home

Paradise lost can only be regained by those who remember it.

—Andre Hardellet

*I*t has been said that romance is unsatisfactory as a religion, but as an approach to housekeeping, I've seen romance perform miracles. Think of how you hustle and bustle around the house when a potential sweetheart is coming to call for the first time. Picking up, putting away, dusting, rearranging objects just so, arranging flowers in a pretty vase, becomes romantic foreplay. Suddenly drudgery is transformed into scene-setting. Approaching almost any tasks we undertake around the home—from cooking to changing the sheets—as if they were romantic preliminaries is how our hearts transform chores into pleasurable tasks.

One of the secret delights in writing my books is the fun I have researching how women have lived since the Victorian era as they've pursued "the art of domestic bliss." Rediscovering and reclaiming lost home-keeping arts is how I ground myself in the Real. Sometimes I'll read a column penned by a literary domestic (women writers who specialized in the home) over a hundred years ago and be reminded of what's still really important to a woman, such as creating a safe haven for hope. Or just for a lark I'll experiment with an old-fashioned remedy that really works and be quite delighted with the results.

But perhaps the real reason I adore revisiting women's past lives through their homemaking books and periodicals is the spirit of cheery optimism in between the lines of practical advice that nurtures, encourages, and uplifts.

Today all women have a multiplicity of challenging roles, but as the English writer Beverly Pagram points out, women three hundred years ago or a century ago had to be even more adept at juggling the chores, and without the modern conveniences we rely upon so much. "In any one day a woman might be called upon to be a child-carer, cook, gardener, cleaner (who had to make her own cleaning potions since they were not available to be purchased in the shops), home-physician, apothecary, perfumer, and cosmetician," Beverly tells us in *Folk Wisdom for a Natural Home,* a wonderful treasury of feminine ingenuity down through the centuries. Beverly believes that "in performing some of the hauntingly fragrant age-old rituals," such as preparing homemade beeswax-and-lavender floor polish or thyme-scented germicide for the pantry, "you can feel part of a female historical continuum that is uniquely satisfying and empowering."

You'll think so, too.

Far-Flung Fantasies

Variety's the very spice of life.

—William Cowper (1785)

*P*arallel realities hidden behind cupboard doors have long been a staple of children's stories. So open your kitchen cabinets and see what adventure awaits you. Behold! Camel caravans are slowly making their way across deserts stretching from Baghdad to Marrakech. If you listen imaginatively, you can hear the traders haggling over prices in the exotic port of Dar es Salaam. A sailor returns from a long voyage and brings his sweetheart a small fragrant package. She slowly opens it and inhales the deep sweet aroma of his love. Why did he take such a risk? She's worth it, he reassures her, as is the cake she'll make him using the green cardamom seeds he has smuggled off the ship.

Like most ordinary wonders, we take for granted the easy presence and variety of spice in our daily lives. Spices are aromatic flavorings gleaned from the many different parts of pungent plants native to tropical locales such as Indonesia's Spice Islands. For thousands of years spices have been as highly valued as an international currency. The pursuit of cinnamon, pepper, and nutmeg sent Columbus westward to the Indies, Vasco da Gama eastward to Africa, and Ferdinand Magellan around the globe. None of them set out to find new worlds. It was new flavors and scents they were seeking.

With few exceptions the many spices we use today can be traced back to use in early human history. Spices have created and destroyed empires, nourished people, cured illnesses, defined cuisines, preserved cultures, provoked wars, warded off evil spirits, and been used to worship benevolent ones. Should all this romance be greeted with a pinch of ennui every time you casually reach for the oregano? I don't think so, and ever since I've adopted this gratefully inquisitive attitude, my dinner hour has gone from rote to reverent.

"True adventures start with desire, an inclination to enter the unknown," the travel writer Kate Wheeler tells us. "In hopes of finding what? More of yourself, or of the world? Yes." A delightful way to discover both yourself and the world without leaving home begins by perusing your spice cabinet. A well-stocked spice rack is a sure cure for suburban wanderlust.

Come to Your Senses

Spice Girl

Careful preparation is crucial for any adventure. This week let's get your spice rack ready to elevate your cooking from bland to inspired at a moment's notice. Organizing your spice rack takes about two hours, but once it's done, you'll feel immediate gratification. First pull out all the jars, bottles, and cans of spices you have and put them on the counter or table. Have a pad and pen handy. Weed out the spices that you've never or rarely used; you'll recognize them because they've not been opened or are extremely dusty. Put them to one side. Now sort out the sometimes-used cans or jars, then the frequently used spices.

Your travel guide is your nose. Open each container and give the spice a deep sniff—the aroma should be pungent. If a ground spice has fossilized, this is not a good sign, nor is the absence of scent. Toss ruthlessly. Crush an herb between your fingers; if it smells grassy or dull, it's no longer potent. Throw it away. As you shift and sort, write down the name of each spice that you'll have to replenish.

The following is a list of dry herbs and spices. This is by no means what every kitchen should have immediately, but rather it is a list to work from and toward.

Allspice (ground); *aniseed; basil* (if you can't get it fresh); *bay leaves; caraway seeds; celery seed; chervil; chili powder; cinnamon* (ground and whole sticks); *cumin* (ground); *curry powder; dill; fennel seed; garlic powder; ginger* (ground); *mace; marjoram; mustard* (dry and ground); *nutmeg* (ground); *oregano; paprika; pepper* (depending on your taste—pepper flakes, hot pepper sauce, cayenne, black peppercorns, or ground white pepper); *poppy seeds; rosemary* (if you can't get it fresh); *sage; savory; sesame seed; tarragon; thyme; turmeric;* and *salt* (French sea salt is the best, or coarse kosher salt).

Spices are still costly, so don't run out and replace everything at once. Instead, first update your frequently used spices, then wait until a new recipe requires a new spice. The better the quality of your spices, the less you will need to use, so consider the best that you can buy as an affordable luxury. Remember, whatever you make will only be as good as the foodstuffs you use. Spices don't usually keep their flavor for more than a year, so consider getting the unusual ones at spice shops or ethnic food markets. Always buy the smallest quantities available of new-to-you spices.

"To be a true adventurer in the realm of taste you do not have to be a gourmet," Oliver A. Wallace tells us in *A Taste for Adventure.* "You must, however, be appreciative and receptive, with a salt and peppering of curiosity and experimentation."

Home Comforts

Ah! There's nothing like staying home for real comfort.

—Jane Austen

One of the reasons that women writing about homemaking a century ago were so self-possessed is that neither they nor their readers were conflicted about the importance of their subject. A Victorian woman's home was her eminent domain, and she ruled over it with as much confidence as Queen Victoria ruled the world. No amount of time, money, emotion, or creative and physical energy expended to make one's home the center of the universe was considered frivolous or extravagant. Women approached the domestic arts—cleaning, cooking, decorating, gardening, handicrafts, and entertaining—not as burdens but as a form of personal expression and deep sources of pleasure.

Today more and more women are acknowledging openly the same pleasure and satisfaction that come from the soul craft of creating and sustaining safe havens—which I call homecaring.

"When you keep house, you use your head, your heart, and your hands together to create a home—the place where you live the most important parts of your private life. Housekeeping is an art; it combines intuition and physical skill to create comfort, health, beauty, order, and safety," Cheryl Mendelson reminds us in her magnificent *Home Comforts: The Art and Science of Keeping House.* "Keeping house has always encompassed knowing and doing whatever is needed to make the home a small, living society with the capacities to meet the needs of people in their private life; everything from meals, shelter, clothing, warmth, and other physical necessities to books and magazines, music, play, facilities for entertaining oneself and others, a place to work, and much more . . . keeping house is a labor of love."

And love's labors are not lost when we endow what we do in our homes, day in, day out, with the respect and reverence this work deserves.

The "sense of being at home is important to everyone's well-being. If you do not get enough of it, your happiness, resilience, energy, humor, and courage will decrease," Cheryl explains. "Being at home feels safe; you have a sense of relief whenever you come home and close the door behind you." Coming home each day is meant to be the "major restorative in life."

But it won't be if we don't honor the role that housekeeping and order are meant to play in the rhythm of each day and week. The housekeeper of yesterday, "the traditional woman" Cheryl calls her, knew that it took more than just dusting and clean laundry to make a home feel warm and alive. "Her real secret was that she identified herself with her home." Her self-respect was reflected "in the soft sofa cushions, clean linens, and good meals; her memory in well-stocked storeroom cabinets and the pantry; her intelligence in the order and healthfulness of her home; her good humor in its light and air. She lived her life not only through her own body but through the house as an extension of her body."

Unlikely Prayers

A well-run home is a microcosm of sanity in a world that is plainly mad. If a home doesn't make sense, nothing does.

—Henrietta Ripperger

For decades Cheryl Mendelson, philosopher, lawyer, and professor, was a woman with a "secret life." Cheryl's passion was the home arts, but she soon discovered that "being perceived as excessively domestic can get you socially ostracized." Perhaps because Cheryl wasn't Martha Stewart, who turned housekeeping into a fashionable industry, she learned the hard way that some guests found her hand-rolled-pasta dinners annoying "as they do not feel comfortable eating a meal that they regard as the product of too much trouble."

However, because the side of Cheryl "that enjoys housekeeping and the comforts it provides is central to my character," her essensual self found a creative way to give her passion its form in a classic book: *Home Comforts*.

Many women writers' passion for homecaring finds its way into their books. The pages of the 1930s novelist Kathleen Norris, of Laurie Colwin, and of Rosamund Pilcher reveal delectable descriptions of food and furnishings. Whenever I can't get back to England for long periods and find myself experiencing symptoms of domestic withdrawal, I reach for Joanna Trollope's Aga sagas, named after the attractive cooking stoves that are so central to the English kitchen.

Perhaps women writers revel in their domesticity because we tend to work from home and putter in bursts and spurts in between organizing chapter and verse. I know that when I'm creatively stymied, I like to polish silver, rubbing away not only tarnish but confusion. Isak Dinesen and Anne Morrow Lindbergh arranged flowers during breaks in their writing sessions. Marjorie Kinnan Rawlings loved to bake pies. When the Quaker writer Jessamyn West couldn't write, "house ordering is my prayer and when I finish my prayer is answered. And bending, stooping, and scrubbing purifies my body as prayer doesn't."

Come to Your Senses

The Caretaker's Cup of Cheer

Caring for our homes is no less a prayer than caring for ourselves or our creative work. The French writer Colette believed that "we only do well the things we like doing," and creating a nest of home comforts was one of her favorites. But in between the writing and the domestic pastimes, she'd put her feet up and savor a celebratory cup of cheer, "the Caretaker's Café au Lait," which appeared in her novel *Cheri*. If there's a home-caring task you're dreading, perhaps knowing this is waiting for you to sip after the floor's been mopped or the refrigerator cleaned can be an inspirational nudge.

Caretaker's Café au Lait

You will need to make one large cup of sweetened café au lait (which is equal parts hot milk and strong coffee, sweetened to taste). Pour it into an ovenproof china bowl. Now place two slices of buttered bread on the surface of the coffee. Place the bowl in a hot oven and bake until the surface of the mixture has become a crunchy crust. Colette advises that before "breaking your bread raft, sprinkle it with salt. The salt gives the sugar bite."

Between the Lines

Honey, I'm Home

Home again. You've been away awhile—a few days, a week, a year or two; it doesn't matter. . . . The house has been empty, shuttered, braced against intrusion. You have the key. Inside all is dim, hushed. You take a few steps forward, drop the bags, and breathe in the slumber of your rooms. The dust has settled, but somehow the air is dense with stillness. Absence has a presence. You feel it and smell it and hear it; you sense it, the way an animal senses, fleetingly, in those first few moments through the door. The rooms are as you left them. But they're not as you remember them. Absence warps, distorts. Everything seems slightly aslant somehow. Bigger. Smaller.

Perhaps you're unable to stand the silence. Or perhaps you can no longer resist the embrace of rooms poised to take you in. You're moved to break the spell. You breathe in the heavy silence one last moment and you reach for a switch. Turn on the lights. You're back.

And you begin the tender work of transforming the rooms of a house into a home again. . . .

When the first home you ever made was with someone else, as mine was with my husband, it can be very difficult to believe that you have a right to call what you are now making by yourself a home. We all have fairly hidebound attitudes about what constitutes home; many of us—men and women—simply dwell in waiting for our next partner, maybe even subconsciously postponing the homemaking. And that's fine. There is no right time to begin again; the spirit has to move you. Returning to a house is the easy part. Bringing a home back to life, that's trickier.

Love does not stop. Energy doesn't stand still. And neither do our homes. They're pulsing with all that we carry in; they vibrate, hum, resonate with every cry and murmur and snap and cheer of our hearts. They are our second skins, the shells we build, like snails, enlarging and encrusting with the whorls of our days, months, years. They are the most private and most telling of places. There they stand, for the world to see. And for us to make of them what we will.

—Dominique Browning
Around the House and in the Garden:
A Memoir of Heartbreak, Healing and
Home Improvement

June

An enchanted hour was filched from the hereafter and
tossed into the lap of the present, as a foretaste of what is to come. . . .
A mystic world, into which we step as soon as we cross the
threshold of the porch.

—Ethelind Fearon (1946)

Thirty days hath perfection, she calls herself the month of June. . . . In case you haven't noticed, there's splendor in the grass and a riot of color in the garden. The fresh fragrance of freedom is in the air and nobody's paying attention to what *we're* doing. Leave the back door open, turn the sprinkler on, and dare to bare. Revel in the unfinished, the improvised, the gloriously imperfect. Dunk strawberries and romance your flaws. Linger in the twilight of a summer's day, dance with the fireflies, wink at the full moon. Believe in Midsummer magic. Bottle a rescue remedy of rose-scented sighs, smudge Chantilly lace on your pretty face. Let each day's brushstrokes reveal the incomparable beauty of *your* stilled life. Moments you once called ordinary now seem infused with grace.

Stilled Life

Art must take reality by surprise.

—Françoise Sagan

*T*he painting is small enough to cradle in your hands. Incredibly simple—an isolated white cup, saucer, and silver spoon. But the astonishing power of its quiet restraint never fails to move me. The first time I saw the French painter Henri Fantin-Latour's still life *White Cup and Saucer,* painted in 1864, I turned to a complete stranger and said, "How dear!" The startled man looked at me, then at the painting, smiled, and said, "Yes, you're right. It is quite *dear.* Isn't that a lovely word to describe a painting."

For whatever reason, *dear* is the word I associate with still-life paintings—groupings of objects such as fruit, flowers, dishes, and books. Perhaps it is because the still-life artist bestows such affection and reverence on the trivial, the ordinary, the everyday, this loving exuberance leaps off the canvas and grabs hold of my heart. Attention must be paid, Life says, through the artist's brushstrokes.

I know that one reason I'm magnetically drawn to still-life paintings is that they're an antidote to my usual state of perpetual motion: sitting still is difficult, standing still virtually impossible, unless it's in front of a painting. These quiet moments of contemplation are a salve for the soul; when I turn away, not only does my sense of sight seem more acute but my sense of place is centered. I am grounded, once again, by what I love—the ordinary.

Creating your own still-life compositions is one of the most delightful and calming of time-outs. You may not be a painter, but you still have the artist's tools to help you see the mundane in a new way—color, light, arrangement, and observation. The next time you're feeling frazzled or fragile, take ten minutes and putter. The painter Paul Cézanne loved creating kitchen still-life paintings—

a yellow pottery bowl with a few apples, a loaf of bread, a colorful blue napkin. For the living room, pull down a vase that has been empty for too long this winter and fill it with a budding branch. One of Vincent van Gogh's most beautiful paintings is *Sprig of Flowering Almond in a Glass.* I always associated dark moods with van Gogh, but this small, exquisite rendering of hope is a poignant testimony to isolated moments of serenity—even brief ones. In your bedroom, why not gather together on a bureau those black satin evening shoes you love (but rarely wear), a perfume bottle, a necklace, and a scarf? Pull a favorite hat out of its box and prop it on the bedpost. (Should someone ask *"Why is that there?"* tell them it reminds you of how much you love hats and how rarely you wear them. But that's going to change, isn't it?)

Above all, play with arranging your belongings. Let the juxtaposition of the ordinary objects surrounding you reveal a visible veracity about you. Life expresses much in the sight of a bowl of cherries, a few stems of flowers, a cup and a saucer. The gift of the everyday *is* very dear.

A Life Less Ordinary

The incredible gift of the ordinary! Glory comes streaming from the table of daily life.

—Macrina Wiederkehr
A Tree Full of Angels (1988)

*S*o what's our problem? Well, for one thing we hover like ghosts over the surface of our days, we don't actually dwell in them. We call our lives *normal* or *ordinary.* Preoccupied with fulfilling the needs of someone or something else, whether it's the children, husband, house, boss, or a telephone call that just won't wait, we float along unfocused.

And during those rare instances when we're not multitasking

with our hands, then we're multitasking in our heads, perhaps while waiting for the kettle to boil or the computer to boot up. Have you ever wondered why you're so shocked when something important has fallen through the cracks, but you could swear you took care of it? You did—in your head. Fat lot of good that did you.

This is not an ordinary life. Not yours. Not mine. Or it shouldn't be. But this common nightmare is why so many women unconsciously choose to "sleep" around the clock, oblivious to time, place, or companions as they sprint, jog, and hurtle from one task to another, whining all the way.

So here's a simple pleasure, especially if we approach it as a game. How about rediscovering what an *ordinary* life looks like for you. Here's a hint: your ordinary life is hiding in a normal day. "Normal day, let me be aware of the treasure you are. Let me learn from you, love you, savor you, bless you before you depart. Let me not pass you by in quest of some rare and perfect tomorrow," the writer Mary Jean Irion implores Life, surely for all of us, in her wonderful book *Yes, World.* "Let me hold you while I may, for it will not always be so. One day I shall dig my nails into the earth, or bury my face in the pillow, or stretch myself taut, or raise my hands to the sky, and want more than all the world for your return."

What Lies Beneath

Freshness trembles beneath the surface of everyday, a joy perpetual to all who catch its opal lights beneath the dust of habit.

—Freya Stark (1942)

*P*eople in many cultures around the world believe that each person has a double walking the earth, known as a doppelgänger. Many of us have had the experience of chasing after a friend on the streets of a strange city, only to discover it was a stranger with an uncanny resemblance to our friend. I once met a French fisherman who could have been my Irish father's twin; it was so unnerving and unforgettable that many times when I recall my father's face, it isn't him I see at all but his Breton double. Why? Because the shock of seeing my father on the coast of Brittany mending fishing nets jolted me out of the near sleep or parasomnia most of us exist in. The only difference between my father and his French doppelgänger was that the fisherman was twice my father's size; he was a giant. But that isn't too surprising because my father was always larger-than-life to me.

Let's pretend that while you were sleeping last night your soul left your body and had a little reentry problem, so you landed in the body of a woman you've never met, your doppelgänger. If you have children and a husband, so does she. If you don't, neither does she. You look alike and think your lives are similar, but they're different enough for you not to know where she keeps the can opener or her deodorant. You'll find out soon enough, but while you're searching through drawers, even the most mundane details of her ordinary life have your complete attention. In other words, you are fully present in her life.

Imagine the scope of your own life if it were gifted with the same modicum of awareness. You wouldn't just scratch the surface of your life, you'd actually know what lies beneath. This is the first step toward dismantling your resignation and disarming your frustration. That's what this month is about. If you want to live a life less ordinary, you have to realize that none of its details are ordinary. Spirit is in the details.

"I think the reason we all get up in the morning, whether we know it or not, is that brief moment during the day when we recognize the beauty in something," the writer Penelope Michler observes. I have no doubt that you'd recognize something beautiful in your doppelgänger's life. Today recognize one moment of exquisite beauty in your *own* daily round. Notice it, rejoice in it, and give thanks.

She Who Should Be Obeyed

*It is by logic we prove, but it is
by intuition we discover.*

—Jules-Henri Poincaré

*W*e've all had occasions when we *know* some choice or course of action is not in our best interest, but we don't know what to do about it. On the surface everything appears to be hunky-dory. But to act on your inner directive will cause a ruckus. So you ignore your qualms. Dismiss them as impractical; second-guess them with the opinions of others. Tell yourself not to be silly. A few months later you're crying in your beer. "Who could have known?" the bartender asks sympathetically, as he pours you another. The sorry truth stings: you did, toots.

As I said, we've all had these occasions. My recurring pattern of "Oops, I did it again" only came to an end when I started acting upon my intuitive prompts instead of spurning the advice. But before that happened, I had to start listening to Her. And then, trusting that She knew a few things I didn't, I took a deep breath, closed my eyes, and jumped into Mystery.

We are always being guided to our highest good and happiness, especially if we ask, "What's next?" Our yearnings, cravings, longings, hunches, impulses, and whims are how we know what we should be doing. For some unfathomable reason you have the urge to clean the hall closet. When you do, you find the lost bracelet you've been mourning for months. On a whim you take a different route to work. After you get to the office, you hear on a news bulletin about a nine-car pileup and a three-hour delay on the highway you normally drive. Your pottery is exquisite and affordable, but the craft shows you've been attending haven't been getting you the sales or attention you'd hoped. One day while you're throwing another pot, the wheel seems to tell you to send this one to a magazine editor. You listen, trust, and act. Three months later your pottery is featured in their "Can't Live Without" column, and the orders start to pour in.

So how do you become more comfortable listening to, trusting, and acting upon your splendid sense of Knowing? With practice, patience, perseverance, and gratitude. By taking small steps, little risks, tiny chances. By indulging in sensory experiments. Remember you've discounted Her advice for years, so you may not recognize the nudges. Today let She Who Knows realize you're finally listening by saying, "I now invite, accept, and act on my intuition with thanks."

The Other Side of Silence

Listen, and attend with the ear of your heart.

—Saint Benedict

*W*e think the other side of silence is only noise: honking horns, piercing jackhammers, ringing telephones, background television buzz, low-flying airplanes, and the chirpy announcement that you've got e-mail. But if we do think that, we haven't really been listening. And who can blame us?

The other side of Silence sounds like a baby's giggle, raindrops on the roof, purring cats, dogs thumping their tails, birdsong, the comforting voice of a good friend, a sigh of contentment, and a grateful gasp of relief.

All too often Real Life's concerto is drowned out by a white screech that relentlessly bombards us, setting off the feminine fight-or-flight response. Since we've learned to pick our battles, more often than we admit we turn tail by "tuning out." The writer Hannah Merker tells us in *Listening,* her moving meditation on losing the sense of hearing, "Psychologists say that deafness, or a severe hearing loss, acquired after a human being has known hearing, can be the single greatest trauma a person can experience."

A sense of this loss is experienced by many women every day in subtle but significant ways. Caught between the cacophony of others' demands and the shake, rattle, and roll of the world, we psychically induce hearing loss. Unfortunately this loss includes Divine sounds, as well as claptrap din. As long as we insist on hearing with our ears, instead of listening with our heart, the disquiet will become deafening.

Every day we make a choice of what we'll take in or tune out. You know what you'll hear on the other side of noise. On the other side of Silence, try listening to the miraculous sound of your own thoughts.

Perfect to a Fault

Pictures of perfection as you know make me sick and wicked.

—Jane Austen

*P*erfectionism has many aliases. *Getting it right. Fixing it. Revising. Tinkering. Micromanaging. Quality control. Anal-retentive. Obsessive-compulsive. Having high standards.* However, "perfectionism has nothing to do with getting it right. It has nothing to do with fixing things. It has nothing to do with standards," the wise Julia Cameron tells us in her classic creativity primer, *The Artist's Way.* "Perfectionism is a refusal to let yourself move ahead. It is a loop—an obsessive, debilitating closed system that causes you to get stuck. . . . Perfectionism is not a quest for the best. It is a pursuit of the worst in ourselves, the part that tells us that nothing we do will ever be good enough—that we should try again. No, we should not."

Images of airbrushed perfection saturate our culture through advertising, the media, and the entertainment industry. And while perfectionism is glamorous, designer-clad self-abuse can still kill. You'll just knock 'em dead in your size 2 shroud.

Do you remember the 1975 thriller *The Stepford Wives,* based on Ira Levin's scary novel about the compulsory perfection of women in a small Connecticut town? Katharine Ross stars as Joanna, a photographer who is startled by her new neighbors after she moves from New York City to suburbia. All of the women are gorgeous domestic dynamos who love nothing more than to stay at home, scrub floors, prepare gourmet meals, and provide their husbands with great sex. Seems that Stepford had been a haven of women's libbers during the sixties, until the men formed a secret association to replace all their rebelling wives with sundress-clad clones happy to serve the perfect martini and canapés at six o'clock with a smile and a wink.

241

The Stepford Wives seems so sinister because on the surface everything looks so wonderfully perfect and happy. Although you know something's terribly wrong, you just can't put your finger on it until the horrifying end. That's exactly what the pursuit of perfection is like. But the really scary thing is that these days it's not men turning us into soulless zombies—we're doing it to ourselves. From now on, think of perfectionism as the Stepford Syndrome—self-loathing disguised as self-improvement. By all means go to cooking classes, but if you break down in tears at 2 A.M. because you're tinkering with a risotto recipe and you run out of Arborio rice, babe, you need to head to the video store to review what *The Stepford Wives* has taught us.

How can something that looks so right feel so bad? could be asked about every aspect of a woman's life: her looks, relationships, work, children, wardrobe, creativity. That's because, from the kitchen to the bedroom, there isn't one human fault that Little Miss Perfect doesn't know how to turn against herself. The pursuit of perfection is a powerful opiate of choice for millions of American women, who are more afraid to live than to die. Unfortunately, it's true that misery loves her own kind, which is why it's not surprising to find feminine perfection clusters—women who support each other in continuing behavior patterns bordering on insanity. I'll never forget the priceless gift of a friend who, after listening to me turn someone else's actions into confirmation that something was wrong with me, said calmly and resolutely, "Sarah, I'm simply not going to support that kind of crazy thinking."

Perfectionism is an addiction that's difficult for women with low self-esteem to recognize because it allows us to run away from our problems but be in plain view, fully present and looking good to the rest of the world, even if it's through sleight of our perfectly manicured hands. Some obsessions are more photogenic than others, and perfectionism is a cover girl.

Just out of curiosity, how many glossy women's fashion or home magazines do you have piled up waiting for you to flip through? Mine go back to February. How huge is that stack of unread self-help books next to your bed? I was once told by the editor of an inspirational book club that I was their *best* customer. (Don't I *wish* I were making this up.) I could pretend I need to "see" everything out there, so I can "stay on top" of my publishing specialty, but the truth is, on my bad days (which occur way too often), depending on the state of my personal relationships (or lack thereof), amount of self-nurturance (or complete absence of), water retention, and how many workout sessions I've missed because I'm overloaded with work, I'm convinced I've missed some obvious personal flaw that will soon be pointed out. Please let me find it first and fix it *fast*.

How many unopened beauty creams, lotions, and potions promising to lift, firm, smooth, soothe, augment, shape, and rejuvenate your looks and your life crowd your bathroom shelves? I've got such an international selection, I don't know whether to open up a day spa or check into a halfway house for the publicly flawless. My favorite "recovery" treatment costs the earth but promises to relax my skin, "leaving it with the same rested and healthy glow that skin has after a long night's sleep." Of course, I could just try to get a good night's sleep, but I know that's impossible; in a few hours perfectionism will be waking me up so that workaholism can crack the whip.

In a memorable (and hilarious) scene from *The Stepford Wives,* the circuitry of one of the women (played by Nanette Newman) goes screwy at a garden party and all she can keep saying to everyone is "I'll die if I don't get that recipe." Remember that line the next time you're tempted yet again by the lure of perfecting *anything.* Like salmonella lurking in the sour-cream dip, perfection can convincingly cloak her insidious intentions in the ordinary, but the stomach cramps that come when you can't live up to your own impossible expectations are just as nasty as food poisoning.

Just the Way You Are

Self-admiration giveth much consolation.

–Gertrude Atherton (1912)

*W*e find solace in our shortcomings when we look at them through the lens of self-acceptance. But isn't that easier read than lived? "Our innate idiosyncrasies are actually more endearing to others than our most glorious personal achievements," Veronique Vienne reassures us in her lovely little book of meditations, *The Art of Imperfection.* However, "the lure of perfection is pernicious. It preys on the best of us."

Still, there "are practical benefits to not being perfect. As scientists today are discovering, quirkiness is a creative force in nature, one capable of neutralizing the otherwise irreversible process of degradation called entropy. In the same way, our faults, weaknesses, and unlucky breaks work to our advantage by making us more resilient, more inventive, and ultimately more efficient."

Happier, too. The secret is to learn to romance your flaws. Cultivate what you formerly censured. Don't finish today what can be finished tomorrow. Do something that makes you shudder as much as it makes you smile. Don't have the last word. Tell the persons least expecting it they've done something wonderful. Abandon the to-do list and see how much gets finished. Flaunt what you're trying to forget. Realize that knowing your weaknesses is your biggest strength. If something's perfect, it can never get better.

"You cannot live your life in anticipation of anyone's approval— someone else's or your own," Veronique Vienne believes. "No one notices whether or not your car is clean, the insides of your closets are neat and your fence is freshly painted." Today, neither should you.

Romancing the Flaws

Your thorns are the best part of you.

—Marianne Moore

For the last several years there's been a California-based decorating style that not only romances a room's flaws or dented furniture, it sells it that way. Called Shabby Chic, this inspired ode to home imperfection was first introduced to Americans by a British woman, Rachel Ashwell, and now her whimsical, practical, "children and dogs welcomed" philosophy has become a highly successful brand, spawning a book series, a television program, and shops.

It should come as little surprise that Rachel found her inspiration growing up in England, where comfort has always been the unifying decorating theme whether it's in a humble cottage or a grand country estate. "Ah, no one does comfort like the English," Henry James is reported to have said, just before tucking into afternoon tea on a lovely June afternoon.

For as well as an appreciation, respect, and love for the old, rumpled, peeling, wrinkled, rusted, worn, faded, and threadbare, the English have always had better things to do than fuss over their decorating style: garden, ride, shoot, walk the dogs, visit the pub, watch the birds, attend the match, put the kettle on. Oh, dear, table leg broken? Then, be a darling and just prop it up with a stack of books until we can get around to it—which, of course, we won't because there will always be better things to do, like opening a really good red and carving the Sunday roast. After a decade the propped-up effect begins to carry off its own patina of classy permanence; the next thing you know, the imperfect "look" known as English Style is being imported by the frazzled, restless colonies and a stack of wooden books as matching end tables sells out on one of the shopping channels.

However, as handy as it would be, slipcovering the soul does not guarantee being able to put your feet up without triggering a panic attack, especially if you need to program the interlude into your PalmPilot. And while you can purchase rugs, pillows, and anything overstuffed, if your obsession to mismatch must produce rave reviews from all who see it, then you've really missed the point.

Forget divorce, menopause, moving, younger men, opening up a B&B. Inviting imperfection is the most radical lifestyle change a woman of a certain age can make. The only way to do it is to do it, almost imperceptibly. Each day, let your guard down long enough for one personal imperfection to slip by without your apologizing, overcompensating, or trying to fix it. The payoff will be to realize that gradually you're grinning more than grimacing through your days, and discovering, as Katharine Tynan wrote in 1919, that in life, in love, in the pursuit of happiness, "Enough is as good as a feast."

Backward, O Backward . . .

I make mistakes. I'll be the second to admit it.

—Jean Kerr

There's a good reason why the Chinese spiritual practice of feng shui—the art of placement for good fortune—is only just beginning to catch on in the Western world even though it's been practiced for thousands of years.

In a word: *compass.* It's the compass stopping all of us from getting our chi, or life-force energy, moving in the right direction. You think I'm kidding? Before you can move the bed or desk to the most powerful position, you need to know if it's in the northwest corridor or southeast corner. But not many of us are carrying compasses in our purses. The only direction the women I know seem familiar with is backward. Over and over again. Unforgiving. Unrelenting. Past redemption. Our mistakes.

The amount of money you wasted buying that hideous dress on sale. Quitting college. Why you "volunteered" your only two free hours Saturday afternoon to organize the eighth-grade car wash. The man who got away (twenty-five years ago). The man who ran away because you were too, too much. The upsetting conversation that flabbergasted you into stunned silence. Next morning you're sorting the laundry or filing paid invoices when the perfect comeback flows—an amusing, articulate wave of sass.

Oh, to be as brilliant and ravishing in reality as we are in rewind. To rethink. Rewrite. Revise.

Or not. "If I had to live my life again, I'd make all the same mistakes—only sooner," Tallulah Bankhead once said. What about you? After much mulling, I think I agree with her. Oh, I've made some doozies in my time, but none that I didn't survive. Horrible haircuts grow out. You can find a job you can love. The dining room can be repainted. The fuchsia eye shadow tossed. You will be able to see him again and feel *nothing*. (I promise!)

A Japanese sensibility that reveres the art of imperfection, as well as the paradox of the inevitability of mistakes, is known as *wabi-sabi* (pronounced "wahbi-sahbi"). Unlike feng shui, this state of mind requires only a shift in attitude—critical to complimentary—instead of furniture.

Look around you. Despite what you might think about the kitchen curtains, nothing is ugly, all is change. So take them down, wash the windows, and let the sun shine in. In fact, the inspiration for *wabi-sabi* is Mother Nature's ever-changing looks. The essence of beauty is the splendor in the ordinary. The overlooked. The disregarded. What's genuine is gloriously flawed.

"*Wabi-sabi* is not about gorgeous flowers, majestic trees, or bold landscapes," the architect and artist Leonard Koren explains in *Wabi-Sabi for Artists, Designers, Poets & Philosophers*. "*Wabi-sabi* is about the minor and the hidden, the tentative and the ephemeral: things so subtle and evanescent they are almost invisible at first glance."

Impermanent. Imperfect. Incomplete. Our spellbinding, Technicolor daily lives. A bouquet of blowsy pink peonies dappled in dew, complete with an ant or two, placed in a mason jar on the kitchen window shelf. A set designer could spend a couple hours "arranging" the beauty it took you ten minutes to achieve by stepping out into the backyard. That half-finished decoupage tray still needing a final coat of lacquer. The faded striped canvas patio-chair covers, which are only starting to show character, rather than wear, including the cigarette burn, which reminds you with a smile why you gave up smoking. A favorite plaid shirt with frayed cuffs from a decade of washing, pressing, loving, living. You got caught in the rain with your husband wearing this shirt on the day he proposed; you nursed your babies wearing this shirt; planted your prize rosebush, changed your first spark plug, and pitched a tent under the stars in this shirt. Few things in life are irreplaceable, but this shirt is one of them.

Never thought of it that way? Neither did I. Which is why Leonard Koren believes that, to successfully introduce the philosophy of *wabi-sabi* into the fabric of our daily lives, we need to think of it as a rescue remedy for the lifestyles of the relentlessly perfected.

"Like homeopathic medicine, the essence of *wabi-sabi* is apportioned in small doses. As the doses increase, the effect becomes more potent, more profound," Koren explains. "The closer things get to nonexistence [read *not a big deal*] the more exquisite and evocative they can become. Consequently, to experience *wabi-sabi,* you have to slow way down, be patient, and look very closely."

Which sounds like a humane approach when our memory rushes backward and our mistakes seem horrendous. Wisdom is also apportioned in small, homeopathic doses. Not enough to kill you, just enough to make you pause an instant or two before pushing forward with a laugh as you leap or overlook. For as Charles Dickens observed about a *wabi-sabi* kind of woman in *Nicholas Nickleby,* "she frequently remarked when she made any such mistake, [that] it would all be the same a hundred years hence."

Today come to the life-affirming awareness that there's really no such thing as a mistake. It's simply that you'd make a different choice *now* than the one you did then, even if *then* was yesterday.

So go ahead, fall heels over head in lust again. But, this time just don't elope until you've seen the whites of his eyes.

Come to Your Senses

Peculiarly Personal

Wabi-sabi celebrates life's crevices and cracks and no one's back is going to break if you step on one every once in a while, but yours might stop hurting.

"To discover *wabi-sabi* is to see the singular beauty in something that may first look decrepit and ugly," explains Robyn Griggs Lawrence, editor of *Natural Home.* "Bringing *wabi-sabi* into your life doesn't require money, training, or special skills. It takes a mind quiet enough to appreciate muted beauty, courage not to fear bareness, willingness to accept things as they are. . . . It depends on the ability to slow down, to shift the balance from doing to being, to appreciating rather than perfecting."

Wabi-sabi also celebrates the senses. "Rough textures, minimally processed goods, natural materials, and subtle hues are all *wabi-sabi.* Consider the musty-oily scent that lingers around an ancient wooden bowl, the mystery behind a tarnished goblet. This patina draws us with a power that the shine of the new doesn't possess."

Just as Mother Nature's showing off right now, you have more beauty blooming in the back of your china closet, attic, or basement than you'd imagine. What makes this ancient point of view so powerful is that it's very particular; no one else can tell you how to do it, and isn't that refreshing? So today, kemosabe, let's play *wabi-sabi*. Get ready to go on a treasure hunt in your own house.

"You might ignite your appreciation of *wabi-sabi* with a single item from the back of a closet: a chipped vase, a faded piece of cloth. Look deeply for the minute details that give it character; explore it with your hands. You don't have to understand why you're drawn to it, but you have to accept it as it is," Robyn Griggs Lawrence tells us. There's no right or wrong way to use *wabi-sabi*. "It can be as simple as using an old bowl as a receptacle for the day's mail, letting the paint on an old chair chip, or encouraging the garden to go to seed. Whatever it is, it can't be bought. *Wabi-sabi* is a state of mind, a way of being. It's the subtle art of being at peace with yourself and your surroundings."

Queen of Denial

Had Cleopatra's nose been shorter, the whole
face of the world would have changed.

—Blaise Pascal

*C*leopatra. A name that no longer serves to designate only one woman, but embodies something more. A name that resonates with an image of feminine power, mixed with an exotic sensuality. An irresistible temptress. A cunning queen. A powerful ruler. A living legend in her own time. A classic beauty.

Wait a minute. Forget for a moment, if you can, the silver screen's version of Cleopatra: Vivien Leigh and Elizabeth Taylor. Cleopatra was many things, but a beauty she was not. This holds wonderful inspiration for the imperfect woman who stares back at me most mornings. The ancient portraits of an unidentified royal woman, formerly considered too homely to be Cleopatra, now prove that the original Queen of Denial was a short, dumpy woman with a huge, hooked nose. But as the French playwright Victor Hugo put it (only one of the countless poets, playwrights, and historians who have had a mad, passionate thing about the woman over a couple of thousand years), "She was not pretty, she was worse."

What both Hugo and the seventeenth-century French philosopher Blaise Pascal meant was that if Cleopatra had been just another pretty face, there wouldn't have been much mystery to her hold on history or on our imaginations. That's because her two greatest conquests—Julius Caesar and Marc Antony—had all the pretty faces they wanted in Rome. But they traveled to Egypt entranced by Cleopatra's *essensuality*—that heady alchemy of intellect and, literally, intoxicating charm. The woman didn't just seduce men; she kindled their passions and addled their brains. Cleopatra was a sensualist who knew that when a person swoons, the eyes close.

In her irresistible book *Essence and Alchemy: A Book of Perfume,* Mandy Aftel tells us that Cleopatra "developed the art of self-adornment into a science" using aromatics as her secret weapon. "She had her own perfume workshop" and would conjure up fragrant formulas combining the erotic with scents that promoted feelings of safety. Caesar might have been drawn to the sweet vanilla fragrance of her skin from her daily milk baths (perhaps evoking a memory of mother), but before he knew it, he was responding to a come-hither muskiness emitted by the kind of woman his mother probably warned him to stay away from.

When Cleopatra wanted to seduce Marc Antony, she floated to him on a sweet, resiny-scented cedarwood barge flapping with perfumed sails. Nothing like making an entrance. As Shakespeare imagined Antony's moment of capitulation: "From the barge / A strange invisible perfume hits the sense." And there went the Roman Empire, not with a whimper or a bang, but a sniff.

Diane Ackerman tells us in *A Natural History of the Senses* that Cleopatra "anointed her hands with *kyphi,* which contained oil of roses, crocus, and violets; she scented her feet with *aegyptium,* a lotion of almond oil, honey, cinnamon, orange blossoms, and henna." In the bedroom where she seduced Antony, the walls were covered in rosebushes secured by netting, and the floor was covered in a foot and a half of rose petals. "Did they use the floor and make love in a swamp of soft, fragrant, shimmying petals? Or did they use the bed, as if they were on a raft floating in a scented ocean?" What do you think? Probably both.

One thing's for certain. Cleopatra's litany of conquests and adoring consorts proves that a woman's allure might begin with the sparkle in her kohl-lined eyes but continues where the nose of her beholder can follow. Which is why on those days when the ordinary woman in all of us seems a bit drab, a little dab of Cleopatra's secret weapon on the pulse points—a combination of cinnamon buns and sin—is bound to induce smiles as well as sniffs of approval all around.

Come to Your Senses

A Little Dab

*T*o prepare this scrumptious oil, use the same methods as for other aromatherapy mixtures. It's easy; it just seems complicated when your eyes are glassing over from the instructions. As with every other suggestion in this book, follow the instructions when you're not frazzled but curious. A *what the heck* approach is an essensual quality when romancing man, child, beast, the daily round—or yourself.

Essential oils need to be mixed with neutral carrier oils for safety reasons. Never apply an essential oil directly to your skin! I like to use dark glass eyedropper bottles (available at drugstores). Always get extra tops. Once a bottle is designated for a particular blend, use it only for that fragrance; no amount of washing will remove a prior scent.

The proportion of base oil to essential oil should be two to one, so fill the eyedropper bottle two-thirds of the way with a carrier oil, such as almond oil, jojoba, or a mixture.

Next add two full droppers of rose oil, one dropper full of cinnamon oil, and two *drops* (not droppers!) of cardamom oil. If you can't find cardamom prepared as an essential oil, you can drop two whole cardamom pods into the bottle. These exotic pods were also Cleopatra's favorite breath freshener. (Suck them, don't swallow!) Cleo's oil can be added to a bath (about four or five drops), rubbed on your wrists, behind ears, or on the nape of your neck. Or you can lightly spritz yourself with it from an atomizer (six drops oil to one ounce springwater). Although intended to drive the Caesars in a woman's life crazy (kids and cats love this, too), a little dab will truly do, or you'll find yourself taking a shower in the middle of the day to get rid of your aura of irresistibility.

The Fusing Grace

There is more here than meets the eye.

—Lady Murasaki (c. 1008)

*W*hile imperfection can seem charming in a dented, blue splatterware pitcher, dimpled knees and wobbly thighs leave much to be desired, especially this time of the year, when it begins to get too hot to stay covered up. But as the shorts come out, not to mention bathing suits, most of us struggle with what Mother Nature has generously—sometimes *too* abundantly—endowed us with, or omitted.

"If only my (nose, hips, legs . . .) were (smaller, slimmer, longer . . .)!!!" Just fill in the blanks. But have you ever looked up at a friend or daughter in utter astonishment when she's complaining about her body? What is she nattering on about?

For the sad truth is that one woman's fault is what another woman flaunts, especially if she's French.

I have a wonderful French friend who's gorgeous both inside and out. Last summer when I was visiting her, we had a frank discussion (at my insistence, if you can imagine, around a pool) deconstructing what makes a Frenchwoman seem so beautiful, even when she's plain, sick, tired, and has a small (or not so small) potbelly protruding over her bikini brief. But this was as difficult as translating the phrase *je ne sais quoi,* that mysterious quality that all Frenchwomen seem to possess but which translates literally as "I don't know what." As Martine was elegantly replacing the top of her bathing costume with a towel, with the confident élan of Brigitte Bardot in *Mademoiselle Striptease,* she insisted she didn't have a clue. But her next question revealed she knew very well the secret of French feminine allure, and it wasn't just how to tie a scarf.

"How often do you go naked?" she asked with a wicked but knowing smile as I was covering up my ankles with another towel. "Frenchwomen are as comfortable with their clothes off as they are on. In fact the only reason a Frenchwoman gets dressed at all is so that she can get naked. . . . There's even an expression for it . . . *bien dans sa peau.* . . . A Frenchwoman doesn't grow up or grow older, instead she becomes a woman who is *comfortable in her own skin.*"

As I looked around me at Frenchwomen of all shapes and ages, basking in the sun and themselves, I was struck by how foreign that thought was—becoming comfortable wearing your own skin or possessing the fusing grace of femininity.

It's fascinating, but when we don't like someone, we use sensory language to express it. *She just rubs me the wrong way.* Well, even if we can't articulate it, most of us "feel" that way about the woman who lives beneath our skin, especially in the summer when her arm crawls out of a sleeveless blouse. But this is a perfect time to begin a little rapprochement; get to know her a little more intimately, one tactile experience at a time, with your inner judge on vacation. Pretend you're French; take your clothes off. (No, not on a beach, in your own home.) If you have to say anything, try the French superlative *pas mal* ("not bad"). Better yet, cover up the full-length mirrors and experience yourself without commentary. After you shower, don't get dressed immediately. Instead, tie a sarong around you (that silk shawl you're saving for a special occasion will do nicely) and sashay around for a while if no else is home. Sleep in the nude, whether or not someone's next to you. When you're alone, wear as little as possible around the house (just keep a robe handy in case the meter reader shows up). Or wear hot pants, with heels and a halter. (The correct answer for *Are you going out dressed like that?* is *Maybe next week*.)

That's because if you start to reacquaint yourself with tactile pleasure—the breeze at night on your bare back, an ice cube down your arm, a gentle stroke on the calf of your leg as you apply sunscreen—in a week's time you're going to *feel* so good just to be alive and living in your own body, you'll be giddy. There seems to be a direct correlation between how comfortable we feel when we're naked even by ourselves or when displaying parts of our body with panache in front of others, and how critical we are when we catch a glimpse of our own reflection.

"She had a credible collection of features, but one had to take an inventory of them to find out that she was good-looking. The fusing grace was omitted," Edith Wharton wrote of a woman who probably couldn't stand to look at herself in the mirror.

This week find your fusing grace when you take it all off. There's much more beauty being reflected than meets your eye, but you'll need to *see* it before you'll believe it.

Speaking of Unmentionables

*It is almost as stupid to let your clothes betray
that you know you are ugly as to have them proclaim
that you think you are beautiful.*

—Edith Wharton

*J*ust as we seasonally buff and polish our homes from top to bottom once the winter has passed, so does our most intimate home need to be aired and washed and lovingly tended. Skin that has been scrunched within heavy garments and is soon to be on display is desperate for exfoliation, come summer. A quick shower or soak won't do it. It's scrub-a-dub time, honey!

Don't be afraid of rubbing yourself rosy. Choose your "weapon" for its unsentimental effectiveness, not pampering softness: a long-handled, natural-bristle brush, a colorful nylon puffball, a coarse loofah. And be sure to lay by a small piece of pumice stone (available in all drugstores and many supermarkets).

Standing in the tub or shower, soap yourself well, and now *scrub,* seeking out every possible inch of flesh. After all, if you were a mirror, you wouldn't polish only a few sections, would you? When you're tingly and rosy, reach for that pumice stone, wet it with a little bit of soapy water, and rub gently at your elbows, heels, and knees. Feel what a difference this makes to your skin. That's just what you've been doing, just a bit more softly, to the rest of you!

Rinse yourself lavishly with strong streams of hot water, to remove all sloughed-off skin. Finish with a quick spritz of the coolest water that you can bear, to close your pores. Allow yourself a joyous yip at the shock of it.

Wrap yourself in a towel or sarong because we're not getting dressed just yet. Let's take a look at what Victorian women called their unmentionables, and what we might as well, too. Remember when Mother warned you about making sure you were prepared for all contingencies, such as emergency-room visits? Is it time for some new undies? As familiar and comfortable as the old reliables might be, even if you are dressing only for yourself, you deserve lingerie that is truly fresh, and that *fits*. Take a good, hard look at these garments, and how *you* look *in* them. Is the fabric or elastic stretched out? Or is it too tight, producing hills and dales where it meets your flesh? Does a component you barely wear look at all like the one you've worn and washed incessantly? What are the chances that you have a matched set? In other words, without even realizing it, are you wearing next to your skin, which protects your heart and your soul, garments that make you feel less than gorgeous?

Do you remember the 1953 film *Roman Holiday* starring Audrey Hepburn as a runaway European princess who bolts from an official tour of Rome, and Gregory Peck as the tough-guy American news reporter who ends up chaperoning her? This captivating fairy-tale romance won Hepburn the Oscar for Best Actress. One of the more delightful scenes takes place when she's being tucked into bed by her lady-in-waiting. Audrey's wearing a prim, severe, old-fashioned nightgown when she yearns for a silk one with rosebuds.

Princess Ann: "I hate this nightgown. I hate all my nightgowns, and I hate all my underwear, too."

"My dear, you have very lovely things."

"But I'm not two hundred years old. Why can't I sleep in pajamas?"

"Pajamas!"

"Just the top part. Did you know that there are people who sleep with absolutely *nothing* on at all?"

Eventually she gets her wish, but what about you?

Do you know how delightful it is to open up a fragrant lingerie drawer and see essensual sets of underwear? To slip into a bra that pleases you to look at, is comfortable to wear, and is flattering? It might seem a little thing, but remember, as the Victorian writer Fanny Fern sighed (probably as she was buttoning up her whalebone corset), "There *are* no little things," especially a woman's underwear. So-called "little things" like brassieres "are the hinges of the universe."

Does yours truly support and shape your breasts, or is it more of a hammock these days, held up by its straps instead of doing its duty of *holding you?* How well does it fit across your back, and how accurate and appropriate are the cup size and shape? Time, child-bearing, dieting or weight gain, not to mention gravity, can change the shape and size of your breasts. If your bras no longer fit you with model-on-the-package smoothness, it's time for a frank reappraisal. Do you know that an astonishing 80 percent of American women wear the wrong bra size? Don't be shy—have yourself measured the next time you're at a department store. If you want an immediate change to your shape without dieting, exercise, or implants, try wearing the right-size bra. I only discovered mine a couple of years ago when a professional lingerie consultant visiting a department store asked if she could help. I told her I was looking for 38C. She looked me over once, turned me around, looked at my back, and tsk-tsked as she wrapped a measuring tape around me. "No, you're not; you're a 34DD."

I protested, I cried. "That can't be right. I'm too small to be that large."

"You're too large to be wearing a brassiere that small."

She was right. But I had to see it to believe it. And when I did, I was so shocked to glimpse flattering curves instead of bulges, it made me stand up straight and I haven't stooped since. "I wait for a chance to confer a great favor, and let the little ones slip," Louisa May Alcott confessed. "But they tell best in the end, I fancy," which is just how you'll feel wearing the right bra. This could be the best advice I've ever given you.

Besides the correct size, form and function *do* go together. If you live in knitwear, for instance, textured lace doesn't look sexy from the outside, just lumpy: go for smooth, seamless styles. Backless, strapless, halter, or T-shirt, you'd be amazed at the clothes you suddenly look wonderful in once you're wearing the correct undergarments.

Same goes for below the belt . . . sagging or too tight briefs usually betray their presence through skirts and trousers, while well-fitted lingerie draws attention to your *body's* contours, not theirs. A three-way mirror in a fitting room will tell you what other people are seeing. Again, take your real-life hip measurement, *now.* If you need a little more spandex, or to change sizes, be honest with yourself and accommodate your body as it looks now, not how it may have looked months or years ago or will when you lose another five pounds.

And, if you've always gone the plain-white-basics route, be so bold it makes you blush. Get yourself a couple of sets of scanties so luscious to the eyes and sensuous to touch, you feel naughty, not nice. A woman's underwear wasn't meant to be an understatement. As Princess Anne lamented before she bolted for the silk panties, "Everything we do is so wholesome!"

The world might only see the pair of jeans or business suit you're wearing over beautiful lingerie, but they'll wonder why you're beaming. You, on the other hand, won't. Modesty might very well be a virtue, toots, but a bra that makes a woman feel bashful is hardly becoming.

Come to Your Senses

Rosebud

*T*he writer May Sarton believed that flowers were "silent presences" that "nourished every sense but the ear." I think she forgot a woman's sigh when she buries her head in a bouquet of roses and inhales Heaven. Sorry, I think there are flowers, and then there are roses. And a rose is not *just* a rose. Roses have been food and drink. Decoration and declaration. Seduction and sedition. Mystery, as well as revelation. How many other flowers can be seen, sniffed, eaten or drunk, and dabbed on?

In the past, roses were valued not for their beauty, but for their fragrance, flavor, and medicinal properties. We only think of roses in the garden or as a dining room table centerpiece. However, for centuries a simple and inexpensive bottle of pure rose water occupied a place of honor on most women's spice racks or dressing tables.

In pre-Victorian times innumerable dessert recipes used this delightful liquid as a flavoring, just as we use vanilla extract. In the Middle East and across South Asia, rose water is still used as a refreshing addition to many culinary delights, from rice dishes to yogurt drinks. And of course rose water is an important ingredient of many cosmetic preparations. In overlooking the boundless gifts of the rose, we are cheating ourselves of romance that women all over the world have cherished since Eve plucked one and tucked it behind her ear. What color do you think it was?

On a hot summer's day, reaching into the refrigerator and dabbing a clean white handkerchief in rose water and then wiping your forehead, neck, and chest will have you swooning first, then revived in just a few moments. While it's possible to create rose-water-like water by slowly boiling down fresh petals in water— and don't even *think* of doing this with store-bought roses, which may be coated with preservative sprays—*genuine* rose water requires a little more complicated but definitely romantic process: distillation. For the real thing, many pounds of roses are set to boil and their vapor is captured and condensed. That small amount of precious moisture is then heated and *its* steam is condensed to create an even more concentrated liquid. This essence of the rose—virtually its warm breath—is what we can buy bottled. Nothing ordinary about that. Spice merchants (especially those that carry supplies for Indian or Middle Eastern cooking), herbalists, and "natural" cosmetics companies are trustworthy sources for rose water that is safe for cooking.

But let's consider its cosmetic use first. Roses contain an impressive amount of vitamin C, so even double-distilled rose water retains this slightly acidic—and therefore astringent—property. An excellent toner for normal skin, rose water combines well with witch hazel (mix one tablespoon of rose water with one teaspoon of witch hazel) for a nonirritating yet thorough cleansing of oily skin.

And then there's Grandma's old standby, rose water and glycerin. Pass by commercial preparations loaded with nonessential ingredients, in favor of simply mixing up your own cool, soothing "gel." In a heatproof bowl set into a pan of boiling water (do not use a metal double boiler), combine one cup of distilled water with four tablespoons each rose water, cornstarch, and glycerin (available from herbalists or pharmacies). Cook, stirring, until a clear gel forms. Remove from heat, allow to cool, and bottle in a glass container with a tight-fitting lid. This gel is excellent for any dry areas of your body, including your face.

A tummy-soothing rose-water potion is the Middle Eastern–style *lassi,* a fragrant and spicy beverage. In a blender, combine one small carton of plain yogurt, one-quarter cup of rose water, one tablespoon of honey, and one-half teaspoon each of ground cardamom and cinnamon. Slowly sip and sigh some more, my lady, sigh some more.

One of my favorite little cookbooks is an Old English volume called *Rose Recipes.* From rose-hip marmalade to pickled rosebuds to rose-flavored sugar, it's quite amazing how many wondrous remedies and recipes relied on roses, especially rose water. From the sixteenth century on, rose water was featured in everything from pound cakes to molded jellies. You can safely add zing to any modern recipe that calls for vanilla extract by substituting a like amount of rose water. Rose water is especially delicious in recipes that also contain lemon flavoring.

So for a sweet June teatime treat, why not "test the waters" with these mouthwatering *Romancing the Ordinary* lemon and rose-water "biscuits"?

Lemon and Rose-Water Biscuits

4 ounces (1 stick) butter, softened
½ cup sugar
1 egg
1 scant tablespoon rose water
¼ teaspoon caraway seeds or dried rosemary
1 tablespoon grated lemon rind
Pinch of baking soda
1 cup flour, sifted

1. Cream butter and sugar together, then beat in egg till light and fluffy.
2. Stir in the rose water, caraway seeds, and lemon rind. Sprinkle with baking soda.
3. Fold in the flour, ¼ cup at a time.
4. Chill dough for several hours or overnight.
5. Lightly grease cookie sheets and preheat oven to 325°.
6. Roll out the dough to ¼ inch thick and cut into circles (a small, scalloped biscuit cutter would be nice). Place the slices 2 inches apart onto the greased cookie sheets.
7. Bake the cookies at 325° for about half an hour, till lightly golden but not browned. Cool on rack. Store in a tightly covered tin or jar. Recipe makes 30 cookies.

Allure à la Mode

Any garment that makes you feel bad will make you look bad.

—Victoria Billings

*W*e've all been through it. The dress that seemed so fabulous in an ad looks downright unattractive or even poorly made when you try it on. But, oh, the glory of a real find at a discount shop or really good consignment sale—something not only stylish, but *sewn* so breathtakingly that it's like holding a work of art in your hands.

Indeed, fine workmanship goes hand in hand with style, in the best of clothing, no matter what you paid for it. You can throw money away on a famous label as well as you can on a no-name.

Learning how to recognize quality construction, fabrics, and trimmings will tell you whether an expensive item might have style but won't *wear,* or whether you've just nabbed a terrific bargain on the labels-removed rack. If you're going to be label conscious, look at the fiber content and care recommendations. Are the fabrics man-made, natural fiber, a mixture of both? Garments wear best if they contain at least some cotton, wool, or linen—the more, the better. Ironically, "easy-care" fabrics don't fare well against repeated washings or body heat. With natural fibers, you might have to do a little more in the way of hand-washing, dry cleaning, or ironing, but you'll have a much better garment.

Give fabrics the "hand" test, too: squeeze a section of cloth for around ten seconds, then release it and smooth it lightly with your fingers. Most quality fabrics (linen is a notable exception) will completely recover, without wrinkling; this means the clothing made from them will look fresh even during the most active day.

In flattering clothing, the "fashioning" will be almost invisible. Superior tailoring may include darts or tucks, subtle interfacings, or shoulder pads to make a garment sit right. Try on different kinds of clothing to discover what touches of fine tailoring work best with your body and personal style. Women would be amazed if they only realized that the best nip-and-tucking available is not from a Park Avenue plastic surgeon but the tailor at the local dry cleaner's. After discovering the right underwear, having clothes properly fitted on *your* body is a secret every well-dressed woman will share. Sometimes just an inch up or down on a hemline or having the cuffs of a jacket end where you find it most comfortable seems nothing less than miraculous and can make the difference between being described as "statuesque" rather than "large," or a "pocket-sized Venus" instead of "short."

Beauty is found in the details. Do braids, piping, zippers, and so on, which are meant to be the same color as the cloth, *really* match it? Have buttons been selected with care for both style and quality? Especially when it comes to trimmings, you can take away great ideas from designer showrooms and apply them to hand-sewn or economical items that you trim yourself. I can't really sew, but anyone can learn to change a button. Look for vintage buttons at antique shops (buying them in sets of at least six) to instantly add elegance or interest to the look of a thrift-store dress, or even a beloved jacket that just looks a bit tired.

You can create your own fashion runway in your mind by visiting the fashion sections of bookstores or the public library, or by looking at historical-fashion sites on the Internet. The origins of famous clothing styles are themselves fascinating, of course, but you'll also see a pattern emerge: the essential elements of chic that made such styles so attractive to the women of their times might still be inspirational in helping you find your own essensual style now. The great French beauty Jacqueline de Ribes once observed that "style is what makes you different," and sometimes it just comes down to a fabulous pin you fashioned yourself from an art deco buckle found at a flea market.

Resourcefulness, imagination, originality, and whimsy are secrets to developing an essensual sense of style. A little nerve. A bit of verve. And money, you're probably saying. Well, if you have no dash, cash isn't going to do you that much good. There's a marvelous story (apocryphal, perhaps, but with a punch) that Coco Chanel wouldn't let a particularly wealthy American client out of her famous *maison de couture* until the woman promised she wouldn't wear everything all together.

Money is "less important than you might think," Annette Tapert and Diana Edkins tell us in their fascinating book, *The Power of Style: The Women Who Defined the Art of Living Well:* "A good example is Gloria Guinness's account of her years with only aspirations to keep her going. 'When I was poor, I would buy a beautiful piece of jersey, cut a hole in the top, put it over my head, and tie an attractive sash around my waist. . . . And everyone asked where I bought my clothes. . . . Elegance is in the brain just as well as in the body and in the soul.'"

Fashion leaves just as quickly as it arrives, but great style is ageless. Perusing books of the great couturiers or fashion photographers from different decades is such a magical way to be reminded that there are as many different ways for a woman to look stunning as there are women. In Carrie Fisher's funny, poignant novel *Postcards from the Edge,* she describes a woman we all know well. "She knew someday she would find the exact right outfit that would make her life work. Maybe not her whole life, she thought, as she got back in bed, but at least the parts she had to dress for."

And as on the stage or silver screen, sometimes becoming a star in your own life is only a matter of a costume change.

The Supporting Cast

Even her eyelashes acted.

−Virginia Woolf

*W*hile we're on the subject of allure . . . can you *walk* in those shoes, or are you just hobbling along? Or, do you spend too much of your time in sneakers or running shoes, as if you're invisible anyplace but at the office or at dinner, where the "real" shoes come out?

How comfortable are you with your other accessories? Does your jewelry compete for attention? Are the pieces neck-to-neck with scarves or other add-ons? Are you constantly adjusting your scarf or hat or eyeglasses because they don't really fit properly? Does your purse resemble the black hole? Do you know that psychologists now say they can tell *everything* about a woman by what she carries in her bag? I've no doubt this is horrifyingly true, but it's not a Rorschach we need to examine today. Still, if you want to get rid of the candy wrappers, Silly Putty, and dog's collar right now, nobody's looking and I'm not asking.

When I think of elegance, I think of accessories, or the lack of them. They are there to support your total look—not just reflect your personal style, but to keep you both comfortable and charming. Clutter, poor fit, or poor maintenance of even the trendiest accessories can actually detract from your appearance, not to mention interfere with some items' most necessary functions.

Let's start with those pinching shoes versus grubby lace-ups. How many pairs of shoes do you own, total (the real count, just between you and me)? A harder question now. How many of your "good" shoes are too high-heeled, too pointy, or too strappy to walk or stand in? Do you wear them anyway? Or, to save your feet, do you favor well-worn or clunky shoes that look dreadful but *feel* great? If there is no happy medium of favorite pairs that both look and feel good, maybe you should rethink your shoe policy.

Do yourself a favor. Find a few classic, moderate-heeled pumps and flats, or even oxfords if you often wear trousers . . . shoes that will go with everything and yet won't make you feel as if you're crossing hot coals if you run for a bus in them. Keep the leather polished and repaired. You'll feel terrific, and the world will see someone confident in her step *and* her appearance.

Now, we've all felt silly fishing about in oversize or overstuffed pocketbooks or just trying to get our fingers into a too small one. An eye-catching handbag that doesn't suit its contents is far less stylish than one that quietly does its job without drawing attention to itself. A beautiful, classic bag that goes with and fits everything will look so much better and make your life simpler, too, because you'll never have to worry that you left your keys in your *other* purse.

As for more decorative touches to your wardrobe, either make only one piece a focal point *or* match a few pieces perfectly. Whichever route you choose, as soon as you do, *forget you've got your accessories on.* A scarf or necklace or hat that needs constant readjustment or feels awkward makes you look distracted, not fashionable! Likewise, a jumble of ill-coordinated pieces, however terrific each individual item is, defeats the ornamental purpose of each. One cancels out the other.

On the other hand, perhaps you've been pulled together too much, too long. Do you automatically reach for the same scarf or brooch or belt when you choose a particular dress or always wear the same gloves and muffler with a particular jacket? Experiment with new combinations. See how a contrasting accessory might perk up garments you've become blind to. Tie scarves in new ways; wear a pin on a different area of a blouse or blazer. Liven up a neutral or stiffly corporate outfit with a single splash of an unexpected color or one whimsical or feminine touch.

Be downright daring. Devise an individual look with vintage or antique jewelry, one-of-a-kind handcrafted items, children's pieces (wear amusing earrings, or replace humdrum buttons with animal faces), or menswear (have you ever tried on hats from the men's department?). Pin a silk flower to a plain hat; wear velvet gloves; use a lace table runner as a shawl.

"Fashion is a playful, sensual, and colorful charade," the delightfully insouciant and very well-dressed Veronique Vienne suggests in *French Style: How to Think, Shop and Dress Like a French Woman.* "Learn to be surprising, not obvious. Dress as you normally would, then take off a thing or two: Remove your earrings and slick your hair back. Take off your jacket and throw a sweater over your shoulders. . . . Replace your jewelry with a fresh flower pinned to your lapel. Hide your hair under a hat, a scarf, or a turban. Remove your watch, hang it on a chain, and wear it as a pendant."

Life is a mixed metaphor. So can your sense of style be. Suggest a lot, reveal little. Be enigmatic. Rid yourself of pretension, so you remember to play. Remember when "dress-up" was your favorite game? No five-year-old ever said, "This doesn't go with that."

You'll know you're on the right track if you grin at yourself in the mirror before setting out.

Come to Your Senses

Midsummer Magic

Midsummer's Eve (June 23) is one of the most enchanting and sensuous nights of the year. Falling halfway between the traditional start of summer on May Day and its end on Lammas in August, it celebrates the power and renewal of the sun at the summer solstice—the longest day of the year. As the extra daylight tiptoes into darkness, Midsummer's Eve is thought to draw us magically closer to the natural world, and over the centuries numerous rituals—usually revolving around romance—have evolved to take advantage of this special portal.

When my daughter was little, we always celebrated Midsummer's Eve. As Shakespeare tells us in his play *A Midsummer Night's Dream,* on this night the fairy realm holds its annual revels. Children who prepared a feast for the fairies were rewarded the following morning with gifts, wrapped in colorful paper, netting, and ribbons, hanging from the branches of trees. During the afternoon Kate and I would make tiny fairy cakes, prepare pink fruit punch, and set out her doll dishes on a little table in the backyard. Glancing back to those moments, I don't know who loved celebrating Midsummer's Eve more. Oh yes, I do.

Which is why I have no intention of weaning myself from the whimsy. I've just made the festivities a little more grown-up—the pink punch now has a champagne kick and the fare is delicious finger food. English folklore has it that fairies are drawn to such herbs and flowers as thyme, verbena, primroses, roses, lilacs, milkweed, and poppies. Create a fragrant wreath for your door, or scatter dried herbs and flower petals on the sill of an open window to invite the wee ones to pay a visit. It never hurts to stay on the right sides of sprites of all types. A flute made from an elderberry branch is supposed to let the fairies know the festivities are about to begin, and they're quite partial, I've heard, to sipping elderberry wine or the nectar from honeysuckle. This year let's find out.

Tradition also calls for scattering protective plants around to ward off bad luck, especially of the romantic kind. They say that fennel, birch, peonies, and the herb rue will repel any *male*volent spirits that may be lurking nearby. And be sure to turn your pockets inside out, to prevent a "changeling," a flirtatious Celtic female spirit (always searching for a human hostess), from climbing in and taking over your life. Admit it, the daily round can't be that dreary if a nymph's jealous.

An enchanting book that can't fail to inspire reveling of all sorts is Dodie Smith's *I Capture the Castle* (1948). A witty romp set in England during the thirties, it tells the story of a bohemian family of eccentrics living in a decaying English castle. Although Dodie Smith (1899–1990) was a successful British dramatist and writer, it was her children's book *One Hundred and One Dalmatians,* published in 1956, that earned her fame in America. *I Capture the Castle* was her first novel and quickly became an English classic, selling over a million copies. Fifty years later, it has lost none of its charm. The future of seventeen-year-old Cassandra Mortmain, as duly noted in her wistful, wry journal, seems bleak indeed. ("My imagination longs to dash ahead and plan developments; but I have noticed that when things happen in one's imaginings, they never happen in one's life, so I am curbing myself.") Cassandra's father, once a literary cause célèbre, is attempting a comeback, but hasn't written a word in twelve years; her glamorous stepmother is a nudist; and her older sister, Rose, is a petulant beauty. When the castle's

American heirs suddenly turn up—two handsome, eligible bachelors—romantic chaos ensues.

One of Miss Mortmain's most engaging quirks is her fervent belief in the power of magic (J. K. Rowling has confessed that Cassandra is her favorite narrator), and she considers Midsummer's Eve sacred. She gathers wildflowers, weaves a garland for her hair, and as evening falls, dresses entirely in green to summon up the earth goddess within. Lighting a miniature bonfire made out of fragrant twigs, she sprinkles dried herbs and salt upon the flames, casting her dreams and fate into the ether. Her ceremony concludes with an offering to Mother Nature of cake and wine (which Cassandra delightfully and dutifully consumes on her behalf), before she runs around the fire a magical seven times and communes with the elements. It's easy to see why generations of girls and women have found a kindred spirit in her. So spread a blanket under the stars. This evening's bewitchment comes but once a year.

When Dodie Smith was in her sixties, she was occasionally appalled that her impetuous nature, whether on the page or in her imagination, still seemed to have a life of its own. "[Am] I the only woman in the world who at my age—and after a lifetime of quite rampant independence—still [does] not feel grown-up?" she wondered.

Not on Midsummer's Eve.

Through a Glass Darkly

*Marlene Dietrich and Roy Rogers are the only two living
human beings who should be allowed to wear black leather pants.*

—Edith Head

*I*n case you missed it, Dietrich and Rogers are dead. Which
means that nobody should be wearing them. Black leather
gloves, elbow length? Glorious. Rumps of a certain age upholstered
in black leather? Forget it. Now. Friendship is simply not possible
between two women if one of them is romping around in black
leather pants. And it's not me. Anymore. But I am not alone. The
British writer Victoria Coren amusingly seconds my scorn: "They
must be stopped. [Women] are marching across the land, squeak-
ing and sweating in this ghastly fabric, and somebody must put an
end to it. . . . Leather trousers are to the Noughties what leggings
were to the Nineties. They're warm and comfy; they beckon from
the shop rail; they pretend to be your friend. But, secretly, their goal
is to make your thighs look like overripe marrows stuffed into
cushion-covers." What's even worse is the message leather pants
blab: "I may be thirty-five, I may be a smart professional woman,
I may have four bathrooms in my house and a cottage for weekends, but goddamn it, I have a sexy side, too. . . . The leather
pleads to be noticed; it struggles to hint at naughtiness; it smacks of
desperation."

Glamour magazine has long had an amusing column in which
fashion dos and don'ts are captured in candid photos. Yet, one
year's do might easily become another year's don't. Do a quick
perusal of family photograph albums and find pictures in which
you looked at the height of fashion at the time, but now seem
ridiculous! How much do you want for that photograph? How
about we just trade?

What strange makeup we used to think stylish! Seductive!

Women poisoned themselves, in olden days, using lead to whiten their skin and belladonna drops to brighten their eyes. Beauty "patches" used to be a big deal for both men and women; placed near the lips or the eyes, they were meant to draw the glance to the wearer's best features. Cleopatra, it is said, had hundreds of faux eyebrows. If this sounds extreme, just remember how Twiggy (and those of us who emulated her) hand-drew eyelashes on the skin under her lower lashes. The green nail polish that Liza Minnelli wore in *Cabaret* kicked off a brief but intense fad. Hey, remember white lipstick? And two-tone lipstick, darker around the rims? Eyeliner drawn beyond the lid to turn up at the sides, like wings on an old Caddie? Bright blue eye shadow, or that brown line strategically placed across your lids to deepen the sockets? How about the equally mistaken notion that drawing in your cheeks and applying a diagonal streak of dark blusher gave you the look of high cheekbones? Just *thinking* about some of these special effects—because I've tried them all—gives me the creeps.

So let's clean out the makeup bag, babe. Here's a hint. If it's older than a year, or your age divided by fifty, throw it out. Eggplant eyelids and tangerine lips are not *now* what they once seemed.

What trends did *you* embrace in your wonder years? You know, the ones that make you wince now? It's downright bizarre the way we can get trapped in an era—a permanent Annie Hall look, for instance, or a graying hippie in denim and suede. It's because we get flooded with happy memories and think they'll never return. Well, they won't. But neither will new ones if we're frozen in a time warp. In fact, best not to embrace any look too tightly. It can be hard, sometimes, to let go of what's become familiar or cost a lot to acquire, especially if we got it on sale. But if my daughter looks better in something from my closet, it's hers.

She's actually sworn never to let me leave the house looking like either the mother of the bride or the bride of Frankenstein, which is our code for "Mother, you're frightening me."

So linger over those old photos again. Or not. Do you barely recognize yourself from year to year? That's the point. Still, better a bearskin rug and a string of pearls than black leather pants. They could prove *very* expensive.

Come to Your Senses

Chantilly Lace

*L*ike the favorite bracelets you've worn so often you no longer notice them, it's easy to become blasé about certain foods, even ones we love, especially if we're used to having them available year-round. However, if you truly want to be happy for the rest of your life, eating seasonally is the simplest way to introduce pure, unadulterated pleasure back into your daily round.

June shows off with two of life's *ordinary* splendors—the rose and the strawberry—kissing cousins of the genus *Fragaria,* which means "fragrant," or fabulous, as far as I'm concerned.

A few centuries ago, people gathered their strawberries from the woods: tiny, winelike fruit, quite different from large and blander modern varieties. In folk legends and fairy tales, *fraises de bois* are said to have magical properties; and elves, nymphs, and wood sprites were believed to be fond of them, perhaps because the fruit is so perfect and tiny. Genuine *fraises de bois* can still be found in gourmet shops. If you've never tried them, prepare yourself for an experience of utter ecstasy, and splurge on a fresh basket. It's an affordable indulgence.

I don't know any sane woman who will turn down a second helping of strawberry shortcake, but don't shortchange your sense of taste. Like mixing and matching accessories, it's the unexpected that draws life's *oolalas* . . . have you ever tried a sandwich of peanut butter and sliced strawberries? Or a side salad of fresh cucumber and strawberry? Peel and finely slice a three-inch length of cucumber (preferably seedless) and toss with an equal measure of thinly sliced strawberries in a few tablespoons of chilled white wine. Another refreshing summer salad idea: omit the tomatoes and add some sliced strawberries to a mixed green salad, and serve with raspberry vinaigrette.

Better yet, my little nymphet, pull the shades and lock the door, for it's time for the Big Bopper of seduction, or some friendly persuasion—the simple, sensuous Crème Chantilly paired with the fruit of love. This can be shared, you flirt, or not. *Au naturale,* it's a babe's choice. But personally, I think you should have pretty frivolous intentions before you invite someone to this party.

Chantilly Lace on Your Pretty Face

YOU WILL NEED:

½ cup double cream
1 tablespoon confectioners' sugar, or to taste
¼ teaspoon vanilla extract
Rinsed whole strawberries, with their leaves

Combine the first three ingredients; whip the cream until glossy but not dry. Transfer to a pretty glass or porcelain dish, and take a moment to appreciate the fluffy whiteness, the fragrant redness, the sheer indolence you have just set before the Queen. *By the way, that's you.*

Now we're ready to begin: dip a strawberry into the cream, holding it by the stem.

No, no, don't bite just yet. We're exploring the spiritual path of tantric taste here. So sustain the soul's pleasure by using your unnibbled berry as a spoon, sipping the now strawberry-touched cream from it and then dipping again.

Take your time, consuming the berries with as many bites and dips as you can, allowing the cream and berry juice to run down your fingers and licking off the drops.

Crush a few berries into the last bit of remaining cream, and use your fingers to finish, as if a child with a bowl of batter.

Don't be in too much of a hurry to wash up: first, sniff the sweet blend of scents still lingering on your fingertips, then the warmth of the vanilla, the roselike berries, the newborn-baby freshness of the cream.

At this point, I don't think a nymph would be wearing more than a grin on her pretty, smudged Chantilly-lace face, but we'll work up or dress down *gradually* as we wiggle and walk our way through the year. Ponytail's optional. It feels like it's going to be a long, hot summer.

Between the Lines

Pas Mal . . .

It's a good thing we don't know how attractive we are. . . . When pressed, we will confess to having a few agreeable anatomical features, such as nice shoulders, strong legs, or slender ankles, but most of us grossly underestimate our physical appeal. We are never fully aware of our real charms—the way we sip our tea, the way we sing off-key, the way we dance till three.

Let's be frank: We all are shy. *In private, most of us have unflattering opinions of our physiques. With reason. We are constantly reminded that our bodies don't measure up to the stringent contemporary standards of perfection. So much so that on bad days our inner micros would have us believe that we are pigeon-breasted and hunchbacked—like the gargoyles of Notre Dame. . . .*

Today, catching a glimpse of one's reflected image is a common enough occurrence, yet we still hesitate before recognizing the person in the mirror as our alter ego. Fixing our likeness in the eyes, we see someone who looks as surprised as we do. . . . Just a few feet away stands a perfect stranger—an identical twin we didn't know existed.

—Veronique Vienne
The Art of Imperfection: Simple Ways to Make Peace with Yourself

Summer weather, like being in love, is a philosopher's stone which turns our ordinary days to gold. But not the whole day. . . . For it is never the whole day, never all our life which is transformed in any happiness, but only the exquisite moments.

—Nan Fairbrother

July, that wildly extravagant Swell Dame, plays matchmaker this month. Sultry, summer senses meet the Babes of Bliss. Let's hang the hammock, lay the blanket, open the hamper, pop the cork, and loaf on the grass with the poet of your choice. Peer into Love's capacious salad bowl, then toss up a salmagundi. Shuck the corn, squeeze the lime, watch the sunset, and wake to wine-soaked cherry mornings. Keep your heart open and your beach bag empty, there are gifts from the sea to be had . . . sand-drenched saunters, backyard showers, and high nooners with hot tomatoes. So walk the shore and hold a shell to your ear. Listen to the erotic echo of the everyday and discover there's *never* too much of a good thing. Life's serving up another portion of bliss.

The Being and the Knowing

The only difference between an extraordinary life and an ordinary one is the extraordinary pleasures you find in ordinary things.

—Veronique Vienne

*W*e know what bliss is, even if we can't define it. Because bliss is a spiritual benediction, unbound by limits of language, the best that even sublime writers can do, such as New Zealand writer Katherine Mansfield, is to describe its sensations. In her stunning short story "Bliss," we are privy to Bertha Young's unexplained sensuous seizure of ecstasy. She "wanted to run instead of walk, to take dancing steps on and off the pavement, to bowl a hoop, to throw something up in the air and catch it again, or to stand still and laugh at—nothing—at nothing, simply."

We often think that happiness and bliss are the same because both induce smiles and laughter. But the smiley face that comes when we're happy is often contingent on external circumstances. Something *happens* outside the normal course of our dreary, repetitive daily round, and suddenly, life's not so bleak. We get the loan, job, lucky break. We make the deal or set the date. However, if six weeks from now the deal unravels and the wedding doesn't take place, we're not going to be so happy. In fact, because so much of what we call happiness is dependent on the whims or choices of other people, you'd think *happy* and *happened* were derived from the same root word.

They're not.

Bliss doesn't involve other people, places, or things. Bliss is bestowed upon us as a gift of grace, the whopping, exultant generosity of Spirit carried to wild, reckless, extravagant extremes. Manifesting as visceral sensations of unspeakable joy, moments of bliss often begin with a ripple of quivering that's, quite frankly, almost unbearable, unaccustomed as we are to sustained pleasure. When Bertha is overcome with bliss, "She hardly dared to breathe . . . and yet she breathed deeply, deeply. She hardly dared to look into the cold mirror—but she did look, and it gave her back a woman, radiant, with smiling, trembling lips, with big, dark eyes and an air of listening, waiting for something . . . divine . . ."

Bertha discovers that bliss is the intense awareness of the sensuous in the ordinary, an erotic echo of the everyday. As she arranges a centerpiece for her dining room table, she begins to notice that even the fruit has a "strange sheen" that hadn't been there before. Or had it?

> *There were tangerines and apples stained with strawberry pink. Some yellow pears, smooth as silk, some white grapes covered with a silver bloom and a big cluster of purple ones. These last she had bought to tone in with the new dining-room carpet. Yes, that did sound rather far-fetched and absurd, but it was really why she had bought them. She had thought in the shop: "I must have some purple ones to bring the carpet up to the table." And it [made] sense at the time.*
>
> *When she had finished with them and had made two pyramids of these bright round shapes, she stood away from the table to get the effect—and it really was most curious. For the dark table seemed to melt into the dusky light and the glass dish and the blue bowl to float into the air. This, of course in her present mood, was so incredibly beautiful. . . . She began to laugh.*

Although down through history, saints, seers, poets, and philosophers have waxed lyrical about the sacred imperative of embracing ecstasy on earth instead of waiting for Heaven, it was the historian and scholar Joseph Campbell who popularized the concept of "bliss" in Bill Moyers's landmark television series *The Power of Myth*. "If you follow your bliss, you put yourself on a kind of tract that has been there the whole while, waiting for you, and the life that you ought to be living is the one you *are* living." Campbell was referring to the hero's quest for desire and fulfillment as a universal theme throughout mythology, romance, religion, and legend. Suddenly, people everywhere were talking about following their bliss, even if they weren't quite sure what their bliss was. Support groups sprang up, coffee mugs wondered why you were doing other people's taxes if you really wanted to be a jazz singer, and bumper stickers in traffic jams jolted awake the sleeping giant of discontent: *Follow Your Bliss.*

Many people interpreted Campbell's advice as only an exhortation to "answer" their calling or life's work. "If you follow your bliss, doors will open for you," he counseled. And, of course, he's right. It's just that the doors aren't always found either in the corridors of power or at the ashram. Often the door to bliss leads to your own backyard, which is probably why we completely disregard it. What? Ordinary bliss?

Like making love, the rapture of bliss involves intermingling senses. Think fantasia to the seventh degree. And while bliss certainly requires us to listen to what truly calls our name, it's not necessarily our life's work, but palpable pleasure beckoning. Bliss is incandescent, but it still sends shivers down your spine. That's the point.

Thankfully, bliss doesn't discriminate against those who decide they must stay with a job they dislike, or in a relationship going through a rough patch. In fact, as Shakespeare observed, often "the contrary bringeth bliss / and is a pattern of celestial peace." I think what he means is that moments of bliss act as the spiritual salve that soothes our souls when our bodies are ravaged and our minds are at the breaking point with the relentlessness of what the world calls "reality." It's been my experience that bliss isn't just a Band-Aid, it's the Divine rescue remedy.

Although bliss, like prayer, is private, peculiar, and deeply personal, because women share the same seven senses, we have similar bliss triggers as well as bliss blockers. One woman's ecstasy might not always be another woman's euphoria (you may not, for example, share my passion for sheep, although I'm at a loss to explain why you wouldn't). Still, I'd hazard a guess that watching the sunset, walking barefoot on the sand, eating a juicy peach, showering outdoors, having an entire day to call your own, and waking up after eight hours of uninterrupted sleep might put a smile on your face as they do mine.

Please notice that these blissful triggers don't require anyone else's presence, nor do they cost money. They will, however, require your active willingness to experiment with idiosyncratic self-indulgence daily until you're reveling in self-rousing.

"What can you do," Bertha Young wondered, "if . . . turning the corner of your own street you are overcome, suddenly by a feeling of bliss—absolute bliss!—as though you'd suddenly swallowed a bright piece of that late afternoon sun and it burned in your bosom, sending out a little shower of sparks into every particle, into every finger and toe?"

Let's find out.

Too Wonderful for Words

Believe nothing. Entertain possibilities.

–Caroline W. Casey

*D*o you wish every day could feel fresh instead of like a replay of the last one? Try brushing your teeth with your other hand. Walk down a new block during lunch, and, for a change, look at what you pass. Wear two pieces of clothing in different colors, ones you've never put together before—such as the chic combo of black and navy so adored by Frenchwomen—or wear contrasting textures such as leather and lace. Try cooking a new dish, especially one whose name you can't pronounce. Take a leap and make *what the heck* this month's new mantra. If you do, you'll discover that most of those insatiable desires you so fervently deny, and so desperately fear, can be satisfied with perfectly plausible pleasures.

Sounds great, you say, maybe tomorrow. Right now there's the camp car pool to drive, meeting to make, deadline to keep. The rest of the world may be on vacation, but not you. Why am I not surprised? Probably because most of my own life has been a future-tense fantasy. Today? Just get through the damn thing. If truth be told, I now realize I existed this way (God forgive me for all the wasted years) because even the thought of feeling good all the time made me extremely uncomfortable. I suspect I'm not alone in crafting a lengthy list of bliss blockers.

Learning to allow yourself pleasure is the most radical celebratory change you will ever make. It won't happen overnight. It won't happen tomorrow. It's taken me half a century of hard work to discover that I could break all the rules, have fun, and still respect myself in the morning. You can, too.

So from this moment on, repeat after me: *There is never too much of a good thing.* Or as our great spiritual Mother, Mae West, teaches: "Too much of a good thing is wonderful." And when we get to the exalted state of bliss where our daily round does indeed seem just too wonderful for words, let's keep it that way with another two: *Thank you.*

Sins of Omission

Desire is prayer.

–Terry McMillan

"*I* want, by understanding myself, to understand others. I want to be all that I am capable of becoming," Katherine Mansfield wrote in her journal in January 1923. "This all sounds very strenuous and serious. But now that I have wrestled with it, it's no longer so. I feel happy—deep down. *All is well.*" It would be the last thing she'd write before her death a few days later from tuberculosis. She was thirty-four years old.

How exquisitely Katherine romanced our ordinary moments on the page. Her second book, *Bliss and Other Stories,* was published in 1920 and shook the British literary establishment with its audacity in form and content. One reviewer was so moved he admitted that Mansfield had convinced him "it was a good thing to be alive on this shining planet."

Katherine Mansfield had dared to completely eliminate plots from her stories, arguing that people did not live plots, they lived through "overtones, half-tones, quarter-tones . . . hesitations, doubts, beginnings," and she was there to eavesdrop on interior monologues and private conversations of her characters or she would zoom into seemingly episodic, emotionally charged moments of sensory discovery that revealed the ebb and flow of ordinary days. "All must be told with a sense of mystery, a radiance, an after-glow." Take this everyday epiphany that you and I have shared with Bertha Young in "Bliss." She walks into her drawing room and lights the fire.

Then, picking up the cushions, one by one, that Mary had disposed so carefully, she threw them back on the chairs and couches. That made all the difference; the room came alive at once. As she was about to throw the last one she surprised herself by suddenly hugging it to her, passionately, passionately. But it did not put out the fire in her bosom. Oh, on the contrary!

Katherine's prose is sparse, but so startling in its descriptive intimacy that reading her work seems almost like self-help therapy. Virginia Woolf confessed that Katherine was the only writer who made her jealous (she'd also adapt Mansfield's technique in *Mrs. Dalloway*). Rebecca West begrudgingly called her a genius, T. S. Eliot believed she was a "dangerous woman," and D. H. Lawrence, with whom she had a tumultuous friendship, based aspects of his fictional women on her. No one was more astonished by her ability to touch the raw nerves of rivals and readers than she was.

The soul of Katherine's writing centered on the cataclysmic effects of the undone and the unsaid, and the necessity to embrace risk if we're to be genuinely happy: "Risk! Risk anything! Care no more for the opinions of others, for those voices. Do the hardest thing on earth for you. Act for yourself. Face the truth."

She believed that our destinies were determined not by fate but by desire, by whether we honored or denied our passions daily. Perhaps because she knew she was dying, her fiction seems fraught with an insistence that her readers live, follow the urgings of their "secret selves," and seize moments of bliss wherever they can be found. Her letters and journals meditate movingly on the inevitability of regret when we don't. "Regret is an appalling waste of energy," she insisted. "You can't build on it; it's only good for wallowing in."

What made Katherine Mansfield so powerfully subversive was her uncanny ability to compassionately reveal our sins of omission, by confessing her own in between the lines. In another story, entitled "Psychology," a woman is serving a teatime treat to a friend. I was so moved when I read it for the first time that I burst into tears; in my entire life I'd never eaten a piece of cake this way. How could I have deprived myself so?

"Do realize how good it is," she implored. "Eat it imaginatively. Roll your eyes if you can and taste it on the breath. It's not a sandwich from the hatter's bag—it's the kind of cake that might have been mentioned in the Book of Genesis . . . 'And God said: Let there be cake. And there was cake. And God saw that it was good.'"

Now when near-missed-bliss episodes are suddenly ransomed back from indifference, I refer to their retrieval as Mansfield Moments, and I have to tell you, they're among my proudest accomplishments. Can you treat yourself to a luscious piece of cake today? I don't care what's swirling around you, make eating a piece of cake imaginatively your most important priority.

After Katherine's death, Virgina Woolf often had dreams about her that were so vivid, they seemed more like ghostly visitations. The emotional aftershocks would stay with Woolf throughout the following day, impacting her in small but significant ways, perhaps even in the way she ate cake at afternoon tea. "Katherine haunted her as we are haunted by people we have loved, but with whom we have not completed our conversation, with whom we have unfinished business," wrote one of Woolf's biographers, Hermione Lee. I think the ghostly Katherine represented Virginia's inability to find pleasure, no matter how successful she became.

"If people are highly successful in their profession, they lose their senses," Virginia Woolf admitted. "Sight goes. They have no time to look at pictures. Sound goes. They have no time to listen to music. Speech goes. They have no time for conversation. They lose their sense of proportion—the relations between one thing and another. Humanity goes."

Not if you eat cake.

Sensing What's Good for You

Well-being is not a state of mind,
or even of body. It is a state of grace.

—Sally Brampton

*W*omen trust and act upon their instincts when it concerns their children's well-being, but then shut down their *sense of knowing* when it's about their own needs. This is a sophisticated form of self-abuse because when we deliberately go against our intuition, we aren't acknowledging or honoring our spiritual gift of Knowing. Usually you deny your intuitive prompts for the best of intentions, which is really the worst: so that you won't inconvenience anyone else, personally or professionally, by even considering, for a change, what's good for *you.*

And you know that I'm right. However, this doesn't mean that following our intuition is easy, especially if the opinions of other people are involved.

De profundis: I am a recovering perfectionist, workaholic, and careaholic, and a damn great one. Give me a project, deadline, or the concerns of a loved one and I'll circumvent the laws of Heaven and earth if necessary to make everything "all right." Part of this steely determination to see things through to the bitter or triumphant end comes from dedication and diligence, but it's often a Pyrrhic victory. By the time I've reached the finish line, I'm too whipped and wiped to do anything but beat a retreat to lick my self-inflicted wounds.

Of course, the leader of the pack should know better, and she does intellectually. But it's hard to change old patterns, to process our lessons emotionally, which is how our lessons stick. Intuitive knowledge—that Divine edge—is useless if we don't listen to it and act.

"It is only by following your deepest instinct that you can lead a rich life and if you let your fear of consequence prevent you from following your deepest instinct then your life will be safe, expedient and thin," Katharine Butler Hathaway wrote in 1946. The holy truth of this observation is stunning.

It has been a tremendous struggle for me to accept that self-interest is the soul of self-preservation. It has required more courage than I thought I could muster to break free of this abusive relationship with myself, and I wrestle with my demons every day. On the days I follow my intuition, I'm constantly astonished. I always think a miracle's taken place, and it has. But the miracle isn't just that Spirit led me to greater good or away from disaster. The miracle is that I didn't second-guess Heaven's "heads-up."

Well-being isn't about the mind or body but the soul. Well-being is how *well* you feel about *being* you. Your sense of well-being is enhanced when you begin to honor your spiritual sense of intuition by following its lead with respect, reverence, resolve, and enormous relief. You're not walking this earth alone unless you want to be.

Bliss Blockers

You look as if you lived on duty and it hadn't agreed with you.

—Ellen Glasgow

The cruelest and most cunning way we deceive and deny ourselves the benediction of bliss is through the concept of duty to others. But "is devotion to others a cover for the hungers and the needs of the self, of which one is ashamed?" Anaïs Nin asks. "I was always ashamed to take. So I gave. It was not a virtue. It was a disguise."

How else do we block bliss? Let us count the ways. Through ignorance more often than not, although we call our bliss blockers by many aliases. However, as the gardening writer Ruth Stout reminds us, "The bliss that comes from ignorance should seldom be encouraged for it is likely to do one out of a more satisfying bliss."

Like our peculiar patterns of making choices and giving promises, our bliss-blocking mosaics are highly developed and very personal. Made up of rogue bad habits, these soul snatchers specialize in changing identity as soon as we recognize them. But I have infiltrated their high command. Often it takes one ignoramus to catch another.

Wanting what you can't have
Not wanting what you do have

Seeing the world as hostile
Believing life is hard
Over reliance on outside circumstances to initiate change
Believing that money is the answer
Believing you're unlucky
Believing that things will never change for the better

Exhaustion
Not eating well
Not exercising
Not listening to your body
Continuously finding fault with your body
Feeling unworthy of happiness, love, success
Not knowing who you are
Not knowing what you love
Self-loathing
Not recognizing addictive behavior patterns or dependence
Workaholism in the name of getting ahead or staying on top
    of things
Perfectionism

Lack of humor
Inability to laugh at oneself

Shyness in social situations
Lack of spontaneity
Thinking you're too inexperienced
Pretending that you're more experienced or worldly than
  you are

Believing the world will fall apart if you're not holding it
  together
Inability to ask for or receive help
Inability to be part of a team

Inability to say No gracefully
Needing to please
Seeing everything as competitive
Confusing being argumentative with being articulate
Always needing to be right

Putting others down so you can feel superior
Not trusting your intuition
Not following your dreams
Believing other people's second guesses are better than your
  first

Making a promise you dread
Making promises you know you won't or can't keep
Making promises just to keep the peace

Thinking that worrying will make it better

Inability to relax

Confusing fatigue and laziness
Procrastination
Inability to self-motivate
Impatience
Rushing
Disorganization
Surrounding yourself with negativity
Remaining in toxic relationships

Setting unrealistic expectations for yourself
Setting unrealistic expectations for others

Looking at the world and life through the lens of lack
Lack of curiosity
Lack of faith
Lack of wonder
Lack of gratitude

Quite amazing to think that all of these bliss blockers have become so familiar we don't even notice them. As Hannah More wrote in 1811 in a little tract entitled "Self-Love," "The ingenuity of self-deception is inexhaustible." This week pick just one bliss blocker (start with the one that made you wince when you read it) and see if you can't exchange these controlling habits with those of contentment.

An Education in Yourself

You're the only kind of knowledge
They don't teach at any college
You're an education in yourself . . .

—Harry Warren, Al Dubin
You're an Education (1938)

*D*uring the twenties, thirties, and forties, when the good life was portrayed on the silver screen in glorious black and white, the highest compliment you could pay a woman was to call her "a *swell* dame." It was an accolade not easily bestowed; beauty, glamour, money, fame, or social position couldn't guarantee being considered swell.

Gee, you're *swell* . . .

A swell dame lit up every room she entered because of her

291

irresistible lightness of being, which is why Life always seemed like a romantic comedy, even when it wasn't. Think Myrna Loy's arched-eyebrow wit in the *Thin Man* series, Constance Bennett's insouciant supernatural naughtiness in *Topper,* or Carole Lombard's sophisticated screwball sexiness in *My Man Godfrey.*

"Swell is the place where spirit and style meet," explain fashion designer Cynthia Rowley and *New York Times* style editor Ilene Rosenzweig in *Swell: A Girl's Guide to the Good Life,* a magnanimous guide to "navigating the world with a little swagger and a lot of grace." And the way to do that is with a little higher education in the things that really matter: climbing into a jeep in a pencil skirt without flashing panty; selecting a single-malt whiskey; playing craps; delivering a punch line that will have them roaring; making a delicious pot of campfire coffee; adopting a runway sashay; changing a flat tire by *yourself* without breaking into a sweat or hysterics.

Yes, you can.

So here's the plan. How about a little home schooling? Along with me, be willing to learn one fascinating thing each month that intrigues. Something you've always wanted to *know* how to do but never got around to learning. Something that sounds like so much fun you can't wait to nail it. Something that makes you stand a little taller, smile a little broader, laugh a little louder, and relax a whole lot more because you're a confident woman who can rise to any occasion with great style. With a swell's insider knowledge, the world becomes your oyster; what's more, you won't look idiotic eating it. As for those little pearls of wisdom, let's just say you have never looked sexier. Nothing in the world is as irresistible as a woman who keeps them guessing.

What should you learn? Well, becoming a swell is "not a paint-by-numbers project," Cynthia and Ilene emphasize. "The secret of swell is having the guts to try some things you might not have before—to do things your own way. What's swell or isn't is up to you."

You've Got It

*It's a sort of bloom on a woman. If you have
it, you don't need to have anything else; and if
you don't have it, it doesn't much matter what
else you have.*

–J. M. Barrie
What Every Woman Knows (1908)

During the Roaring Twenties, a silent-movie sensation named Clara Bow embodied allure—the mesmerizing power to entice and attract through personal charm and mystery. Loved by millions as the "It" girl, Clara was happiness personified, exuding innocent sex appeal on the screen and off. With a heart-shaped face, hourglass figure, flaming red hair, and big expressive eyes, Clara wowed 'em coming or going. The writer F. Scott Fitzgerald wrote, "This girl was the real thing, someone to stir every pulse in the nation." A studio messenger boy put it this way: "I've never taken dope, but it was like a shot of dope when you looked at this girl."

However, hidden behind Clara Bow's captivating smile and vivacious manner was a sad, disillusioned, and lonely young woman who wished she really could be the It girl. "She's much happier than I am," Clara once wistfully confided in an interview. The reporter would hear none of it. Clara Bow lonely? Balderdash!

Once in a season when I appeared to have it all, my mind and heart begged to differ; my soul knew the truth, but you know how hard it is to butt into an argument. During the day the world often sang my praises, but at night, all I could hear were the deafening harpies of self-doubt and derision. Others may think you have It—but if you're not a true believer, toots, it doesn't much matter what they say.

Being possessed of your reason, what do you do when you're bombarded by insistent noises drowning out Life's melody? Try listening to something else, which is exactly what I did. I tuned out the shrill lies of self-loathing and began listening to the resounding truth of my Essensual Self.

Self-loathing seems to sneak up on us when we've become spendthrifts of the soul. Whether you're single or married, eighteen or eighty, there are days when our shortcomings seem magnified, nights when our inadequacies intensify. Even if you're in a wonderful relationship, there are times when love is not expressed, although you desperately need to hear it. If you're not part of a pair, you begin to doubt that anyone else on this earth could ever love you. You can't even remember what love sounds like.

If you're feeling this way today, take heart. I have a *guaranteed* remedy to help remind you that all you think is lost and lacking is really waiting to be found and cherished—within you. Do you remember the old Roy Orbison classic "You've Got It"?

> *Anything you want, you got it.*
> *Anything you need, you got it.*
> *Anything at all, Baby, you got it . . .*

Well, you do, too. You've just forgotten you've got whatever It represents to you. So let your sense of hearing be the portal to this new understanding. Start with the sound track to the movie *Boys on the Side,* which includes two versions of this great song—a rock-and-roll rendition by Bonnie Raitt and a slow, soothing ballad sung by Whoopi Goldberg. When I'm down on myself, I'll boogie to Bonnie in the morning, which is a fabulous way to begin any day. At night, just before I go to sleep, I'll listen to Whoopi reassure me that, indeed, I still have It.

Behavioral psychologists tell us it takes twenty-one days of repetition to exchange a bad habit for a healthy one. Try this as a bliss-blocker experiment. There is simply no way that you'll feel the same way about yourself at the end of the month as you do right now if, day in and day out, you're reminded just how much you're loved by the One who truly knows you best.

A School for the Senses

How should tasting touching hearing seeing breathing . . .
doubt unimaginable YOU?

—e. e. cummings

Since antiquity there have been forbidden foods. From the apple to aphrodisiacs, certain foods have always been associated with danger and risk. However, in recent years, all foods seem to have become suspect for one reason or another, because now we focus on health rather than taste. Once a source of enchantment, food has now become a source of entrapment. And while our cholesterol levels have never been lower, so are our spirits.

"The soul needs to be fattened," Thomas Moore tells us in his exquisite contemplation of the ordinary, *The Re-Enchantment of Everyday Life.* "The idea of feeding the soul is an old one, which can be found in mystical literature from around the world . . . spiritual food for the soul is closely connected to the body's food."

One of the ways that we nourish both our body and soul is by seeking out different ethnic restaurants or recipes in order to taste life around the world. For months my daughter raved about a Moroccan restaurant that she and her friends had discovered. The menu was the same every night. But no matter how many times she ate there, she never became bored. Instead, when she returned home, her face always seemed flushed with wonder. One evening she surprised me by whisking me off to dinner. Twenty minutes later we were standing in an unpromising part of the city and knocking on the door of a windowless stucco building, adorned by only one word written in Arabic. The door opened, a young man wearing a fez—a red, cone-shaped hat with a black tassel—peered intently at us both. Recognizing Katie, he smiled and waved us into Marrakesh.

For three hours we reveled in our senses: luxuriated on low

sofas and plump pillows, sipped mint tea, ate moist, succulent garlic chicken with our fingers. In between courses we were mesmerized by the beauty of an exotic belly dancer and the illuminated darkness that was pierced with so many votive candles, it seemed as if fireflies were lighting the room. I can't remember what we talked about; I do remember we laughed until my sides hurt. This simple, inexpensive meal was the essence of magic. The evening was intoxicating because we experienced tasting touching hearing seeing breathing as one mystical expanse. Katie and I have returned to our local Casbah many times since. For those of you who might wonder, there are no unsightly bulges when the soul is fattened up. Enchantment becomes us.

"Tasting is a form of knowing, a school for the senses," Thomas Moore reminds us. "Food is an implement of magic, and only the coldhearted rationalist could squeeze the juices of life out of it and make it bland."

Come to Your Senses

The Glamour of the Grill

O ne of the things I have always loved was grilling during the summer. When I was growing up and while I was married, my family would have a barbecue or "cookout" at least a couple of times a week. But after I was divorced, I didn't enjoy it once. I know this is true for a lot of women who find themselves on their own. That's because we associate the grill with testosterone— heavy, oversize tongs and forks, great gauntlets of oven mitts . . . the stoking of flames . . . and great, blackened slabs of meat or wild boar roasting on a spit.

Time out for a small gender-change chat. "While the male of the species seems to like the idea of doing fires for barbeques, there's something divine about a lady taking charge of this masculine preserve. Don't be afraid of this," the English writer Titania Hardie reassures us in her book of magical feasts, *Witch in the Kitchen*. "The word *perfume* reminds us that scent was originally released *par fumée*—by smoke. This is therefore a delicious opportunity to seduce through the flames themselves."

But not just him. Seduce yourself with the glamour of the grill. It can be a magical, romantic, and quite feminine experience, too! And you don't need to feed crowds to do it.

First, choose your equipment. While the traditional large charcoal or gas-burning grill might be fun for company, it does seem rather strenuous for preparing a solo meal, taking upward of half an hour just to heat, and Heaven knows how long to clean! Instead, if you're on your own, treat yourself to a small hibachi or a tabletop electric barbecue grill. Even the broiler of your range or toaster oven will do fine, if you want the taste of barbecue without needing the literal cooking-on-a-grill activity to complete the experience.

Hamburgers, steaks, and hot dogs are standard, boys-will-be-boys barbecue fare. Shish kebabs that alternate meats with vegetables or fruit, and fish grilled in foil or on skewers, allow you to mix and match whatever you might have on hand. Whatever your selection, keep the grill or broiler temperature low, so that meats can cook through without charring. All the following recipes are for one person, so if you've got company, increase the amounts.

Grilled Fish

You will need:

1 teaspoon lemon juice
1 teaspoon crumbled fresh rosemary, dill, thyme, or parsley
Pinch each of salt and freshly ground pepper

1. Select a fish steak less than 1 inch thick. Score the skin all around.
2. Lightly oil one side of a piece of foil large enough to enclose fish.
3. Place fish on the foil and sprinkle with the lemon juice, herb, and seasonings.
4. Wrap the fish, sealing all seams well to avoid leakage. (If grilling over an open flame, wrap a second piece of ungreased foil around the first.)
5. Grill for 15 minutes, turning once (or oven-bake at 400° for 15 minutes, no need to turn).

Shish Kebab for One

You will need:

½ pound beef, lamb, or boneless chicken breast, cut into ¾-inch
   chunks
Small quantities or ¾-inch chunks of small onions, red or green
   pepper, cherry tomatoes, zucchini, button mushrooms,
   pickles, olives *or* small quantities or ¾-inch chunks of
   pineapple, maraschino cherries, apple, pear

1. Marinate meat in any of the following sauces, in a glass,
   ceramic, or stainless-steel bowl, for at least 2 hours before
   grilling. Overnight is even better.
2. For the same length of time that the meat is marinating,
   immerse wooden skewers completely in water (a tall
   pitcher is a good container for this), or have metal skewers ready.
3. Alternate meat and other ingredients upon skewers. Leave
   a smidge of space between ingredients so that their side
   sections will cook; also, leave enough room along the
   skewer to lift it off the grill while you're wearing a padded
   oven mitt!
4. Brush kebabs with sauce. Grill or broil for 5 minutes on
   each side, brushing with additional sauce at each turn.
   (Don't use as a dipping sauce any marinade that had contained raw meat without reboiling leftover sauce first.)

While the following sauces can be used as basting liquids for
steaks, chops, or chicken parts as well as for kebabs, they are
quite delicious as marinades. Whichever sauce you prepare, be
sure to use a nonreactive (glass or stainless-steel) pan. Each recipe
makes around ½ cup.

Traditional Barbecue Sauce

You will need:

1 teaspoon butter
2 heaping tablespoons finely minced onion

¼ cup bottled tomato ketchup
1 ½ teaspoons light brown sugar
Pinch of salt
¼ cup water
½ teaspoon yellow or Dijon mustard
1 teaspoon bottled Worcestershire sauce

1. Over low heat, melt the butter in a small saucepan and sauté onion until transparent.
2. Add all other ingredients. Raise heat and bring to a boil, then reduce heat to low and simmer for 10 minutes, stirring occasionally.

White Wine Sauce

Good for chicken or lamb.

You will need:
¾ cup dry white wine
2 tablespoons olive oil
1 tablespoon butter
¼ cup grated onion
1 clove garlic, crushed
½ teaspoon salt
½ teaspoon dried rosemary

Combine all ingredients in a small saucepan and simmer over low heat for 30 minutes.

Sweet Teriyaki Sauce

You will need:
¼ cup soy sauce
⅓ cup water
¼ cup sugar
2 tablespoons white vinegar
1 clove garlic, crushed
1 teaspoon grated fresh ginger

1. Combine all ingredients in a small saucepan and bring to a boil.
2. Reduce heat and simmer for 10 minutes.

Savory Asian-Style Marinade

You will need:

½ cup tamari or soy sauce
1 clove garlic, crushed
¼ teaspoon freshly ground black pepper
¼ teaspoon ground cinnamon
1 tablespoon oil, preferably peanut oil

Combine all the ingredients.

When you're experimenting with grilling, also experiment with your fuel, adding a little wood to your charcoal to impart a scrumptious scent and flavor. Titania Hardie recommends pinewood, juniper, or cedarwood if you can get some. Some of her other suggestions to "scent the air pungently with wild and wonderful imaginings" are herbs such as rosemary, sage, lemon, verbena, lavender, myrtle, thyme, and citrus fruit peels. Be sure to add the herbs only after the coals are glowing rather than burning.

I think that one of the reasons women alone become lonely is that suddenly, without warning, we recall moments of bliss we once shared with others that we don't allow ourselves to enjoy any longer, such as the intoxicating fragrance of a summer night's cookout. Our lives become blissful when we realize, as L. E. Landon wrote in 1825, "We make ourselves our own distress / We are ourselves our happiness."

The Moveable Feast

The faint semblance of Eden,
The picnic in the greenwood.

—Herman Melville

The Anglo-Irish novelist Elizabeth Bowen believed that once we lose our innocence "it is futile to attempt a picnic in Eden." Perhaps. However, if you're feeling a little too sophisticated for your own good, a sure way to restore a sense of innocent wonder is to go on a picnic—in a shady lane or a park, by a lake, on a riverbank or a hillside. Some place where it's green and leafy.

Although both occur in the open air, a picnic is not to be confused with eating outdoors. We eat outdoors on the patio, deck, or in the backyard, and during the warm summer months, we should try to do it as often as we can. We picnic away from our home, and even in the summer we don't seem to do it often enough. That's because picnics can seem like productions, and while they do involve a bit of planning, they don't have to be three-ring circuses. Picnics possess romance and ritual—the day, the place, the menu, the accoutrements, the clothes, the blanket, the companion, the keep-in-minds and don't-forgets. But there are splendid rewards for she who delights in the ceremony of the picnic.

Where shall you go? Somewhere a little away from the routine (unless your everyday path beats a retreat through the backwoods) that's picturesque, quaint, or charming. Some place where you've often thought, "That would be a lovely spot for a picnic." If no place immediately pops into your head, pretend you're a location scout for the movies, or a painter. You want a spot with a view that doesn't include power generators, aerials, or satellite dishes, if possible. If you're in a large park, settle down where you can feel somewhat secluded, even if other people are around. You'll want level ground and a fair balance between sun and shade. I really love to have an ancient tree anchor any picnic setting because I like to lean my back against it. Indulging our quirks is the secret of contentment. Some people prefer to picnic in a favorite location, others love the thrill of the unknown. Adventurous friends of mine make a picnic day part of every vacation they take and can recommend shady nooks from Kansas to Kenya. Their annual picnic reports (the local food, ambience, what went wrong, and the heavenly unexpected bits) are great fun to listen to and inspiring.

Another friend found a beloved hideaway on a drive once a few years back. In a field off a twisting road, there was an old, abandoned house that in its day must have been glorious. Pulling over to get a better look, she took a walk around the house. The grass was high and unkempt, and some of the windows were boarded up. During the rest of that summer she found herself going out of her way to drive by this place, again and again. There was something about it; it had a certain charm, peacefulness, and romance. Soon, though, only a look wasn't enough, so one afternoon she mustered up the courage to make a special visit. Bringing along a book and a picnic, she settled herself down, deciding to play innocent if someone came along to ask her what she was doing. But she's never met another soul and her secret respite remains. One caveat here with abandoned, old houses: a Do Not Trespass sign means just that.

What to lay on the ground? A blanket. Perhaps you won't need one if you choose a place with picnic tables, but that's more "outdoor eating" than picnicking. Picnics take place on the ground, which is why an old, soft blanket is preferred. I recommend taking a blanket thick enough to give your natural padding a pad of its own. Keep in mind that your spot, however warm or sunny, may be a bit damp (which is why a water-repellent pad such as the liner for the kids' sleeping bag is handy). Pillows are optional for some people, I suppose, but not me. Take two at least. And you? On top of one end of the blanket, the romantic will spread a pretty tablecloth and, dreamer that she is, will have brought along a small vase for the wildflowers she's going to gather later. Women often sigh wistfully, "I wish my life could look like it was out of a magazine, just once." Well, it can, occasionally, and a picnic is one of those times.

The menu. Entire books have been written on the subject of

picnic food. However, simple food that stands up to hot weather arrives at the picnic site in better shape than elaborate courses and fragile foods, which are more suited for when you're dining alfresco on the patio.

Now, what separates the women from the romantics is whether you have a picnic "hamper." Creating one for yourself with thrift-shop finds of assorted china plates, flatware, real glasses, vintage linens, blanket, all outfitted in a lidded basket, is a delightful indulgence and a charming hobby for the summer. I keep one packed and ready by the back door. Because it's there and ready, deciding to go on a picnic seems so much simpler and light-hearted. The hamper also reminds me how long it's been since I took it anywhere.

Even though we're planning a picnic for one, that doesn't mean you can't have a companion. Of course, it can be another person or child. But it also could be a pet, book, or journal. It's nice to have someone or something to share your thoughts with. But it's also refreshing to be able to hear your own.

Keep in mind and don't forget: Being a woman who does not travel light has its advantages. I have usually stashed away the very thing everyone else forgets in the effort to be spontaneous. That includes (especially if there's a small entourage) paper towels, napkins, a damp sponge in a plastic bag, as well a large plastic garbage bag for litter.

In the great outdoors, it's easy to remember that we are all part of the great web of Life. Wondrous as this might be in poetry and song, it does complicate the picnic experience. I've found that it's the mosquito, the ant, and the bee that generally create trouble when eating outdoors. Ants, while a nuisance, are harmless and can be swept away with a brush of the hand and a few crumbs thrown afield. Bees and wasps are a bit more stubborn; take care not to plant yourself too close to a nest. A little trick that has worked for me is to take along an extra plate, pile it with something sweet (applesauce, pie, anything, really), walk it about thirty feet away from your spot, and let them have a picnic of their own. No one wants to be left out of Life's party, and why should they?

Always bring along bug spray and a small first-aid kit to treat bee stings. Don't forget a light jacket or sweater, a travel umbrella, bottle opener, and pocketknife. I have needed every one of them at one picnic or another. Always, always take a few spare bottles of water.

"I loafe and invite my Soul; I lean and loafe at my ease, observing a spear of summer grass," Walt Whitman entreats us with an invitation too irresistible to refuse. "Loafe with me on the grass..."

Come to Your Senses

Romancing the Salad

Could be the heat, but I can't stop ruminating on the peculiar way male poets muse about women and their salads. What *was* Robert Louis Stevenson nattering on about when he whispered to his "wine scented" maiden fair, "There's much more to be devoured in your capacious salad bowl." A plea to hold the mayo and chopped celery?

Don't blame the man. At least it's a more imaginative way of saying "Chicken salad again?" Six weeks into summer and the tongue longs for culinary novelty—sharper tastes, brighter colors, contrasting textures, mysterious scents.

One old recipe dating all the way back to the time of King

Henry VIII will produce a portion of the most amazing chicken or turkey salad you or he might ever have tasted. It's delicious enough to inspire verse worthy of ransoming a queen. Unfortunately, the two of Henry's six wives whom he beheaded for "adultery" obviously didn't spend enough time in the kitchen. Anne Boleyn could have told him she was only exchanging recipes so she'd have something tasty to set before the king.

Unadulterated Summer Bliss Salad

YOU WILL NEED:

⅓ cup white wine
3 tablespoons sugar
4 tablespoons honey
¼ teaspoon ground cloves
¼ teaspoon cinnamon
2 heaping tablespoons raisins
1 teaspoon grated lemon or orange peel
1 cup cooked and finely chopped chicken or turkey
Shredded lettuce or cabbage (optional)
Cinamon-raisin bread (optional)

1. In a small, nonreactive saucepan (glass or stainless steel) combine the wine and sugar, bring to a boil, and simmer over low heat for 10 minutes.
2. Add the honey, cloves, cinnamon, raisins, and peel, and simmer for 2 more minutes, stirring to mix thoroughly.
3. Remove from heat, stir in the chicken.
4. Pour into a small heatproof bowl, cover with a piece of foil, and chill thoroughly.
5. Invert onto a pretty salad-size plate lightly lined with shredded lettuce or cabbage, or serve as a sandwich made with two slices of cinnamon-raisin bread.

A tasty lunch or teatime egg salad, while it does contain mayonnaise, takes its cue from the colonial days of the British raj, when Victoria was not only queen but Empress of India.

Colonial Raj Curried Egg Salad

You will need:

3 tablespoons prepared mayonnaise
1 tablespoon prepared mango chutney (chop any pieces of
    mango)
1 teaspoon curry powder
2 tablespoons golden raisins or chopped dried apricots
2 hard-boiled eggs, cooled

1. In a small mixing bowl, whisk together the mayonnaise,
   chutney, and curry powder until well blended. Mix in
   the fruit.
2. Chop or coarsely mash the hard-boiled eggs.
3. Stir eggs well into the mayonnaise mixture. Mound onto
   a salad dish, or serve inside a lightly toasted pita pocket.

But my favorite summer salad is the always changing, never
boring salmagundi. Say what? Pronounced as it's spelled, versions of this dish have traveled all over the British Empire for hundreds of years because it's so adaptable. "You may always make a
Salmagundi of such things as you have according to your fancy,"
Mrs. Hannah Glasse reassured feminine cooks at their wit's end,
in her book, *The Art of Cookery Made Plain and Easy,* published in
1747.

Think caterers' platters or Cobb salad elevated to an art form.
Salmagundi is something like that, a visually pleasing arrangement
of small hills or curves or sprinklings of finely shredded, chopped,
or grated ingredients chosen for their contrasts of color and flavor.
And they are such fun to concoct on a scale for a single diner!

Start with a dinner-size round plate, placing a small saucer
upside down at the center (for more 3-D structuring). Now, pretend you are creating a bird's-eye view of a colorful garden, or an
Oriental rug. Starting at the center of the bottom of the over-
turned saucer, place the following kinds of foods in concentric rings
or symmetrically balanced small scoops (say, finely mashed potato
salad positioned at three o'clock, six, nine, and twelve), aiming as
much as you can to alternate colors and bland/tangy tastes:

shredded chicken, ham, or cold beef
cooked shrimp or strips of anchovies
minced hard-boiled egg yolk
hard-boiled egg whites sliced into rings or finely chopped
grated raw or pickled beets; grated raw carrots
sliced olives (contrast green and black)
green and red seedless grapes or raisins
finely chopped, colorful peppers, grouped by color
individual peas or wax beans or string beans
tiny florets of raw cauliflower and broccoli
heaps of corn kernels . . . the list could go on and on

Ornament your creation with sprigs of parsley, dill, or with edible nasturtiums.

The point is, take your time creating your salmagundi; enjoy your talents as a food arranger and the potential of whatever you might have on hand in the house. When you're done, sprinkle your composition with a little oil and vinegar, and as delicately demolish it, working your way in rings or along a radius or in symmetrical leaps, however you please. Eating with your fingers is encouraged.

"It's certain that fine women eat / A crazy salad with their meat," Yeats wrote. "Whereby the Horn of Plenty is undone."

Now, what do you suppose he meant by *that?*

Love Like Breakfast

*Love wants to enjoy in other ways the human being whom
it has enjoyed in bed; it looks forward to having breakfast.*

—Henry Fairlie

A long list of things comes to mind when I hear the word
bliss: Sundays and afternoon naps, bare feet on warm sand,
and banana splits for supper. But some of life's true moments of
bliss are to be found at breakfast. Not the everyday breakfast,
which for some may not exist at all, but those long, languorous
occasions where there isn't any rush or place to be, except break-
fasting.

The bliss of a real breakfast is unlike that of any other meal
because now it's all been relegated to the quaint and exotic. The
generation of women who used to time the eggs gave birth to
daughters who, for the last two decades, have also had to bring the
bacon home before frying it. Now we don't even do that anymore,
choosing instead to fill up the grocery cart with fat-free cereal and
soy milk. Mornings on the move mean little more than a gulped
cup of tea or coffee, a piece of fruit, prune yogurt, a cereal bar, or
a can of Red Bull.

Still, this socially enforced Spartanism has its advantages, Barbara Holland points out in her wry and wise book of essays,
*Endangered Pleasures: In Defense of Naps, Bacon, Martinis, Profanity,
and Other Indulgences.* "For one thing, it elevates a number of
previously routine matters into the realm of illicit thrills. What
was once an ordinary, underappreciated breakfast—two eggs over
easy, bacon, and a well-buttered English muffin, for instance—
now packs the guilty wallop of adultery, or starting the day with a
slug of Napoleon brandy."

When was the last time you treated yourself to a sensuous,
completely satisfying breakfast? No, not when you had overnight

company or were someone else's guest; not when you were on holiday and managed to make it downstairs in time to the hotel's all-you-can-eat buffet breakfast. Not when you had a business meeting over your oatmeal. But when did you prepare a scrumptious breakfast for *yourself* on an ordinary morning? All right, even an ordinary weekend morning.

Thought so. I hadn't either until recently, which is a startling realization, especially for a woman who cooked thousands of meals during a nearly two-decades-long marriage. However, the meal I concentrated on was rarely breakfast. That's because my husband ate only his own homemade granola in the mornings, and so, after the cats were fed (even before the kettle boiled) and my only child's needs were taken care of, no one else in the house said she was hungry. Maybe she didn't know. Hunger denied for years on end eventually quiets down. But hungers don't disappear; if not acknowledged, honored, appeased, they will devour their torturer through depression, addiction, despair. The soul starves before the body does. In her poem "The Fury of Abandonment," Anne Sexton, who would eventually take her own life, recalls the anguish of solitary morning hunger:

> *I know that it is all a matter of hands*
> *Out of the mournful sweetness of touching comes*
> *Love like breakfast.*

It is all a matter of hands, really. Hands that squeeze the oranges, beat the eggs, butter the toast, spread the jam, pour the tea, carry the tray out to the patio, deck, or table near a sunny window. Hands that serve up Love for one—bliss that tastes like breakfast.

Come to Your Senses

Basking in Bliss

"Just a cup of tea. Just another opportunity for healing. Just the hand reaching out to receive the handle of the cup. Just noticing hot. Noticing texture and fragrance. Just a cup of tea. Just this moment in newness," the metaphysical writer Stephen Levine points out this summer's morning. But it's not just another cup of tea for me, and it doesn't have to be for you, either. Each morning is another opportunity for us to accept with gratitude the gift of being here by taking care of ourselves so that we can stay a little while longer.

But self-nurturance, or learning to bask in bliss, is an acquired art form. It requires commitment (just as in a relationship with another person), patience, and a few tricks. Try preparing your breakfast tray at night. Learn to rehabilitate your cooking for a crowd to creating sensuous single portions. The English cook Delia Smith tells us in *One Is Fun* (and it really is with her recipes) that overcoming the single person's psychology of *It hardly seems worth the bother just for me* takes time and a willingness to experiment. "It *is* worth the bother, but until you've bothered you won't discover the satisfaction. It isn't easy to break out of the instant convenience-living syndrome" that so many people barely survive on, "but it can be done by stages. For instance, instead of downing your thin, half-cold cup of dreaded instant coffee—cold because it's too boring to gain your attention"—investing in a good, small coffeemaker so that you can "sit down to really enjoy sipping and *savouring* a cup of freshly ground coffee" will pay you back in pleasure that you can't put a price tag on.

Perk up your percolator by trying new coffee blends. You need not hit the gourmet shops: test what your local grocer carries of French roast, 100 percent Colombian coffee, or even just a brand you've never had before. See how your coffee tastes with almond or rice milk, especially the flavored varieties (vanilla nondairy milks and coffee are a sweetly fragrant combination; chocolate milks mixed with coffee produce . . . mmm, mocha!). If dining alfresco, bring along your coffee premixed with any milk and sugar, in a thermal carafe, for no-fuss pouring.

If you drink tea, you could easily enjoy a different flavor each day, until the one you reach for is the one you really want. This week treat yourself to seven small boxes of different teas: China, Indian, Irish, English, green, herbal, and fruit.

If you blindly reach for the same thing each day, wake up your *imagination,* too! Even if you prefer just toast . . . what about sampling a new bread, such as a nutted or fruited one? Have you ever toasted rye or pumpernickel bread? Toasted brioche bread tastes so sublime, you'll be turning around to make sure you don't have to share it with anyone else.

Whatever the grain, have you ever tried it with butter and honey? Almond or cashew butter? Is there a bagel topping that you've never had? (If you've eaten only poppy-seed-topped bagels for the last year, be bold and try the garlic!) How long has it been since you tried a new jam? If you've become locked into one flavor, buy yourself a sampler set of small jars and see if a new favorite emerges. Or enjoy a roll or croissant as the Europeans do, unornamented and dipped into a bowl-sized cup of coffee with hot milk.

Prefer cereal? Discover the new crunch and flavor of a cold cereal made from a grain you have never bought before—or try mixing your own all-natural muesli of sweetened oats (toss oatmeal flakes with a little all-natural maple syrup and oil, and oven-toast briefly at low temperature until dry) with dried fruits, nuts, seeds, coconut.

Yes, you can have a piece of peach pie for breakfast, honey-drenched figs, or something wildly decadent like wine-soaked cherries and pears over pound cake, which you prepare the night before.

"The moment when you first wake up in the morning is the most wonderful of the twenty-four hours. No matter how weary or dreary you may feel, you possess the certainty that . . . absolutely anything may happen," Monica Baldwin wistfully wrote in 1950. "The possibility is always there."

Who knows, it might even be a serving of bliss for breakfast.

Breakfast Bliss

You will need:

½ cup of good red wine (the better the wine, the better the sauce)
½ cup sugar
Zest from ½ lemon
¾ pound cherries, pitted
2 pears, peeled and sliced
Pound cake
Butter, softened
Freshly whipped cream

Combine the wine, sugar, and lemon zest in a medium saucepan. (Cooking the wine evaporates the alcohol, leaving only the taste of the grapes.) Stir until the sugar dissolves and add the cherries. Bring to a boil and then quickly reduce heat and simmer for 10 minutes. Add the pears and simmer an additional 5 minutes. Refrigerate overnight. While the coffee's brewing, toast the pound cake and warm up the fruit sauce in the microwave. Spread your sexy "toast" with a touch of butter, top with the cherries, the sauce, and some freshly whipped cream.

Gift from the Sea

The cure for anything is saltwater; sweat,
tears or the sea.

—Isak Dinesen

"*T*he Beach is not the place to work; to read, write or think.
I should have remembered that from other years. Too
warm, too damp, too soft for any real mental discipline or sharp
flights of spirit. One never learns. Hopeful, one carries down the
faded straw bag, humpty with books, clean paper, long over-due
unanswered letters, freshly sharpened pencils, lists and good intentions," Anne Morrow Lindbergh softy chides me this morning as
I begin to pack my beach bag. But we both know she is right. "The
books remain unread, the pencils break their points, and the pads
rest smooth and unblemished as the cloudless sky. No reading, no
writing, no thoughts even—at least, not at first."

One of the books in my bag, however, is Lindbergh's master-
piece *Gift from the Sea*. Originally published in 1955, her exquisite
midlife memoir has been like a spiritual compass for millions of
women; the pages Anne Morrow Lindbergh began for herself
remain a comforting, enduring classic of inspirational literature.
When I first discovered the book in the eighties, I reread it each
summer on my annual beach visit. But it's been five years since the
last time. I know because on some of its dog-eared, sunblock-
stained pages there are passages highlighted in yellow, along with
my dated comments in the margin. It was the last summer before
my marriage ended; the last beach vacation we would take as a
family, but I didn't know it, although coming events do cast their
shadows. One afternoon my husband lost his wedding ring and
we spent several frantic hours on our knees covering every square
inch of grass looking for it; he was so angry he'd lost it and I was
so fearful that if we didn't find it, I'd have to give him another,

and that thought filled my heart with dread. By then the long disquiet between us had become deafening; each in an inarticulate but telling way knew that neither of us could repledge a future together. But, smiling wanly at each other, we found the ring, relieved that we'd both been given a reprieve from the inevitable.

For thirty years I'd been coming to this beach village on the eastern shore of America, always staying at the clapboard home of my dear friends. And in all that time, the rhythm and rituals of my beach idyll remained as constant and as reassuring as the waves on the shore. Sunny days began around 7 A.M. with the first cup of tea on the screened porch before anyone else awoke; then a walk to bring back freshly baked, fragrant bagels and breads, still warm, for breakfast. Later I'd meander around town, wandering in the little shops in the morning. Buying one new Christmas ornament in July.

Returning to the empty house around noon, I'd change into my bathing suit and head out to meet my friends at their eminent domain of sand, unchanged in its location since we'd been coming to the beach. Not too surprisingly, my friends Tom and Dawne have spent practically every weekend of their lives here because they are "beach people"; I'm only a beachcomber for a few hours annually, and then I look as if I were crossing the Sahara. Since I'm Irish and fair-skinned, any summer beach sojourn requires a large hat, sunscreen, cover-up, and beach umbrella.

Time for lunch. Will it be an ice-cream cone, a piece of greasy (and fabulous) pizza, fries with salt, or a tomato sandwich? Today it's fries. The seagulls want to share and I have to move down on the beach away from everyone else to toss the beggars their treats. On my way back, I stroll the boardwalk and try my luck at the amusement games. Oh, the time, energy, emotion, and money spent winning stuffed animals for the children over the years. I excelled at it, and everyone always got a prize or two, in turn, over the week. This year no one's entreating Mommy and Auntie for a cheaply made toy elephant, but that doesn't mean I won't play the water-balloon chase.

A few magazines flipped through and most people are packing up. Finally, I can come out from underneath the umbrella and stand on the shore, letting the waves wash over my feet. Dawne and I pick up a conversation that began long before either of us was married, when we were roommates, and continues today. She threatens that she will someday reveal all—men whose very names now invoke an involuntary sign of the cross; the night I danced on the bar at the hillbilly joint and *never* knocked over one glass; the time I paid a storefront psychic $500 to remove a curse on my romantic life. (She told me to put an egg underneath my bed and wait. A week later I had no money to pay the rent, the man I thought I couldn't live without had gotten married to someone else, and the apartment reeked of sulfur.) Now we roar with laughter until we're both in tears and it feels *so* good. "There will be nothing left to tell, I've told all the good stories," I inform her. "I'm not worried," she teases relentlessly, as we slowly head back to the house, balancing beach bags and folding chairs, the sound of our flip-flops hitting the hot pavement. "I've got tales you don't even remember." No doubt she does. I look forward to hearing them.

I wait until last to wash off the remains of the day because it means I can linger in the bliss of their outdoor shower. "In all the years when I did not know what to believe in and therefore preferred to leave all beliefs alone," the Norwegian novelist and Nobel Prize winner Sigrid Undset reminisced in 1939, "whenever I came to a place where living water welled up, blessedly cold and sweet and pure from the earth's dark bosom, I felt that after all it must be wrong not to believe in anything." She could hardly have been describing my friends' backyard, but showers taken in doubt and faith come cascading in memory. The summer I miscarried; the summer I was pregnant and, thank God, stayed that way; and Katie's first trip to the beach. The two summers when *Simple Abundance* was rejected again and again; the July when my agent called to tell me, at last, we'd found a publisher; the summer I made the bestseller list. Moments of pain and happiness, like drops of water down my back, merge into the holy, palpable present.

Back on the screened porch, I'm shucking corn, sipping a margarita, and sucking the salt off the rim of the glass. The steaks are grilling, the wine is "breathing," and we're laughing again. In a few hours, I'll sink into the oblivion of a saggy mattress and deep sleep, the breeze off the ocean lightly brushing my body until I tingle. Blessed am I among the blissful and once again I know it.

So often after a parting of the ways in life—a relationship ends, our children grow up, we move, we change jobs, friends divorce or die—we abandon the personal passions and pleasurable pursuits we once enjoyed and associated with those particular people and places. The bistro where every morning, over the best café au lait you'd ever tasted, you prepared yourself for the day's gauntlet at the office. The summer concert tickets. Celebrating the Chinese New Year. The reading group. Putting up a real Christmas tree.

"I believe most people are aware of periods in their lives when they seem to be 'in grace' and other periods when they feel 'out of grace,' even though they may use different words to describe these states," Anne Morrow Lindbergh wrote fifty years ago. "In the first happy condition, one seems to carry all one's tasks before one lightly, as if borne along on a great tide; and in the opposite state one can hardly tie a shoe-string. It is true that a large part of life consists in learning a technique of tying the shoe-string, whether one is in grace or not. But there are techniques of living too; there are even techniques in the search for grace. And techniques can be cultivated."

When we recall the sensory pleasures that once swaddled our souls, we can use them as bliss triggers. Like a "little hermit crab, who has run away, leaving his tracks behind him like a delicate vine on the sand," Anne Morrow Lindbergh reminds us, we can find our way back to the protection and benediction of momentary bliss. "There is no pattern here for permanent return, only for refreshment." I scribble today's date in the margin next to that quote. Who knows what the next year will bring? When I first started coming to the beach, I wanted life's every step laid out before me; now I'm grateful there's rarely even a glimmer. But I *do* know today I'll have a tomato sandwich for lunch.

Beauty and the Beach

Clothes and courage have so much to do with each other.

–Sara Jeannette Duncan (1900)

*I*magine—were we at the seashore a hundred years ago, we'd be wearing, for modesty's sake, thick, striped woolen suits down to our knees, or layered bloomer dresses . . . and mobcaps, perhaps even stockings! What on earth would our great-grandmamas have thought of today's swimwear? Utter shock, perhaps. Or . . . just maybe . . . a wee bit of envy. Then on second thought, it's *their* bathing costumes that seem enviable, especially this morning as the mirror reveals more of my lusciousness than I wish, modest woman that I am. All that lip-smacking salt has settled on my hips.

If there is a feminine torture worse than finding a new bathing suit, I can't imagine it. This is probably why we wear the same one until it falls off.

Most modern swimsuits are made from nylon, a polyester blend, some kind of elastic fabric containing spandex, or some combination of all three, flattering only to stick-figure dolls, who don't need to wear one-piece swimsuits anyhow. It was the great fashion editor Diana Vreeland who spotted the first bikini on the French Riviera in 1946; she asked an American sportswear designer to copy it and thrust a green-and-white, itty-bitty, teensy-weensy polka-dot bikini upon the world with the May 1947 *Harper's Bazaar.*

During the thirties, forties, and fifties, the era of the glamorous Esther Williams, bathing suits came with little skirts or shorts. Should a woman want to show off a flat tummy, she chose a "sheath" swimsuit (with a flat, skirtlike panel on the front).

Making peace with your body is the first step toward finding a bathing-suit style that's as comforting as it is flattering. Imagine the bliss of *wanting* to put on a swimsuit. Yes, with a little sleuthing, peace in our lifetime. And the way to lasting contentment is to decide which part of your body you want to play up or down.

If you have cleavage even in a turtleneck, now is the time to show off. During the Victorian era, it was a compliment to be described as a woman possessing "those." Just be sure your bust is well supported, in a suit that considers the overall shape of the chest, and not just your breast size. There's a bandeau top, a front-crossing wrap style, or a color pattern that breaks across your chest. Experiment with cleavage: a deep V versus a scoop neck will have very different effects. Basic, solid-color tank suits of a firm fabric can minimize a large bust.

If you are small breasted, try on contoured suits, styles with a V shape of color extending slightly broader than you do, a suit with a lighter top and darker bottom, or bold prints. If you are not actually going into the water, think about wearing a suit with a little extra coverage and, under it, a padded bra, a trick a friend swears by.

The old adage that vertical lines are slimming is true. A new twist is that high-cut legs can be flattering on large-hipped or heavy-legged women, precisely by drawing more attention to the vertical line. Side stripes or central panels on a one-piece suit are also slimming, lengthen short torsos, and can give thick-waisted bodies more of an illusion of curves. Diagonal effects at the waist, cutouts, or prints that break up the line also add or highlight curves. If you have a long torso whose length you'd rather minimize, try a top and bottom of two different colors, or a print on one piece coordinated with a solid on the other.

The hourglass figure looks lovely in a halter, sweetheart, and wrapped necklines were made for you, as well as—surprise!—one-strap suits. Suits that don't cling too tightly will actually help you appear shapelier.

Whatever your figure, don't forget the dramatic beauty of a low-cut back. It will make a difference in how you feel about yourself if you stop trying to hide your hips and start showing off a beautifully curved set of vertebrae and velvety-smooth skin.

Before you buy it, examine the fit of your suit carefully to see how it stretches and moves with your body, before a three-way mirror. And that goes if you've already owned the suit for years—

diet and gravity do make a difference. The same amount of energy required to suck in your stomach could be expended more pleasurably licking an ice-cream cone! If you're constantly fiddling with a suit's leg openings or straps that won't stay in place, this is *not* the right suit for you. However you look, or think you look, you need to feel comfortable enough to forget how the suit fits once you're wearing it, and that goes for skimpiness, too: if you feel self-conscious or actually embarrassed, you'll look it.

Ideally, a good swimsuit fits like a second skin. Become accustomed to your suit by wearing it around the house a little before going public. "Sometimes idiosyncrasies which used to be irritating become endearing, part of the complexity of a partner who has become woven deep into our own selves," Madeleine L'Engle wrote in *Two Part Invention*. Although she was writing about lovers accepting each other with benevolence over time, as I get ready to head to the beach, it occurs to me that she could just as easily have been talking about a woman and her bathing suit.

Come to Your Senses

Ode to Salt

"**D**ust of the sea, in you / the tongue receives a kiss / from ocean night," wrote Pablo Neruda in his poem "Ode to Salt." I wonder if he'd been sipping a margarita.

The ancients considered salt holy. Romans offered salt to their gods, and the Old Testament also contains allusions to salt. In Ezekiel 16:4–5, we learn that in biblical times newborn babies were routinely washed with salt water (as a protection against evil). For many centuries, infants being baptized had a few grains of salt placed beneath their tongue, to ward off Satan. During medieval times, salt was believed to repel witches and was carried upon one's person or thrown upon the fire. To keep an unwanted visitor from returning to a house, salt was sprinkled on whatever areas he or she had walked upon, then was swept up and burned. The superstition about throwing salt over one's left shoulder after spilling it derives from the belief that it would counteract the gathering of evil spirits come to take advantage of the accident.

Salt was such a valuable commodity that it's not surprising there are many references to it throughout history. Jesus called his followers "salt of the earth," a phrase we use to this day to describe the dependable. In Latin, *sal* means "salt": Roman soldiers were given a salt ration called a *salarium*—the origin of *salary*. Salt was so precious as a preservative in Renaissance times that, when a bowl of it was placed upon a banquet table, the most honored guests sat "above the salt," while the more common folks sat "below" it . . . a culinary equivalent of being on the right or wrong side of the tracks. In many cultures, too, salt represented hospitality or peace; friendship oaths or treaties often involved the sharing of salt by the participants; and the Russian word for hospitality means "bread-salt."

Salt contains two valuable components: sodium, which helps to distribute fluids throughout our bodies at the right pH level; and chloride, which aids digestion. Too little sodium can cause headaches, dizziness, or cramps; on hot days or after a bout of turista, a pinch of salt in tea or fruit juice helps restore our equilibrium. However, it is far more likely that we consume too *much* of a good thing: high sodium is one of the causes of hypertension and bloating. To stay healthy, we really only need about half a teaspoon a day, total, to be fit, but probably ingest many times that. If you need to cut down on salt, there are many delicious ways to do so. Opt for desserts that rely on beaten egg whites for leavening (rather than baking powder or soda). In place of salty bottled sauces, mix oil and vinegar (or lime or lemon juice) with freshly ground pepper, a small amount of Dijon mustard or horseradish (these condiments contain salt, but far less than prepared dressings), freshly crushed garlic, or herbs. Eggs, for instance, look and taste lively sprinkled with a little sage or paprika.

Top pasta with salt-free pesto: in a blender, puree one cup of fresh basil leaves with one clove of finely chopped garlic, one teaspoon of lemon juice, and one-quarter teaspoon of pepper, then whirl again with one teaspoon of olive oil, for a single, yummy portion of sauce. An excellent salt substitute that provides much of the healthy goodness of salt with almost *no* sodium is seaweed: powdered black nori or red dulse flakes, sold in health food or gourmet stores. Sprinkle onto salads, pastas, baked potatoes, and so on, instead of salt.

I jump a dress size when I reach for the salt shaker, which is why I'm only an occasional user. Like champagne and chocolate, salt can become a special treat, all the more so because when you do indulge, it's consciously and with great enthusiasm. That's why I opt for natural sea salt, sold by gourmet or health food stores. Don't be alarmed if it is silvery gray instead of white; colors vary by region. Coarse sea salt can be made finer by grinding it in a salt mill or by spreading it between two sheets of waxed paper and crushing it with a rolling pin.

Use a dash in a vase to keep cut flowers fresh, rub cups with damp salt to remove tea or coffee stains, freshen sponges by soaking in cold salt water. Even if you haven't any evil spirits to drive away just now, use a line of salt to repel ants!

Mystical rites aside, salt is certainly useful for many kinds of bodily purification. Equal measures of salt, baking soda, and dried sage make a natural, tooth-whitening tooth powder. Dip a small, natural-bristle brush into a small bowl containing two tablespoons of wheat germ oil (an excellent source of skin-soothing and skin-smoothing vitamin E) and then into one-quarter cup of sea salt, then rub—without excessive scrubbing—any dry or rough areas of your body. Rinse well with warm water.

External-use-only Epsom salts—named for its original region in England—is a traditional skin-softening, muscle-cramp-relieving soaking agent, especially when combined with other legendary softeners. For several baths' worth, mix one cup of Epsom salt, one-quarter cup of borax powder, one-third cup of powdered milk, and one teaspoon of the floral essential oil of your choice. Store in a tightly covered jar, and use about one-third cup per warm-to-hot bath, stirring water well. Soak, and feel blessed and protected.

However, my favorite way to experience the bliss of salt comes during the summer—tomato sandwiches for lunch, margaritas and corn on the cob for dinner. Call us self-indulgent; we won't deny it.

"We cannot make bargains for blisses," Alice Cary wrote in 1876. "Nor catch them like fishes in nets." But we can reach for just a pinch of salt or two.

Tomato Sandwiches and Margaritas

You might think making a tomato sandwich is straightforward. You would be wrong. Like many bliss triggers there is a ritual, and anticipation is very much a part of it. You must wait until July to partake of this bliss, because only then will you get the tomato at its most sublime. After you have thought about a tomato sandwich for a minimum of one week, on the appointed day take two pieces of extremely soft white bread. Spread both slices with real mayonnaise. Slice ripe summer tomatoes and pile them on the bread. Sprinkle freshly ground salt and pepper on the tomatoes. Cut into quarters. And eat them as slowly as possible. Now make yourself another.

There are different versions as to how the margarita got its name. My favorite tells of a showgirl during the twenties named Marjorie King, who had an allergy to all alcohol with the exception of tequila. A bartender in a Mexico City nightclub created a drink especially for her, calling it the margarita—her name in Spanish.

A margarita for one: Lime wedge; coarse salt; 2 ounces of tequila; 1 ounce triple sec; 2 ounces of lime juice. Rub the rim of a stemmed glass with the lime wedge and dip it into a saucer filled with salt. Shake the tequila, triple sec, and lime juice in a shaker with ice and strain into the glass. Sip it slowly. Preferably while shucking corn and as the sun sets.

Between the Lines

Becoming Self-Centered

With a new awareness, both painful and humorous, I begin to understand why the saints were rarely married women. I am convinced it has nothing inherently to do, as I once supposed, with chastity or children. It has to do primarily with distractions. The bearing, rearing, feeding and educating of children; the running of a house with its thousand details; human relationships with their myriad pulls—woman's normal occupations in general run counter to creative life, or contemplative life, or saintly life. The problem is not merely one of Woman and Career, Woman and the Home, Woman and Independence. *It is more basically: how to remain whole in the midst of the distractions of life; how to remain balanced, no matter what centrifugal forces tend to pull one off center; how to remain strong, no matter what shocks come in at the periphery and tend to crack the hub of the wheel. . . .*

But how? Total retirement is not possible. I cannot shed my responsibilities . . . I cannot be a nun in the midst of family life. I would not want to be. The solution for me, surely, is neither in total renunciation of the world, nor in total acceptance of it. I must find a balance somewhere, or an alternating rhythm between these two extremes; a swinging of the pendulum between solitude and communion, between retreat and return. . . .

It is a difficult lesson to learn today—to leave one's friends and family and deliberately practice the art of solitude for an hour or a day or a week. . . . For me, the break is the most difficult. . . . And yet, once it is done, I find there is a quality to being alone that is incredibly precious. Life rushes back into the void, richer, more vivid, fuller than before.

—Anne Morrow Lindbergh
Gift from the Sea

325

August is a wicked month.

—Edna O'Brien

R eckless, wanton, sultry, too hot to handle . . . August's breathing down your neck and it's not even noon. Hold it right there. When it's one hundred degrees in the shade, and heat shimmers off the blacktop, babes turn bad, if they know what's good for them. Leave the group tour on the motor coach and chill. Strip down to your essensual femme fatale. Heed the hammock's siren call to sensuous solitary sojourns: shady nooks, racy books, egg cream sodas. Just pull a veil over your eyes and let the shenanigans begin with an irresistible assortment of do-try-these-at-home romantic escapades. Discover that distance lends enchantment, that the past isn't really where you thought you left it, and that no woman can ever eat too many peaches. So turn the page. Love lurks where you'd never thought to look. Plenty of time left for a summer fling.

In Good Company

*Most of us are only bad girls in our dreams. But there's
a pattern in the bad-girl lifestyle that deserves contemplation.
Bad girls buy what they want to buy, eat what they want to eat,
wear what they want to wear, sleep when they want to sleep.
Bad girls do not have therapists because they don't need them.
Instead bad girls have housekeepers and masseuses.*

—*Simple Abundance*
November 22 entry

When my daughter was getting ready to go to college, I had great fun gathering together some books that I thought might help when I wasn't available to offer sage advice. One of the books that caught my eye was a lavender primer called *The Bad Girl's Guide to Getting What You Want.* However, while standing in the long line waiting to move her into her dorm, I started perusing it. And giggling. Three hours later, it was clear who needed this book, and it wasn't the gal who had guys she'd met only minutes before unpacking her boxes.

"Don't worry, Mom. Got it covered," she said with a wicked grin and a wink.

"Bad girls make it happen. A bad girl knows what she wants and how to get it. She makes her own rules, makes her own way, and makes no apologies. She knows when to work a room, when to work the angles, and when to work her curves or do all of the above. A bad girl is everyone's dream date and nobody's fool," Cameron Tuttle tells us in her cheeky *Bad Girl Guide* series. "She's attitude in overdrive, coast-to-coast confidence, and fast-forward fun. She's your boldest dreams and your inner wild. A bad girl is you at your best—whoever you are, whatever your style."

And whatever your age. That's because "once you light your

badness fuse, you'll start to hear the muse—that sassy little voice inside your head reminding you to go for it, trust your instincts, and find the G-spot of your own life."

Those of you who've read *Simple Abundance* know of my deep admiration for the bad girl in all of us. "There are no good girls gone wrong," Mae West confides. "Just bad girls found out." Unfortunately, for too many of us, Bad Girl's not quite out of the closet in all her dazzling spandex splendor. That's because we often confuse bad girls with the archetypal feminine shadow—the brazen, wanton hussy. The bitch. The witch. Strumpet, wench, trollop, tart, floozy, nympho, hooker, libertine.

Yes, historically that is what men have called women who rule, women they couldn't control, and the women of rock and roll. "Great women throughout history were bad girls. They were passionate about what they wanted. They were dreamers, risk-takers, and visionaries who defied the norm of their times," Tuttle points out. "They didn't conform and they didn't take no for an answer. They weren't afraid to break the rules or scare the hell out of men to get what they wanted. You don't have to change the world to find your badness. But you'll definitely change yours."

Let's free-associate for a moment. When you think of a Bad Girl, who immediately comes to mind? Probably not the twelfth-century queen Eleanor of Aquitaine, the wife of England's Henry II, my personal bad-girl mentor. Eleanor was so "bad" (ambitious, strong-willed, independent, calculating, commanding, and seductive) that her husband had to keep her locked up so she wouldn't incite rebellion when she disagreed with his plans. It took Katharine Hepburn, who was always playing bad girls, both on and off the screen (and won the best-actress Oscar playing Eleanor in the 1968 film *The Lion in Winter*) to convey the queen's high spirits. When asked the secret to her success, Katharine said, "I liked to look as if I didn't give a damn." So did Eleanor. There's bad girl advice to live by.

What other bad girl screen images come to mind? Thelma and Louise? Thought so. Unfortunately, a lot of women would agree. That's because we fear the consequences of bad girl behavior—speaking up for ourselves, putting our preferences first, saying no, and going after what makes us happy, whether it's moving to a strange city or a man our friends don't like.

Thelma and Louise were *good* girls who erupted like a volcano and went beserk because they didn't acknowledge or honor their magnificent "inner wild." They tried to bury their passion. When a good woman tries to completely snuff out the spark of wildness that nature gave her to keep her alive, she ends up "dead" in some sense, whether it's through chronic depression, debilitating illness, addiction, or by driving off a cliff. A woman shouldn't have to be diagnosed with breast cancer to take up mountain climbing or landscape design. Nor should she feel it necessary to pretend she's having a root canal in order to get a haircut. However, I've known one too many good girls who've had to do just that. Maybe you have, too.

Cameron Tuttle suggests we reconsider our concept of Bad Girls. Think "Cleopatra cruising the Nile . . . Dorothy Parker at the Algonquin . . . Rosa Parks in the front of the bus . . . Miss Piggy hitting the high notes . . . Aretha getting some respect . . . Tina strutting her stuff . . . Xena kicking some ass."

How about Lucy in *Peanuts*? The turn-of-the-century rebel rouser of Nova Scotia, Anne Shirley in *Anne of Green Gables* ("It's so easy to be wicked without knowing it, isn't it?"), or Pippi Longstocking?

Oh, don't forget Tinker Bell. Now that babe was so bad, she'd fall down, hold her breath, and pretend to be dead until she got her way. Jane Austen? One of the most subversive women ever to lift a pen ("I always deserve the best treatment, because I never put up with any other"). Marilyn Monroe. The greatest sex symbol there ever was but, sadly, she wasn't a bad girl. She just *wanted* to be. Really bad girls might wear only Chanel No. 5 to bed, but their survival instincts are admirable.

Still, for women of a certain age whose deepest, unarticulated fear is that someday they'll end up alone, homeless, and on the street, the shadow of the fallen woman hovers menacingly. Don't bad girls grow up to be bag ladies?

"The word *shadow* itself suggests a dark, secretive, possibly malevolent countenance that looms in the background of our nature, ready to do harm to others as well as to ourselves," the brilliant writer and pioneer in spiritual-energy medicine, Carolyn Myss, explains in her book *Sacred Contracts: Awakening Your Divine Potential*. However, "a much more appropriate understanding of the shadow aspects" of our personalities is "that they represent the part of our being that is least familiar to our conscious mind."

And for many women the least familiar part of ourselves is the girl who just wants to have fun. It's quite illuminating when you make the discovery that often what women call the search for true love turns out to be the suppressed hankering to do the hokey-pokey. Or strictly ballroom. There's a wonderful Yiddish proverb that says, "The girl who can't dance says the band can't play."

Granted it's a big transition from the "me, too" mind-set to "me, first," but sometimes the orchestra's been playing our tune for so long we can no longer hear it or we're afraid to want to.

"Do you have the idea that it's unladylike to want? Snap out of it!" Cameron Tuttle admonishes us. "Don't be afraid to want things, to yearn, crave, or lust for anything. And don't be afraid to go after what you want. If you can't satisfy yourself, then how can you expect anyone else to satisfy you?"

Playmates

Shall we play the wantons . . . ?

—William Shakespeare

*I*n the dictionary, as well as in the boudoir of Life, the word *play* comes before *pleasure*. But this is how little women know how to play: in one of my favorite bliss triggers, *The New Beacon Book of Quotations by Women* (edited by Rosalie Maggio), there's not even a category for "play" quotes, which means that not many women have been musing or writing about the importance of play down through the centuries. Maybe it's because we call it other things. Adultery. Shopping. Internet chat rooms. Running away from home to join the circus, a temptation even princesses can't resist, as Princess Stephanie of Monaco, who bolted from the castle to live with a circus elephant trainer, dramatically demonstrates. Surely the Big Top was not the life her mother, the former Grace Kelly, had envisioned for little Stephanie. But being royal and removed from the everyday world was obviously not the life the princess wanted either. Even if the tiara's diamond encrusted, all duty and no whoopee makes a woman self-destructive.

In other words, when we play dumb about our perfectly plausible passions, we pay a high price for denying our wants. Then comes the morning when we just can't play safe anymore in a game where we never get to pass "Go" or even toss the dice. By this time we're so angry, frustrated, and enraged that playing around, playing with fire, or playing fast and loose (even with a married circus ringmaster), looks preferable to playing martyr.

Time for some tango lessons.

Jumping into Each Day's Deep End

A sheltered life can be a daring life as well.
For all serious daring starts from within.

—Eudora Welty

*D*o you remember when you were little and jumping into the deep end of the pool was one of the most daring things you could do? You always got such a rush when you buoyed back to the surface of the water. Wow! Let's do it again. Once a sense of play introduces a little deep-end jumping into each ordinary day, you'll want to keep doing it again and again. And you're meant to.

In her mesmerizing book *Deep Play,* the scholar, scientist, siren, scribe, and Renaissance woman Diane Ackerman breaks feminine silence and meditates on the sacred meaning of play in our lives. Women will encourage their children to play because we know it's how a child learns to navigate her way through the universe. But when we grow up, we begin to "think of play as self-indulgent and irresponsible." However, play is one of the most sacred experiences, because in play, as in Love, we encounter the sacred, and "deep play thrives on a romance with life."

"In rare moments of deep play, we can lay aside our sense of self, shed time's continuum, ignore pain, and sit quietly in the absolute present, watching the world's ordinary miracles. No mind or heart hobbles. No analyzing or explaining. No questing for logic. No promises. No goals. No relationships. No worry," Ackerman writes movingly. "With innocent surprise, one regards life's spectacles and underpinnings. All one feels is affectionate curiosity for the whole bustling enterprise of creation. It doesn't matter what prompts the feeling—watching albatrosses court or following the sky-blown oasis of a tumultuous sunset. When it happens we experience a sense of revelation and gratitude. Nothing need be thought or said. There is a way of beholding [in play] that is a form of prayer."

One of my favorite ways to play is to putter, the pleasant meandering of the mind when a woman starts rearranging the objects that surround her. I don't know about you, but I can start dusting one tabletop or fixing a crooked picture on the wall, and in what feels like a fleeting few minutes, I've lost a couple of hours to serenity. Several days ago I was roaming in an antiques market and found a fabulous flower-patterned parasol from the twenties in perfect condition. It was unique, so colorful and so much fun that I knew I couldn't leave without it. I couldn't wait to get home and find the perfect place for it. Actually, what I wanted to do was use it as a parasol; I played in front of the mirror, loved how romantic it looked, but felt a little awkward. So finally I hung it from a corner of my living room ceiling where it catches the sunlight during the day and splatters patterns of roses and berries on the wall. It makes me smile every time I see it. Puttering among my household objects has become a profound ritual for me, a form of sacred play that is always surprising. I never know what ideas, thoughts, connections, or conversations I'll have while I do it.

"Many quiet rituals have submerged into the sea of everyday life to the point of invisibility—dressing the children for school, going out jogging, pausing for tea and sweets each afternoon, crawling into bed with a glass of warm milk, getting dolled up before an evening out. Rituals of self-care, planned and savored, can rise up like a shimmering oasis at the end of a long dry day," Diane Ackerman reassures us.

"There are real holidays, of course, sprinkled throughout the year. But I prefer personal, everyday rituals. Taking a rambling blind sort of follow-the-road-wherever-it-leads mystery trip on Sunday afternoons, sharing breakfast and secrets with a good friend by telephone on Saturday mornings." While some activities are more apt to trigger a sense of deep play than others, "what matters is the mood, not the activity. One can hunt mushrooms with an enthusiasm bordering on mania, find bliss in building a wall of perfectly balanced fieldstone. . . . Deep play can be solemn or rich with laughter.

"On the other hand, one can turn bronco riding into drudgery. One can create mildly. We can live at a low flame. Most people do. We're afraid to look foolish, or feel too extravagantly, or make a mistake, or risk unnecessary pain. . . . But one does need to invite deep play into one's life. A lunchtime bike ride or violin sonata can be intense enough."

The Call of the Wild

Adventure can be an end in itself. Self-discovery
is the secret ingredient that fuels daring.

—Grace Lichtenstein

*I*n today's world, it's hard not to marvel at the thrill seekers, the daredevils, the risk takers, those who push themselves to extreme limits of physical and psychic endurance for the sake of adventure. Whether we see them on television, in films, or on the cover of a magazine, women of all ages seem to answer the call of the wild. Does their audacity, zest, verve, and passion for adventure bring out the green in my eyes? Of course it does. It should in yours as well, because it means we still have a pulse. Even when women like Diane Ackerman admit that these days their adventures are closer to home—cultivating delight in the backyard and outwitting the wild deer determined to dine in the herb garden—I am wistful as I turn the page. The spirit of Diane's exploits never diminishes, just the locale. She has much to teach me and I am so ready to learn.

Today's lesson. Heaven doesn't rank courage, so why do we? Comparing the exploits of heroines, adventuresses, sky divers, explorers, and survivors diminishes every day's profound feats. The ordinary stuns with soulful intensity. In a simple television commercial for an arthritis drug, a woman in her late sixties confides as she goes about her daily round, "I don't want to climb a mountain, I don't want to fly an airplane. I just want to walk up the stairs."

Anyone facing the daily challenge of pushing past the constant pain of a chronic and debilitating illness knows exactly what she means and how much courage even getting out of bed requires. And if we're unable to do that, how much more moxie must be summoned to accept another "useless" day in bed and to be grateful for the hidden gift. "The only courage that matters is the kind that gets you from one moment to the next," the writer Mignon McLaughlin tells us, especially if you're trying to get across the room. You might as well be trying to reach the summit of Mount Everest.

For another woman I know, whose life has shrunk because she's terrified of flying, taking a class to overcome her paralyzing fear is a monumental achievement; and the shuttle from New York to Boston is possibly all the adventure she can handle right now.

A dear friend of mine has a dread of driving because she lived in the city for twenty years and never drove. Recently she moved out to the country, and she can't go grocery shopping, drive her young daughter to a birthday party, or pick up her partner at the train station. I have a similar problem. Although I have a license and feel comfortable driving in the Maryland suburbs, I've barely driven my car in England. This is because I have to learn how to drive on the left-hand side of the road, and I haven't "had time" to get to it. This leaves me dependent on others or a hired cab,

335

which means I can't be spontaneous or visit friends as often as I'd like.

Still, neither of us has done anything yet. Eventually our discomfort and inconvenience will become the instruments of deliverance and we'll stop procrastinating, pick up the phone, and schedule some driving lessons. Then we'll show up. "It's a sad day when you find out that it's not accident or time or fortune but just yourself that kept things from you," the writer and playwright Lillian Hellman tells us in her memoir *Pentimento.* I wonder if she left all the driving to Dashiell Hammett?

We all have our own levels of adventure and excitement within us, and what might be easy for one woman can be excruciating for another. Dining alone; taking up a new sport; redecorating a room in a bold new style; treating yourself to something expensive and totally unnecessary and refusing to feel guilty; cooking for a new group of friends; calling up an old but distant friend; offering an apology to heal an estrangement; standing up for yourself; wearing a dress that calls attention to your attributes, especially if you think you don't have any!

"Was there no one over thirty-five who had not some secret agony, some white-faced fear?" the writer Helen Waddell asked in her novel *Peter Abelard,* written in 1933. "Half one's life one walked carelessly, certain that someday one would have one's heart's desire: and for the rest of it, one either goes empty, or walks carrying a full cup, afraid of every step."

Love Between the Lines

*We read books to find out who we are. What other
people, real or imaginary, do and think and feel is an
essential guide to our understanding of what we ourselves
are and may become.*

—Ursula K. Le Guin

*I*t was a literary seduction. Two writers, both incurable romantics, cross paths in a used-book shop. Unfortunately one of
them had been dead for over a century, giving new meaning to the
expression *foxed with age.* So the woman finds herself enveloped in
the slight sweet, musty fragrance of aged leather and paper, instead
of arms. Nonetheless, the page-perfect adventures she shares with
Sir Richard Francis Burton are pleasurably keeping her up at
night.

While I'm always open to infatuation, I really don't fall in love
too easily with either men or books. I'll flirt like mad, but if a first
conversation or paragraph doesn't give me chills of curiosity or
leave me breathless with anticipation, I lose interest. Still, when I
fall head over heels in love or in lust to learn something new, I fall
hard. While it's true that we read books to find out who we are, we
also fall in love for the same reason. Whether the romance is real or
imaginary, with another person or on the page, we fall in love to
better understand who we are and what we might become.

A Victorian novelist's wildest imagination couldn't have conjured up a hero as dashing and romantic as my latest amour—
Sir Richard Francis Burton—or concocted the magnum opus
that was his life. Burton (1821–90) was a soldier, scientist, spy,
scholar, swordsman, writer, linguist, and the last great British
explorer of the nineteenth century. Darkly handsome and dan-
gerously inquisitive, he pursued women and life's secret mysteries with an ardor that scandalized English society as much as his

exploits enthralled them. Rudyard Kipling based a character in his novel *Kim* on Burton, but only after the English reading public had a frame of reference; otherwise Kipling feared his fiction wouldn't be believable.

Eventually there would be enough true-life adventures to fill more than fifty books by Burton. The intrigue that made him a legend in his own time was a covert pilgrimage in 1853 to the sacred Islamic holy cities of Mecca and Medina, which were forbidden to Western "infidels" or foreigners. However, with his bravado, dramatic flair, and fluency in Arabic (he spoke twenty-nine languages), he was able to pose convincingly as an Afghan physician, even participating in religious rituals undetected. His vivid account of his triumph, *Personal Narrative of a Pilgrimage to El-Medinah and Meccah,* brought him fame around the world. Four years later Burton made headlines again when he became the first white man to venture into the interior of darkest Africa searching for the source of the Nile, a challenge as mind-boggling to the Victorians as walking on the moon would be a century later to their great-great-grandchildren.

However, according to biographer Edward Rice, the most riveting adventure Burton ever undertook was his own safari of the self and spirit. "Burton's adult life was passed in a ceaseless quest for the kind of secret knowledge he labeled broadly as 'Gnosis,' by which he hoped to uncover the very source of existence and the meaning of his role on earth," writes Rice in his masterly biography *Captain Sir Richard Francis Burton.* This restless search led Burton to thoroughly investigate the cabala, alchemy, many religions, the erotic path called tantra, theosophy, spiritualism, and altered states, including extrasensory perception. In fact, Burton coined the term *ESP,* which he described as our "extra-sensuous perception."

Burton's passion pulled him in a thousand different directions, but he always returned to writing. He worked on so many projects simultaneously that he needed eleven separate desks, so that he could turn his attention to whatever undertaking matched one of his many moods. Burton's greatest literary legacy is his uncensored translation of two obscure, exotic, and erotic canons: the Persian *Arabian Nights* (with its tales of Ali Baba, Aladdin, and Sinbad the Sailor) and a Hindu love guide known as the *Kama Sutra.* Here again, Burton went where no Western man had gone before. Rice tells us, "In his writings, Burton opened sexual vistas that Victorian England dared not enter. He was adamant that women enjoy sex as well as men, this at a time when Victorian brides were told at marriage, 'Lie still and think of the Empire.'" Indeed, Burton "helped bring about new attitudes toward sex in the Western world."

I never intend to get over this man.

There's a story that Burton's future wife, Isabel, spent their prolonged engagement (due to his travels and her mother's objections) actively preparing for their marriage by learning to pitch a tent, milk cows, and ride bareback. She even sought out a celebrated English fencer and demanded he take her on as a student. "Whatever for?" he asked. She answered, "So that I can defend Richard, should he be attacked."

One of the greatest joys of armchair passions is that we get to try on different lives of mystery, intrigue, fascination, and romance in the privacy of our homes and different kinds of lovers in the privacy of our hearts. Sometimes long, balmy summer nights can overwhelm us with loneliness; it's so beautiful and there's no one to share it with. Oh yes, there is. Does it *really* matter how you get that gleam in your eye?

By the way, I've taken up fencing. As they say, in love and life one wonderful thing usually leads to another.

Shady Nooks and Racy Books

She would read anything from a dictionary
to a treatise on turnips. Print fascinated her, dazed her,
made her good for nothing.

—Kylie Tennant

*W*hen I was a child, among the great joys of summer were the languid mornings when I would peek my eyes open and realize I didn't have to be anywhere but in bed with a new book. Having no school to go to or specific place to be, I might even finish one book and start another before the rest of the house was up and about. That, to me, was absolutely the best way to start any day. "Only one hour in the normal day is more pleasurable than the hour spent in bed with a book before going to sleep," Dame Rose MacAulay wrote in 1926, "and that is the hour spent in bed with a book after being called in the morning."

The way I see it, as well as being the season for recreation and renewal, summer is also the time to catch up with the reading I've yearned to do during the rest of the year. Inevitably, when I go on vacation, I pack more books that I do clothes (which is saying quite a lot) and certainly more than I could ever read. I'm getting to the point where I can almost leave unopened paperbacks in hotel rooms to lighten the homebound load. Almost.

Part of the pleasure of summer reading is the yearlong anticipation. Deciding what books you'll take along with you on holiday is almost as crucial as deciding what person might make an interesting travel companion. All year long I make lists and tear out clippings from newspapers and magazines: books with appealing reviews, books that were recommended by friends, books by authors I've loved in the past, books about a place or culture that fascinates me, books on topics that have relevance to my life, books by authors I heard interviewed on the radio. As my annual late-August holiday approaches, I take out my list and cull through the clippings, reveling in the selection.

How to choose? This is a nice combination: one or two nonfiction books that will challenge your mind and introduce you to new information; a book of short stories in paperback for those interludes when you're waiting somewhere; a contemporary women's novel; a novel about a place you're visiting that summer, whether it be the hills of Italy or the shores of the Chesapeake; a classic that you want to reread or one you wish you'd read instead of Cliff's Notes when you were in high school. Two or three mysteries, so you have a choice, depending on your mood—one new-to-you sleuth, and an old favorite; maybe one story set in the present and one historical. And finally, one utterly trashy, bad-girl tome—and not this season's saltwater taffy that everyone else is chomping on the beach. You want classy trash: racy (unauthorized) biographies, erotica, perhaps an aphrodisiac cookbook, something so outrageously out of character that it makes you blush to pay for it. Perhaps *Becoming a Sex Goddess in Less Than an Orgasm* or *The Trouble with Boy Toys*. Sadly, these tantalizing titles are pure conjecture, but you get my drift. We all need a little more color in our cheeks and I'm not talking about sunburn. Trust me, the only comment you're likely to get at the cash register is "Cool." Think of this as an exercise to warm up your adventuress reflexes.

But remember, you must leave room on your traveling bookshelf. For what, you ask? For rainy-day trips to local bookstores in resort towns, for slow scavenges through used and rare collections, for the book a friend presses upon you with enthusiasm at the end of a summer barbecue.

For women who love to read, there's nothing better than a vacation that includes long hours spent picking through piles of books and finding the perfect gift for yourself or someone you love. I have a friend who times her yearly trip to a small town in New Hampshire to coincide with a book drive sponsored by the local library. She contributes $20 to the library's coffers and in exchange has the right to take away—for free—as many books as she likes from the thousands piled under tents on the library's front lawn. The books are all donated by townspeople, who themselves come to the drive in search of new books to transport them to other places and times during the next cold New Hampshire winter.

If you think of holidays as opportunities to read books that warm your heart, broaden you mind, carry you away, touch your emotions, or make you think, then you're my kind of gal. "We raked books off the shelves by the dozen and hauled them along on picnics, to haylofts, up oak trees, to bath and to bed," the novelist Kathleen Norris reminisced about summer reading in 1941. "The one terrifying possibility was to find oneself without a book."

But that won't happen to us.

Come to Your Senses

Unsuitable Ladies

"*T*ravellers are always discoverers," Anne Morrow Lindbergh wrote in *North to the Orient,* her memoir describing the exploratory flight she made, as copilot, with her husband, Charles A. Lindbergh. "Our route was new; the air untraveled; the conditions unknown; the stories mythical."

Ever since Eve fled the Garden, intrepid women travelers have been pushing up against man-made boundaries, recording their exploits and scandalizing society. The first woman to write down her adventures—a travel guide on the Holy Land—was a nun named Etheria, who in A.D. 381 traveled to Jerusalem and Egypt in search of what women have always been in search of, the freedom of choice. From Elizabeth Thible, who, in 1784, became the first woman to travel in a hot-air balloon, insisting that the sky was not the limit, to Nellie Bly, the Victorian American journalist who beat the record of Jules Verne's fictional adventure hero Phileas Fogg in *Around the World in Eighty Days,* making the trip in seventy-two days, six hours, and eleven minutes, there's a woman adventuress to inspire each of us.

For centuries women travelers have been behaving boldly with a wink and a wave—crossing deserts, scaling mountains, tramping through the tropics, defying anyone to say they couldn't. We're used to thinking of our life as being limited by outside circumstances, but the tug of war between duty and desire has been a feminine constant. Reading about women who became romantic heroines, sometimes privately, sometimes before the eyes of the world, gives you an entirely new perspective on your own possibilities. "I have accomplished the task which I marked out for myself," Julia Archibald Holmes wrote in 1858 after climbing Colorado's Pikes Peak. "Nearly everyone tried to discourage me from attempting it, but I believed that I should succeed."

If women explorers are new to you, three favorite collections guaranteed to bring out latent wanderlust are *Spinsters Abroad: Victorian Lady Explorers* by Dea Birkett (Oxford, England: Basil Blackwell, 1989, out of print, but worth the search), *Living with Cannibals and Other Women's Adventures* by Michele Slung (Adventure Press/National Geographic Society, 2000), and *Unsuitable for Ladies* by Jane Robinson (Oxford University Press).

A delightful way to travel and see new horizons, from the Arctic to the Amazon, without ever leaving the hammock, is to read about one woman at a time, with both your imagination and your atlas at the ready. Absorb her experiences vicariously. "Often when one sets out on a journey one travels by all the roads according to the latest maps, one reaches all the places of which the history books speak. Duly one rises early and turns one's face towards new countries, carefully looks and laboriously one tries to understand, and for all one's trouble one might have well stayed behind and read a few big archaeology books. But I have you know that is not the way that I have done it," wrote Gertrude Bell, who in 1907 became the first European woman to travel to some parts of the Middle East. There "is a world of history that one sees with the eye and that enters into the mind as no book can relate it."

Hat Tales

I think tomorrow is a say-something-hat day.

—Vida Boheme
To Wong Foo, Thanks for Everything,
Julie Newmar

*B*reathes a woman with soul so dead that never to herself hath said, "I need another hat to adorn my head."

Not on my watch.

Probably what I love the most about intrepid Victorian adventuresses is that these women didn't travel light, and not a one of them would dare venture past her front step without a hat. On my dresser sits a late-nineteenth-century brown tin hatbox painted with the inscription "Lady Sarah's Summer Hats." Much glee, hooting, and hollering when I chanced upon it. For some curious reason, I couldn't negotiate the price. But that, as they say, is another lesson for another day.

Once, I like to imagine, my hatbox traveled on trains and steamers, in sampans or *dahabeeyahs,* on the backs of camels, mules, or elephants, in the hands of her porter or personal maid, ensuring that the mysterious Lady Sarah's crowning glories would arrive safely, no matter where her wanderings took her. Now it safeguards the accoutrements of my future adventures—pastel silk flowers, bits of tulle and netting, a curvaceous scarlet ostrich feather, vintage Bakelite buttons, silk ribbons, sequined swirls, lace, a rhinestone shoe buckle, and hat pins rescued from oblivion on different outings at flea markets and antiques venues. Charming coquettes wait patiently in my millinery fantasies for reincarnation when I trim my next hat.

There is no point of departure for a woman like the one that occurs when she tries on a hat. "A hat is a shameless flatterer, calling attention to an escaping curl, a tawny braid, a sprinkling of freckles over a pert nose, directing the eye to what is most unique about a face. Its curves emphasize a shining pair of eyes, a lofty forehead; its deep brim accentuates the pale tint of a cheek, creates an aura of prettiness, suggests a mystery that awakens curiosity in the onlooker," Jeanine Larmoth writes in *Victoria: The Romance of Hats*. "Few women have ever been able to resist the temptation to try on a hat and discover in the mirror a person they never suspected was there. A hat alters the image we have of ourselves, and the image others see as well. For the hours we wear it, it brings out different dimensions in our personality, much as a costume aids an actress in her role."

The right hat encapsulates our personality. It may also enliven our imagination of the past. Though we might not be comfortable walking around in some garments that were the height of fashion in another era (such as a bustier or bustle), an old-fashioned cloche, a picture hat, or a toque trimmed with a pouf of polka-dotted veiling is just enough to make us *feel* as if we were living in another, romantic age.

Years ago, there were shops devoted solely to millinery. Now, there are so few that a good accessory department must do. Visit several (some stores with small hat departments stock only a few styles), and try on a broad palette of designs and colors, turning them this way and that to discover what flatters your face, head shape, and hair, as well as what looks best for your overall fashion style and body scale. Try brims of different widths, hats with crowns of different depths, caps with visors of different degrees of projection. Tilt a beret or boater, try it smack-dab horizontal. Check your profile in a three-way mirror, if you can. Some fancy hats are deliberately asymmetrical, so don't be thrown by a roller-coaster brim or one of varying widths. When in doubt about what is the front, be guided by the hatmaker's label or the seam of the crown, both of which should be at the center back.

But don't feel you must wear a hat exactly as the manufacturer imagined it. Turn a trimmed chapeau along its circumference to see where its ornament might look best. Flip soft brims up, down, or part up and part down. If the hats of a certain era appeal to you, look for models whose styling you might enhance with a bit of fiddling or extra trim.

Natural straw hats tend to be fairly stiff and also tend to shed; and such hats do not take well either to attempts to reshape or to pack them. Much as I hate most things synthetic, some mixed-fiber hats have more "give" in the crown, allowing you to change the position of the brim, and protecting against the crush in a suitcase. And don't overlook the wonderful new hats made from woven paper or a mixture of paper and cotton. While they don't stand up well to rain, alas, they are softer and lighter than straw and are available in scrumptious shades. If you like a tailored look, test lightweight fedoras and panama hats offered by men's haberdashers, which, by the way, often have a broader range of hat sizes than a woman's store will carry.

I adore buying plain, inexpensive hats and trimming them on languorous summer afternoons. There are few crises that can't be completely forgotten, at least for a little while, when I'm trimming a hat. And it's so easy. Simple off-white or tan straw ornamented with something that picks up the color of your eyes or outfit makes you feel very pulled together, especially when you're not. Suddenly you're chic. Insouciant.

A veil can bring on more shenanigans than forgetting your silk underpants.

And goodness rarely has *anything* to do with what happens next. Just remember, a *lady* never removes her hat. Or so I've heard.

Once you find a favorite, flattering shape—and you will, that's the fabulous thing about hats—you simply change the band. Take care that trimmings are securely fastened; a secret safety pin or two, fixed from inside, will keep a scarf or blossom just where you want it. If you want to be sure, however, simple basting with thread will keep your trimmings in place.

I've learned the sad way that storing hats on a flat surface rather than on a hook maintains the shape. I've also learned that it is almost impossible to reshape a straw hat that has been distorted or squashed. Longer-term storage of any hats (except all-fabric or crushable-fiber) is best in inexpensive cardboard (not plastic) hatboxes. Lightly stuff the crown of the hat with crumpled white tissue or a bit of netting to help keep its shape.

The English critic J. B. Priestley believed that when it came to women and fashion, particularly their hats, there was one grand illusion we all shared: that "with necessary swaps and alterations, beauty and witchery can emerge, that somewhere here is the beginning of an enchanted life." Or at the very least, another grand adventure.

Come to Your Senses

Here Comes the Sun

"*P*assion is what the sun feels for the earth," the Victorian poet Ella Wheeler Wilcox wrote in 1888. "When harvests ripen into golden birth." Bite into a golden peach or

August-ripened plum and you will have no trouble whatsoever understanding why the ancients worshiped the sun.

When summer fruits are in season, solitude can be one of life's most heady pleasures: juice dripping down our chin, cheeks smeared with the concentrated indulgence of a toddler discovering the multisensory pleasures of her first Popsicle. Making love to Life with an intoxicating food can be *such* a messy business. Don't worry, no one is a voyeur in an orchard.

All deep yellow and golden fruits are not only succulent, but good for what ails both the soul and our often undernourished bodies. Mother Nature's passion fruits are loaded with vitamins A and C, and minerals, including potassium, that are easily depleted in the heat. But don't be *too* quick to eat them: get fruit not fully ripe and let it swell in flavor near you, to appreciate its perfume for its own sake. Let your mouth water in contemplation of the tastes awaiting you. Allow your fingers and lips to be surprised by the fruit's almost liquid tenderness.

Velvety apricots and peaches—both of which date back to ancient China—and their fuzzless sister fruit, nectarines, really come into their glory this month. They can be enjoyed on their own—soft, tart skin and sweeter flesh forming a perfect complement—or added for a fresh burst of flavor to a wide variety of desserts—oh, the deep-dish pies and cobblers of summer!

These fruits are also superb sliced or diced and combined with a small quantity of matching brandy (e.g., apricots with apricot brandy) or an orange liqueur such as Cointreau mixed half and half with white wine—indulge your eye by serving them in a champagne glass for extra elegance.

Should a fresh purchase prove disappointingly bland, despite your expectations based upon scent and appearance (alas, rosy flesh is not a dependable indication of sweetness or intensity), you can enhance the flavor. Briefly simmer apricots, peaches, golden plums, or nectarines over low heat in a concentrated lemonade (per cup of water, one-half cup sugar plus one tablespoon fresh lemon juice)—just enough to cover—and then chill them in the liquid.

The arrival of sultry weather provides the perfect atmosphere and opportunity in which to explore the magnificent golden fruits of the tropics:

Mangoes (although imported into the States year-round) are

marketed homegrown from Florida in early summer. When fully ripe, their soft kid-leathery skin strips off to reveal yellow-to-deep-orange flesh as luscious as custard; in fact, you can simply punch a hole in the skin to "drink" the fruit! The scent is simply sensational, evocative of peaches and yet totally distinct.

Passion fruit is a native of Brazil, but is also available in its Floridian variety come summer. (Although its name certainly does well to describe its deliciousness, it derives from the fruit's flowers, whose various parts are thought to represent aspects of the Passion of Christ.) Pale violet, gold, or red, and egg-sized (think nonfuzzy kiwi), the dull-rinded fruit can be deceptively bland in appearance. But cut through the skin—when it begins to "give," the fruit is ripe—and you'll be rewarded with juicy, golden pulp studded with dark, edible seeds . . . and a scent simply out of this world! Use sparingly, almost as a flavoring agent, in fruit-based drinks, salads, or sauces, as both the taste and the fragrance can easily overwhelm milder ingredients.

The green or rosy, thin-skinned papaya, whose sweetly, almost floral scented flesh of deep yellow cups a cluster of edible, peppery black seeds, is a relative of the passion fruit. Sliced, it is a wonderful addition to fruit salads; seeds scooped out, it also forms a lovely little boat for savory fillings, such as a scoop of poultry- or ham-based salad. If not too ripe, it can also be cubed for summer shish kebabs, alternated on skewers with marinated meat. Sprinkle the seeds upon salads for a delightfully spicy lift.

The flavor of guavas, like that of kiwis, has been compared with that of strawberries, bananas, and pineapple—but it is uniquely its own. The heavy perfume of the fruit might take some getting used to, as might the surprisingly spicy edge to its taste—keep in mind that it is related to allspice and cloves! The gloriously pink flesh makes a lovely addition to sweeter drinks, sauces, or salads made from yellower fruits of the season.

Here's a sun worshiper's Golden Goblet for One:

You will need:

1 ripe peach, skinned
½ ripe papaya, skinned
¼ ripe cantaloupe
1 teaspoon lemon or lime juice

Pinch of salt
1 tablespoon culinary-grade rose water

1. Cut fruit into ½-inch cubes. Combine all ingredients in a glass bowl, cover with plastic wrap, and chill for several hours.
2. Slowly and blissfully devour.

The Adventure of Accomplishment

She listens to her own tales, laughs at her own jokes, and follows her own advice.

—Ama Ata Aidoo

Several years ago I met a woman in Italy who was so accomplished it was thrilling to be in her company. Chief among her many talents was the ability to change a flat tire by herself on a pitch-black country road dressed in a long, flowing skirt. *Uno, due, tre! E molto facile!* Afterward, over a glass of grappa, I confided that when I grew up, I wanted to be exactly like her. She laughed because we're the same age. "Life seems to throw many more adventures your way when you're prepared," she said. "It's very sexy knowing how to take care of yourself." Since Sylvania never seemed to lack for charming admirers, I did not dismiss lightly her cosmic word concerning some of Life's overlooked adventures. Wouldn't it be wonderful to:

Go to a party alone with contentment, not resentment
Write a love letter
Recite three poems
Deliver five new jokes a year
Tell a captivating story
Give a toast
Accept a compliment
Complain effectively
Distract a child
Calm a fear
Disarm an adversary with wit
Recover from criticism with grace
Make the perfect comeback
Offer a suggestion, instead of advice
Belt out a great torch song

Administer CPR for both adults and children
Perform the Heimlich maneuver on others and yourself
Stop profuse bleeding
Dress a wound
Treat severe burns
Make a splint
Remove a tick; soothe a bee sting; extract a splinter

Pitch a tent
Build a fire
Bait a hook, catch a fish, fry it in a pan, and fillet it on the plate
Mark a trail

Change a tire; check the oil
Replace a fuse
Use a fire extinguisher

Pop a champagne cork
Order wine in a restaurant
Mix a perfect martini
Prepare a soufflé
Get the garlic smell off your hands and breath
Throw a cocktail party

Eat an artichoke
Give a dinner party for eight and enjoy it!

Put on a condom
Self-examine your breasts
Buy the right-size bra
Wrap a sarong

Use a drill, choose the right screwdriver, hammer a nail and
    not your thumb
Hang a picture alone
Tie three different kinds of knots
Thread a needle; sew on a button
Program the VCR
Swim a lap; stay afloat
Drive in snow; handle a skid
Read a map; give flawless directions
Protect your privacy on the Web
Play chess and two card games—one naughty, one nice
Know three after-dinner party games other than charades
Place a bet, roll dice
Shoot pool
Throw a dart, land a punch
Serve an ace, swing a bat, bowl a strike, dribble a ball, make a
    basket, sink a putt
Saddle, mount, and ride a horse
Understand the etiquette of watching ball games
Behave well at a gaming table

Strike up a conversation; keep up your end of it
Ask interesting questions
Make a graceful exit
Flirt with a stranger across a crowded room
Be conversant in a second language and polite in two more
Convey "Sorry, not interested" convincingly
Say "You had your chance" with a smile. Mean it
Know you accept or extend an apology only once
Take a good picture (both as subject and photographer)
Pack for a two-week trip using only one suitcase

"She was learning to love moments. To love moments for themselves," is how the poet Gwendolyn Brooks described a woman who sounds like the girl I want to be when I grow up. How about you? As we begin to exult in our adventures in self-possession, we'll know just how she did it.

Past Forgetting

How we remember, what we remember, and why we remember form the most personal map of our individuality.

—Christina Baldwin

*W*hen we think of embarking on an adventure, many of us picture packing, plane tickets, and maybe even donning a pith helmet, à la Karen Blixen in *Out of Africa*. But rainy summer afternoons can provide us with some unorthodox adventures on the wings of memory.

Attics are great August destinations. Even if you, unlike the rest of womankind, have everything neatly packed away in labeled boxes, "the past is never where you think you left it," the novelist Katherine Anne Porter tells us. When we depart on sentimental journeys, we discover how right she was.

Where is your past? Is it in your attic or basement, or at your mother's or sister's? Was it accidentally left behind at your former husband's house? If remnants of your childhood or your life as a young mother aren't physically located in places where you can easily retrieve them, you might want to gently broach a conversation with the past. This is especially important if you, like a woman in Carrie Fisher's novel *Delusions of Grandma,* have become "a chronicler of absence," only recalling what is missing from your life. When our lives feel empty and lacking, it's often because we're giving too little notice to all that we've lived through or that's surrounding us or all that we're so desperately trying to overlook. You'd be amazed at how forcefully Denial persists until we finally pay attention; how less frequently migraine headaches, heart palpitations, or spasmodic lower-back pain occur when the emotionally unarticulated at last gets to have a brief chat with us. Think of the past as a swirl of psychic energy hovering just above your head. Now push it down forcefully. Where do you think it goes? I've gotten to the point where I ask, "Who'd like a word with me?" and head out the door for a walk before I automatically pop a painkiller. Often by the time I'm back, whatever was bothering me isn't anymore.

But beyond therapeutics, revisiting our past through sorting our memorabilia can be thrilling. A friend was helping her father sift through the contents of her grandmother's attic when suddenly they found a dusty projection reel along with a shoe box full of film. They had long been thought lost, unrecoverable, and her dad was jubilant at having found them. Suddenly the day took a delightful detour. While her father fiddled, her mother rearranged furniture and her sister prepared popcorn, my friend wondered what all the festive fuss was about. As unfamiliar faces flashed in front of them, moving soundlessly in outdated bathing suits and funny glasses, my friend's oohs and aahs were punctuated by the sound of her parents' laughter. The film revealed a personal history my friend had no prior knowledge of. Suddenly a little boy ran in front of the camera, chasing a herd of yellow baby chicks. The boy, of course, was her father, though it certainly took my friend a few minutes to recognize him. She told me that she felt as if she'd suddenly inherited a priceless family heirloom, which is a beautiful way to think of memories that pay a surprise visit. "Even though you've given up a past it hasn't given you up," Susan Glaspell wrote in 1939. "It comes uninvited—and sometimes half welcome."

I've also watched spellbound as an exuberant little girl leaps in plastic pools, curtseys in daisy crowns, stars in backyard musicals, preens and adroitly prances in lace-trimmed ankle socks and her mother's high heels. "You were *so* cute," I tell her with genuine admiration. "You still *are*," she says, returning the compliment.

When we sort through personal memorabilia, retrieving mementos and photographs from banged-up, battered, and anonymous boxes, and placing what's still precious in suitable *labeled* containers, our sense memories are triggered. Like distant cousins at a family reunion, each eager to share a recollection, the old letters, snowflake paperweights, matchbooks, and playbills can transport you immediately back to another time, another place, another you. But if they don't, be willing to let go of them. The bottle of your grandmother's perfume? Of course, save it. The empty box from an old Christmas cosmetic freebie? No, it won't come in handy to hold your daughter's barrettes because you'll forget you put them there. Better choice: a clear, plastic shoe box.

You can't reproduce or replace your son's first finger painting (or your own), but don't leave it squirreled away. Instead, frame it and hang the memory where it will trigger a smile. But one macaroni pin is really all you need. All right, two. One for you and one for him. But that's it.

The scent of love enveloped in a folded handkerchief, the feel of plush bears, flannel shirts, an old beach blanket (still with sand after all these years!), a pair of go-go boots, or a pressed flower found in a book of poems reunite us once again to what we were never meant to lose. It may only be up or down a staircase, but as the Victorian novelist Sarah Orne Jewett says, "The road was new to me, as roads always are, going back."

Come to Your Senses

Soda Fountain Sojourns

*S*ometimes when we travel back, memories we'd just as soon not recall come flooding in. We remember the young girl who always felt like an outsider, who served punch at the dance rather than taking to the floor herself, who quickly passed the popular kids' hangout so that no one would suspect how much she wanted to be invited to join them. If there's a flashback that makes you wince, just fast-forward to stop at something sweetly wistful, such as a sentimental sojourn to the soda shoppe.

When I think of the frothy fountain treats from my wonder years, it isn't just the jukebox or black-and-white ice-cream sodas I remember. It's the bad girls! Ponytails, poodle skirts, bobby socks, saddle shoes, and pointed breasts sticking out of cotton sweaters—mountains looming large above the landscape of unattainable love—as Moon Doggie shared his Coke float with Gidget. Was there ever a femme fatale as impossible to live up to as Sandra Dee? Thank God we stopped trying.

Remember instead the heavenly sipping and slurping: shakes, malts, egg creams, floats, and ice-cream sodas. When was the last time you had one? When was the last time you made one? How about this afternoon?

For the ice-cream soda you'll need flavored syrups (chocolate, vanilla, or fruit-flavored) and whatever flavor ice cream you love, remembering that fruit sodas, such as cherry, will taste best with vanilla. The basic proportion and method is easy. Take two tablespoons flavored syrup, one cup seltzer or any flavored soda (except ginger ale, which often turns unpleasantly scummy when mixed with ice cream), and one large scoop of ice cream.

Place the syrup and seltzer in a tall glass and stir. Be sure the glass is big enough to allow a couple of inches above the mixture for the ice cream. Now carefully "plop" the scoop of ice cream on top of the liquid. Let it settle slowly so that a foam top rises, then sip through a straw. Now I'm not one for suggesting fancy gourmet equipment, but the minor investment of an ice-cream scoop really is necessary to achieve the desired effect—time travel.

The exotic egg cream contains neither eggs nor cream, but is rich in nostalgia. One sip has been known to induce visions of ceiling fans, dark mahogany booths carved with pledges that Sal will love Angela forever, and elongated shadows swing-dancing on the cool mosaic-tiled floor. It also couldn't be easier to whip one up:

You will need:

2 tablespoons chocolate syrup (traditionally, Fox's U-Bet, but
    others will do)
¾ cup cold milk
½ cup seltzer (and it must be seltzer, not fizzy springwater)

Layer into a tall glass in order of list, and stir gently.

"Pictures of my life stretch back," the English writer Sheila Kaye-Smith wrote in her 1937 memoir, *Three Ways Home.* "They are not movies, nor are they talkies, but they are quite distinctly feelies." Especially when August tastes of egg creams.

Travels of an Independent Woman

*The Possible's slow fuse is lit
By the Imagination.*

—Emily Dickinson

"*M*ost of us, I suppose, have had at one time or another the impulse to leave behind our daily routines and responsibilities and seek out, temporarily, a new life," Pulitzer Prize winner Alice Steinbach admits in her charming memoir *Without Reservations: The Travels of an Independent Woman.* "I daydreamed about having the freedom to travel wherever chance or fancy took me, unencumbered by schedules and obligations and too many preplanned destinations." However, even though she was single, her sons were grown, there was money in the bank, and her career was assured, she dismissed her desires as impractical, unreasonable, and undoable.

The fantasy begged to differ, and "sprang out at odd times. In the middle of the night, I would get up and start figuring what such a plan might cost and how to finance it. I spent hours in the bookstore's travel section poring over possible destinations. At dinner, talking and laughing with friends, I would wonder about my capacity to be a woman in a strange city, without friends."

Alice began to have vivid dreams, both day and night versions. "They seemed to signal a willingness on my part to go where the moment took me and to trust it would take me to an interesting place. They also reminded me of how it felt to approach every day as I once had, guided less by expectations than by curiosity."

Finally, the day came when her fantasy gathered the momentum of a tropical storm named Alice and demanded her attention: "*Take the risk. Say 'Yes' to life instead of 'No.'*" Alice decided to make real her lifelong dream to go to Paris and live for a month in a little hotel on the Left Bank. "I wanted to take chances. To have more adventures. To learn the art of talking less and listening more. To see if I could still hack it on my own, away from the security of work, friends and an established identity. Of course, I also wanted to lose ten pounds, find the perfect haircut, pick up an Armani suit at 70 percent off, and meet Yves Montand's twin, who would fall deeply, madly in love with me."

Instead, she fell in love with herself and with Life.

The expression *independent woman* or *woman of independent means* used to describe a woman who could take care of herself financially. But money doesn't make a woman independent, and the lack of it can't prevent her from being independent. What makes a woman independent is her imagination, and that she doesn't consider her fantasies mere whims but holy whispers of what's Possible.

I'm not heading off to Paris today, and probably neither are you.

Doesn't matter. What matters is that you give your fantasy the respect it deserves.

Distance Lends Enchantment

One should know the value of Life better than to pout any part of it away.

—Hester-Lynch Piozzi (1789)

"*I* like any place that isn't here," the writer Edna Ferber sighed in 1922. So do I, today. But here I am and here it looks like I'll be at least for the foreseeable future.

Is there a place that tugs at your spirit, but you just can't make the trip? Whether we're kept at home due to a lack of money or circumstances that rule out travel—perhaps the country is too dangerous right now, or the terrain too daunting for us to visit comfortably—there are still many ways to visit. Time might be a problem as well; not just taking the time to get there, but finding the right era when you arrive. Perhaps you'd really like to have visited fifty or a hundred years ago. All my life I've been waiting to see the Pyramids, but for the last couple of years I haven't felt it was really safe to travel there. After my trip up the Nile was postponed once again, I watched *The English Patient* for about the tenth time, longing to check into Cairo's Shepard's Hotel as Kristin Scott Thomas and Ralph Fiennes did. Michael Ondaatje's characters were there in 1939. Unfortunately the hotel burned to the ground in 1952. When you feel a pout coming on, it's important to be specific about the source of your discontent. The Egypt I really want to visit can now only be reached through my imagination, or the imagination of authors and filmmakers.

The plot is secondary. What you're looking for is a "fix" of the place itself: the scenery, the language or accent, the sounds and action of the street life that could only take place *there*. If you've exhausted the resources of your video store, you can search out local universities, which often organize minifestivals of foreign or small independent films. Use Internet search engines to locate films with a particular setting. And much vicarious experience can be had through cable or radio stations aimed at particular ethnic audiences or people who enjoy those cultures.

Another great way to keep your finger on the pulse of another city or region—in our own country or a foreign one—is to search for the Web sites of local newspapers. Read the supplements to immerse yourself in what's really going on *there*. What are the upcoming events this week, what plays or concerts have just been reviewed, what restaurants have recently opened? Is there a "living" section that discusses local food, decor, clothing, child care? Is there a classifieds section? Reading job and housing listings is a great way to indulge a fantasy. If a periodical dealer near you carries a magazine or newspaper from your dream place, you might find it worth the investment to buy it regularly—actually to hold in your hand what *comes* from there.

Satisfy yourself with books, especially novels, set in your dream locale. Hold off on the travel guides for now; they might make you feel more miserable if you really can't buy a plane ticket or find time to go. However, books of photos, regional art, food, costume, architecture, social issues, even children's books set in or about another land, are amazing placebos. And don't overlook recordings that capture the indigenous music. Or if you ache to hear someone else speaking another language, audiobooks in that language can be bought or rented.

Do you miss products that you used while visiting another country or that come from a specific region of your own country— a particular kind of chocolate bar or soap, A1-size writing paper? Here's where travel guides can come in handy with the names of shops that might do mail order. You can also look on the Web for on-line sources. If you live in or can travel to a large city, see if a specialty or ethnic shop there might have your favorite product. Even medium cities across the country have stores carrying Central and South American, Indian, Middle Eastern, Russian, and Chinese products to serve their local immigrant population: everything from spices to fabric to cookware can be found.

The point is, where there's desire, there never really are that many degrees of separation. As Queen Marie of Romania tells us, "Nothing's far when one wants to get there." It's only despair, not delay, that does dreams in.

Vacationing at Home

The great and recurrent question about abroad is, is it worth the trouble of getting there?

—Dame Rose MacAulay

"This is what holidays, travels, vacations, are about," Shana Alexander reminds us this morning. "It is not really rest or even leisure we chase. We strain to renew our capacity for wonder, to shock ourselves into astonishment once again."

Well, dear Reader, we don't have to go very far to do that.

What's a secret pleasure of every vacation? Coming home. That's right. And guess what. We're already here! Rediscovering your own town or city, or a neighboring area, as if you're a tourist, can be a wonderful vacation. You'll have so much fun, you'll wonder why you didn't think of this years ago.

Or even last week. Perhaps our day in, day out drudgery and *Who'd want to live here?* attitude is a killjoy?

Can you spend a weekend at a local inn or that darling little bed-and-breakfast with a reputation for beautiful decor and service? You may have passed these places all the time thinking, "Gee, that place looks like fun." How about finding out?

Pretend you're a tourist and you've selected your hometown as the perfect spot to visit for an unpretentious, relaxing, and delightful getaway. Work with me here, babe. I've been here and done this and had a ball. So will you. Are there museums and galleries or famous buildings that, again, you sort of know about, but not really? So many people who live or work near landmarks haven't even glanced at or in them. Visit your chamber of commerce and learn what tourists who are visiting your area seek out *on purpose*. Read about the history of important local buildings, their architecture, their unique archives. See which registered landmarks offer guided tours of their interior. Are there statues commemorating battles, famous people? Do you know what or whom they represent? Find out.

And while you're at it, read up on the history of your town. Who founded it? What area developed first? What industries was it known for, perhaps is still known for? Did your family come to the area generations ago? Where did your grandparents or parents live? In what house was your great-aunt born? Where did your ancestors go to school, or work? If your family has lived in the same area for a long time, a terrific walking tour could be designed around your family's history. Start the route where the oldest member lived and work your way toward where you now live. How many layers of change have there been on the streets and in the buildings you pass through on that tour? Have meadows given way to pavements, and then those to malls or plazas? Are old family homes still standing? If you are lucky, the current residents might let you inside for a peek.

When I went back to visit my first home, I was so shocked to find out how tiny it was! In my memory it was a mansion. And the three-block walk to my grammar school was one of the most satisfying trips I've *ever* taken. You can't imagine how wondrous it was to tell that little girl, still walking slowly by herself, dawdling because there was really no place to go, that she had in fact moved on. It was as if I'd discovered a small, bewildered ghost, neither here nor there, still lollygagging in longing. We laughed, we cried, we were both so grateful she could cross over from mourning to memory. "I have learned this strange thing," Helen Bevington wrote in *When Found, Make a Verse Of.* "One may return to a place, and quite unexpectedly, meet oneself still lingering there from the last time."

Look up your ancestors' school yearbooks, go to the local library and find newspaper articles about their marriages, births, deaths in the town archives. What were your favorite streets when you were a kid? Which house did you always wish you lived in?

Are there parks, town squares, market areas, that you have never taken the time to sit in? Spend a sunny hour on a bench or stoop, watching the world—your world—go by. It's especially interesting to do this early in the morning, just before shops are opening or business begins or while an outdoor market is just setting up: watch the streets come awake, *become* the place you perhaps take for granted.

What about the restaurants you've been wanting or meaning to try and haven't? Even if they are pricey, sneak a look inside. You might be able to get away with ordering very little (soup or coffee, for instance), for the experience of sitting there and soaking up the atmosphere. One friend who lives in New York on a freelance writer's budget took another friend along to the famous Russian Tea Room and all they ordered was . . . tea! Yes, their tea cost them $25, but it came with scrumptious petits fours, and it made them feel like a million dollars.

What shops in your town or neighborhood hold the most appeal to tourists? Again, you may often have passed such stores without even quite seeing them. Museum shops are a great place for vicarious travel and are wonderful places to find gifts. What would a tourist bring home to remind her of where you live? Amuse yourself by trying to find the kitschiest example (no, you don't need to actually *buy* it!). Or, become genuinely knowledgeable about a local crafts industry that you were perhaps unaware of.

Create a memory of your "vacation" by getting some postcards of local scenery that you had never thought to photograph; keep a paper napkin or take-away menu from a restaurant you tried; save the floor plan or exhibit information from a museum. In fact, it would be nice to create a small album of *your* history within this town. What you've seen here, what you've done. How much you've overlooked and missed until now.

As the poet Cynthia Ozick succinctly put it when describing her weariness with travel, "Finally one tires / of so many spires." But we *never* tire of unexpected pleasure.

Come to Your Senses

Memories Are Made of This

*A*t the end of the summer we ask ourselves how many long afternoons and evenings did we savor? Or we should. How many seasonal pleasures did we seek and luxuriate in? How many summer tastes were not only indulged but encouraged? "Summer's freedom has its own flavors: watermelon from the farm stand and suppers that are just a matter of boiling water for the fresh-picked corn and slicing some tomatoes. It's the season for impromptu desserts, for chasing the drips down the cone or slicing the red strawberries and pouring the cream," Catherine Calvert reminisces. "It's finally baking that pie, the one with all the nutmeg, when the peaches arrive. Has anyone ever had too many strawberries or peaches, or too many blueberries eaten from the bucket while perched on a stone wall? Even ice pops, in colors nature never knew, have their place."

How about a new dessert to close the season? The sublime English Summer Pudding. Like the Christmas pudding, this treat is an annual event.

Authentic summer puddings include raspberries, blackberries, and red and black currants; however, other kinds of berries that are at their brightest and juiciest wherever you live will also provide a tasty dessert. Just make sure that it's a mixture of berries. This recipe is an especially fine way to deal with a batch of fresh berries that are a trifle too sour for raw consumption: cooking them down in a syrup of their own juices mixed with sugar banishes their acidity while heightening their very berry-ness. The following recipe will make two generous portions. Begin your preparations the day before you plan to serve or consume it yourself.

Summer Pudding

You will need:

1 pint (2 cups) mixed berries
½ cup granulated sugar
About half a dozen ¼-inch-thick slices of plain white bread or challah, crusts removed

1. Place berries and sugar in a small, nonreactive saucepan (glass or stainless steel) and bring slowly to a boil over low heat, stirring constantly. Continue to cook for around 5 minutes, until fruit is soft and juicy.
2. Line a 1-quart, round mixing bowl, small casserole, or nonaluminum pudding basin with 2-inch-wide strips of bread (cut the crust off), covering base and sides completely.
3. Pour in the berry mixture, and top with a layer of bread. Cover with plastic wrap.

4. Set another bowl of slightly smaller diameter than the first bowl upon the top layer of bread, and weigh down with something heavy (a few large cans, perhaps) so that the bread presses deeper into the mold.
5. Place the weighted bowl in your refrigerator to chill and compress overnight.
6. To serve, run a knife around the edge of the mold, place a rimmed dish or shallow bowl upside down upon it, and invert. The juices will have soaked through the sides and base of the bread for a jewel-colored soft pudding you will be glad not to have to share with anyone else.

Between the Lines

Running Away to Serenity

Though many a house has sheltered me in the course of summers past, one memory serves to tie them all. It's early afternoon and all is sweet peace. Just a shift of the pillows sets the porch swing swaying gently—pillows covered in faded chintz with the slight musty scent that attests to their long winter's nap in the shed. The book lying tented across my chest is slightly musty too, foxed with the brown spots of age, since it was left downstairs in the bookcase thirty or forty years ago. You may be sure there's nothing in it to tax the brain: It's a romance and Cressida and Percy are settling their futures over a game of tennis. But I shall simply revel in the pleasures of the present, listening to the burr of the lawn mower down the road, watching the hornets busy themselves with their nest, biting into the slice of lemon I've finished with my iced tea.

Ah, the joys of a summer place! . . . Making our house our own was always easy. We could add what we liked—and subtract. Sometimes we'd spend the first few hours hiding the owners' plastic lobsters, fake fishnets, and seagull mobiles in the deep dark closet to allow a clean sweep for our time there. . . . Drape a Marseilles spread over the sofa, swap the lamps around, drag the softest chair into the landing that overlooks the lake—all is permissible, all is comfortable. . . . Someone would gather a bucket of irresistible shells, as pink as the first light of morning, and scatter them along the mantelpiece. There were always tomatoes ripening on the windowsills and handfuls of berries found on country lanes. A seagull feather was dropped on the duck decoy, and wildflowers filled every jelly glass, shedding their petals on the table. . . . We'd line the sideboard with jars of beach plum jelly from the Ladies Beautification Committee Fair and hang a watercolor of a rose discovered at a tag sale— and consider all of it quite beautiful indeed (if anyone had paused to look in between dashes to the tennis courts or bike rides to the beach).

> —Catherine Calvert
> "Porch Swings, Old Novels, and Memories
> of Summer Past"
> *The Quiet Center: Women Reflecting on Life's
> Passages from the Pages of Victoria Magazine*

Autumn . . . asks that we prepare for the future —
that we be wise in the ways of garnering and keeping.
But it also asks that we learn to let go — to acknowledge
the beauty of sparseness.

—B. W. Overstreet (1947)

September's sweet afterglow reminds us that sometimes it's difficult to distinguish between bad luck and new beginnings. Let the turning of the seasons gently instruct you in the art of choosing your losses. We're swapping tales of mythical women . . . honoring secret anniversaries of the heart . . . healing with tender mercies . . . cozy naps, scented sleep pillows, sensuous sulking, apple dumpling days. So lead yourself into temptation with perfectly plausible passions. Life's only sin is a day without desire and a night without thanks.

The Season of Relinquishment

There is a time, when passing through a light,
that you walk in your own shadow.

—Keri Hulmee

The English poet Elizabeth Barrett Browning believed that her husband, the poet Robert Browning, whom she married when she was forty, had loved her into "full being." For most of my life, I assumed that this sublime sense of completion was only found in Love's reciprocal promise. But the coming of autumn makes me wonder if Loss hasn't also been an attentive suitor. Why? Because it was only during the lonely and bereft times that I finally learned how to love myself; only during the seasons of relinquishment that I could clearly discern between my needs and my wants; only by searching through the rubble of what was missing that I discovered the overlooked; only after sorrow isolated me from the world that I was forced to become a woman of my own devices. But when I did, I began to reach toward an intimacy that I always sought in others. Now I've found it with the least likely person—myself.

It was extremely comforting to discover that this was always part of the Divine Plan for woman.

In *Eve's Diary,* as translated "from the original" by Mark Twain, the first female is having a difficult time adjusting to her surroundings. The man, whose soul mate she's meant to be, resents her presence and is doing his best to ignore her. Eve is left to explore Eden on her own, but she's so bewildered by her first loss she doesn't quite know what to do.

My first sorrow. Yesterday he avoided me and seemed to wish
I would not talk to him. I could not believe it, and thought there
was some mistake, for I loved to be with him, and loved to hear

him talk, and so how could it be that he could feel unkind
towards me when I had not done anything? But at last it seemed
true, so I went away and sat lonely in the place where I first saw
him in the morning that we were made . . . but now it was a
mournful place, and every little thing spoke of him, and my
heart was very sore. I did not know why very clearly, for it was a
new feeling; I had not experienced it before, and it was all a
mystery, and I could not make it out.

But when night came I could not bear the lonesomeness, and
went to the new shelter which he had built, to ask him what I
had done that was wrong and how I could mend it and get back
his kindness again; but he put me out in the rain, and it was my
first sorrow.

Four days into Eden and woman is asking man what's she's
done wrong.

Well, sometimes there's nothing to do but make the best of it.
Eve wanders off by herself and chances upon a beautiful moss-
bank where she can sit and put her feet into the water. When she
does, she catches her own lovely reflection. Still pining for the sighs
wistfully. "But it is something and something is better than utter
loneliness."

But then Eve discovers this unexpected Other is responsive to
her. "It talks when I talk; it is sad when I am sad; it comforts me
with its sympathy; it says "Do not be down-hearted, you poor
friendless girl; I will be your friend," and "it *is* a good friend to
me and my only one."

Suddenly, a passing cloud blots out her reflection. Eve panics at
the thought of losing her only true friend. The man's rejection was
one thing, but to lose herself is a despair she cannot even begin to
cope with.

She was all I had, and now she is gone! I cannot bear my life
any more! . . . and so I hid my face in my hands, and there was no
solace for me. [But] when I took them away, after a little, there
she was again, white and shining and beautiful and I sprang into
her arms! That was perfect happiness; I had known happiness
before, but it was not like this, which was ecstasy. I never doubted
her afterwards. Sometimes she stayed away—maybe an hour,

maybe almost the whole day, but I waited and did not doubt; I
said, "She is busy, or she is gone a journey, but she will come."
And it was so: she always did. . . . Many and many are the visits
I have paid her; she is my comfort and my refuge when my life is
hard—and it is mainly that.

Although grief is a universal passage, loss is deeply personal. But we are not meant to bear it alone. The clouds may cast temporary shadows, but your Essensual Self, the companion who has been with you from the beginning, is still patiently waiting for you, like the lovely reflection who comforted Eve.

Taking Stock of Your Losses

As is often the case with losses, she did not notice
that anything was missing for some time after it had gone.

—Naomi Royde-Smith

*W*e are far better dealing with the big losses—death, divorce, debt, and debilitating illness—than with the daily onslaught of little losses. The big losses stun us into response; the litany of little loss saps us physically and psychically. But there is an "art of losing," the poet Elizabeth Bishop tells us, and it "isn't hard to master." In fact, "so many things seemed filled with the intent / To be lost that their loss is no disaster."

Have you ever gotten so worked up over a misplaced set of keys that you flipped? What about a past-due bill that you could swear you'd paid, and then you find it stuck in the back of your calendar (so you wouldn't forget to pay it)? I once tore apart my house (and fought with my daughter for twenty-four hours) because she'd mislaid a handbag she'd borrowed that I desperately wanted to wear for a special evening. I was so angry I could barely contain myself; actually I didn't. Of course, looking back, I'm appalled at the serenity siphoned by an empty purse. I found the darn thing after a few hours combing her room, but the ranting and raving wasn't worth it. When it was time to get dressed, I was an emotional wreck and didn't even want to go out.

Think about all the little losses that agitate you during a typical day—a missed phone call, the letter that doesn't arrive, a glove gone astray, an appointment canceled at the last minute. How do you react? Are you quick to erupt or do a slow burn? Do you seem to take it in your stride, only to brood secretly and become increasingly aggravated? (Heaven help anything or anyone who crosses your path one hour later.) Unfortunately, once the day unravels, it's nearly impossible to wrestle it back or ransom any pleasure in its return, which is why it makes sense to learn a new response to what I call "gnat losses." They might sting, but it's *our* scratching that makes them red, swollen, and so irritating that amputation doesn't seem too extreme. So let's try something different, shall we? You've heard the phrase *choose your battles?* Well, I say, "Choose your losses."

A woman I know almost canceled dinner plans with a good friend after an exasperating day of gnat losses—bad traffic, grand-jury-duty summons, disappearing sweater at the dry cleaner's, constant interruptions. The entire day was lost in the morass of minor annoyance. When she got to the restaurant, she discovered that her dinner companion was upset and frustrated as well. But her companion's angst was due to an overbooked day at her medical practice that had inadvertently kept her from attending the first chemotherapy session of a young, frightened leukemia patient. Although the child had made it through the session with his mother, the little boy was disappointed in my friend for not being there and told her so. Loss surrounded Arlene's no-win decision: ask ill patients to come back another day or be with her young chemo patient. In either case, someone would lose her professional attention and compassionate presence, and she would gain only guilt. The seriousness of her dilemma makes you wonder about the small losses that automatically throw us for a loop.

It's called putting lost purses into perspective.

Too often we elevate the inconsequential into the influential— as influencing the quality of our day—by reacting without reflecting. How hard would it be to ride the ripples of inconvenience, acknowledge imposition's presence privately, and dispatch irritation on its way with a self-preserving shrug? Not as difficult as you might think.

Do you remember the character in Charles Dickens's *Nicholas Nickleby* who used the span of a century to decide how bad a mistake was? *Will it matter a hundred years from now?* Now here's a woman with a balanced view of life. But we can gain her perspective by using a year, a month, or even a day. Next time you're frustrated in the post office line, stuck in traffic, or caught behind an extended "price check" in aisle 5, ask yourself if you'll ever remember this incident. If the answer is "probably not," then don't focus on it now unless there's something you can do to improve the situation. Little by little you'll notice a difference in how you react to things—the inconsequential will stay that way and you'll have more reserves of psychic energy when you really need them.

"Lose something every day / Accept the fluster of lost door keys, the hour badly spent," Elizabeth Bishop advises. "The art of losing isn't hard to master."

Getting Defensive

No day is so bad that it can't be made better with a nap.

—Carrie Snow

*I*n our defense, may I just point out that probably one of the reasons you're at the breaking point is that you're exhausted. Beatrix Potter described feminine fatigue as being "worn to a raveling," and I don't know a woman today who isn't sleep-deprived and threadbare. In fact, we're not just sleep-deprived, we're sleep-abused. Often, a woman's fatigue is more emotional than it is physical; like a toxic relationship, it's impossible to remedy before acknowledgment of the problem or pain.

There's something pleasant about the kind of physical tiredness that comes after an afternoon of cleaning closets or planting rosebushes, but emotional exhaustion is so debilitating, no amount of sleep at night seems to revive you. What's more, emotional exhaustion is laced with just enough distress and desperation to poison you slowly but not kill you off.

I know women who've never had a hand raised in anger toward them, but I'd still describe them as battered. Women battered senseless from living up to the exasperating expectations of others and the impossible burden of delivering on their own good intentions. To be born a woman is to be chosen to nurture; calming the fears of our family and friends is a feminine prime directive. We accept it, even enjoy it. But that doesn't mean we aren't often exhausted by it. Every time we reassure another that it will be all right, we automatically start trying to figure out how *we* can be the one to make it so. Have you any idea of how much a ton of "There, there" weighs? This isn't to say that we should turn our backs on the very real needs of our loved ones or our obligations (we couldn't if we tried). But we should at least give ourselves permission to redistribute the weight so that we can carry it more easily. Even the mythological Atlas shrugged as he attempted to balance the world on his shoulders.

This revelation came to me after I found the courage to take a nap in the midst of a day that was overwhelming me. "You become courageous by doing courageous acts," Mary Daly tells us. "Courage is a habit." And sometimes it comes wrapped in a blanket in the middle of the afternoon.

Many women would find it easier to admit to having sex in a phone booth with a complete stranger than to napping. The shame of being caught with their pants down is nothing compared with being caught with their eyes closed. "Adult napping should not have a bad connotation. Many people feel that napping is only for children, the sick, the lazy, and the elderly. The phrase *caught napping* reflects people's belief that, for healthy adults, napping is the most blatant manifestation of sloth," William C. Dement, M.D., Ph.D., a pioneer in sleep medicine, explains in *The Promise of Sleep*. But "naps can make you smarter, faster and safer than you would be without them. They should be widely recognized as a powerful tool in battling fatigue, and the person who chooses to nap should be regarded as heroic." Tell that to a woman so tired she shouldn't be allowed to cross the street by herself.

Because I work from home, I've long used naps as a creative tool. If I find myself blocked and unable to write, I lie down, close my eyes, and see myself "reading" the piece I'm trying to write. Invariably, within fifteen minutes to a half hour, I start envisioning a few sentences of the piece I'm working on. As soon as I'm able to "read" what I'm supposed to write, I jot down notes on a pad next to me. Feeling refreshed, I'm eager to resume work. For a long time I thought unraveling a creative block through napping was an embarrassing peccadillo. Then I discovered that Johannes Brahms regularly napped at his piano in composing sessions, waking up one day to transcribe the world's most famous lullaby. Of course, because creative napping is productive, I've never felt guilty about it. But the very thought of excusing myself midday because I'm weary, confused, overwhelmed, or cross-eyed with a stress headache still seems so indulgent it nearly triggers a panic attack. I'll have to get over that and I'm not alone. Some of history's most successful and formidable individuals were dedicated nappers: Winston Churchill, Albert Einstein, Thomas Edison, John F. Kennedy. They were also men.

"There is a fatigue so great that the body cries, even in its sleep," the choreographer Martha Graham admitted. But its muffled sobs while awake are the ones that break the spirit.

If they're yours, you could use a little snooze.

The Defense rests.

Bring On the Night

Sleep is no mean art.

—Friedrich Wilhelm Nietzsche

I've absolutely no doubt the nineteenth-century German philosopher Nietzsche had this epiphany in the middle of the night. The man was a chronic insomniac. No wonder he declared, "God is dead."

"The experts say that most of us will suffer a bout of sleeplessness at least once in our lifetime, an irksome spate of waking nocturnal hours related to personal crisis, worry, grief, or passion—or even a particularly potent espresso imbibed too late in the evening, or a bit of bad beef," Lisa Russ Spaar tells us in her introduction to the wondrously comforting poetry anthology *Acquainted with the Night: Insomnia Poems.* "But many people—a third of the population, at least—endure sleep disorders that are chronic and debilitating."

However much we'd like to think that insomnia is part of the modern condition, it's not. The word comes from the Latin meaning "inability to sleep." "The Hittites, ancient Greeks and Romans, and medieval Europeans all recorded cures for sleeplessness, ranging from a night spent in the temple of one's favorite god to sleep potions concocted from mandrake and lettuce juice to special talismanic bedside candles made from mummified hands."

Haven't tried that one myself, but as they say, the night is young. As I write, it's 2 A.M., and if you're up with me, we're in great company. The poets John Berryman, Elizabeth Bishop, Louise Bogan, Emily Brontë, Samuel Taylor Coleridge, Emily Dickinson, Gerard Manley Hopkins, John Keats, and Robert Frost were all literary insomniacs. Ideally, this would be a fun group to hang out with, but not tonight.

I can't sleep; no light burns, the Russian poet Aleksandr Pushkin begins his "Lines Written at Night During Insomnia." *What do you mean, tedious whispers?*

And while sometimes our inability to sleep is due to stress or personal crises, other times, it's all the things we're doing to relax that snap us to attention like a rubber band.

A new sleeping position or place might help you drift off. Sleep with your head at the base of the bed and your feet at the headboard; or, if you have a king-size bed, try sleeping crossways. Sometimes it's the temperature. Even on chilly nights, sleeping in the nude beneath sheets of natural fabrics—linen, flannel, or silk—envelops you in a cozy cocoon of your own body heat. Settle yourself into the mood for sleep by avoiding exciting television, videos, or reading late at night. Or, play yourself a piece of quiet-down music every night—soothing nocturnes, Indian ragas written specially for night, or a CD of lullabies. Even the sound of a fan can help you drift off if you gently focus your attention on listening to its whir, rather than rehashing the day or continuing that argument in your head. Except in the depth of winter, when I'm sleepless, I often open up the windows and listen to the night; the chirping of the crickets or the buzz of cicadas comforts me throughout the autumn.

What if you try these tricks and still can't get to sleep? Well, checking your e-mail is not an option. In his provocative book *The Promise of Sleep,* the physician and writer William C. Dement makes the case that one of the reasons we can't sleep is that we think of it as a duty rather than a pleasure. And while insomniacs can make a variety of behavioral adjustments, perhaps the simplest one could be to give ourselves permission to embrace pleasure. "Enjoy your sleep. I think many people tend to feel guilty about sleep; staying in bed any longer than absolutely necessary feels like sheer laziness. That is wrong," Dement reassures us. "Sleep is an essential part of life—but more important, sleep is a gift. . . . There are few things more exquisitely pleasurable than giving [yourself] over to sleep at the end of the day or lying in bed half asleep slowly waking to the new day. . . . In order to grasp the fullness of our waking life, we have to make the most of our sleeping time."

Lights out now. Maybe tomorrow night, you'll write a poem.

Come to Your Senses

Rest Assured

"*I* love sleep because it is both pleasant and safe to use," Fran Leibowitz recommends. I heartily agree. However, sometimes our problem isn't falling asleep, but staying there. If hot nights or too busy days have you awakening too soon and keep you from drifting off again, you might want to consider some ancient sensuous therapies that really work.

Rabbits do not suffer from insomnia, as Beatrix Potter pointed out in her Victorian adventures of Peter Rabbit and his friends, probably because "the effect of eating too much lettuce is *soporific*." I love that wonderful old-fashioned word that means "inducing drowsiness." The beloved children's writer may have discovered for herself that the medieval English remedy of lettuce tea works wonders. That's right. Lettuce contains the same sedative properties found in warm milk and is a lighter nighttime drink. Take a few washed leaves of any variety, bring to a boil in a saucepan filled with a cup of water; then take off the flame and let steep for at least ten minutes; add a drop of peppermint extract or stir with a sprig of fresh mint; and, hippety-hop, sip your way to dream-land. You can even bring a small pitcher of the brew up to your night table, drinking it at room temperature if need be.

Medieval women stuffed their pillows with sweet grasses to ensure sweet dreams. As far back as the sixth century, hops were a dependable pillow stuffing for this purpose . . . but rinsing your bed linens in beer won't have *quite* the same effect. Instead, here are some traditional herbal recipes for a good night's sleep.

A scented sleeping pillow is my first suggestion. But, strong fragrances placed close to your face might create too great a sensory effect and actually keep you awake, however pleasant they are. And herbs and spices, however finely ground, can be a bit lumpy or gritty to snuggle directly upon. The ideal sleep pillow is a flat casing (no extra fluff or padding) containing loose herbs, which is tucked *beneath* your regular pillows. As crushing dried leaves and buds releases their scent anew, every time you lay your head upon your pillow or turn over, you will revive the scent of your sleep pillow.

Leaving an inch or two open along one straight edge to insert the sleep mixture, sew together two plain men's handkerchiefs, or two pieces of plain cotton broadcloth or muslin (an old sheet, cut up, is perfect for this purpose). Fill with the herbs of your choice, then sew the casing shut. Sewing along three sides, create a prettier outer casing of calico or linen or any soft, plain broadcloth to enclose the sleep pillow and protect your bedding from fine siftings of powder.

Another way to scent your pillow area, if you are all thumbs at sewing, is to put your herbs in the foot section of several infant-size cotton socks and then pin them clothesline-style on a ribbon that you string across your headboard. Or you might place your herbs at the center of a few pretty handkerchiefs, gather each sachet hobo-style, and tightly tie it with a ribbon. Then suspend your homemade sachets from your headboard. Squeeze the sachets as you lie down, to release their scent.

And now for the recipes. Half a dozen flowers, herbs, and spices, always used in various combinations rather than singly, typically recur in centuries' worth of instructions for sleep pillows: rose petals and leaves, lavender, cloves, rosemary, peppermint, and lemon verbena. Each is a relaxant, and perhaps not coincidentally, each is also reputed to have disinfectant properties. Lavender and peppermint especially are legendary for repelling mosquitoes and gnats. And, of course, be yet one *more* reason you've been staying awake! Orrisroot, which smells faintly of violets and is available from herb shops and spice companies, is a small but vital element: it serves as a fixative, extending the potency of the other scents with which it's combined.

Grind the dry ingredients well with a nonmetallic mortar and pestle . . . or make your own pestle from a flat-bottomed glass kitchen herb jar; and for a mortar, use a small, deep glass or porcelain bowl. *Don't pound;* use a pressing and rolling motion, as if walking on the ball of your foot, to create as fine a powder as you can. Isn't it delicious to feel like a medieval alchemist? Now use a plastic fork or throwaway wooden spatula, such as an ice-cream stick, to stir in the essential oil thoroughly. Store the mixture for several weeks in a jar set in a cool, dark place, shaking every few days to redistribute the oil. Then spoon the mixture into your sachet casing.

Lavender-Rose Mix

You will need:

2 tablespoons dried lavender
2 tablespoons dried rose petals
1 tablespoon dried rosemary
1 teaspoon ground cloves
1 tablespoon orrisroot powder
1 drop rose essential oil
1 drop lavender essential oil

Rosemary-Lemon-Mint Mix

You will need:

2 tablespoons dried rosemary
2 tablespoons dried lemon verbena
2 tablespoons dried peppermint
1 tablespoon finely ground, dried lemon peel

Leg cramps can strike during the night, and if you've ever had them, you have my sympathies. There's no way to sleep through a spasm. An old English preventative is to place a basin of cool water beneath your bedstead; if your room needs extra humidity, this might make you sleep more comfortably. Eating a banana before bed or blending it with skim milk will give your body badly needed potassium, the lack of which is often the cause of muscle cramps. You might also want to keep on your night table a vial of chamomile oil, should you suddenly need a leg massage. Place one-quarter cup of dried chamomile flowers into one-half cup of olive oil, and leave to steep in a covered jar for several weeks. Strain, and place in a fresh covered jar. Use a few drops to stroke achy limbs.

The English mystery writer P. D. James has described sleep as "a sensuous gluttony of oblivion," and as far as I'm concerned, every woman should aspire to be a wanton hussy in this regard. If the bliss trigger that might help you stop losing sleep is still a mystery, be willing to experiment until you find the right one. Often, it's right under your nose.

Sensuous Sulking

There is hardly anyone in the civilized world – particularly
those who do just a little more every day than they really have
strength to perform – who has not at some time regarded bed
as a refuge.

–J. E. Buckrose (1923)

O f all the rooms in her house, a woman's bedroom is the most
personal expression of the state of her soul. For her bedroom
reflects a woman's truth—her past, present, dreams for the future,
or lack of them. Her hopes, her sorrows. Her passions, pleasures,
peccadilloes. What she believes about herself, what she thinks
she's hiding and, obviously, is not.

For most of my life I occupied a bedroom that was small, dark,
overcrowded, messy, dreary; a hodgepodge of the unresolved, it
was a Rorschach test of my emotional, psychological, physical,
and spiritual health. From the moment I awoke until I closed my
eyes, every moment spent in that room was an inarticulate expression of deep despair. And believe me, it doesn't matter whether
you're sharing the bedroom with someone or not. A man may leave
a mess on your floor, but the real question isn't who should be picking up his dirty socks or shorts, but why is he throwing them
down? Is it because you are not caring for your room or yourself
either? Buried beneath that answer is the real heartbreaking mess
that's slowly snuffing your soul. A woman's unkempt bedroom is
a distressing SOS for an ûnlived life.

And since we're on the subject of inarticulate despair, just what
are you doing in your bedroom? Don't tell me you're sleeping
because I won't believe you. Other reasons for having a bedroom
include repose, rest, relaxation, reading, and of course, romance.
But somehow I doubt that's on your list, either. Sadly a woman's
bedroom has become not the refuge for which it was intended, but

the communal rec center—the place we end up ironing or mending clothes, bill paying, e-mail answering, exercising, television viewing, and watching the kids play where you'd rather they not.

In times past, women of some means also had an agenda beyond lounging around, but their duties and other activities took place in a little sitting room off their bedroom, known as the boudoir. Here the lady of the house held court to her household staff (today she'd be making to-do lists), visited with her children, kept her household records, withdrew to dress, read, or write letters, and otherwise maintained a personal space quite apart from her bedroom.

Most significantly, a woman's boudoir was where she "retired" or beat a classy retreat. The writer Judith Thurman tells us that the boudoir was literally "a room in which to sulk, for *bouder* in French means 'to sulk.' This is a wry and rather elegant way of signaling a need most women share but don't in reality admit to: the need to be invisible."

Why would a woman want to be invisible? So you can psychically putter and pull yourself together. And how? Judith offers this sensuous sulking selection: "staring at a fire, watching the rain, listening to music through a set of headphones, reading catalogs, stenciling a picture frame, fantasizing about an old flame, doing a double-acrostic while drinking an entire pot of espresso, trying to explain oneself telepathically to one's mother, writing a seductively critical letter to a famous novelist that will never get mailed, sorting one's panty hose by color, studying palmistry or ancient Greek, making an evening purse from the scraps of some old silk ties . . ." In other words, doing nothing important to the rest of the world, but something vital for your sanity.

Just as *night* and *sleep* are not synonymous, neither are *bedroom* and *boudoir*. Not many women have separate rooms for their boudoir, but creating one is more a state of mind than of space. Perhaps the computer, exercise equipment, or ironing table can't be moved somewhere else (but don't give up trying!). However, it might be screened or curtained away from your sleeping area. Try to keep your bed for the bliss of a good sleep or lovemaking (if you do, you may find you get more of both). Use a chair, daybed, or desk for serious reading, writing, or work, or even just some sighs over a last cup of tea.

If you've a taste for it, lace and frills are welcome here, but a boudoir need not be fancy or overdressed to be feminine. Nonetheless, you'll find yourself more relaxed if you can "drop a curtain" over your workday. So when they're not in active use, drape the computer monitor and exercise bike, if you can't get rid of them, with a pretty fabric; tuck papers into decorative trunks, hatboxes, or baskets.

Let the things you already own and love (but don't trot out too often) decorate your boudoir: rarely used evening handbags, or china; silk scarves or crocheted shawls recycled as dresser scarves or tablecloths, for instance. Frame doilies or other small heirloom pieces of fabric such as Grandma's lace gloves, a vintage handkerchief or collar. Hang a fluttery negligee or an evening wrap over the edge of a closet door; display a fancy hat. It does delicate clothing no harm to get some air from time to time and it does your soul so much good to remember life needs "fancies" as much as the practical. Experiment with curtains that allow cascades of moonlight or streams of sunshine to dance on your floor—a double layer of lace or tulle might be all you need, in place of stuffy, nature-blocking fabrics. For even more atmosphere, use a low-wattage light blue bulb as a night-light and feel yourself let go when you turn it on. *Always* indulge in a bouquet of scented flowers for your boudoir. Take the time to find a fabulous throw for the end of your bed, to encourage naps; group your perfume bottles on a pretty silver or decoupage tray; ransom some gorgeous candleholders from a thrift shop; plant a window box even if it overlooks the backyard; find the prettiest *Do Not Disturb* sign you can and hang it on the door, then supplement it with an inside chain lock.

A woman's boudoir is the perfect place for family photos and children's mementos, memorabilia from trips, or other sentimental objects . . . things that might seem too intimate, delicate, or twee for more public areas of the home, but still provide the comfort and company of a good friend. If you've got lots of curios, rotate your collection, displaying only a few objects at a time; you'll be giving yourself a chance to really *see* why you chose and love each one. And if suddenly you lose your affection, you know what to do!

No need to leave the boudoir for late-night or early-morning tea. Keep a bed-and-breakfast-style bedroom tray with a cup and saucer and one-cup water heater at the ready. Here is unadulterated indulgence: making a cup of wake-up tea and then crawling back under the covers to sip it! Only the first time do you feel that you're committing a sin; afterward your early-morning assignation becomes redemptive. A few more minutes in bed and slowly she's able to rise . . . step by step she's able, perhaps reluctantly, to return to the world.

Even if they must share the same four walls, begin to imagine a boudoir in your life rather than merely a bedroom, and you'll be creating a decompression zone where, even when busy, you are in a unique setting devoted to being privately awake and in attendance to your own thoughts, even the odd sulk or two.

"Sulking—refusing to be cajoled or intimidated by the demands of other people or of reality—has been vastly underrated as a balm for the stresses of a woman's life," Judith Thurman believes. A woman's boudoir allows her the sanctuary of "spiritual *dishabille.* And just as a boudoir needs its perfumes, its draperies, its divan, and its locked door, it needs to deserve a title—a secret, about which [we] will say no more. For a woman's mystery is not always what a man might imagine."

Come to Your Senses

Your Fondest
Bedtime Companion

*H*ow you make your bed is often more revealing of how you feel about life than whether or not you see your glass as half-empty or half-full. But more important, a woman's bed uncovers her secret feelings about herself. It's always the small, subtle inferences that are the most telling.

This is the place in our home that touches us most intimately, sometimes for as long as a third of each day. It is the place to which we give ourselves freely when we're most vulnerable, ill, sad, or weary. We trust it to support our escape from this world or our transport to others. "It is in bed that we bear the inevitable," J. E. Buckrose wrote in 1923. "We are learning this all the time we lie with our face turned to the wall thinking we are doing nothing."

When you change your sheets, is it just a laundry chore, gathering together the creased or unclean, an *un*making of your bed?

Or is it an opportunity to *re*make your bed, to *prepare* a silken, scented setting for your body and your dreams?

Poets find almost inseparable the notion of sleep and sweet bedding: "And still she slept an azure-lidded sleep, in blanched linen, smooth, and lavender'd," wrote Keats in "The Eve of St. Agnes." One of the most romantic poems ever written is "The Great Lover" by the English poet Rupert Brooke, who died in the First World War. In it he describes Life as our soul's true lover, and details all the ways that Life attempts to seduce us with simple splendors every ordinary day: "The cool kindliness of sheets, that soon / Smooth away trouble; and the rough male kiss of blankets . . ." Could you wax as lyrical about your *own* bed's attire?

Whether or not your sheets are pretty is almost a moot question, but what about how they *feel* against your skin? Are they stiff, unforgiving? So worn-thin or slithery that you fear to damage them? Is that lace trim lovely . . . but also scratchy as all get-out? Is your blanket pilled like an old sweater, or your comforter too lumpy to comfort much?

Nothing dies harder than a bad habit or ratty linens. Why we think that hanging on to them is virtuous, I'll never understand, but every woman I know does until she's hanging by a thread. If there's only one thing you do this month to make yourself feel better, get rid of the raggedy sheets and towels. Even the coziest, most attractive linen once upon a time has a shelf life, and twenty years is long enough.

If it's time to replace the worn, you have a wonderful range from which to choose: fabrics that will not only match your decor, but will feel soft and inviting to your skin. Personally I think a woman should be rapturous about her bedcovering, and obsessive about what lies beneath it. Silk sheets cost the earth, but they wash and wear well *for years* without showing their age, keeping you warm in winter and cool in summer, especially if you sleep in the buff. (And you will if you're on silk sheets.) But there are some wonderful white sales in mail-order fiber catalogs come January and July. Take advantage. Or outfit your bed by season: good quality flannel for winter, pima or Egyptian cotton for warm months. Take care to read the fiber content. Synthetics, jerseys, and satin/sateen weaves wear poorly and also tend to stick to the body. What you want in cotton sheeting should be a fine, close weave in the 180–280 thread-count range: high enough to feel smooth, but still low enough not to thin quickly with everyday use.

As for blankets or duvets, several layers of lighter coverings might feel much better to awaken to than one heavy quilt that is snuggly at bedtime but becomes stifling by dawn. Here again, natural fabrics will "breathe" more, too. Be sure blankets and the undersides of comforters have enough texture not to slither off you in the night.

Experiment with pillows: firm? soft? How many do you sleep with now? As far as I'm concerned, a bed can rarely have too many of them. Is your mattress hard? It's quite amazing, but for so many years I bought beds without testing the mattress and then suffered silently. Think of yourself as the princess and give yourself the pea test. Try out quilted liners (sold for pillows as well as mattresses), an "egg crate" foam layer for your mattress, a goose-down feather bed or an eiderdown. Buy extra-small pillows if you need neck support. Work toward assembling a nest that will hold you gently but firmly, as you might cup a bird in your palm. No, it's not possible to be too extravagant when it comes to pulling together your bedroom. It's where a woman begins to discover self-nurturance and divine the sacred in the ordinary. Become a disciple of the spiritual English poet John Donne, who was praising God when he wrote, "This bed, thy center is / These walls, thy sphere." Heaven knows my happiest, most heartfelt gratitudes go wafting skyward after I wake up from a good night's sleep. Yours will, too.

Lavender, as noted Keats, is an excellent scent for linens, and a natural disinfectant. Its name derives from the Latin word *lavare,* "to wash." Use lavender water (available from bath shops or herbalists) as a final rinse when you launder your sheets, or tuck the following sachet in your linen cupboard: Combine one-half cup each of dried lavender and rosebuds, one-quarter cup of thyme, and one teaspoon of ground cinnamon; sew the herb mixture into small, closely woven bags (here's where scraps of old sheets and dish towels can be recycled). If you have trouble falling asleep, try this sachet remedy, which dates back to the seventeenth century: Combine one-half cup rosebuds, one teaspoon of dried peppermint leaves (you can use a pure mint tea), and one-half teaspoon of ground cloves. Again, mix them together and sew them into bags. And be sure to freshen your bed every morning by simply throwing back the covers and opening your bedroom window to air the room. Yes, even in winter . . . *especially* in winter, when steam heat and heavy layers can make even the most orderly beds uncomfortably fusty.

Make the changing of your sheets a time of rejoicing. Set your body swaying with music to inspire you to graceful movements with sizzling romantic tangos. Go ahead, gather that used bedding into your arms as if it were a lover, and give it a spin about the dance floor, dipping and gliding, before placing it in your laundry bag or basket. It served you nobly through the night; don't be too eager to part with it! Sensuously stretching to match your motions to the music, unfold your fresh sheets and pillowcases . . . float and whisk them through the air. Press the fabrics to your cheek, to feel, to sniff. Caress your sheets, smoothing them upon your mattress. Fluff your pillows high. Now mist them with lavender-scented sheet spray. Give it a minute or so to dry as you breathe deeply, then pull the covers up.

Atop the covers, add decorative cushions . . . an elegant throw or cozy afghan folded at the foot . . . to keep your bed company while you are away from it during the day, or to pull up over you when you pay a midafternoon visit. Above all, make your bed with some of the passion and devotion you bestow when you're making love. Emily Dickinson says it best: "Ample make this bed / Make this bed with Awe."

A Good Cry

Let your tears come, let them water your soul.

—Eileen Mayhew

*W*hy is it that so many women are ashamed to shed tears? Is it because after years of struggling for equality with men, exposing our fragility suddenly seems too threatening? Have you noticed that in the last few years, even though women have been encouraging their sons and partners to get in touch with their emotions, including crying, we've started to shut down ourselves? Not good. Not healthy. Not wise. As I hear woman after woman begin to apologize as she starts to well up, I can't help but think of my Southern granny, who warned when I was fussing and fretting too audibly, *I'll give you something to cry about, young lady.* Invariably, her threat simply escalated my weeping and wailing.

Maybe it was the Irish banshee side of the family staking claim to my sensibilities. For centuries in the west of Ireland, women were traditionally taught the proper way to wail, or *keen,* which is a long, high-pitched cry of wrenching loneliness and grief. To really sob, to truly cry, is to open yourself up to those emotions struggling for expression and relief; the anger wrestling in the pit of your stomach; the despair caught in your throat; the sorrow tightening across your chest. I think that some of us resist the release of crying because the truth is it hurts. Heartache is real.

Far from being self-indulgent, crying is a form of articulated prayer. In Catholic and Orthodox religions tears have always been considered one of the special gifts of the Holy Spirit, and in the Hebrew Old Testament, an entire book of the Bible is devoted to crying—the Book of Lamentations.

Consider the phrase *have a good cry.* Sometimes it isn't sorrow that induces our tears but joy or disbelief. Yet even when the origins of our tears are sad, crying is good for us, especially the crying jags that mangle our features and remind us of how we cried when we were young and didn't know how to stop, especially if our granny was telling us to hush.

Stop it, child, you don't cry pretty. Well, guess what? Now I do. Or rather, I revel in the knowledge that self-control has the opposite effect on a woman's looks. The great nineteenth-century beauty Natalie Clifford Barney believed that "Time engraves our faces with all the tears we have not shed." Give me a box of tissues over Botox anytime.

The Soul Remembers When

We all need the waters of the Mercy River.
Though they don't run deep, there's usually enough,
just enough for the extravagance of our lives.

—Jonis Agee

To give yourself permission to cry is to bless your body with the benediction of healing. Although you may feel wiped and wrung out after an intense crying jag, you also feel cleansed after a dip in the Mercy River.

Sometimes we're so shut down that a single unexpected word, a line from a song, or even a stray thought can trigger our tears, especially when a situation feels exasperatingly nebulous or downright overwhelming. Often our conscious mind might not remember the source of our sorrow, but our soul does. The poet Henry Wadsworth Longfellow believed that "the holiest of all holidays" are not the ones on our calendars, but the ones we observe "in silence and apart," and in private tears. He called these special days our "secret anniversaries of the heart."

Secret anniversaries often reveal, in mystical ways, our place in the world and our relationship to ourselves and others. They can be joyful or sad, major turning points or minor epiphanies. You might remember the day you got a coveted part in the school play, received a special love letter, sent your child off for his first sleepover, or accidentally bumped into a stranger who would change the course of your life. Or you might recall a painful loss: the due date of a baby who was never born, the day an adored parent passed away, the day you abandoned a dream. Sometimes, it takes many years to recognize the importance of a secret anniversary—or even to know that you have one to commemorate.

Often our secret anniversaries are tied to the seasons, and because our senses are the conduits of these soul memories, they are the favorite messengers. Scent is an especially potent harbinger. The mother of a friend died suddenly in the spring when my friend was only ten; she remembers walking into her mother's bedroom immediately after hearing the sad news and being overcome with the fragrance of a vase of lilacs on her mother's dressing table. Now each spring, my friend remembers and mourns her loss by buying an enormous bouquet of lilacs, carefully arranging them, then bringing them to her own dressing table. It's her sacred ritual, a tender mercy.

Every autumn when I smell leaves burning for the first time, I experience a total eclipse of the heart, and the loss of my first love feels as if it's just happened. I recall Edna St. Vincent Millay's sonnet:

> Time does not bring relief; you all have lied
> Who told me time would ease me of my pain!
> I miss him in the weeping of the rain;
> I want him at the shrinking of the tide;
> The old snows melt from every mountain-side,
> And last year's leaves are smoke in every lane;
> But last year's bitter loving must remain

And she's right. Time does not always bring relief. But tears always do.

Perhaps the opposite situation torments you—you wish that you *could* cry, but the tears just won't come. Your heart feels as dry as twigs inside, ready to snap. You feel so arid in the pit of your soul that it's as if you have been roasted. We've all known such hollowness, such emptiness . . . and irrigating your spirit can do much to ease such pain.

Yes, it can actually be a positive experience to consciously trigger tears. Read the saddest poetry you can find, listen to the saddest songs. If you are mourning a person or a tragic event, dredge up memories or mementos that will unlock the floodgates, or immerse yourself in what others who shared the tragedy have expressed. Go to a dramatic performance—a play, an opera, a movie—and allow it to carry you away in the privacy of darkness. The old Greek playwrights well understood that theatrical tragedies allow the audience to leave feeling refreshed, not depressed, after having vicariously experienced a fictitious sorrow worse than any they have known themselves.

What you seek is what the Greeks called *catharsis,* which literally means a purging. Not lasting grief, but losing control *in a controlled fashion* that permits you to return from a deep plunge into darkness. I'll never forget the release I felt after seeing the films *The English Patient, Somewhere in Time, Out of Africa,* and *Truly Madly Deeply.* I have videos of all of them, and if I've got a bad case of the blues, I prescribe myself one of them, have a good cry, and avoid a call to the doctor in the morning.

"Tears are a river that take you somewhere," the Jungian analyst and storyteller Clarissa Pinkola Estes reminds us. "Tears lift your boat off the rocks, off dry ground, carrying it downriver to someplace new, someplace better."

Your future.

Come to Your Senses

Tender Mercies

*W*hen a crying jag is over, it's a bit like coming back from a deep-sea dive. But instead of decompressing, what your body needs is to *compress:* your red, swollen eyes and puffy face.

Brew some chamomile tea and, after you pour yourself a cup, soak a man's large white cotton handkerchief in the tea, fold it in thirds, and use it as an eye compress for your tender lids. If you can enjoy the luxury of lying down, place a chilled cucumber slice on each eyelid and "chill," yourself, for fifteen minutes in a darkened room, listening to soothing music.

A blotched face will benefit from a cucumber-and-tea rinse:

You will need:

½ cucumber, peeled and seeded
¼ cup hot, prepared green tea
¼ cup hot, prepared chamomile tea

1. Puree cucumber in a blender, and strain out the juice.
2. Mix the teas together and add the cucumber juice. Stir well and place in the fridge for at least half an hour. (If you've been crying on and off, make this and keep it on hand for a day or two!)
3. Pat face with mixture.
4. Rinse face with cool water, and pat dry with your softest towel.

Sometimes a good cry leaves us feeling headachy. Ease the throbbing with a little aromatherapy by inhaling the scent of an essential-oil combination of ginseng, violet, peppermint, orange peel, or marjoram. You don't need all of them, but a combination of two or three works wonders. And, of course, don't forget the scent of lavender. Sometimes the best thing after a good cry is the nap that follows.

Getting Through Getting over It

Part of getting over it is knowing that you will never get over it.

—Anne Finger

"What were they thinking?" is a favorite magazine and newspaper headline often used as a commentary over funny or bizarre photographs. But frequently when I think of famous women I admire, I find myself wondering the same thing, and perhaps you do, too. What were they thinking as they faced the challenges, crossroads, changes, and choices that shaped the trajectory of their lives? When sorrow slapped them down? How did they feel after achieving a long-desired dream and then found no one could share in their joy because of jealousy? What were they doing when their lover walked in and said, "We've got to talk"?

"There was a time when my life seemed so painful to me that reading about the lives of other women writers was one of the few things that could help. I was unhappy, and ashamed of it; I was baffled by my life," Kennedy Fraser admits in her luminous collection of essays on women's lives, *Ornament and Silence.* "Even now, I feel I should pretend that I was reading only these women's fiction or their poetry—the lives as they chose to present them, alchemized as art. But that would be a lie. It was the private messages I really liked—the journals and letters, and autobiographies and biographies whenever they seemed to be telling the truth. I felt very lonely then, self-absorbed, shut off. I needed all this murmured chorus, this continuum of true-life stories, to pull me through. They were like mothers and sisters to me, these literary women, many of them already dead; more than my own family, they seemed to stretch out a hand."

Do you remember the comfort and joy of an imaginary playmate when you were a child? Just because the rest of the world couldn't see your constant companion, it didn't mean he or she wasn't real. Reassuring companion spirits can still be an immediate presence in our daily round—guiding, inspiring, guarding, and loving—even if it's been a long time since you made mud pies in the backyard. The way we communicate with our unseen friends is through our sacred imagination—the love child of knowing and wonder. I remember when First Lady Hillary Rodham Clinton became the object of ridicule because it was revealed that she held "fantasy" conversations with Eleanor Roosevelt. "She usually responds by telling me to buck up, or at least to grow skin as thick as a rhinoceros," Mrs. Clinton responded. Wonderful advice, and it sounds as if Hillary followed it all the way from the embarrassing darkness of the moments of disgrace of her husband's presidency to living by her own lights as a senator from New York.

"Women, I believe, search for fellow beings who have faced similar struggles," the distinguished author and critic Carolyn G. Heilbrun observes in an essay entitled "Unmet Friends." She was writing about the kinship she shared with Maxine Kumin, a close friend "only in my mind" and between the lines of Kumin's poetry. "Why do I feel, not having met her but having read all her work, that she and I are closer in the destinies we have chosen than I am to many friends personally known?"

While every woman needs flesh-and-blood friends, occasionally it's comforting to be able to ask the advice of someone likely to give you an answer you don't already know; someone who's been where you find yourself now. At a few times in my life I've felt completely isolated and alone, although my close friends and family would beg to disagree. But they couldn't understand what I was going through—an unrequited love that became a tortured, secret obsession, the shock of becoming an overnight success (after struggling for acknowledgment of my work for twenty-five years), the isolation of a harrowing illness that appeared to others as malingering until it was properly diagnosed. Because my circle of intimates had no frame of reference in their lives, they couldn't offer any advice to help me navigate my way through these unexpected shoals; it was easier for them to pretend the distress I was going through didn't exist or to advise me to "get over it."

And it was easier for me simply not to talk to them, so I turned on the spiritual blessing of the telephone answering machine. Then I tuned in to the hints, whispers, asides, echoes, resonant ripples, and consolation of women who have written on the page a path out of despair, a path that helped me find my way back to sanity and solace, one sentence at a time.

Each week I would set out to another new-to-me used-book store and search for a new page friend. I particularly sought out women I'd never heard of before (that's why concentrating on books published from the thirties to the sixties provides rich plundering). I didn't limit myself to biographies, but also explored poetry and plays, cookery books and gardening collections. I'd set myself a limit of $10 to spend and only bought books by or about *one* woman a week.

Although I call this self-help treatment bibliotheraphy, seeking Divine guidance through books is an ancient form of prayer. "Divination is the means by which you engage in dialogue with the Divine. Communicating with the deity provides proof that you are not alone, that the Universe is alive, and that it is aware of your presence, your longings, fears, needs, wounds, gifts, and truest self," the spiritual writer Phyllis Curott tells us. One of her favorite sources of Divination is consulting her "library angel" by going to a row of books in her home or at a friend's house, as well as to libraries and bookshops all over the world. In each place she would ask to be led to the right book to give her the guidance and comfort she sought at a particular time. This is her prayer: "I invite the numinous spirit that resides within these volumes to guide my hand, and my inquiry. Please help me find wisdom." She then closes her eyes, moves her hand back and forth and up and down over the bookshelf, and, when the moment is right, honors the gentle pull toward a particular volume. She waits to see if there's a feeling of certainty and then takes it from the shelf, saying, "I acknowledge you as my guide."

Phyllis asks her question of the book before opening it. Then she suggests, "Allow the book to open in your hands. Open your eyes and let them light upon the page. Read what is before you. It may take time to meditate upon the answer you have received, or the message may be absolutely clear immediately. . . . Write down the passage you received and, even if it does not seem immediately meaningful, let it evoke feelings. And end the divination by giving thanks to the book, the library angel, and the Divine for their assistance."

I have been exploring a similar prayer ritual for decades and have never failed to be nudged toward the next step or given the knowledge that I needed. When I'm searching for new women friends on the page to guide me through rough or daunting life passages, I start meditating on the type of advice I need even before I leave for the bookshop. And the swiftness of the Divine Librarian's help makes me smile through my tears with thanks.

Until you try it, you can't imagine how comforting this rite of passage can be when you're stuck in the *getting through the getting over it* stage of loss. In truth, I don't believe we're supposed to *get over* loss because whether we like it or not (and we don't), the loss is shaping our future. But we do need to *get past* loss, and more times than I like to admit, I get caught up in one scene and replay it over and over in my mind until I think I'll go mad.

But it's virtually impossible to be in two places at once, so if I'm rolling out piecrust with Marjorie Kinnan Rawlings, the Pulitzer

Prize–winning author of *The Yearling,* who cooked to blunt the pain of bad men, or planting bulbs with Katharine White, who was the gardening editor at *The New Yorker* for over thirty years, then I can't be frozen in my own distress.

I discovered Katharine's collection of gardening essays *Onward and Upward in the Garden* on one of my bibliotherapy soul searches. It was years ago when all I knew about plants was that you kept the green part on top of the ground. But Katharine's passion for gardening was so infectious, it encouraged me to give bulb planting a try. I had been particularly moved by her husband E. B. White's remembrance of watching her plant bulbs in the garden of their Maine home the autumn she was dying: "her studied absorption in the implausible notion that there would be yet another spring, oblivious to the ending of her own days, which she knew perfectly well was near at hand, sitting there with her detailed chart under those dark skies in the dying October, calmly plotting the resurrection." That passage never fails to move me forward in my own journey, even if it's only one more step.

Today Katharine's book has mud splatters on it, as well as tea and tear stains. Today she and I are planning to plant scores of bulbs over the next few weeks around Newton's Chapel. Underneath them I will bury a small box containing all that's left of a loss so devastating that I'm not sure I can get past it. Katharine assures me it can be done, one bulb at a time. I'll take her word for it. I may still be unable to believe that this pain will ever end, but I can plant my heart's resurrection, and the sight come spring should be breathtaking.

Spirit willing, next April I'll be back to sit in my garden, sigh, and give thanks. The sigh will come from the sight of an undulating, sensuous wave of daffodils and tulips, gracefully bending in the gentle breeze, welcoming my return. The thanks will come from knowing and wonder. Not only did I get through the getting-over-it stage of this September's crushing sorrow, but in so doing, only the beauty of this season of relinquishment remains behind.

Mythical Woman

*H*ave you ever lost yourself so completely in a novel or a movie that you became part of it? Something about the story struck a deep chord in you. The nineteenth-century German writer Thomas Mann called these pleasantly perplexing occasions "a smiling knowledge of the eternal, the ever-being and authentic."

I call them secret rendezvous with "my old flame." Once again an ancient spark has been rekindled. I'm invited to sit at the hearth of my heart; the Teller of Tales has arrived and is about to reveal the next installment in a riveting romance—my personal myth. It's a story as old as time: the kingdom of a solitary queen is being threatened by sinister forces. Does she marry for safety or does she hold out for true love? Eventually, the brave and beautiful lady is going to live happily ever after—for the love of all that's Holy— because she believes that she deserves nothing less. But right now, she must be more heroic than she ever knew she could be.

Each of us has a personal myth. Do you know what yours is? You should because it's your internal compass, a sacred birth gift meant to help you find your way through life's labyrinth. The way you've weathered crises, taken risks, made choices, or recovered from loss has been determined by your belief system. Think of your personal myth as your soul's prime directive for the spiritual lessons you need to master at different stages in your life.

From ancient times, myths and fairy tales have contained more spiritual truth in one telling than we can even process, which is why the soul keeps asking to have them told once again. Remember how Jesus told stories or parables to the crowds that followed him? He was trying to use their daily round to help them understand the sacred in the ordinary. The seed that falls on rocky ground and cannot grow; the shepherd who protects his flock; the lilies of the field, who neither toil nor spin, but are beautiful; the sorrow that Heaven feels even at the fall of the sparrow.

The only thing more real than a myth is a dream.

Your history begins with the facts: where you were born and when, who your parents were, where you lived. Your factual history includes the ethnic, cultural, and religious traditions of the family that bore and/or raised you, along with any superstitions and bigotry that may have been handed down over the generations. And while this miasma certainly colors the way we view the world and life, it's not our Truth. But personal myths are.

If you're not consciously aware of your personal myth, take heart. The great Swiss psychologist Carl Jung didn't begin to explore his "personal myth" until he was eighty-three. Ironically, his life's work was helping the world understand mythical archetypes—universal and timeless images and themes common to the human experience. Why so long, Dr. Jung? Probably because he was so busy helping everybody else take care of his or her "Self" (another Jungian legacy) he couldn't find the time to take care of his own. (Sound familiar?) I didn't start searching for my personal myth until after my marriage ended. Why only then? Because that's when I needed to know what I believed in, confirming the poet Maxine Kumin's observation that "when Sleeping Beauty wakes up, she is almost fifty years old."

My mythical awakening came the first time I glimpsed the painting *The Meeting on the Turret Stairs* (1864) by the Irish artist Sir Frederick William Burton. This mystical moment was so potent that recalling it gives me goose bumps, for I experienced "synesthesia"—the fusion of all seven senses—so acutely that I felt as if I were there on the turret stairs. In the painting, a knight is kissing the sleeve of his lover's dress as she turns away. I knew instinctively the story of these two people. But what was it? Mesmerized by their mystery and my need to understand why it was affecting me viscerally, I set out on a trail that continues to enthrall my heart, as it guides, protects, and nurtures my soul.

While there are many books on personal mythology, the most sensuous way to begin your search is with a picture. Somewhere, in an art book, on a gallery wall, or in a box of old photographs at an antique stall, there's an image that will stop you cold. This is your first clue. To find it, you'll have to take a delightful detour to libraries, museums, or flea markets. By all means seek out places you've never been before, but don't discount what's nearby either. I recently began rewatching videos I'd bought and enjoyed years ago, and I'm astonished at what they reveal now because I'm taking the time to stop, look, and listen.

One caveat. Discovering your personal myth is a sacred undertaking. But you are not alone. Your senses of vision, knowing, and wonder are your mythical guides. The writer Ursula K. Le Guin tells us that when our genuine myth rises in our consciousness, the spiritual message is always the same: "You must change your life."

Especially if you want to live happily ever after.

The One Story Worth Telling

May stillness be upon your thoughts
and silence upon your tongue!
For I tell you a tale that was told at the
Beginning . . . the one story worth the telling . . .

—Traditional Celtic storyteller's prologue

"*T*he one story worth the telling is the one that strikes most nearly to the heart. For each person, that story will be different, for each heart is like a harp with its own distinct tuning," Caitlin Matthews, the respected teacher of Celtic traditions, explains in her glorious book of enchanted love fables, *Celtic Love*. "When the melody of love vibrates the strings, that one story is the distinctive music we shall make."

While other people's love stories can inspire us or illuminate our path, the one story we always hunger to hear is our own love story. The Irish poet William Butler Yeats believed that there was only one romance: the soul's. And the soul's romance is our personal myth.

After I discovered *The Meeting on the Turret Stairs,* I framed a print of it for my bedroom. Frequently, I'd gaze on it and think, "You really must find out about this." But I didn't. Several months passed and while I was still captivated by the image, I also started feeling vaguely uncomfortable, a sure sign that we've disregarded our intuitive prompts. I put the picture away. A year later, during a season of relinquishment, while cleaning out a closet, the picture found me again. This time I sat down and really spent some time looking at the lady and her knight. This was a painful parting, and yet they couldn't look at each other. I started imagining all the different scenarios that caused their forced separation (clearly, they parted unwillingly), and I ended up recalling moments in my own life when I'd turned away from a love that frightened me. The painting seemed to have become a mystical mirror reflecting my own unresolved regrets and remorse. But there were no recriminations, just feelings of release and healing as I acknowledged my resistances to love. I felt so blessed afterward. All of us have resistances to love whether we're in a relationship or not. However, by learning to love Life, we learn to trust and open ourselves up to relationships on a deeper level.

This was such a gently powerful epiphany that I decided to continue to use the image as a point of departure for a new kind of meditation—a soulful pilgrimage from the loss of love toward an affair that would never end, my Great Romance with Life. But first I needed to create a sacred space for this journey—physically and psychically.

Mythologist Joseph Campbell described sacred space as a place where wonder can be revealed. The form sacred space can take is as varied as Spirit: a garden, poem, painting, room, altar, shelf, a circular bench underneath an old apple tree, and, of course, a book. And that is how I created what I call the Wonder Book.

Those of you familiar with my work know my use of journals as meditative insight tools, such as the Simple Abundance Journal of Gratitude and the Illustrated Discovery Journal. The Wonder Book was the next step toward my essensual blossoming and can be for you as well if you're game to try it. Basically, it blends key elements of the earlier journals and then takes it a step farther on our spiritual journey. The spiritual practice of the Gratitude Journal was to write down five things every day for which you're grateful. With the Illustrated Discovery Journal, you created a visual auto-biography of your authentic self by crafting collages that reflected your long-forgotten passions and preferences. Now that you have a clearer idea of who you are, it's time to acknowledge, honor, own, and revel in the wonder woman you're discovering as you learn her personal myth.

What I would like you to do is to find a large, beautiful blank book that speaks to your senses. (Mine is a peach-colored journal with long leather ties that wrap around.) Everything about your Wonder Book should appeal: the size, the cover's texture, the color and weight of the paper. Search until you find one that thrills you with its look. To give you an idea of what I mean, when we were putting together the cover of this book, I searched for a long time for the image of a woman that would convey the exquisite bliss that comes when we honor a spirituality of the senses. When I found the nineteenth-century Scottish painter Keith Henderson's gorgeous red-haired "Ydelnesse" (1907), she became *Romancing the Ordinary*'s cover girl, expressing more in her blissful swoon than words could ever say.

Books are living presences and reflect on every page and in between the lines the love that has gone into their creation. This should be the same visceral experience you have with your intimate journal. Feeling magnetically drawn to your own Wonder Book is part of a romantic mystery that will slowly unfold before your eyes. After you find both your mythical image and your book, set aside a special time when you can be alone. Light some beautiful candles, listen to some exquisite music, and sip something festive. Glue your image on a page in the beginning of your book. Gaze upon it gratefully and reflectively. That's all for now. Both you and your image have traveled far to find each other. Each day, as you say your prayers or meditate, or just before you go to sleep, look at your picture and ask it to begin to tell you a story. It will, and as it does, write that story in your Wonder Book. As your story progresses, you'll discover (as I did) that you'll want more pictures to illustrate the tale. Keep searching and they will come to you as if carried by angels.

If you begin creating your Wonder Book during a season of

relinquishment, don't be dismayed if the pictures you choose to illustrate your story seem dark. When we are shrouded in sorrow, we are in the dark.

But as you continue to live your romantic adventure with Life, the images will become brighter, more hopeful. Trust me, this process is magical.

"There is for every man and woman, some one scene, some one adventure, some one picture that is the image of our secret life," W. B. Yeats tells us. "For wisdom first speaks in images and this one image, if we would brood over it our whole life long, would lead our souls disentangled from unmeaning circumstances . . . into that far household where the undying gods await all whose souls have become simple as flames."

There will be many wonderful revelations in the days, weeks, and months ahead as you are drawn deeper into the mystery of your personal myth. But for now, simply be grateful that you are being gently led back to the luminous future, one reflective glance, one heartfelt chapter, at a time, of the one story worth the telling. Yours.

The Essensuality of Desire

Desire accomplished is sweet to the soul.

—Book of Proverbs 13:19

"When Eve bit into the apple, she gave us the world as we know the world—beautiful, flawed, dangerous, full of being. She gave us smallpox and Somalia, polio vaccine and wheat and Windsor roses," Barbara Grizzuti Harrison muses in her meditation on Eve included in the provocative collection of essays *Out of the Garden: Women Writers on the Bible*. "All we know of heaven we know from Eve, who gave us the earth. . . . Without Eve there would be no utopias, no imaginable reason to find and to create transcendence, to ascend toward the light. Eve's legacy to us is the imperative to desire. Babies and poems are born in travail of this desire, her great gift to the loveable world."

Like the apple that came to represent Eve's audacity, the sweet flesh of desire is encased in the taut, bittersweet skin of loss. For there can be no desire without loss; just as loss couldn't exist without the ache for what it once had. The baby's first knowledge of life is loss, the warmth of her mother's womb. But the baby will abandon the breast after the first taste of ice cream. The poet knows that to put desire on the page is to lose intimacy with the Great Creator, but she'll stand up a private date with Divinity any day for a public reading.

In his engaging book *The Botany of Desire: A Plant's Eye View of the World,* Michael Pollan, a prizewinning writer on horticulture, argues that, long before humans understood what was happening, certain plants—particularly tulips, marijuana, potatoes, and apples—seduced by casting a mesmerizing spell over our senses through desire. The four desires he explores are sweetness, beauty, intoxication, and control, which go a long way toward explaining why man and woman have carted these plants around the world to perpetuate their existence.

Isn't that a marvelous thought?

Because what this means is that the apple seduced Eve.

Eve wasn't the mother of Original Sin. Eve was the mother of Essensual Desire.

For who created the apple? The Great Lover. And who made Desire part of woman's nature? The Great Lover. Eve's leaving Eden was always part of the Divine Plan, necessary so that you and I might know Heaven on earth. Paradise. To fulfill our desires, Spirit was willing to endure the first loss of love. As the French mystic Simone Weil expressed it, "Grace fills the empty spaces, but it can only enter where there is a void to receive it, and it is grace itself which makes this void."

Loss creates desire and it's only desire, to live and love again, that heals loss.

Come to Your Senses

Lead Her into Temptation

O ne hesitates to let historical facts stand in the way of a good story, but there seems to be some wrangling (by scholars rather than poets) over whether it was indeed the apple that Eve desired over Eden. Some biblical historians argue for the pomegranate. In his fascinating culinary history, *Apples: The Story of the Fruit of Temptation,* Frank Browning tells us, "Although apples may have grown in Palestine at the time the biblical texts were written (Ramses II apparently received a gift shipment of apple trees from Palestine in the thirteenth century B.C. and Egyptians offered apples to the high priests, the keepers of knowledge and wisdom), no one thought to hang them on the tree of knowledge of good and evil until the fourth or fifth century A.D., when apple trees began appearing in woodcuts and ecclesiastical drawings. The Eastern Church favored figs as the forbidden fruit, while others in the Roman Church argued for the grape. Apples, however, do recur repeatedly in early visions of Paradise throughout the

Indo-European world, and possession of them almost always has to do with desire, fecundity, and the reward of immortality."

Of course, the best way to enjoy an apple is unadorned, as Eve did. Come to think of it, why not evoke Eden in the privacy of your own home. Let your hair down and luxuriate in the last of the summer's heat while nibbling the fruit "in the flesh."

Seriously, my dear, whichever flavor, peel color, and shape takes your fancy, eating that proverbial "apple a day" is healthy for you: low calories, blessed with vitamins A and C, potassium, and fiber. Whenever possible, eat the skin, as much of the nutrition is there rather than in the flesh. Apples have an unfortunate tendency to brown when cut, so if you are using the fruit raw in salads, sprinkle the pieces with a little lemon juice . . . or buy Cortland or yellow Delicious apples, which brown less than the other species.

But sweetness is one of the original desires. So here are two unexpected ways to be led into temptation.

Classic Baked Apple

You will need:

1 large cooking apple, washed and cored
3 tablespoons dark brown sugar
2 tablespoons raisins
1 tablespoon butter
Water

1. Preheat oven to 375° F.
2. Cut a 1½-inch circle of skin off the top of the apple, and also slit the skin around the fruit's "equator," to allow for expansion while baking.
3. Mix the brown sugar and raisins.
4. Place apple in a small ovenproof dish. Fill cored opening with the sugar and raisin mixture, then top with butter.
5. Pour enough water into the pan to come halfway up the side of the apple.
6. Bake the apple for around 45 minutes, or until soft.

Buttery Mulled Cider

1 cup fresh apple cider
2 teaspoons sugar
1 cinnamon stick
1 whole clove
Pinch of ground allspice
½ teaspoon butter
¼ cup calvados

1. In a small saucepan over low heat, bring all ingredients except the butter and calvados to a light simmer, taking care not to let the mixture boil. Stirring occasionally, continue to simmer over low heat for another 15 minutes.
2. Strain into a mug, and stir in the butter and calvados.

Between the Lines

All About Eve

Let me tell you the other story of Eve. Eve did a brave and beautiful thing. She reached her arm past the injunctions of the Father God, she picked the apple from the tree, and bit into its ripe and ready flesh. She knew that it was good, and she passed the apple on to Adam, that he might taste the goodness of it also. In that moment, Adam and Eve awoke from the primordial dream, and their eyes were opened. They saw the beauty of their form in the splendour of their own light.

Now Eve was wise from the beginning . . . because she was able to listen deeply. Eve listened, and beneath the clamour of the Father voice which told her to do its bidding without questioning she could hear the softer whisperings of a truer life. Eve chose this way of life, according to her own conscience, and she took the fruit. In that one moment, Eve blessed all generations to come with the gift of being able to take part in the creation of their own world. . . . Eve "knew" to take the apple. She had the greatness of heart to reach out her hand in the face of all reason. Eve had courage because she knew that in eating the fruit of a conscious life, she would be living the pain as well as the joy.

—Roger Housden
Soul and Sensuality:
Returning the Erotic to Everyday Life

October

October is a symphony of permanence and change.

–B. W. Overstreet

*W*hile we've been making other plans, the year's brazen hussy of a month scatters our good intentions with a haughty laugh. So stop, look, listen, taste, touch, smell the turning of the season. Indulge in sensory *entre nous*. Become bewitched, bothered, and bewildered, one golden autumn afternoon after another. Trifle with the uncanny, let the inexplicable nudge, take a chance on coincidence. Play with the notion of pausing, exchange the day planner for daydreams, rendezvous with romance. Your future's extending an intimate invitation for a heart-to-heart between your present and your past. October is the go-between. What's next? Only tea will tell. But this much is certain. Wonder can be your oyster and the Ordinary is your pearl.

Making Other Plans

Life is what happens to you while you're busy making other plans.

—John Lennon

*D*o you know how to make God laugh?

Try telling Her *your* plans.

Is there anything women love to do more than making plans? We organize from the inside out, careen from the right brain to the left side of the calendar, prioritize from top to bottom. Don't you get a thrill when you pick up a pen and crisp yellow, ruled legal pad? I know I do. And why? Because planning reinforces the feminine hallucination that we are "in control."

Ha!

And then what happens? Life—that series of unexpected, seemingly unconnected events—ricochets right through our reasonably well-thought-out schedule. Of course, being the glorious women that we are, we rise to the unexpected with great style (take a bow, ladies). But then, after we've saved the day and caught our breath, we pick up the pencil again for a few revisions, usually crowding even more into our week or month than before. Einstein believed insanity was continuing to do the same damn thing over and over especially after you know it doesn't work. Does the woman still clutching the To Do list underneath her straitjacket agree?

Life hasn't actually gone the way I've planned this past month. When I have an especially demanding work schedule, which I do right now, I take great pains beforehand to juggle everything carefully so that my commitments and obligations fit together as neatly as a jigsaw puzzle. At least on paper. In fact, until recently, I've been rather proud of my ability—albeit secret—to compartmentalize my life so efficiently. But lately the more I plan, the more I seem to attract fierce psychic opposition. Something or Someone seems determined to upend the table as the demands of home, career, finances, child, love, duty, guilt, prior commitments, intense yearnings, rest, and health fall helter-skelter to the floor. In the ancient Hindu sacred book *The Upanishads*, it's written that the Soul is the "Inner Controller." She "who controls all things." I'm beginning to sense that She doesn't find my planning helpful. Could it be that the more women plan, the less we live?

Consider for a moment that there are only three catalysts for change, whether it's for better or worse: crisis, chance, and choice. Women frequently associate chance with chaos and control with choice. But if, like me, you're sitting on the floor surrounded by a thousand plans gone awry, I suspect it's not chance that got us into this mess. However, choice can get us out of it. Circumstances may often be beyond our control, but there is no such thing as not having a choice.

What is called for is a completely different approach. A radical departure. A spiritual experiment. How about choosing *not to plan anything* for the next week. Go about your business, carry out your tasks, but don't plan to do or add anything extra. Not one more appointment penciled in the margin of the day planner. No, you can't do an extra car pool, volunteer an extra two dozen cookies for the bake sale, or agree to anything that doesn't make you break out into a huge grin. Instead, you're going to pause and do nothing.

That's right. Nothing, except *observe* how destiny, particularly yours, unfolds on its own. Be willing not to *make* anything happen this week. Instead, allow happenstance to help you. Life's sublime mysteries only become our everyday miseries when we insist on creating a detailed blueprint that leaves nothing to chance, especially our happiness. "Who is to decide between 'Let it be' and 'Force it?'" Katherine Mansfield wondered in 1927. Today realize that this miraculous, life-changing choice is yours.

Getting out of Your Own Way

Thousand upon thousand of human plans
are not equal to one of Heaven's.

—Chinese proverb

"*G*od's plans for our lives are always so much better than our own. The day I stopped making plans, the plans began making me," Cristina Carlino, the cofounder of the innovative, imaginative, and inspirational personal-wellness company *philosopy* confides in her book *The Rainbow Connection: How to Use Color and Energy to Transform Your Life*. "By trusting in the mystery, my life became miraculous."

Although Cristina had achieved success developing skin-care products for plastic surgeons, she longed to be able to push past the boundaries of the commercial cosmetic industry with a beauty line intended to nurture a woman's inner radiance as well as enhance her looks. Cristina wanted to package not just collagen but daily reminders that emphasized gratitude and the belief in miracles— and a woman's inherent power to make them happen. "God speaks to us through so many mediums, including mathematics, science, music, literature, nature, and yes, even color," she says. Then, why not cosmetics? I agree with her because it's difficult not to smile or say a little prayer when you reach for a moisturizer called Hope in a Jar, shower with Saving Grace, or dab on a night cream called Eye Believe.

"Miracles occur when we align our soul, our heart, our thoughts, and our actions with conscious choice, and with God," says Cristina Carlino. But more important, miracles happen "when you get out of your own way."

Getting out of your own way is everywoman's hardest hurdle, especially if you're used to making things happen, which seems to be the daily round for the gals I know. But all too often, we're so busy making things happen for other people, we're oblivious to the dangerous taxing of our own mind, body, and spirit. Until the day comes when we can't take it anymore, or give it, and we get desperate enough to cry for help. I call it asking for grace. You may call it giving up. But no matter what we call it, the miracle is that, finally, we're getting out of our own, and Spirit's, way.

Entre Nous

We will only understand the miracle of life fully when we allow the unexpected to happen.

—Paul Coelho

"At one time or another most of us have experienced strange and inexplicable happenings: someone rings just when we're thinking of telephoning them; a letter arrives containing exactly the information we need that day; a book falls off the shelf, we open it, and the words we read hit us right between the eyes; we find ourselves sitting next to someone on a train who turns out to be a vital catalyst for future events. How do such things happen and, more importantly, *why* do they happen and *what* are they for?" Deike Begg asks in *Synchronicity: The Promise of Coincidence,* which is the best book I've ever read explaining the mystery of unexpected coincidences as a spiritual gift. "Quite often synchronistic phenomena are announcements of important coming events; at other times they are signs of comfort, which assure us that 'all shall be well.' They can also be signposts that show us which way to go next, or which way *not* to go next. Again and again they give us the feeling that we are in contact with something that looks out for us, which has our own best interests at heart and which will be present whether we invoke it or not."

Outside of Newton's Chapel, there's a very old apple tree, and I sit underneath it as often as I can, leaning against the trunk.

Each time I do, I'm struck by the happenstance that led me here, linking my ordinary daily round with one of the world's most cosmic coincidences: the apple falling from the tree while Sir Isaac Newton sat under it, disappointed and exhausted because every experiment he was doing so painstakingly right was going so terribly wrong. In the late summer and fall, when the fruit is heavy on the branch, I sit carefully because apples tumble down regularly, and after my head injury, I've got a thing about fast-moving orbs. And an apple falls down very directly. No veering to the left. No sashaying to the right. Plop. Plummet. Straight down. Newton had seen many apples drop before, but on that particular day during the summer of 1666, the apple's fall became a catalyst for one of science's most significant moments. Too tired to be anything but receptive, Newton understood this ordinary occurrence in a new light.

One Newton biographer, L. T. More, wrote in 1934, "It was a trifling incident which has been idly noticed thousands of times; but now, like the click of some small switch which starts a great machine in operation, it proved to be the jog which awoke his mind to action." Today scholars discount the story as apocryphal, doubting its authority because it's too simplistic. But it's fascinating that the word *apocryphal,* which comes to us from the Greek, originally meant "hidden" and "secret." And indeed, Newton kept the story of the apple to himself for twenty years. The workings of the universe may well be encoded in enigmas, but the conundrums are common ones. And the revelations that help us understand our place in it are always as *simple* as they are stunning, especially to the person experiencing them, even if it's all Greek to the rest of the world. Deike Begg, a British psychotherapist and astrologer, explains, "A synchronistic event not only has something uncanny about it, something otherworldly, inexplicable, and wondrous, but it also has an important meaning for the person involved."

In 1929, the Swiss psychologist Carl Jung first introduced the world to the concept of synchronicity—the intersection of two totally independent events, that when put together, like missing puzzle pieces, take on deep personal significance particular to an individual. The soul of synchronicity is the meaning *we* attach to the events. Spirit is very specific.

Certainly the mystical chain of chance that led me to be writing this book in Isaac Newton's sacred hideaway, nearly 350 years later, were synchronistic. But I was open, receptive, even eager for it, and by following each weird (to the rest of the world), intuitive nudge, I was led smiling all the way to wonder. *"How* we interpret the signs depends on how sensitive we are to the callings from a world that lies beyond our physical limits," Deike Begg says. That's because we can just as easily "deliberately block out synchronistic occurrences" as allow them to edge us in another direction. We're more likely to disregard our sense of "knowing" when we feel as if we're in control of our lives, when our plans work out. But when our best-laid plans run amok and we're panicking, we often hesitate; confusion creates a small cosmic chasm between reason and soul, thank Heavens. Chance is given a window of opportunity. "Some people are comforted by synchronicity, for it suggests to them that they are under the influence of divine guidance. Others are petrified, because to them it means that they are not in control—at any moment Fate could step in and deal them a nasty blow."

I've often used the term *everyday epiphanies* to describe luminous moments of sudden insight that transform our view of the world. Most of the time what we're processing is the world's static— more information than any of us needs, disturbing news, other people's opinions, and a jumble of contradictory cacophony. But every once in a great while, an "aha" transmission makes out the soul's impassioned Morse code—the dots and dashes of our daily round—tapping out messages to be discerned in the small, the simple, the common, and the ordinary. What's right before our eyes.

Think of everyday epiphanies as synchronistic events which are *entre nous,* a marvelous French expression meaning an intimate secret exchanged just between two people. *Entre nous* between you and *Whom?*

"Is it possible that there exists another 'self' that lives alongside the self we know and does this self know more than we do?" Deike Begg wonders. "There seems to be an altogether 'other' that knows more than us, can see into the future, and also has the ingenious ability to find the quickest route to return us to our destined path."

Yes, and she's called your Essensual Self.

As Begg notes, "We have been well trained and socially conditioned to trust only what we can experience with our five outer senses. Yet, genuine synchronistic events can only be registered when our normal, everyday consciousness is off-guard and their meaning can only be understood if we allow ourselves to 'think' with that other mind of ours, that mind which can make connections that are not obvious at first glance. The trick is to learn to use that other mind with a free spirit and an open heart."

The Pause That Refreshes

Since her childhood it had seemed to her that
the movement of all laws, even natural ones,
was either suspended or accelerated on the Sabbath.

—Ellen Glasgow (1925)

*W*hen you pause to make room for Mystery in your daily round, an astonishing thing occurs. Life begins to fall beautifully into place in ways you could never have imagined and could certainly never have planned. I've been blessed to have many of my dreams come true. But my sweat, tears, and toil often weren't enough. Learning when to be stubborn and when to surrender tipped the Divine scales in my favor.

And while it's true that most often the only way to get something done is to work our butts off, Spirit seems to offer more imaginative suggestions and constructive shortcuts to those who believe that self-help isn't a solo act but a Divine collaboration that can only happen if the Self asks for help.

But frankly we don't consider that until we become too exhausted to continue fiddling, fussing, planning, and plotting. Often we think that we're abandoning our dreams, giving up, when in reality what we're doing, or being forced to do, is clear cosmic space. The Universe abhors a vacuum. Sometimes when we cease struggling, our surrender cues synchronicity's entrance.

Good luck, perfect timing, and amazing coincidence are meant to be available to us as frequently as our daily bread, once we start cooperating with the Cosmos and use the fulcrum of faith to move our lives in the right direction.

Synchronicity likes to hang out with serendipity, which is the discovery of wonders you weren't looking for. For example, synchronicity will get you and an antique dealer to the same flea market; serendipity whispers to you to go look at that stall you just passed by because a cursory glance suggested it wasn't very interesting. Five minutes later you've discovered something so fabulous you can't live without it, like my Victorian hatbox, or the treasure trove of nineteenth-century women's and children's magazines that became the foundation for *Mrs. Sharp's Traditions*.

The great mythologist Joseph Campbell described the spiritual graces of synchronicity and serendipity as "a thousand unseen helping hands." Any given Saturday or Sunday is a perfect opportunity for us to discover how right he was by becoming reacquainted with the Pause that refreshes, renews, and recharges. The Pause of rest, rejoicing, and reconciliation. The Pause that ends the estrangement between your body and soul. The Pause that gets results when we can't. The Pause that delights in delivering dreams to our doorstep or redirecting them toward our essensual passions instead of toward other people's preferences.

"Wonder begins in the senses, comes alive in the imagination, and flourishes in adoration of the Divine," Frederic and Mary Ann Brussat tell us in *Spiritual Rx: Prescriptions for Living a Meaningful Life*. You may not be able to pause today. If you can't, then plan to do so in a few days, even if it's just for a few hours. Today just wonder what your life might look like, sound like, taste like, smell like, and feel like, if you gave it and yourself a rest.

In the Nick of Time

The Sabbath was made for man,
not man for the Sabbath . . .

—Mark 2:27

"*G*od does not want us to be exhausted. God wants us to be happy," the spiritual writer Wayne Muller reassures us persuasively in *Sabbath: Restoring the Sacred Rhythm of Rest.* The "Sabbath is a time for sacred rest; it may be a holy day, the seventh day of the week, as in the Jewish tradition, or the first day of the week as for Christians. But Sabbath time may also be a Sabbath afternoon, a Sabbath hour, a Sabbath walk—indeed anything that preserves a visceral experience of life-giving nourishment and rest," Wayne explains. "Sabbath time is time off the wheel, time when we take our hand from the plough and let God and the earth care for things, while we drink, if only for a few moments, from the fountain of rest and delight.

"Sabbath is more than the absence of work; it is not just a day off, when we catch up on television or errands. It is the presence of something that arises when we consecrate a period of time to listen to what is most deeply beautiful, nourishing, or true. It is a time consecrated with our attention, our mindfulness, honoring those quiet forces of grace of spirit that sustain and heal us."

But Wayne Muller knows that this isn't easy today, which makes it all the more necessary. "In our drive for success we are seduced by the promises of more: more money, more recognition, more satisfaction, more love, more information, more influence, more possessions, more security. Even when our intentions are noble and our efforts sincere—even when we dedicate our lives to the service of others—the corrosive pressure of frantic overactivity can nonetheless cause suffering in ourselves and others."

Wayne Muller felt compelled to write *Sabbath* after his own relentless work and unceasing good intentions brought him close to death. Felled with an often fatal bacterial infection (the same one that killed Jim Henson, who created the Muppets), he became so exhausted he could not lift his head or open his eyes. Only a month before he had been living "a typical life," seeing his psychotherapy patients, traveling around the country lecturing and teaching, and running his nonprofit organization, Bread for the Journey, created to support the poor, the hungry, and others in need. But Wayne couldn't take time to respond to his own need to rest. "This one little conversation, this one extra phone call, this one quick meeting, what can it cost? But it does cost, it drains yet another drop of our life. Then, at the end of days, weeks, months, years, we collapse, we burn out, and cannot see where it happened. It happened in a thousand unconscious events, tasks, and responsibilities that seemed easy and harmless on the surface but that each, one after the other, used a small portion of our precious life."

Although *Sabbath* is a wonderfully soothing and healing book, it was difficult for me to read because its truth literally triggered panic attacks. Was it a coincidence that I was reading it in bed during a frustrating time of convalescence that didn't fit into my plans or anyone else's? I don't think so. Anytime we have a visceral reaction to something we're reading, we're meant to pay attention, especially if our reaction is to slam the book shut. Think of it as your future extending an invitation for a heart-to-heart between your present and your past. Your body is the go-between.

Of course, it's glorious when we agree with another writer's observation. But don't discount a negative response—anger, annoyance, or even vague unease—that is the easiest reaction to ignore. Be willing to reread the trigger passages slowly, meditatively, and with thanks. Then put away the book and mull over the message.

We, and I'm referring to most of the women I know, are so overworked and overwrought we don't know how to help ourselves any longer. How about realizing that we can't unless we stop, not dead in our tracks, but while we're still alive? "Sabbath does not require us to leave home, change jobs, go on retreat, or leave the world of ordinary life," Wayne Muller reminds us. "Sabbath time is not spiritually superior to our work. The practice is rather to find that balance point at which, having rested, we do our work with greater ease and joy, and bring healing and delight to our endeavors."

And we resist at our peril. "If we do not allow for a rhythm of rest in our overly busy lives, illness becomes our Sabbath—our pneumonia, our cancer, our heart attack, our accidents, create Sabbath for us," he warns. "If we forget to rest we will work too hard, and forget our more tender mercies, forget those we love, forget our children and our natural wonder. God says: Please, don't. It is a waste of a tremendous gift I have given you. If you knew the value of your life, you would not waste a single breath. So I give you this commandment: Remember to rest. This is not a lifestyle suggestion, but a commandment—as important as not stealing, not murdering, or not lying. Remember to play and bless and make love and eat with those you love, and take comfort, easy and long, in this gift of sacred rest."

She Wears It Well

No good poem, however confessional it may be, is just a self expression. Who on earth would claim that the pearl expresses the oyster?

—Robert Cecil Day-Lewis

Recently, while excavating the dark recesses of my guest-room closet, I happened upon a red leather jewelry box that was a gift to me at age thirteen. It's been with me through puberty, motherhood, and menopause, unintentionally serving as a repository for costume-jewelry discards—you know, the pieces that defined the era and made you look and feel like part of the pack, even if you weren't.

Inside were sentimental favorites—plastic Pop-It beads from the fifties, the circle pin worn on round-collared Villager shirts through college, and African shell strings that witnessed the sit-ins of the late sixties. On the suede bottom of the case, hidden behind a chorus-girl collection of single earrings waiting patiently to see if their mates would ever return, my fingers found a timeless treasure that I'd forgotten I'd had: my grandmother's pearls. They'd gone missing over thirty years ago. I probably "borrowed" them from my own mother's jewelry box without asking permission and then *forgot* to return them. Daughters have been known to do that sort of thing.

Oddly enough, through the years, especially after my mother died, I resigned myself to this sad loss. But I often longed for the comfort those pearls provided and for their singular beauty, especially as I would occasionally search for their replacements, which I never found. Their sudden reappearance now is a good example of serendipity, which always seems to bring us gifts wrapped up in understanding.

It takes a long time for a woman to grow up and bloom into herself. As the great Pearl Bailey wrote in her memoir, *The Raw Pearl,* "There's a period of life when we swallow knowledge of ourselves, and it becomes either good or sour inside." There's also a period when we can wear the jewelry of that knowledge— pearls of wisdom—with pride and pleasure. In many families a girl receives her first string of pearls for her sixteenth birthday. It's a sign that she's becoming a young lady. But I believe that only a grown-up woman can carry off pearls with panache.

I am beginning to appreciate parts of my body that I've been oblivious to until now, and my neck is one of them. I have a lovely neck, and considering how many times I've stuck it out on my behalf, I'd like to adorn it with something fitting.

We associate pearls with maharajas, award-winning fiction, and glorious women: Jacqueline Kennedy Onassis, Princess Diana, and Audrey Hepburn. Cleopatra wanted her pearls buried with her, Elizabeth I had pearls ground up and used for medicinal purposes, and they were considered appropriate payment for the ransoming of royalty. After a particularly ugly breakup, a dear friend of mine purchased one single, exquisite pearl on a gold chain. She wears it as a lucky talisman—a reminder of her self-worth—and as a sacred promise never to let herself be emotionally or psychically trampled upon again in a relationship. I always admire how gracefully self-respect plays up a woman's best feature: her soul.

The fascinating thing about pearls is that they are conceived through irritation and grow slowly in layers, just as our lives do. Something foreign such as a piece of grit or a parasite gets beneath the shell of an oyster, embeds itself in the oyster's soft lining, and years later emerges in a new form, as effortlessly, it would seem, as a butterfly from its chrysalis. But consider the oyster. It had to put up with discomfort and discontent. As I finger my grandmother's exquisite necklace—a set of luminous balls strung together—I marvel at their creation and wonder if these "irritations" aren't eloquent testimony to the becoming of a woman. How many of us are relentlessly nudged by discontent and discomfort, just as pearls are shaped by gritty sand, then lie hidden in cocoons of complacency, only to emerge more intact, wholly wondrous after decades of being lost?

Of course, the cardinal rule about taking care of pearls is never to leave them unworn in a jewelry box; I'd hazard a guess there might be a string of pearls you've been saving for a special occasion. How about today? Like Life and love, pearls thrive on skin contact and will lose their luster if not worn. Although pearls grow in darkness and distress, the luminosity of their beauty—born of imperfection, irritation, and, sometimes, neglect—like the woman who wears them, is only visible in the Light.

Come to Your Senses

Every Woman's Gem

*W*hether with casual clothes or when we need to feel "dressed," pearls, worn lovingly, are my definition of perfect, flexible jewelry. They announce that we have taste, sophistication, and a sense of style. There are pearls to fit your mood, the occasion, and to showcase your physical attributes to their best advantage.

The best part is that they don't have to be "real." While pearls were once affordable only by the wealthy, technology and popularity conspired in the last century to make them a gem for all seasons. Basically pearls come in three broad categories:

Natural—produced by shell-boring parasites in mollusks, without human assistance. (Extremely expensive!)

Cultured—farmed in underwater fields after artificial insemination and then harvested. (Affordable to expensive.)

Faux—(French for "fake" and found in all price ranges) also known as simulated, costume, and imitation pearls and created by repeatedly dipping beads into a pearly varnish solution. You might remember that the necklace many of us most associate with Jackie Kennedy was her triple string of faux pearls.

Natural and cultured pearls are considered products of nature and are more likely to be called "real," but truly great costume pearls make a "real" statement. A quick check—rub pearls against your teeth. Cultured and natural pearls are gritty; faux pearls are smooth.

There are many different aspects to consider besides price when buying pearls. The first thing to look for is color. Natural and cultured pearls come in many shades—white, pink, silver, cream, gold, and black. Pink tones are the most highly prized at the moment, but trends change. The best thing to do is try them on to see which hues complement your skin tones. After color, consider the luster of the pearls. Look for a rainbow or iridescent glow when the pearls catch the light. And finally size and shape. Perfectly round pearls are extremely rare, but most cultured pearls are close enough. Oval, blister, X-shaped, baroque, and teardrop shapes are usually less expensive and are frequently reserved for brooches, bracelets, and other ornaments.

Strings of pearls come in many different lengths, and what you choose depends on your budget and the neckline of the out-fits with which you want to wear them. Here's a fun way to think about a pearl wardrobe.

The Little Black Dress. This is the fourteen-to-sixteen-inch-long simple strand. The starting place for most women's pearl wardrobe, it hangs to midclavicle.

Collar. Or choker à la your pet poodle. This sits higher on your neck. Every night Empress Josephine wore hers to bed.

The Princess. This string of pearls is sixteen to nineteen inches long. Slightly longer than the simple strand, it hangs to about the top of your lovely décolleté and does wonders with a plunge.

Bib. Barbara Bush's three-graduated-strand mainstay. The top strand is collar length; the bottom, the length of the simple strand.

Matinee. Cleavage-gracing with its twenty-inch length. Best over higher necklines.

Opera. At thirty inches, this long strand can be doubled or tripled and worn in overlapping rows around the neck. Dowager queens went for these, but so does Sharon Stone. These are for times when more is better.

There are many reputable sources for pearls: department stores, jewelry stores, and specialty retail outlets for cultured brands such as the celebrated Mikimoto. Pearls can also be found on hundreds of Web sites, at gem and jewelry shows, and even at local gift shows. (Just be a smart consumer and ask for the store's or dealer's refund and return policy, and get a full, written description of what you're buying on the bill of sale.)

But the biggest fun of pearls is trying on a variety of strands to find out what looks best on you, and for this I love antique shows, shops, and flea markets, which are great venues for the bargain pearl hunter. I've ransomed a couple of different costume-jewelry pearl necklaces, and my favorite is a faux five-strand from the fifties. It cost me more to get them restrung than to buy them, but was well worth it because they're a knockout and look glorious with everything from an old tweed jacket to my best cocktail dress.

Remember, though, that it's how pearls make you feel that counts—not what you paid for them or the label on their box. Everyone assumed that Jacqueline Kennedy's signature pearls were genuine, and everyone was wrong. A set of faux pearls worn three times a week with love and great style is worth more to the daughter or granddaughter who'll inherit them than the fancy set that cost two months' pay but just sat in a cushioned box, too dear to be displayed and enjoyed. What makes a string of pearls "real" is the woman wearing them.

The Familiar Revisited

The cream of enjoyment in this life is always impromptu.
The chance walk; the unexpected visit; the unpremeditated
journey; the unsought conversation or acquaintance.

—Fanny Fern (1872)

*A*s the daylight hours decrease and the air turns crisp, we're reminded that it will soon be too cool to take leisurely strolls through our ordinary Edens (though I'm sure the original had four seasons). Searching the back of the closet to unearth the scarf we bought on sale late last winter, we suddenly fast-forward to a few weeks from now, coat wrapped tightly around us, face muffled against the elements, already grumbling about winter. In about thirty seconds we've already tossed away the gift of these autumn days without opening it.

It's time to revisit the familiar and invite Spontaneity to come along with us. She's the babe who always brings the party with her. While synchronicity can't be scheduled and serendipity pouts when we push her, both of them are easily seduced into good moods by Spontaneity. It's been my experience that one of Spontaneity's favorite excursions is into Soft Time, that spiritual dimension when unexpected pleasure jolts us from being a detached observer into Life's lover. And often just a simple walk someplace new triggers it. "Soft Time is warm and moist and earthy," British writer Gill Edwards explains in *Pure Bliss: The Art of Living in Soft Time*. "It gently reaches deep down into our roots, our core, our very soul. Life becomes an almost unbearably rich experience." One of the reasons is that we get to hang out with our wild, essensual Self, who helps us "reestablish balanced cycles of work, play, creativity, and sexuality—like the rhythms of nature. Without our wildness, we don't know how to pace ourselves. We are too 'nice' and make life-sapping choices, giving away our power to others. When we reclaim our wild Self, we are wise, powerful, creative, and intuitive. We are fearlessly individualistic. We are passionate and spontaneous."

So let's open our eyes to the streets we travel through every day but don't really see, listen to acorns drop from the trees as squirrels busily store food, and jump into a pile of leaves. The longer we live or work in a community, the more we drift into spending our days on automatic pilot, programmed to go to the office, the grocery, our own front door, without noticing our surroundings. And what a shame it is, because right nearby there are wonders at every turn! We don't need to go far afield to be surprised, exhilarated, and delighted. Whether we live in the city or the country, we need only to observe, to sniff, to listen. To sigh with pleasure at a new view, a fresh perspective, and an unexpected break—the spontaneous bliss of soft time.

"When we're in Soft Time, we might feel intense joy at catching a falling leaf, seeing a pale wintry sun, hearing a child laugh or a skylark sing, or stroking the mossy bark of a tree. We feel whole and complete. We feel connected. Our mind is peaceful and still. There is no desire to search, to act, to do. Everything we need is right here—in this moment," Gill Edwards tells us. "Soft Time is 'recreation' in its true sense—time in which we re-create the Self by coming back to ourselves, by deeply relaxing, by simply 'being' for a while."

Come to Your Senses

Backwoods Babe

"Nature has been for me, for as long as I can remember, a source of solace, inspiration, adventure, and delight: a home, a teacher, a companion," Lorraine Anderson writes in *Sisters of the Earth*. But I'm just a newly born backwoods babe, which is funny considering that I spent many years trying to run away from a small rural New England town. However, now that I have finally come to my senses, I've discovered that the only woman who gets bored is one who doesn't know where to take a walk, the surest way to shift gears from overdrive into soft time.

Armed with vintage nature books, like travel guides to exotic locales, I set off for new horizons, which to my neighbors look just like their "ordinary" fields and hedgerows. Perhaps you, too, may have stopped taking in all the wonders burgeoning beyond your doorstep. It's time to discover that no day in Mother Nature's playground is exactly like any other. Allow me to show you around, toots.

Take plant life, for example. Perhaps you know the names of the flowers and shrubs you've planted in your own garden. But do you know what's growing on the paths you pass every day? Living amid greenery in all directions, do you actually take nature walks to meet grasses, flowers, bushes, trees . . . perhaps even edible fruits and nuts . . . that any passing bird or squirrel probably knows better than you do? Break away from your routines. Stop to see what's growing on the road you walk or drive down every day. Snoop along roads and paths that you rarely encounter, simply to see what's there.

Are there bodies of water nearby? No lake or river or stream is exactly the same, end to end. Follow it with your eye, walk its shoreline. What color is the water? How does it change as the hour and time of month vary? Can you see deep into the water? What's visible below the surface? Can you see your reflection? If you float a paper boat or leaf in the water, where does it go? Is the shoreline sandy, rocky, grassy? Can you find small, interesting objects at its edge—shells, coral, pretty wave-washed stones? Are there gulls or other seabirds overhead? Does the place have an air of peacefulness, of turbulence, of stagnation? What about two hundred yards down?

Wander off the path into fields or woods. Listen. Can you hear the insects, birds, small woodland creatures, rustling and whispering together? Can you keep so still that they will come forth to continue their daily activities in your presence? What greenery and flowers can you find in natural symbiosis with each other? Are there mosses on the trees? Can you spot insects at their work, or birds preparing to fly south as the days grow chilly?

If there is a botanical garden or nature preserve nearby, spend some time there, and contrast what you find with what is growing about outside its gates. Are there marked nature trails, helping you to learn the names of plants or creatures you wouldn't otherwise recognize? Are there historic, even ancient features of the land that have been set apart, untouched by time? As the leaves fall, the landscape changes drastically from the lush coverage that crowned summer days. In fact, it's a whole new world.

Stroll toward a single tree or clusters. Look up and appreciate the tapestry of changing colors of the greenery from a distance; look down at the range of colors of individual fallen leaves upon the ground. Isn't it amazing how trees that are solidly green all summer can produce so many different tones: pale yellow, golden yellow, warm tan, russet, puce, rose-red, maroon, even purple? Perhaps the nineteenth-century poet Anne Mary Lawler describes it best: "October dresses in flame and gold / Like a woman afraid of growing old."

Linger, explore, and grow younger with every glance. Wherever you go, pretend that you are seeing the land, the water, the sky, for the very first time (in many ways, perhaps you are), dropped upon Earth for a one-day visit. Take it one sense at a time: close your eyes and smell the smells. Listen. Touch everything you can possibly reach, for texture and softness and wetness and weight.

Don't be in too much of a hurry to dismiss what you assume is familiar. Nature is not perfect: branches may be ragged, animals have more stripes on one side than on the other. Have you ever really examined what a plant's individual components—stems, leaves, seeds, and so on—look like? Are trees old, gnarled, with split and knobby trunks, or young saplings covered with smooth bark? Are there birds' nests? Are stones beneath your feet all of the same material, or of different colors, different shapes, striated or shot through with glitter? Is the earth itself dusty taupe, brown, even red? Have you looked closely at an insect's body structure, at just how it moves to run or fly? Can you identify what it is that distinguishes one breed of bird from another? Notice how the coat of a deer changes color to camouflage itself from predators as the woodland colors around it run to rusts and browns. When was the last time you lay on the grass and saw pictures in the clouds? If you find a favorite spot, return to it regularly, as even the passing of a day may bring new riches to explore.

Bring along a cassette recorder and tape the rushing of water, the chirping or hum of bugs and birds, the conversations of furry creatures. Play it back when you're indoors, and watch the visuals of the scene come flowing back as you listen. Create an autumn symphony that you can savor when cooler weather stills your outdoor music to a creak and hush.

In Victorian times, women often sketched "studies" of nature. Bring along a pad and pencil or even watercolors; create a sense memory of this new world. Capture the individuality of a leaf, a beak, a cloud. Or, again as the Victorians did, bring back small souvenirs to touch and smell: brilliant fallen leaves, handsome stones, a spray of dried golden grass. But leave what is still growing in its place, to continue uninterrupted. You'll want to come for another sensory indulgence soon.

A Sunday Kind of Love

*Sunday is sort of like a piece of bright gold brocade
lying in a pile of white muslin weekdays.*

–Yoshiko Uchida

*W*hat did your last Sunday look like? Mine was a stopped-up toilet, an emergency rewrite of a magazine article that had been sitting on an editor's desk for three months, and six loads of dirty laundry. And I sure didn't find a piece of bright gold brocade hiding among the week's sheets, towels, and socks. Perhaps that's because the gold brocade tablecloth sat on a dark shelf in my linen closet. Patiently waiting to be spread out, eager to soak up spilled wine, gravy, and warm candlewax, longing to be privy to laughter and shared confidences. Instead, the gold brocade was haughty in her abandonment, her crisp folds reproachful in their disuse. "Next week," I told her. She doesn't believe me anymore and I can't blame her. Neither do I.

Remember our wonder years when Life was so generously apportioned into five days on and two days off? Back then, Sunday afternoons were a bit wistful, even if you hadn't done much at all and were bored to tears. It was because we knew that the next day we had to go back to the daily grind of school and homework. Now those *were* the days.

Not long ago I spent a Sunday in a hospital emergency room

waiting for a couple of stitches and a tetanus shot after nearly severing my thumb while trying to pry a can of orange juice open with a butcher knife (don't ask). I shared the cubicle with a woman who'd sprained her ankle in a nasty spill. Because our medical needs were low in priority (thank God), we spent a few hours waiting to be seen and dozing. Every so often, a nurse would pop her head in to see how we were doing. Don't worry about us, we'll be fine, we'd tell her. Finally she needed our vital statistics: "How many kids do you have?" My cubicle mate told the nurse she had three under five, including a two-month-old. "Who's with them?"

"Their father."

"You worried?"

"No."

"And you?" the nurse asked. Since I only had a pile of paperwork waiting at home, I saw the doctor first. It was the least I could do for womankind.

"We live in a culture that denigrates rest. We think that we need to fill every moment with action. Some people have difficulty with even an instant of silence," Rabbi Naomi Levy writes persuasively in her wonderful *Talking to God: Personal Prayers for Times of Joy, Sadness, Struggle and Celebration.* "Now, because of cell phones, e-mail, and pagers, the borders between work and home have disintegrated. Colleagues can reach us wherever we are. There are people who cannot turn off their cell phones, who cannot hold a conversation with a live human being in front of them without stopping to take a call. Our work always hovers; stress follows us while we walk or drive or even sit in a movie theater. Having no separation between work and rest is unhealthy for our bodies and for our souls. Constant work leads to a lack of creativity. You can have all the drive in the world, but if you never stop driving, you will never know all the wonders that have flashed by your window. Life becomes a blur."

Although all the great religions teach the importance of honoring the Sabbath, those women who have grown up in more orthodox spiritual traditions such as Judaism or Islam are blessed because the idea of a day of sacred rest is fundamental to the ordering of their week. If they have lapsed in keeping the Sabbath, a return to the practice feels healing and right, a source of redemption rather than guilt. But if, like me, you've not been raised to set aside one day a week for sacred rest and renewal, incorporating one into your life and keeping it will be a difficult challenge. Rabbi Levy suggests we approach it deliberately. "You can't wait passively for the Sabbath to arrive. You have to *make* the Sabbath. You have to prepare your body for receiving the Sabbath; you have to bathe and choose Sabbath clothes that make you feel special. You have to prepare your soul; you have to put away the cares of the week and welcome the precious gift of rest. You have to prepare your home for receiving the Sabbath; you have to fix Sabbath food and welcome Sabbath guests. The atmosphere is magically transformed. Holy rest is an art form. It's not simply the absence of work. It is the presence of all the sacred pleasures you can partake in: a festive meal, family and friends, a good book, a little romance, a walk in nature, a prayer to God."

It is searching for, and finding, a beautiful piece of gold brocade, in the back of the linen closet, or at the beginning of your week.

Come to Your Senses

The Passionate Flea

?

*I*t's been said that hobbies protect us from passions and passions protect us from obsessions. Tell that to a woman hunting and gathering in the serendipitous atmosphere of a flea market.

Most collectors and bargain hunters look forward to these free-wheeling retail experiences, while others are fearful that they'll make naive, irreversible mistakes. A friend whose expertise has earned her the nickname "the passionate flea" has given me some of the best advice ever on surviving open marketplaces. Thanks to her, I've never felt that I'm being "had." I have confidence doing business in a setting that might not be there tomorrow, and I've learned to trust my own flea market savvy. You can, too.

As with every other aspect of your life, the most crucial element in any shopping transaction is you. You know what you're looking for, what you love, and what you want. You probably don't need another thing. You also know what you're willing to pay and whether you have to hide your purchases in the trunk of the car. So only you can arbitrate a détente between the passionate and the practical, although admittedly, there have been flea market excursions where I thought I was the caretaker of multiple personalities.

Normally we like to leave our mind behind on fun outings, but it can help get you outfitted for the adventure. It can remind you to wear practical shoes (through muddy fields) and carry sunscreen, sunglasses, or a hat (not all dealers are under tarps), bottled water, tissue packs (get used to a Porta Potti), and an umbrella in an expandable bag. Spring and fall excursions also require layered clothing that rivals the gear you might need striding through the Alps. Weather-sensitive shoppers would do better in indoor antique shops or on the Internet.

I prefer to go to flea markets as a meditative practice, roaming alone so that I open to serendipity. If I go with a friend, we'll separate to explore on our own and check back with each other every hour or so. It's all about your personal style; other women like to comb flea markets and antique shows in groups, looking for specific items. If you know exactly what you're searching for, it's a good idea to bring multiple photocopies of a picture or sketch that includes your contact information. If your china pattern or treasured object appears weeks later, a conscientious dealer can find you, and it can still be yours.

Remember the size of the show and pace yourself. Some people like to start at the farthest point and end up conveniently near where they parked their car; some like to retrace their steps to see if any prices have been lowered since they last asked. Still others set off on a speedwalk, scouting out the whole show before opening their purse. There are those who believe that they should never buy what interests them at first glance, while others snap up immediately something that catches their eye. Both approaches balance risk and loss. So if you suspect you can't live without it, walk away slowly.

Serendipity can fill your cupboards with things you truly love and never expected to. Open your eyes and rejoice in the visual cornucopia before you. Wander and give yourself some time as your "eye" becomes seasoned. You may find yourself in hot pursuit of a transfer-ware bowl, only to end up with the crystal jam pot next to it. But don't forget that the bowl called to you, too. Check out its price (because you liked it) and see how it compares with similar ones in the show. By the end of the day your eye will tell you what you like and you'll have a general idea of a fair price. The jam pot will be useful, was a great buy, and you would never have seen it if you hadn't followed your eye.

You can gauge the intensity of your lust by bringing just so much cash with you (although some shows take plastic and checks). But these questions are pretty insightful:

Where will I put this treasure? Visualize the display/shelf/garage space at home. Make sure that when you get home, some empty space can be created with a little sorting and shifting. But if there's no room, move on.

How will it complement my life/collection/decor?

Is it the perfect gift for someone in my life?

Can I live without it?

Price doesn't have to set off a panic button, although sticker shock has its value, too. Dealers mark their inventory in two ways. They add a percentage to what they paid for the item or they research current literature (eBay's "Past Sales" on similar pieces is a great source for such info). Then they price according to the current market value. It's always wise to ask if they can do better than the stickered price ("Is this the best you can do?"). If you're serious about buying, ask if you can make an offer, but don't be insulting (20 percent is a usual dealer discount). You never know how long the item has been in inventory and how anxious the dealer is to have cash in hand. *Caveat emptor* should be on your mind at all times, and remember that your knowledge of authenticity and value may prove your find to be a real bargain. While dealers are usually aware of what they're selling, you might just know better! And in any case, you have an emotional set point in your mind for what something's worth *to you.*

One last bit of advice: If you can't get it home easily and the dealer doesn't have a shipping policy, I'd take it as a sign that it's just not meant to be yours.

Tea Will Tell

We grow in time to trust the future for our answers.

—Ruth Fulton Benedict

"Our faith in the present dies out long before our faith in the future," the anthropologist Ruth Fulton Benedict observed in 1915, which explains perfectly why women are so addicted to the fantasy of micromanaging *mañana*. Actually, what we really want is a break, so why not just take one? Put the kettle on and put the day planner down. Let's indulge in a different daily dose of destiny—tea leaf reading.

Perhaps you've been too embarrassed or skeptical ever to step into a gypsy tearoom, but I'd wager you have always been a bit curious about this traditional form of fortune-telling, which can be performed in private right in your own home. Spangles and head scarves are optional; all you need is a cup and saucer, and loose-leaf tea.

Opening a tea bag won't work, as the tea is too finely ground. You need the real thing for this ancient form of divination, the kind with lumps and stems, sold for brewing in a pot or tea ball. Buy a flavor you like, as you'll be drinking the tea first—no sugar or milk, please!—before reading the damp leaves. But brew the tea in your cup without using the tea ball, so that the leaves settle at the bottom as you sip.

Drink all but a teaspoon or so of your tea. Then, holding the cup in your left hand, swirl the liquid three times. Immediately turn the cup upside down to drain into its saucer.

When the cup is drained, turn it right side up and hold the handle in your right hand (three-o'clock position). Look at the position of the leaves, reading from left to right. It's good luck to have a fairly even scattering of leaves over the sides of the cup; although traditionally a lot of leaves at the bottom is bad luck, it may only mean you need to swirl your leaves more skillfully next time! (Are there no leaves left in the cup? A lucky sign indeed—this means you will have no problems!)

According to old-fashioned fortune-telling guides, stalks and stems indicate people. Thin, small stems mean women, thicker or longer stems mean men (sorry, but traditions tend to slip into stereotypes!). Stalks that are upright represent friends, those that are jumbled or tilted mean mischief or trouble from these people.

A single dot means a letter, a cluster of dots means money is coming your way, and a big dot means you should expect a gift. Tea leaves that group into a solid square stand for peace or joy. A circle also means happiness, but if it is incomplete or is pierced by other leaves, it foretells a disappointment in love. A wheel means that an opportunity should be seized.

Fortune-telling guides place significance upon letters or numbers that the leaves seem to write. Single letters are initials of people who will have a great influence upon your life. As for numbers, their meanings are fairly similar, but with subtle differences:

One means happy days are on the way; two, that something good will occur twice in the near future; three, that a great wish will soon come true; four, that you will have success in your work; five, that you will receive a pleasant surprise; six, that you will make a new friend; seven, that a period of contentment is approaching; eight, that a disappointment is on the horizon; and nine, that better times are coming.

You might also see pictures formed by the leaves. Birds or fish mean good luck; an egg shape means a change is coming; a key shape, that you will learn something that will be useful to you; knives or a cross indicate you're worried about something. A crescent moon is a lucky sign, promising romance; a deeper arch means that something unexpected is about to happen. A tree means a relocation is in your near future. A star is another lucky sign, promising prosperity.

Many other shapes might suggest themselves, in solid form or in outline. Use your imagination; often they are literal symbols of the professions of people you know, or of objects that will concern your life in some way. A ship can mean a message coming from far away, or a journey, for instance.

And should you be able to discern only one large lump of

uncertainty? Well, I think this is the best prediction of all—a future, as Maya Angelou describes it, "plump with promise." So many good things are coming your way, you'd better free up some space in your calendar.

Between the Lines

Finders Keepers

A woman at a retreat shared how she had devoted her whole life to spiritual seeking. She had traveled to sacred sites, attended countless retreats and workshops, sought teachers and guides. It had, she confessed, been a time of much striving; it had been fruitful in some ways, yet she felt tired, weary. She was getting older. She wondered how much stamina she had left to continue her search.

"You have been a seeker for so long," I said. "Why not become a finder? At this stage in your life, what if you imagined you were ready to let go of seeking, and begin finding?" She remained silent for a time, a look of deep confusion on her face, her head slightly tilted, as if she were trying to hear a sound far away. Then, suddenly, a laugh exploded from deep in her belly. A finder! What a delight! How could she have never imagined it before? She had always been so focused on the search, she had never taken time to rejoice in the blessing, the gift of finding.

When we are trapped in seeking, nothing is enough. Everything we have mocks us; we see only what is missing, and all that is already here seems pale and unsatisfying. In Sabbath time we bless what there is for being. The time for seeking is over; the time for finding has begun.

—Wayne Muller
Sabbath: Restoring the Sacred Rhythm of Rest

443

All That Is Hidden
Should Be Revealed

*Since nothing is so secret or hidden that it cannot be revealed,
everything depends on the discovery of those things that manifest
the hidden.*

—Paracelsus (1493-1541)

One Halloween when my daughter was small, she wanted me to wear a costume when I answered the door to greet the trick-or-treaters. The problem was she got this idea Halloween morning. I told her it was too late for me to put together anything. "I know who you can be," she said, disappearing from the table mysteriously. A few minutes later she came back with the costume I wore when giving workshops on Victorian family celebrations. "You can be Mrs. Sharp, Mommy."

Her father looked up from the newspaper, smiled, and said, "Whoa, Katie. The perfect mother. Now that's *really* scary."

Of course, he was right. Perfection is probably one of the most frightening of all masks women wear, and not just at Halloween. Even our most cherished image of perfection—sexual equality— has turned into something macabre, as we find ourselves unconsciously hiding or even snuffing out our femininity to achieve it.

Suspend disbelief for a brief moment and imagine that you could spend the day revealing and reveling in your natural birthright, your feminine powers—sensuality, sexuality, and sensitivity—as well as your intelligence, business acumen, and cleverness. Dare I say it: competence could be curvaceous. You could opt for being a brazen hussy as well as a brilliant manager.

The point is that many women have forgotten how to access the eternal source of Mystery that is our strength. "We don't even realize that our ancient feminine heritage is still alive and well inside that GAP-clad unisex world of ours," Barrie Dolnick, Julia Condon, and Donna Limoges gently chide us in their provocative *Sexual Bewitchery and Other Ancient Feminine Wiles.* "You need to remember that your feminine power is with you everywhere you go. The source of the feminine is all around you—in nature, the moon, the earth. . . . The more you notice and bring nature into your life, the more natural using your feminine powers will be. Don't worry, you won't be trailing scarves and scent wherever you go. Your feminine allure will parallel your own personal style. Katharine Hepburn was sexy and she didn't get too frilly."

What she did get, however, was just about whatever she wanted, in the nicest possible way.

"Every woman is born with mystery: the magic of creation, allure, and magnetism," the ladies remind us. "It's such an innate force you don't even notice it, which simply means that you're not using it to its fullest potential. Bewitchery is the power to enchant, and all women have that within them. . . . Being feminine does not mean kowtowing to anyone or tying yourself to the railroad tracks." Instead, it means doing what comes naturally and not denying or fearing it.

So how do women begin to access this ancient power? "Stop trying to be like a man" because "for the Goddess's sake you're not." And don't forget, as that first-class agent provocateur Erin Brockovich so succinctly put it, "They're called breasts."

Come to Your Senses

Bewitched, Bothered,
and Bewildered

A fabulous way to begin gently exploring the spiritual path I
call Feminine Wiles is with an ancient Celtic beauty ritual
known as *glamoury*. A *glamour* was a magic spell that enhanced,
enlarged, and magnetized a woman's aura so that she could convey any quality she wanted with her demeanor. From the Celtic
warrior queen Bodaecia (who gave us the luscious feminine
adjective *bodacious*) to the Old Testament temptress Bathsheba,
there are as many women in each of us as facets in a precious
diamond.

All Hallows' Eve is a night traditionally set aside for magic,
which makes it a powerful night for a woman to begin getting
comfortable with her feminine wiles. Bewitchery is a highly personal art form. Don't forget that magic is a sensual spiritual ritual,
so it's important when casting a glamour to engage all your senses:
sight, sound, taste, smell, touch, knowing, and wonder. I've

adapted my glamour ritual from Edain McCoy's books *Bewitchments: Love Magick for Modern Romance* and *Enchantments: 200 Spells for Bath and Beauty*. Think of a glamour as a spell your Essensual Self is casting to awaken you to your own beauty. Every woman needs a little sorcery once in a while to be reminded just how irresistible she is to Life.

In fairy tales, the looking glass is a powerful conduit of magic, and it's the truest tool of glamours as well. Start with a special mirror that you love to look at and gaze into. It took me time to find one, but seek and yours will show up as well. Mine is a beautiful, curvy picture frame that I turned into a mirror. It stands on my dressing table, but I only use it for glamour casting or to give myself compliments.

The only light in the room should be candlelight, placed at your back so that it reflects a soft, hypnotic golden glow. Music is important and you'll want something that is energizing but at the same time allows you to drift away into a sensual reverie. Remember the point of this ritual is to turn yourself on, so give yourself good vibrations. For glamours, I especially like to listen to the English film composer Anne Dudley's CD *A Different Light* or Caroline Lavelle's haunting *Brilliant Midnight*.

Before the glamour take a salt shower to get rid of whatever negative energy you're holding on to without realizing it (and we all do). From the emotional bruise of a thoughtless casual remark to the heartbreaking blame for a love that never materialized or the soul-bludgeoning shame of a relationship that failed, women hold on to negative energy better than a skunk's scent. So mix a paste of coarse, natural sea salt and a little almond oil and rub it all over your body. Then scrub it off with a loofah under a hot shower. Next, take a long, luxurious soak in a bath scented with a combination of rose, jasmine, and lavender essential oils. After you're completely relaxed put on your prettiest negligee. I have a silky ivory nightgown worn only when I'm glamour casting.

"To make your glamoury work its best, you must remain realistic about what this spell can and cannot do," Edain McCoy tells us. "A glamoury cannot make everyone who sees you fall madly in love with you, though it will draw to you more eyes than you ever expected. Almost no one will think you're not, at the very least, a very attractive woman."

And the most important person to think that is *you*!

And what are you supposed to be doing as you sit in front of the mirror? Basically hypnotizing yourself with an incantation that has a kernel of believability. This one is powerful. Be sure to insert your name at the end of each sentence.

THE BLESSING OF BEING

By the power of fire, be magical, ————!
By the power of water, be beautiful, ————!
By the power of earth, be who you are, ————!
By the power of air, be all you wish to be, ————!
By the power of the Goddess, so mote it be.
Blessed Be, three times three: Past, Present, Future.

Edain McCoy suggests you "gaze at yourself in the mirror and feel the pull of your attraction growing stronger. Cock your head with a flirtatious air. Laugh with insouciance. Let your eyes dance and sparkle. This is the moment where the glamoury first starts to take shape and begins the path to manifestation. Allow the spell to take the self-image of your fondest imagination from the world of the unformed. From here you will pull it right from the mirror into the world of form for all to see." In her books Edain suggests some wonderful incantations, and here's my favorite:

Radiant health and confidence shine
Illuminate this face of mine;
Bold, beautiful, sassy, brave and smart
I inspire faith while winning all hearts.

Now finish your ritual with a sip of something festive, and as a proud daughter of Eve, eat a luscious apple. Offer thanks to the Goddess for her guidance in the coming days as you grow more comfortable in your own skin (such a blessing!), and you will.

Falling in love with yourself is a lifelong affair. But I find that after I've cast a glamour (which I do as regularly as getting a haircut), I'm always more inspired to take better care of my outer woman. Pampering seems the least I can do for myself. After a glamour I exercise more (and notice more results), eat better, and find time to experiment with home beauty rituals such as facials.

I'm also inclined to wear more colorful, feminine clothing (instead of my uniform of black slacks and sweater) and perk up my spirit with makeup even if I'm completely by myself.

It goes without saying, but I'll say it anyway: a glamour is a woman's *private* magic rite. Secret. Sacred. Not open to snickering or discussion. This means no coven of curious onlookers surrounding you. If necessary, plan your glamour as part of a locked-bathroom ritual.

"You are beautiful by virtue of existing, just as you are magick," Edain McCoy reminds us. Casting your own glamours until you've no need to ask the mirror who is the fairest of them all is an enchantment no woman should ever want to break.

November

The love of bare November days
Before the coming of the snow . . .

—Robert Frost

November loves the pilgrim soul in you and longs to erase the fretting from your frazzled face. With the holidays fast approaching, have you already grumbled away this month's gifts of grace? Family, feasting, and fussing might be en route, but November knows how to take care of you. So let her, with cold comfort charms, a winter's tale or two, sumptuous pajama suppers, and splendor in the glass. The stunning Ordinary in the simply overlooked. Let that cup runneth over with sensuous self-preservation.

You Were Meant for Me

To love oneself is the beginning of a lifelong romance.

—Oscar Wilde

"*T*ruly choosing to be single is very different from being single and looking for a partner or just waiting for one. After ending a long-term relationship I realized that I had never chosen to be single, it had just happened," reveals the artist and writer Sark in *Eat Mangoes Naked: Finding Pleasure Everywhere and Dancing with the Pits,* with the disarming candor that makes her so beloved by all her fans, including me. "So I embarked on a real love affair with myself, a mad passionate one which involved having a very singular focus on myself and my capacity for self-love. I had always been afraid to explore self-love for fear of what I would find, or not find there, or being thought of as selfish! Also, who would I be without someone to love? Could I really stop 'looking' and just look at myself? And if I was not enough for myself, how could I be enough for another? Could I be my own someone?"

Sark's question is one that every woman understands she *might* have to ask one day, but we never expect it today. Surprise. Love's pop quiz is on the agenda right now, and it isn't multiple choice. So crib from me. You are your own someone (whether or not you're in a relationship with someone else). And though it might be a clandestine affair at the moment, it's time to go public with a little love magic called dating yourself.

"Dating yourself is quite possibly the most satisfying way to date. You know from the start that you're building a relationship that will last. You don't have to worry about infidelity. You always get to choose the restaurant and you never have to pretend you're in the mood to see *Baywatch* or anything else. You win every argument, and you'll never lie awake in the wet spot feeling unsatisfied," bad girl Cameron Tuttle assures us.

Whether you're single or married, eighteen or eighty, you can date yourself. However, as Cameron points out in *The Bad Girl's Guide to Getting What You Want,* "When dating yourself, it's important to communicate clearly, just as in any other relationship. Make time for pillow talk a few nights a week. If you set an appointment with yourself, you'll know you have a sacred and safe place where you and your hand mirror can spend some quality time together in bed. Make a ritual of it: turn on soft romantic music, light a candle, and then speak from the heart to your own reflection. 'I love spending time with you. You're the best thing that's ever happened to me. It's fun getting to know you. You make me so happy. I've never loved like this before. You complete me.' When you say the words out loud, your feelings resonate and actually become more real."

I confess I snickered when I first read that passage. But skeptics make the best evangelists. "Self-seduction *does* sound a bit mad, doesn't it?" Anna Johnson admits with a sensuous smirk in *Three Black Skirts: All You Need to Survive.* But "romancing your life creates energy, energy makes you happy, being happy brings back your sense of humor, and laughing makes you pretty. Everyone is suddenly asking you, 'Are you in love?' and all you have to say is, 'Yes, in fact, I am in love—with snails and poems and pastry flour and a cloud shaped like Mozart's ponytail and Lyle Lovett's voice and my nephew's big toe and the smell of fresh sheets and the squish of wet earth in the garden and the way I feel singing Etta James on my bicycle . . . but other than that, no, not really.'"

When you date yourself, you get to try on all sorts of different personas. A little bit of country. A little bit of rock, or roll over Beethoven. Are you a secret bombshell or a sassy bluestocking? The singleness of purpose behind trying to woo yourself is twofold: you get to have fun, and should the occasion arise, you know how to convey your pleasures to another. Pretend you've met the perfect partner who adores plotting and planning your pleasures (just the way you do for others). You read the Sunday papers together, and as you see events that pique your interest, you rip out the listing or review. *What shall we do this week, darling? What sounds like fun, pet? All right, my sweet, I'll take care of it.* Suddenly your Essensual Self is behaving in a mad, impetuous manner that delights you: ordering tickets to that chamber music concert;

walking down a street lined with art galleries and registering your name in the guest books for invitations to openings; attending a reading on a subject that fascinates you but that you've never explored; signing up for motorcycle lessons (motorcycle optional). This past year my Essensual Self nudged me into a fling with Scottish football (Americans are the only ones in the world who call the sport "soccer"). I knew I was well on my way to becoming a romantic adventuress when I was the only woman among a hundred Scotsmen attending a televised football match in a New York City bar on a Saturday morning at 7 A.M.

"Follow the phosphorescent thread of intuition that moves toward delight. So many things to learn, things to learn from," Rainer Maria Rilke encourages us. "Love is an art, like music, dance, or painting pictures. It thrives on light and imagination and daring. The heart of the lover learns wisdom from a stone, a song, a blossom, a breeze." Or an offside penalty kick.

Come to Your Senses

Just One

"*A*lone, alone, oh! We have been warned about solitary vices," the Quaker writer Jessamyn West complained, but "have solitary pleasures ever been adequately praised? Do many people know that they exist?"

We don't have to ponder this conundrum very long.

How about exploring the enticing possibilities of our "just one" theory? To wit: Romantic diversions are not like the Ark, to be enjoyed only two by two. Sometimes one will do nicely. Like today.

Of course, there's a catch. The treat has to be something totally frivolous. A trifling you can live without, but why? Let's see. What single, perfect indulgence might just hit the spot? Certainly chocolate must be right up there at the top of the list. How about a single, frightfully expensive bonbon from a luxurious chocolatier? Pretend you just walked into Madame Vianne Rocher's shop in *Chocolat,* the novel by Joanne Harris about a single mother who changes the destiny of a small French town through her chocolate love magic. Vianne is psychic, so when customers enter her shop she "senses" what malady of the heart ails them. As she recommends a particular sweet, chocolate becomes more of a homeopathic romantic remedy than a sin, especially as the novel takes place during Lent, the season of denial. So when you enter a chocolatier, take your time choosing, inhaling the entire fragrant ambience of the shop. Which confection whispers, "Try me . . . test me . . . taste me"? What is the name of the sweet that seduces? Take another moment to appreciate how the single candy you've selected is placed in a tiny package, as if it were a jewel. Unwrap it as if you have *no idea* what's inside. Sniff it. Finger its smooth whirls or geometric ridges. Nibble, don't scarf. Make the experience last as long as you can, and savor the aftermath—the taste of the chocolate on your tongue, the scent now transferred to your own breath.

Or, visit a fine grocer to discover what delicacy might be just right for a single serving. How about the tiniest jar of quality caviar? Save it until you're curled up on your bed in a sexy nightie, and eat as slowly as you can, licking the soft roe off the tip of a finger. The writer Barbara Holland describes her favorite breakfast as a "glass of cold champagne and a perfectly ripe pear, perhaps with a spoonful of caviar eaten straight from the jar." And I can assure you that her breakfast menu makes a scrumptious supper for one. Or, what about the smallest container of a pricey gelato or sorbet? Sip dabs off a demitasse spoon, allowing the lusciousness to literally melt in your mouth, before taking another tiny bite. Or, treat yourself to a miniature bottle of a liqueur you have always wanted to taste: licorice-flavor anisette, perhaps, or minty crème de menthe. Transfer it to your prettiest, smallest goblet, and take your time holding it to the light, sniffing its aroma, rolling it in your mouth before swallowing. Or, for total decadence, sample it only a few drops at a time, in coffee, or over ice cream (not frozen yogurt!).

Fabric and trimming stores are a virtual carnival of touch and sight. Visit the bolts of tapestry prints and velvet, commune with the ribbons and edgings, treat the imaginatively molded buttons as a gallery of miniatures. Choose "just one": a single button shaped and painted like a cat's head, or cast in brass to resemble a rose . . . a single yard of exquisite braid or bridal lace . . . as small a piece of beautiful fabric as the shop will cut for you (I like to get a yard).

Once your selection is home, place it where you can see and touch it: drape fabric or trimmings over a mirror or swirl them upon a shelf; treat a button as a jewel, propped amid your earrings and brooches, or pin it from behind to ornament a drapery. Don't find a *use* for such things, enjoy them purely for what they are. A glimpse of something that triggers a personal sigh of appreciation.

When was the last time you stopped in at a fine-arts store or museum shop to look at the prints and cards? Browse, then buy just one postcard-size print of the piece you like best. Tuck it into a frame, get a discreet magnet and decorate your refrigerator door, hang it in your office cubicle.

Now for a solitary vice that I probably engage in a couple times a week, especially if I'm stressed out and haven't made it to the gym. If you know all the words to a favorite album, the next time you're home alone, why not turn the music up and lip-synch before a mirror? I've got "Every Breath You Take" down and I'm ready for my duet with Sting as soon as his calendar permits. Or, go one step further: put on a music video, turn *off* the sound, and supply the vocal dubbings yourself. (Even if you aren't Audrey Hepburn, who didn't do her own singing anyway, you can take the starring role in *My Fair Lady* in the sanctity of your own living room!) Or, put on the most romantic movie you know and say all the lines aloud to your screen lover. "Whisper sweet nothings into the air, then spin around really fast to catch them in your ear," Cameron Tuttle suggests.

Anna Johnson thinks private babe time should be the crazy stuff that can trigger a *Really? I can do that?* response. How about "watching four pretaped episodes of *The Nanny* back to back; doing your housework in a crocheted bikini, an apron, and a raspberry-colored beret; teaching yourself to two-step with a broom; speaking Italian to your plants; or taking Polaroids of your breasts for future generations to admire? . . . You are not crazy," she insists in your sexy solitude sojourns. "You are, hopefully, charming the pants off yourself."

The Secret Marriage

When it's over, I want to say: all my life
I was a bride married to amazement.
I was the bridegroom, taking the world into my arms.

—Mary Oliver

"*A*fter you've dated yourself for a few months, you'll feel rejuvenated and ready to date other people," Cameron Tuttle assures us. "Or you may feel rejuvenated and realize you've found your soul mate, the love of your life, and you never want to date anyone ever again. But either way, you'll feel rejuvenated."

You'll also have gleaned important information about yourself. I've been in a committed relationship with myself now for about two years, and in that time, thank Heavens, I've learned that if I want to be happy for the rest of my life, I'd better not dillydally with anyone who doesn't like the English countryside, rare sheep, horses, dogs, and Scottish football, among other surprising pursuits. My personal passions are precious to me because they bring me bliss whether I'm by myself or in the company of others who share them. It's taken me a lifetime to learn this, but hopefully my new insider knowledge will shape the rest of my life.

A few years ago, after my divorce, I was invited to the wedding of a close friend. Both she and her fiancé were in their fifties and both were getting married for the second time. As they exchanged their vows, I was struck by the enormous responsibility these two people were taking on in the name of Love; not only each other but their new partner's children, health, finances, opinions, obligations, habits, passions, preferences, and priorities. The courage that marriage requires! When you're young and in love/lust, courage is the last thing you connect with marriage because you believe that anything's possible if you have each other. When you're older, you know that the most precious gift you can give another is emotional courage.

It's wonderful to be committed to another soul's happiness. But it's *wondrous* to be committed to your own. The truth is that our relationships are only as emotionally healthy, happy, holy, and content as we are. Can you imagine how splendid and rich your life would become if you married yourself before another? Imagine what choices you would make if you were deeply devoted to your own well-being before another's. Can you pledge before Spirit to be faithful to your own passions the way you would be to a partner's? Can you imagine celebrating life with your own soul for better or worse, for richer or poorer, in sickness and in health?

I do.

And I hope you can, too.

"Aroused by beauty, moved by its poignancy, the sensuous woman embraces life, inviting it to enter like a lover into union— a marriage of one, unique Woman with all-mysterious Life, a marriage of earthly delights. This passionate sense of connection, this encompassing sensuality, celebrates life with mindfulness and joy," the English writer Elisabeth Millar observes in *The Fragrant Veil*. "The sensuous woman reaches out to the world with her senses and through her senses receives its marvels. . . . She is sentient, sensitive, alive with perception."

Night Vision

There is in God, some say,
A deep but dazzling darkness.

—Henry Vaughan (1650)

*W*hen I moved to the country, my most surprising adjustment was learning to live according to the rhythm of natural light. Day is for activity, night is for rest. "There's a certain

Slant of light" on winter afternoons, Emily Dickinson points out, and "When it comes the Landscape listens."

In the city, electricity makes it easy to blur the boundaries between day and night, winter and spring, and I do, usually by burning the candle at both ends. But on winter nights in the country, when I'm in the back of beyond, the only candles meant to be burning are on my dining room table.

Simmer down now, the shadows seem to say. By five o'clock the curtains are drawn, the fire is blazing, and the lamps are lit, throwing off golden slivers that creep through the cracks between the windows and doors. The cares of the day are set down by the front door, sure to be picked up in the morning. But for now, the conviviality of evening awaits my company.

Outside, it's dark. And dark as you have never seen dark before, unless you grew up in the country. The startling absence of artificial light reveals a sky as black as a raven's wing. As deep autumn slowly moves into winter, the sky reveals a darkness so deep, yet so full of light, it's dazzling. Part of the luminosity comes from the stars, like a thousand blinking eyes, watching to see how earth is doing, when they are not waiting on Lady Luna. Nighttime used to be a time of apprehension for me, especially if I was alone. But since I have allowed Life to romance me, I have known some of the most serene, sweet, and poetic hours sitting on the bench in the dark, underneath an apple tree in my garden, conversing with Night. Sometimes I'm bundled up, sometimes I'm barefoot, but always I am content. The Darkness has become a dear friend to me, a comforting presence, not to be feared, but to be embraced.

Like everything else in the natural world, the horizon changes with the seasons; becoming familiar with the mysteries of light and darkness is an exquisite seasonal splendor. The light in November is crisper than in the warm haze of June, but November's velvety darkness has just as distinctive a beauty as July's gossamer nightshade.

One of the ways you can discover this is to take up shadow walking. Learn to experience the world through night vision. This week on a clear, crisp night, take a walk at dusk where you feel safe (bring a friend if you'd like, a dog if you have one). Observe how the shadows fall, how dusk turns into twilight through a progression of eventide hues—steel gray to smoky blue to charcoal ash. On another night, take an early-evening saunter after supper; save a midnight stroll for a full moon. As the nights progress and the seasons change, what nocturnal wonders are revealed for your eyes only?

Learning to love the nights of our lives as well as the days is the beginning of contentment. "For the night was not impartial," Eudora Welty observed in 1949. "No, the night loved some more than others, served some more than others." My guess is, if Night has her favorites, it's because the romance is reciprocal.

Come to Your Senses

This Delicious Day

*C*an you remember the last time you tasted something so scrumptious that the first bite triggered a squeal of delight or spontaneous prayer? *Oh, God, this is good!* In her marvelous food memoir *With Bold Knife and Fork,* M.F.K. Fisher recalled such a tasting *sixty* years after it occurred. "I can taste-smell-hear-see and then feel between my teeth the potato chips I ate slowly one November afternoon in 1936, in the bar of the Lausanne Palace.

They were uneven in both thickness and color, probably made by a new apprentice in the hotel kitchen, and almost surely they smelled faintly of either chicken or fish, for that was always the case there. They were a little too salty, to encourage me to drink. They were ineffable. I am still nourished by them." She went on to explain that the sense memory remained so powerful she was rarely tempted to eat potato chips again. Honoring our sense of taste actually "cultivates restraint."

Give us this day our daily taste, the poet Robert Farrar Capon asks. To which we all say, "Amen."

It's true that our senses become jaded as we get older—requiring new, fresh, and frequent jolts to awaken them. Every adult has about ten thousand taste buds in the mouth (primarily on the tongue, but also on the palate, pharynx, and tonsils). Throughout our lives, every ten days or so these taste buds wear out and regenerate. Unfortunately, as we enter middle age, they don't regenerate as frequently as we might hope. This could be taken as a bitter pill, but I think it's a cause for celebration. Use it as just the excuse to introduce a new, guilt-free taste sensation once or twice each week. Think of it as regeneration rejuvenation, especially if you aim for a mouthwatering memory as palpable as Miss Fisher's potato chips.

Today simply bring your awareness to the way you approach food. Do you really taste or just eat what's put in front of you? "Anytime we eat it's holy," M.F.K. Fisher reminds us. "We should have ritual and ceremony, not just gobbling down some food to keep us alive."

Fisher's words are, for me, vast food for thought. Care to join me in a bite?

Delicious Day Potato Chips

I couldn't locate the recipe for M.F.K. Fisher's epiphanous potato chips, but this one is inspired by the glorious handmade chips once served in the bar of the Hotel Lancaster in Paris. Yes, they are fried. No, they are not low-fat. But oven-baked chips do not trigger religious experiences. These do.

4 russet baking potatoes
About 4 cups canola oil
Salt
A deep-fat thermometer

Peel the potatoes and submerge them in a bowl of cold water. Pat each potato dry as you use it. Manually slice potatoes as thinly as possible, and let them soak in another bowl of cold water. Drain the potato slices, and spread them out on a triple layer of paper towels without overlapping. Blot the slices completely dry with another triple layer of paper towels.

In a deep fryer or a 3-quart saucepan, heat the oil until a deep-fat thermometer registers 380° F. Working in small batches of 8 to 10 slices, fry the potatoes, turning twice until golden (about 2 minutes). Watch out for spattering oil. Slowly lift the fried chips out of the pan or fryer with a large slotted spoon and place them on a clean layer of paper towels to drain. Blot twice with fresh paper towels to absorb as much oil as possible. Sprinkle with salt.

As you continue frying, make sure the oil returns to 380° F before adding the next batch of potato slices.

They say these potato chips can be kept in an airtight container for up to 2 days. I suppose some things must be taken on faith. They've never lasted longer than an hour in my house.

How Do You
Keep the Music Playing?

*Who hears music, feels his solitude
peopled at once.*

—Robert Browning

I spend so much of my life in the company of good music that, when I venture out into the world, it's often startling to realize how much of my time is spent alone. I won't kid you; occasionally a brief wistfulness comes over me when I see happy couples talking and laughing together. But then I'll see another couple sitting in resigned silence, and suddenly I feel grateful I'm not part of *that* pair. Once back home, the thrill of a heady romance is just within earshot and always beckoning. Like Robert Browning, my solitude is very convivial these days, largely because of music.

At some point in each day, every woman should be able to feel home alone, especially if you share your space with others. Listening to your favorite music is an easy way to carve out a private interlude.

Music is one of the most sensuous ways in which Life flirts with us. As I'm writing, an amorous tenor saxophone is wooing me with the thought that I'm somebody's one and only love. Jazz great John Coltrane may be the messenger, but I know the Sweetheart who really sent this reassuring reminder.

Enjoying music that makes us feel good, or feel better, is an important way to pamper ourselves. But how many women actually revel in this sensory pleasure? Having different kinds of music readily available so that you can listen to your own mood music when *you* want may not sound like much. But if you don't recognize the value of music, you *don't know* what you're missing.

And sorry, flipping on the radio when you drive to work or cook dinner doesn't count.

I know that I didn't understand the power of personal audiotherapy until the ordinary began romancing me. A few years ago, I was sorting my CDs. Since there was no particular love interest in my life, I found myself weeding out my favorite romantic love songs from the thirties, forties, and fifties—Cole Porter, George and Ira Gershwin, Jerome Kern, Rodgers and Hart—to be packed away. "What are you doing?" my Essensual Self asked. "You love those songs!" *I only allow myself to have pleasure when there's someone to share it* wasn't an acceptable answer for that Babe, so I started listening to my favorite love songs right then and thankfully haven't stopped.

It's funny, but when we're in love and we hear a refrain in a song with the word *you* in it, we immediately associate the song with the object of our ardor. But when we're not in a relationship and a love song is playing, it's hard not to feel empty. That is, until you put a new spin on the experience. Choose to believe that Life is serenading you.

Here's a great way to get started. This week go through your CDs and tapes. First, sort out your romantic favorites, as well as those that get you going when you're weary or relax you when you're overwrought. Weed through the rest, and put aside the CDs that have only one or two tracks you like (Doesn't that drive you crazy?). Recycle the ones you no longer listen to by bringing them to work and leaving them at the coffee machine with a note that says, "Free to a good home." As soon as you can, invest an hour to make your own compilation tape by recording the scattered favorites on a new tape or CD. It's fabulous to have your own selected music so readily available. You'll wonder why you didn't do this years ago. Well, years ago we didn't know how to indulge ourselves, or even if we should. Now we do, and that's how we keep the music playing.

Come to Your Senses

A Plea to Stop Whining

*W*hen we think of wine and cheese, the word *party* can't be far behind. If you, like me, have always hated to go to parties alone, it's crucial that we learn to bring the party with us. One of my favorite long weekends is a winery tour, and I absolutely adore wine tastings, so I've learned how to adapt the pleasure to suit my circumstances right now. "Think, for a moment, of an almost paper-white glass of liquid, just shot with greeny-gold, just tart on your tongue, full of wildflower scents and spring-water refreshment. And think of a burnt-umber fluid, as smooth as syrup in the glass, as fat as butter to smell and sea-deep with strange flavors. Both are wine," the famous British wine authority Hugh Johnson tells me.

Don't you want to taste the difference?

One of the more amazing things we discover when we finally decide to adore Life is that every pleasure we assume or insist it takes two to enjoy can be transformed into a passionate romp for one. *You don't* always need the company and commentary of others to—why not say it?—to *drink in* the subtle aromas, colors, and flavors of romance. A party of one is just right, when the pursuit is pure sensation. So shall we take the pledge to stop the whining? Even though we think no one can hear us, Spirit can.

Since we're only entertaining one today, we don't want a staggering amount of leftovers, so let's think about quality rather than quantity—say, three cheeses, three wines. If you've been unable to differentiate between similar wines or cheeses, why not invite them to a "panel discussion"? A frank, side-by-side comparison might clarify particular features you had overlooked before. Or perhaps you've been playing it too safe, buying only a few familiar, middle-of-the-road products. Treat this as an opportunity to explore new ground: creamy mild versus sharp cheese, goat cheese, blue cheese; robustly mature versus young, dry wines, fruity or spicy wines, sparkling wines.

For best flavor, buy your cheeses freshly cut. Avoid precut, prewrapped, processed brands. If you rely on your wine merchant for brand or vintage, be firm about the price range you would be willing to spend on each bottle. A responsible dealer should be able to make good suggestions that won't blow your budget. In fact, I recommend you find yourself your own vintner. The way to do that is to meander into an interesting-looking wine shop (not on a Saturday afternoon) and ask someone to help you.

Here are some general matches preferred by vintners:

- Mild Brie, Camembert, Edam—cabernet sauvignon, merlot, pinot noir
- Mature Brie, Camembert, Edam—zinfandel
- Swiss, Emmentaler, Gouda, Gruyère—chardonnay, Riesling, gewürztraminer, sauvignon blanc, or a Rhône wine
- Muenster—zinfandel or Beaujolais
- Port Salut, taleggio—red or white burgundy, or pinot noir
- Mozzarella—pinot blanc
- Cream cheese—champagne
- Chèvre, feta, or other goat cheese, sheep's-milk cheese— sauvignon blanc, chenin blanc, Pouilly-Fumé, or any other very dry white wine
- Blue cheese, Gorgonzola, Roquefort—sauternes, Riesling, sweet and fruity red wine

- Aged Parmesan or aged provolone—Chianti or burgundy
- Mild cheddar—merlot or chardonnay
- Aged cheddar, Stilton—port or muscat

Remember that this is going to be a wine *viewing* as well as a tasting. Put away your cut or tinted glass for another time, and don't even *think* of using plastic. Large, clear glass goblets will best show off the color and taste of your wine. Use a separate glass for each wine bottle, and place by it the cheese you have selected to be its partner. Appreciate how each pairing looks.

Now, *look* at your poured wine, under a good light. Young, dry white wines will be clear or pale yellow or green; fruitier or more aged white will be golden, even almost tawny. A young red will be a uniform color, but an aged red will be darkest near the rim of your glass and contain more purplish, orange, maroon, or brown overtones.

How would *you* describe the color of each liquid? Does a white wine suggest precious platinum or humble celery? Does a zin-fandel remind you of a particular rose-colored carpet? Does an aged red bring back a memory of the pony you dreamed of riding when you were twelve? (Here's where not needing to announce your impressions to others might actually give freer rein to your imagination!) Sniff wines quickly, for a "first-blush" reaction. Smelling them for too long actually deadens your sense of smell. Instead of prolonging the sensation, take a breather and then come back to sniff again, as if testing a new fragrance. Get a little notebook and jot down your impressions.

Don't neglect communing with your cheeses: Which looks creamy, even runny; solid, crumbly? Are holes round or crackle-edged? Is that blue cheese really blue, or is it parchment flecked with aqua-green? What texture and body does each cheese present to your knife or fingers? (Be sure to serve fairly bland crackers or a simple baguette, so as not to cloud your sensations with extra flavorings.)

Working from mild to strong, try a small slice of cheese followed by a sip of its companion wine. How does the aroma of the one blend with, complement, or heighten the other? What lingers in your nose and throat once you have swallowed and taken a few breaths? If you have chosen well, the scents and flavors will be in balance and won't fade too fast. This last is a sign of a good wine: the same impressions you received upon first impact should remain after a few moments have passed.

As wine is so sensitive to air, it is essential to purchase *before you begin your tasting session* several vacuum corks, used to preserve the wine you don't drink at the first sitting. Store the leftover red at room temperature and the white in the refrigerator. Strong young wines and sweet wines keep longer than mature or very dry ones; try to finish the latter within a day or two, and the others within a week. Don't even *think* of using a spoiled wine for cooking.

Store leftover cheese in the fridge, too, tightly wrapped in plastic or foil; stick a little label on each to identify it, until you learn to recognize your cheeses. Then pop them all into a lidded plastic container. Cheese does not keep forever, either. A small icing of mold can be cut away, but resist convincing yourself that a cheese that is going bad is simply turning into blue cheese—leave fermentation to the experts.

One of the most thrilling compliments I've ever received was from a Frenchman, who was not a lover but became a close friend. "You have a very sensual soul, Sarah." (Imagine it said with a French accent.) I'm still blushing. When I asked why he thought this, he said, "You revel in your own pleasure. Your house wine is always a good vintage. You can tell more about a woman from the wine she serves when she's at home alone than you can from her perfume." We then had a wonderful conversation about the habit many people have of always reserving "the best" for others, which has nothing to do with money, and everything to do with believing that personal pleasure is not important. I confessed to my new friend that it had not always been that way. Learning the art of Life is a bit like learning the art of wine. One sip at a time. For only when you generously fill the cup of happiness for yourself is there plenty left over to quench the thirst of others.

Lovespeak

The real thing creates its own poetry.

—Anzia Yezierska

For many years I've used poetry as a form of meditation. This practice started when I was writing on deadline for newspapers. Convinced that I didn't have twenty minutes to quiet my mind or take a walk, I'd open a book of poems instead and randomly pick a poem. As my list of deadlines has increased over the years, so has my poetry collection grown, especially with the help of secondhand-book shops. My latest coup was finding the complete oeuvre of Rod McKuen, which I snapped up for nostalgia's sake.

I fell in love with love and in love with poetry because of Rod McKuen, and I'm not embarrassed to admit it, although I probably should be. But Willie Yeats and I wouldn't be such a hot item today if I hadn't fallen under the rapture of *Listen to the Warm, Caught in the Quiet, In Someone's Shadow, Stanyan Street and Other Sorrows.* Do you remember Rod? As I reread his poems today I understand why for decades my love life didn't stand a chance. How could it when my concept of romance came from the fantasy of someone telling me, *"If you cry when we leave Paris, I'll buy you a teddy bear all soft and gold."* God knows, I wish I were kidding! But we all have to begin somewhere, both in discovering what we need from love and in moving from clichéd sentiment to great writing.

Many of us resist the power of poetry to illuminate our lives because we have such bad memories of high school English class: "Quoth the Raven, 'Nevermore.'" Get past it. You're cutting yourself off from one of life's great pleasures. More of us have an inferiority complex about poetry that we need to get over: we view poetry as an esoteric art that only the well educated, literate, and erudite can appreciate. Interestingly, poets are the first to disagree. As everyday alchemists, they know that life's hours of lead are base metal waiting to be transmuted into wisdom's gold. "Poetry connects you to yourself, to the self that doesn't know how to talk or negotiate," Rita Dove, America's first African-American poet laureate explains. Once, on the radio, I heard her read a poem about waiting to board a flight home. I was standing at the stove one moment, and the next I was boarding my own flight. It was an exquisite sensory experience and I've never forgotten it.

Recently the power of poetry changed my life again when I was reading David Whyte's collection *The House of Belonging*. Because poetry is written for the soul not the mind, it pulls no punches. As I read Whyte's verse *This is the temple of my adult aloneness and I belong to that aloneness as I belong to my life,* I was shaken, rattled, and rolled into a personal awakening. Suddenly, I understood that I had been isolating myself from love in ways I hadn't realized. David Whyte was writing about his life, but the message was meant for me. That is the mystical power of poetry. Poets are Spirit's agents provocateur. Now, hanging on the wall at the landing of the staircase leading to my bedroom, there's another verse from *The House of Belonging:*

> *This is the bright home*
> *in which I live,*
> *this is where I ask*
> *my friends to come,*
> *this is where I want*
> *to love all the things*
> *it has taken me so long*
> *to learn to love.*
>
> *There is no house*
> *like the house of belonging.*

"Because poets feel what we're afraid to feel, venture where we're reluctant to go, we learn from their journeys without taking the same dramatic risks," the poet, Diane Ackerman, reveals. "Think of all the lessons to be learned from deep rapture, danger, tumult, romance, intuition. But it's far too exhausting to live like that on a daily basis, so we ask artists to explore for us. Daring to take intellectual and emotional chances, poets live on their senses." And sometimes "we need to be taught how and where to seek wonder, but it's always there, waiting, full of mystery and magic." Wrapped up in the heartstrings of a poem.

Come to Your Senses

Dearest and Best

*B*eing an incurable romantic, I've sent more love letters than I've ever received. I regret almost none of them because I always put my best writing in a love letter. I'm not alone. Michelle Lovric, editor of two luscious anthologies of famous love letters, as well as a delicious primer, *How to Write Love Letters,* explains why the story of most women's lives is written in *X*'s and *O*'s. "We write letters because they last, even when the love that inspired them has gone, leaving little other trace. . . . We write letters because we are all insecure. We cannot hear often enough that we are loved. . . . We can scarcely believe our luck. . . . Writing love letters are graceful palliatives for the lonely, the lustful, the needy, and the disbelieving."

Women also write love letters because words are potent, passionate, persuasive go-betweens, able to woo potential lovers far more successfully, we believe, than we ever could in person. Frances Wilson tells us in *Literary Seductions,* "In literary seductions it is writing that seduces and not the writer." And so in September 1846, when the poet Robert Browning saw his soon-to-be runaway bride, Elizabeth Barrett, outside her house for the first time—they were eloping to Italy—he was already besotted. Despite being forty, and an invalid with an overprotective father, Elizabeth had managed to seduce Robert with her passion on the page. In the previous eighteen months they had exchanged 573 letters, each more sensuous and erotic than the one before it. On the page each could reveal his or her true self to the other. Their clandestine affair was kept alive with the love letter, and with wry acknowledgment their affectionate nickname for their son was Pen.

As modern life becomes ever more mechanical, factual, impersonal, how much more necessary to our souls is the secret whisper, the intimate nickname, the caress in just the right place, the voluptuous cataloging of every small detail of a moment shared or anticipated or of the body's delights. . . .

Are you swooning just at the thought? Well, as with so many other things, for a job well done, you'll just have to do it yourself. A love letter. From you. To you. To the you that, perhaps, few if any know well enough to write what you would most wish to read. A letter from the one person who has the boldness to address you with the specificity of sensuousness and the insight you deserve from a lover. (Wouldn't you like to receive one perfect one before you die?)

"Before words," Michelle Lovric explains, "there is, of course, desire. Language is the thread joining that desire to its object, explaining its needs, expressing its cries. The love letter is our heart on our sleeve, our battle standard, our essence, our indelible signature, our emotional fingerprint, our private well of memory, our own ghost of kisses past, our true secret self."

Consider the romantic letters exchanged by Nicholas and

Alexandra, collected in *A Lifelong Passion*. In one, the czarina informed her husband, often absent for affairs of state, "Your precious letter and telegrams I've put on our bed so that when I wake up in the night I can touch something of yours." Or the letters of Oscar Wilde to his wife, Constance (whom he loved very much, despite his infamous extramarital behavior). Separated from her, briefly, in 1884, he wrote, "The messages of the gods travel not by pen and ink and indeed your bodily presence here would not make you more real: for I feel your fingers in my hair, and your cheek brushing mine."

Written while in the absence of their loved one, many love letters are in fact a recording of the heights and depths of the writer's own feelings while he or she is *in solitude*. They contain sensuous details about the place where the writer is, or fond memories of physical pleasure, sweet pet names, and perhaps even silly endearments, confessions . . . everything that *you* are in a perfect position to provide for *yourself.*

Don't feel self-conscious. Instead, feel conscious of your *self.* Gather your most beautiful paper, your most flowing pen, your thoughts. Sit by a window flooded with sunlight, or sit in a garden; tuck yourself into a cozy nook. Remember. Feel. Yearn. And now, write.

Dearest and best, my own sweetheart, Heavenly creature, ma Chérie, My One and Only Love, Pet . . . What do you wish someone would call you, but once? Describe where and how you are seated, what you are wearing, in a way that will allow the reader of your missive to picture you longingly from afar. Use the most luxurious language you can summon to perfectly capture this moment. *I am in the large wing chair, the little wine-red velvet pillow tucked beneath my elbow to hold my hand steady, my darling, as I thrill to write to you. . . .*

Recount a special memory, confess a hope or wish, lavish praise upon an accomplishment, languidly stroke your body with the imagery spun from a well-wielded pen . . . express what joy you take in knowing this person, the recipient of the letter, how much you treasure her. Close with kisses and flowery, fond superlatives. Sign the letter with a secret, romantic pseudonym or password. *May you bloom forever, garden of my heart, I remain, forever Your Own Girl.*

Address an envelope to yourself. Affix a stamp. And, yes, mail the letter to your home.

When it arrives, wait a week, then open it and read it. Giggle. Blush. Reread it incredulously. Reread the *juiciest* bits aloud. Sigh. Dry a tear. Press the page to your heart . . . and then press it in a book, perhaps a collection of love letters itself, or an anthology of love poems, to come back to and read yet again . . . or write more letters, and tie them together with a ribbon, as if you were the heroine of an old romance novel. Go about your day aglow with the feeling of being loved by someone who will always be there for you. And imagine what a riotous uproar the letters will cause someday when they're discovered after you're gone.

Cold Comfort Charms

I, singularly moved
To love the lovely that are not beloved,
Of all the seasons most
Love winter.

—Coventry Patmore

*H*ow *long* it has taken me to learn to love winter. Probably as long as it's taken me to learn the difference between solitude and loneliness. The secret, I think, was realizing that if I was so inclined, there could always be singular winter pleasures waiting to cajole me into good cheer. The Danish writer Isak Dinesen, who spent many years alone in between passionate liaisons, referred to the country house near Copenhagen where she was born in 1885 as a cherished refuge of a "hundred summers' sweet-

475

ness and winters' comfort." We can try to create such a seasonal sanctuary for ourselves.

While snowy days may leave us feeling that we'd rather stay in bed where it's warm, there are cold comfort charms available only to those who venture outside in the early morning. The first snow is here. So throw back those covers at daybreak. Bundle up and get outside while the snow is smooth and fresh, still unmarked by footprints and unsoiled by the snowplow. Tonight's dessert:

Snow Sherbet

YOU WILL NEED:

1 cup heavy cream
½ cup superfine sugar
1 teaspoon pure vanilla extract
8 cups of fresh snow (remove the ice crust on top and scoop up
    the soft, wet snow immediately beneath it)
Chocolate and nutmeg, shaved, for garnish

Combine the cream, sugar, and vanilla. Beat well until frothy. Place the mixture in a large bowl and gradually add the snow until the liquid is completely absorbed. Place in freezer until serving. Garnish with shaved chocolate and nutmeg.

Now, wasn't it worth getting up and out for?

Come to Your Senses

Romancing the Cold

The last thing a woman wants to think about when she's
about to drop into bed—eyes burning out of her sockets, red
and runny nose, raspy throat, hacking cough—is how fetching she
looks, unless of course her name is Camille.

While we might aspire to look ravishing when we're caught up
in a romantic fever, if the fever precedes the flirtation, please,
really, darling, we just want to be left alone! But on the other hand,
your body is aching for extra pampering, a loving touch, and rest.

Happily, many soothing solutions are right at hand. No need
to struggle out to shop, no need to call for reinforcements.

Let's start with your sleeping arrangements. Slip into something
light and loose. If you still feel cold, add another easily removed
layer or two. Don't trap achy limbs within garments that bind or
stick. The same goes for your bedding: lightweight, layered covers
that can be drawn up or kicked off is what the lie-a-bed lady
needs. Have a couple of extra-comfy pillows close by, so that you
can hug one when you thrash to the left or heave to the right. Raise

your head with an extra pillow. And keep some extra bedding (sheets, blankets) and nightclothes nearby, so if you become at all uncomfortable, hot, sweaty, or stinky, you can remake your bed and change into a fresh set.

You'd be amazed at how quickly a runny nose, fever, or upset tummy can deplete your body of essential fluids. Drink as much noncarbonated mineral water, juice, and decaffeinated herbal tea as you can.

Staying fresh and clean when you're sick seems impossible, but it makes you feel so good. When I was little, my mother would wash my arms, face, and neck with a moist cloth, wiping the "sick" away, as she called it, and I always believed her, as did my daughter when I carried out the loving ritual with her. But if you can muster the energy, a long, warm shower or leisurely eucalyptus-scented shampoo will do wonders for respiratory ailments. And I love having a humidifier moisten the bedroom air with a scented mist. You can sweeten and moisturize the air by simmering a few drops of lavender, eucalyptus, peppermint oil, dried rosemary, lavender, or ground cinnamon in a pot of water. Then place it on top of the radiator in your bedroom. It's something a Victorian nanny would do for her little charges.

Your nose is *so* sore, poor thing. Are you using the softest tissues? Keep a pot of lip balm and skin lotion on your nightstand. Pure almond oil is soothing, as is petroleum jelly for your lips. All of these things can be collected in a small pretty basket and stored in your linen closet, so you don't have to search for each one when you're sick.

Drink through a straw if you have cold sores; have a small jar of flavored honey to dip a little spoon into and every so often suck on it.

Remember to wash your hands frequently (all winter long); a lovely lavender-scented liquid soap in a pump bottle at the sink is a good reminder, even if you're too stuffed to smell its fragrance. And remember to wash your glasses, cups, and towels frequently. You don't want to pass your own germs back to yourself!

There are stages in the progress of every cold or flu. To fill the hours when you're too bleary-eyed or feverish to read, listen to soothing music that lets you drift in and out of pleasant hallucinations. During one nasty bout of what felt like malaria (but wasn't),

Johnny Mathis kept me company, just as he did during my high school years. It was great. Chances are that old favorites you haven't heard in a while can induce pleasant reveries for you, too. I also keep a "Wonder Years" box—Nancy Drew novels (the originals), comic books, and a couple of old issues of *Seventeen* that I found at a flea market. They're so amusing to flip through when I'm feeling poorly. The whole point, when you're sick, is to treat yourself as wittily as you can.

"The sad truth is that there is no point to getting sick when you're a grown-up. You know why? It's because being sick is about you and your mother," Adair Lara reminisces. "Without that solicitous hand on your forehead, there is no one to confirm that you are really sick."

Except your Essensual Self.

Come to Your Senses

Pajama Food

Comfort food, nursery food. Whatever evokes that image for you, it's likely to be soft, and warm, and prepared with love. A snuggly flannel "jammies" food that tucks in your hungry spirit.

What do you reach for, or yearn for, when you're sad or sick or have had a hard day? What memories are associated with that food? Memories that soothe you as you sip or sup?

For some, it's a happy recollection of their mother or grandmother making a favorite treat *just for them,* a culinary confirmation that all was well. They can still see the beloved cook standing in her apron at the stove, stirring. They can smell the aroma of comfort waiting in the wings, feel the special comfort that a repetition of the predictable and familiar brings.

To others, comfort food is what they proudly learned to make themselves, in a magical ritual of transforming ordinary, everyday ingredients into a single, heavenly whole. Butterscotch pudding. Buckwheat pancakes. Tuna-and-noodle casserole.

It's the rare comfort food that doesn't involve milk and some kind of starch, our very first nursery foods. What wonderful unconscious feelings of safety and satiation lie just below the surface of delicious memories; no difficult excavation process here to get at these comfort icons.

Is your happiest treat a chilly-morning porridge—oatmeal, Cream of Wheat, farina . . . thick with milk and sugar or maple syrup? Sweet-potato pie or nutmeg-topped whipped squash, served only on Sundays or special occasions? Cream pies? Old-fashioned peanut butter cookies, the kind squashed flat with a fork?

Creamy puddings rate high on the nostalgia list. In England, where many homey desserts fall under the name *pudding,* the cry "What's for pudding tonight, Mummy?" might encompass anything from a gelatin parfait to a sophisticated layer cake. English steamed or boiled puddings, such as fruit-laden Christmas puddings, are actually moist cakes. What Americans think of as puddings, the Brits call custard. Sure enough, the British-manufactured Bird's custard (a basic cornstarch pudding mix dating back to Victorian days) remains a huge seller over there and you can find it in some large American supermarkets. It's positively redemptive when consolation is called for.

Traditional milky puddings such as tapioca, junket, rice, and bread-and-butter are also feel-good foods. An important contributing factor to most is that to properly make them, one must assemble them from scratch . . . so their comforting quality comes not only from the listed ingredients, but from the gentle touch of the hand that stirred the spoon.

Gift yourself with this loving attention. Make yourself a pudding, and while you do it, take pleasure in anticipating the delight the eater (you and you alone) will take in the finished dish. How "warm and fuzzy" it will be to make it for her. What good care you are taking of her . . . and of her memories.

There, There Rice Pudding

You will need:

¼ cup long-grain white rice (regular or basmati)
¾ cup water

Pinch of salt
2 teaspoons unsalted butter
1 egg, at room temperature
3 tablespoons granulated sugar
1 cup milk (vanilla soy milk will also work well)
½ teaspoon vanilla extract
¼ teaspoon each ground nutmeg and cinnamon
¼ cup raisins

1. Place rice, water, salt, and 1 teaspoon of the butter in a medium saucepan, and bring to a boil. Cover pan, lower heat as far as it can go (use a "flame-tamer" pan beneath, if you own one), and cook for 15 minutes. Remove from heat, do not remove lid, and allow to stand for 15 minutes longer. Then remove the lid and allow the rice to cool in the pan. Rice can be made up to a day in advance this way (refrigerate, covered, if not using immediately).

2. Preheat oven to 325°. In a 2-quart bowl, combine the egg and the sugar, and beat several minutes, until light. Stir in the milk, vanilla, a dash of each spice (reserve rest), and the raisins. Stir in the rice.

3. Coat a 1-quart casserole (ovenproof ceramic or glass) with the remaining 1 teaspoon of butter. Pour in the rice mixture, level it off, and dust with the reserved spices.

4. Place the ovenproof ceramic or glass pan into a large, high-rimmed baking pan, and fill the pan with enough water to come halfway up the sides of the casserole.

5. Bake at 325° for 1 ½ hours, or until set. Eat warm or cold.

This recipe makes 3 standard portions or 2 extra-comforting big ones. I've also served rice pudding as dessert for grown-up dinner parties, and the clamor only subsides after I pass on the recipe.

Come to Your Senses

A Winter's Tale or Two

*A*t the end of a long day, how do you turn a pleasant rendezvous with a wonderful new book into a winter splendor? Start by turning the lights down low and tucking yourself in
bed, with a cup of warm cheer. Now sink your weary head back
on a pile of plump pillows, and play footsie with a hot-water bottle while *listening* in the dark to one chapter of an audiobook.
My favorite bedtime storytellers include Jan Karon and her
enchanting Mitford series, about small-town life and middle-age
romance (beginning with *At Home in Mitford*). Other sweet
dreams came after listening to the English writer Rosamund
Pilcher's *Winter Solstice* and Joanna Trollope's *Marrying the Mis-
tress*. Besides the cozy domestic details that I adore, these novels
are filled with the reassuring affirmation of how rich our ordinary
lives are. And we can never hear that often enough.

As far as I'm concerned, movies are either spiritual mentors or
self-medication. Depending on the moment, mood, or time of
the month, hunkering down in the dark with popcorn can seem

like the answer to a prayer or feel like the cure for whatever ails you, from boredom to feeling betrayed. "As we women know, movies are more than entertainment," Nancy Peske and Beverly West remind us in their witty and wise reference tome *Cinematherapy: The Girl's Guide to Movies for Every Mood.* "A good flick is like a soothing tonic, that if administered properly, in combination with total inertia and something obscenely high in fat grams, can cure everything from an identity crisis to a bad hair day to the I-hate-my-job blues."

This month let the snows and breathtaking fashions of yesteryear woo your sensibilities with these sweeping winter-set sagas of star-crossed lovers: Omar Sharif and Julie Christie in the film adaptation of Boris Pasternak's *Doctor Zhivago,* set in the days of the Russian Revolution; Ralph Fiennes and Liv Tyler in *Onegin,* a sumptuous dramatization of Aleksandr Pushkin's nineteenth-century novel in verse, *Eugene Onegin,* about a man who becomes obsessed with the love he once scorned; and a stunning rendition of Edith Wharton's heartbreaking novella *Ethan Frome,* written in 1911, starring Liam Neeson and Patricia Arquette. As Peske and West put it: "Indulge in the forbidden pleasures of enmeshment without having to pick up the emotional check."

Romance the ordinary experience of home videos by imagining that you are one of the characters in a film. Pick a character early on, before you know how the film will evolve, but make sure it's someone you feel a connection with whether it's because she's gorgeous, or because she reminds you of a favorite aunt. Or find a character living out your dark side: the less-than-good girl, the not-so-perfect mother, the ruthless executive. Then follow the twists and turns of "your fate." If the film is adapted from a book, read it later to fill in the blanks of the character you've chosen. You'll be amazed at how enlightening and fun this reflective reverie can be.

For, as the philosopher Marsha Sinetar observes in her fascinating book *Reel Power: Spiritual Growth Through Film,* "Movies mirror us and invite us to go beyond the obvious. Their themes and images can powerfully equip us to see ourselves as we are at our worst, and at our best, or to help us invent new scripts about who we hope to be."

484

Going Back to Your Roots

Had we but world enough, and time . . .
My vegetable love should grow
Vaster than empires, and more slow.

—Andrew Marvell (1652)

I grew up thinking that there was only one vegetable in the world—mash. This is not too surprising because from the time I could hold a fork, every vegetable that ended up on my plate looked the same, boiled beyond recognition. It took a trip to France in my twenties to discover how miraculous vegetables truly are and it was an epicurean epiphany. Suddenly vegetables had color, flavor, texture, and aroma. I had to be *shown* how to eat an artichoke at a dinner party, but instead of being embarrassed, I was giddy with possibility. Thus did my vegetable love begin to grow. (A friend later told me that whenever she has a group of relative strangers to dinner she serves artichokes, putting a large bowl or two at the center of the table for discarded leaves. The tossing of leaves into a communal bowl always breaks the ice, she says.)

While most people wax lyrical about spring's first asparagus or summer's tomatoes, my praise goes to root vegetables, which are at the peak of their flavor during the winter. "Few pleasures are more satisfying than coming in from the cold to a warm house filled with the aromas of freshly baked bread and slowly simmered soups, or the earthy smell of overroasted vegetables," Darra Goldstein argues persuasively in her luscious cookbook *The Winter Vegetarian*. "Winter need not be a time of gastronomic deprivation, a season to be weathered, a culinary gap to be endured year after year. The cold season can and ought to be an opportunity to luxuriate in the comforts of hearth and home."

Vegetables that grow underground are known as root vegetables, but go way beyond the familiar carrot and everybody's favorite, the potato. They include beetroots, Jerusalem artichokes, celeriac, fennel, turnips, yams, parsnips, and the much maligned rutabaga. One of the more seductive ways that Life attempts to woo us each month is with seasonal foods. Until a few years ago I was unacquainted with the particular charms of these winter marvels. But love that grows slowly always takes root. Why not expand your old boundaries by preparing one new-to-you vegetable a week? This suggestion sounds so inconsequential it's easy to overlook or dismiss, but please don't. The return on your investment of curiosity will be delicious. Each root vegetable has its own distinctive flavor and requires little ornamentation; and each provides a sense of being cozily content when dished up hot and soft. Root vegetables absorb nutrients from the ground as they grow, and they retain this goodness during storage and cooking, unlike more fragile, leafy vegetables that fade with time or heat. This makes them a terrific means of getting your daily vitamins and minerals in large, delicious doses.

French-fried sweet potatoes have become a café sensation, but how often have you had them whipped, like the lightest and creamiest of white mashed potatoes? Sans marshmallows, sans syrups, sans spices except salt, pepper, and a bit of fresh thyme? Here's how to rediscover the taste of the sweet potato. Scrub one medium sweet potato well, poke a few holes in it so it won't explode, then oil it lightly with olive oil. Bake at 350 degrees for one and one-quarter hours, or until easily pierced with a fork. Remove and discard the skin and puree the flesh (cut into chunks and use a blender on low). In a small saucepan, melt two teaspoons unsalted butter. Add the melted butter and one-half teaspoon fresh, finely snipped thyme (an herb traditionally used to cleanse, stimulate, and yet soothe digestion), and give it a quick whirl. Pour into a bowl and top the fluffy treat with a sprinkling of salt and freshly ground pepper.

Carrots, beets, and other root vegetables can be prepared similarly, using a blender or a food processor. But instead of baking the vegetables first, cut them into chunks and steam them, then whip them. A tablespoon of cream cheese added to a turnip puree is divine. A touch of bourbon in a carrot puree is wickedly good. See what happens when you combine different root colors and flavors, and in different proportions: beets and turnips, or carrots and parsnips. Whip small amounts separately, and build yourself a vegetable landscape of white, pink, and orange scoops (just the way your mother might have!). Play with your roots. They've been patiently waiting for you all this time to reveal their true nature.

Come to Your Senses

Vegetable Love

*D*iscovering and preparing simple meals that induce sighs of contentment is one of life's unsurpassed pleasures. Rich in vitamins and minerals, void of fat, low in calories, high in flavor, vegetables are *good* for you—body and soul. Mother might have known best, but she just didn't know how to cook them. Darra Goldstein does. Her roasted winter-vegetable medley will pique your palate as well as your spirit.

Roasted Winter-Vegetable Salad

This is so simple, satisfying, and scrumptious you'll designate it a "company" dish. Peel and slice an assortment of vegetables in whatever combination you want. Go wild and mix together raw *beets, carrots, celery root, fennel* (trimmed and sliced), *garlic cloves* (peeled and left whole), *yellow onions* (peeled and cut into wedges), *parsnips, potatoes* (peeled and cut into small wedges), *rutabagas, shallots* (peeled and separated into sections), *sweet potatoes* (peeled and cut into small wedges), *turnips,* and *winter squash* (peeled, seeded, and sliced).

Preheat the oven to 425° F. With good olive oil lightly grease a baking dish large enough to hold the vegetables without crowding. Toss the vegetables with a little more olive oil (about 6 teaspoons) and balsamic vinegar (about 3 teaspoons), and season with salt, freshly ground pepper, and a teaspoon each of dry savory and thyme. Put the dish in the oven and roast for about 45 minutes, turning the vegetables every 15 minutes until they are tender and browned.

With a loaf of crusty French bread (to push the vegetables around on your plate!) and a nice glass of red wine, this dish makes a meal well worth staying home for.

We'll Take Romance

Is not this the true romantic feeling — not to desire to escape life, but to prevent life from escaping you?

—Thomas Wolfe

*I*n her delightful essay "A Plea for Flirtation," written for *Vogue* in 1964, the writer Marya Mannes points out that the purpose of flirtation is "to warm, to amuse, to titillate, even to excite" our drab daily round. "And it would make this impermanent life a lot more fun if more of us learned the art of keeping the spark alive, and glowing."

It would seem that learning the art of keeping sparks alive is a lifelong occupation for every woman.

If truth be told, I'm a woman born for relationships, and yet, to my great bewilderment, I'm alone. Glancing back, I suppose I've been alone all my life, especially when I've been *in* relationships, and that is the loneliest kind of lonely. It astonishes me to confess this, because it sounds so sad. And it *was* very sad—for about half a century. But then one ordinary day, like the ordinary day I discovered the miracle of gratitude, I got tired of my own misery. To others, I effectively hid my secret sorrow, but the emotional exhaustion of carrying and concealing my loneliness became more than I could bear alone. So I turned to Spirit.

Knowing the transformative power of gratitude to redeem every situation, especially the impossible ones, I started a brand-new Gratitude Journal devoted to romance. I began by listing the reasons that I was grateful, at that particular moment, to require a table only for one. The holiday season is especially hard on single people, so if you're lonely because you're no one's sweetheart this Thanksgiving, here are a few entries to help you stop enduring your loneliness and begin embracing your at-one-ness:

1. I don't have to stop what I'm doing to take care of anyone else except my daughter.
2. I don't have to hide my purchases in the trunk of the car.
3. I can stay in my pajamas all weekend long.
4. I can eat pizza for breakfast, or make pancakes for dinner.
5. Waxing can wait until spring (both floors and legs!).
6. I can spread all my papers and books on the other side of my bed and leave them there until I'm finished.
7. My decor needn't accommodate jarring departures from my exquisite personal taste.
8. I don't have to make an appointment to spend half an hour in the tub.
9. I can watch a wonderful old movie at 3 A.M. without keeping the volume down.
10. I don't have to share my closets with anyone.
11. I can dress up for the fun of it without anyone asking, "What's the occasion?"

12. I can tear pages out of magazines and newspapers without waiting for anyone else to read them first.
13. I don't have to tune out the clamor of someone else's choice in music, television, or videos.
14. I can spend Saturday reading and catch up on the housework whenever.
15. I can eat anything in my own refrigerator at any time.
16. I can celebrate any darn thing I want to with an expensive bottle of wine.
17. I'm always happy with my own birthday present.
18. I'm not working overtime to pay for someone else's frivolities.
19. I don't have to stop everything to catch the score, unless I want to.
20. I don't have to explain myself, ever.

None of this may sound like the stepping-stone to living romantically, but trust me, the experiment has to begin somewhere. At this moment you may be feeling sorry for yourself because of loves lost. But discover a few new-to-you reasons to be grateful for your singleness of purpose right now—your determination to find your own essential, long-overdue happiness—and who knows what you'll be grateful for tomorrow?

Between the Lines

Love After Love

*I*f you wake up feeling depressed because you're alone, especially during the holidays, the Nobel Prize–winning poet and dramatist Derek Walcott's poem "Love After Love" becomes an eloquent prayer expressing gratitude for the unexpected blessing that comes when we are ready to take a chance on Life's true romance.

The time will come
When, with elation,
You will greet yourself arriving
At your own door, in your own mirror,
And each will smile at the other's welcome

And say, sit here. Eat.
You will love again the stranger who was your self.
Give wine. Give bread. Give back your heart
To itself, to the stranger who has loved you

All your life, whom you ignored
For another, who knows you by heart.

Take down the love letters from the bookshelf,
The photographs, the desperate notes,
Peel your own image from the mirror.
Sit. Feast on your life.

December

December, the diamond-frosted clasp
linking twelve jeweled months to yet
another year.

—Phyllis Nicholson

*T*he Old Year wanes. No more yearning for what might have
been. Instead, open December's generous gift of what *is*. . . .
Let the darkest day shed new Light as you rediscover old-fashioned
reasons for a heartfelt season of simple splendor. Hang the stocking, trim the tree, get in line for Santa's knee. Believe us, you've
been *too* good this year. What can True Love bring, if the turtledoves go missing or there's no golden ring? An opulent month of
ordinary miracles wrapped up in a reverie of romance. Glad tidings
of comfort and joy.

Marvelous Truth

Marvelous Truth, confront us
at every turn,
in every guise . . .

—Denise Levertov

This dark, cold, and wet December morning the annual feminine tug-of-war between hope and experience is in earnest. A reluctant participant in this year's skirmishes, I burrow beneath the bedcovers wishing the holidays away. Ten minutes later their imminent arrival still lurks. The thought of the day's first cup of tea coaxes me down the stairs.

Unfortunately, the kitchen table is exactly as I left it last night. Not even room to sit down.

Here before me, the metaphysical manifestation of a woman's holiday duplicity—anticipation and dread. A ramshackle assortment of cookbooks, women's magazines, mail order catalogs, boxes of cards, and reams of lists. On the chairs, gifts to be wrapped still in shopping bags, a huge pile of vintage ribbons that need to be pressed. "As Christmas approached the usual mysteries began to haunt the house," Louisa May Alcott wrote in *Little Women*. She might have been referring to the large brown boxes labeled "Xmas/Misc" that engulf the kitchen and spill into the dining room, waiting to be opened and sorted. The very thought of their contents is terrifying. Of course, the sorting and labeling should have been done last year when Christmas was packed away. In her guide *How to Survive Christmas,* the brilliant, funny English writer Jilly Cooper describes women caught in the crossfire of enforced celebrating as *Xmasochists*. Clearly, I must be one.

Wishing rarely makes anything so, but it's been my experience that acceptance can change most situations, probably because it rearranges our thought patterns, even if our circumstances remain

things become more beautiful when lit from within) and there's a man standing at the second-floor window, holding a cat in his arms. What a handsome man, I think. Wouldn't it be nice to live in that house?"

Standing outside the boundaries we have erected in our lives to protect us or keep us propped up is a gentle spiritual, creative, and practical way to reawaken wonder. "The most common things can yield startling surprises when we give our attention to them," Rebecca McClanahan reminds us. Especially the holidays you're dreading.

On Your Marks, Get Set

There is no doubt . . . that being prepared is the secret to a more harmonious Christmas. If Joseph had booked a room in advance, Jesus would not have been born in a stable.

—Jilly Cooper

"*A* perfectly managed Christmas correct in every detail is, like basted inside seams and letters answered by return, a sure sign of someone who hasn't enough to do," Katharine White-horn reassures us. I don't think that's our problem.

Actually, I had every intention of writing us both a brilliant schedule of preparation for the holidays *that really works!!!!!* However, none of our schedules ever does work, because we never implement them until about December 20. Did you know that the holiday issues with those fantastic week-by-week organizing articles were prepared by magazine editors in August? This always makes me feel better. The point is, it's too late for schedules and countdowns whether you celebrate Chanukah, Christmas, or Kwanza. Instead, let's count all the things you love about the holidays.

Yes, you *do*.

What are your five happiest holiday memories? I'd bet they're all sensory ones. The fragrance of pine, oranges, and cloves; hitting the high note in "O Holy Night"; lighting the menorah; the first bite of warm gingerbread; the touch of tinsel as you decorate the tree. Savoring the gift of each sense is how you romance the season and rediscover the art of celebrating.

Once upon a time, you believed that Christmas was the most magical time of the year. It can be again. I think the real miracle of Christmas is that it allows the mystical child slumbering in each of our souls the chance to be reborn every year, awakening a sense of wonder that even eleven months of grown-up doubt, derision, discouragement, or disappointment can't snuff out. All that's required of us is that we believe.

Believe in what? How about starting with whatever you can see, hear, taste, smell, and touch that brings you contentment this time of year?

"Time was, with most of us, when Christmas Day encircling all our limited world like a magic ring, left nothing out for us to miss or seek; bound together all our home enjoyments, affections, and hopes; grouped every thing and every one around the Christmas fire; and made the little picture shining in our bright young eyes, complete," Charles Dickens reminisced in a charming essay, "What Christmas Is, As We Grow Older," written in 1851. "Therefore, as we grow older, let us be more thankful that the circle of our Christmas associations and of the lessons that they bring, expands! . . . Welcome, old aspirations, glittering creatures of an ardent fancy, to your shelter underneath the holly! We know you, and have not outlived you yet. Welcome, old projects and old loves, however fleeting, to your nooks among the steadier lights that burn around us. Welcome, all that was ever real to our hearts."

The Ghosts of Christmas Past

There are few sensations more painful, than in the midst of deep grief, to know that the season which we have always associated with mirth and rejoicing is at hand.

—Mrs. Sarah Josepha Hale (1835)

*L*ife's firsts are either the best or worst of times. There's no middle ground. The first Christmas you spend with a lover or a new baby is wondrous. The first Christmas alone is a cavernous echo and ache. "Christmas is a time of sentimental triggers," the British writer Catherine O'Brien reminds us. "Other memories blur and fade, but one can almost always call to mind where one was for Christmases past."

Perhaps. For the last few Christmases past I have been pulling a Scrooge—shutting down or fleeing from memories too painful to confront. One year of defection blurs into another; denial doesn't seem to have any distinguishing features, except that it doesn't feel good. A desktop Christmas tree in a hotel room is unlikely to make one merry, even if it's in Paris. We can run until we're out of breath. We can hide for a while. But eventually we become too emotionally exhausted for fight or flight, and that is always a good sign. Besides, my Essensual Self really loves Christmas and missed it.

My reckoning came when I asked my former husband (who kept the house we lived in while married) to give me the boxes of holiday decorations so that I could go through them and sort things out. Of course, I couldn't, even five years after my divorce, which is how the boxes became marked "Xmas/Misc." Even when we move past the shock of enforced life changes, the pain of Christmas Past has a particular sting. Still, I wanted to retrieve a few special ornaments, such as the angel my parents put on my first Christmas tree and the one I had put on my daughter's, as well as a few more decorations that carried more pleasure than poignancy in their resurrection.

It was then that I came upon my idea of reclaiming Christmas by editing out whatever I considered a burden or too painful, and keeping only the holiday pastimes that I have always cherished. In so doing, I was rewriting the holiday—giving both Christmas and myself the miracle of another chance. We think that traditions are carved on stone tablets, but really they're like recipes, and they'll adapt beautifully, if you'll let them, to your new circumstances. Introducing new-to-us festive rituals each year as our lives change is how we continually open ourselves up to wonder, ensuring that our future memories of Christmas Past bring contentment and renewal.

But first, you must go back. "Linger on the memories that made one particular Christmas or even just a moment at one Christmas a positive and spirited experience. Perhaps, when you were a child, a visiting relative gave you a new book and read to you on Christmas night. Stay with that memory until you can feel the quiet reassuring love and the pleasure of being read to," Judith Blahnik suggests in *Checklist for a Perfect Christmas* (a title that's really too trivial for her deeper and important message of how to personalize Christmas). Write the memory down because it will become the foundation for a holiday that's *perfect for you.* Or as close as you can get it.

"Then go back to collect more memories. Stay with each memory long enough to understand what about it still has meaning for you.... Continue to do this until you have a list of important memories: the moment of mailing the letter to Santa; learning all the words to 'The First Noel'; the smell of a favorite aunt's perfume; hearing the applause after your appearance in the school play; lighting the candle of the Advent wreath; searching for the perfect tree, cutting it, buying it, strapping it to the car, and enjoying its fragrance all the way home; leaving a note for Santa and actually finding it gone in the morning; feeling the leap in your heart on Christmas morning when presents that weren't there when you went to bed appeared miraculously under the tree."

When I excavated my memories of Christmases Past, one of the shockers was that I was always ruining my surprises. From October to Christmas Eve, I'd be snooping all around the house until I found everything that Santa was planning to bring me, and then I'd wonder why I was disappointed on Christmas morning. Now I wait until Christmas Day to open gifts. One small step for babes in toyland, but one big leap for woman's wonder. I also realized that my need to know the future extended far beyond Christmas presents. It derived from a fear that Love would forget me. My recognition that as long as I didn't forget how to give Love, I'd never be forgotten, was one of the best gifts Spirit has ever bestowed. As I've said before and will keep on saying until you believe me, our past only asks to be remembered so that our wounds can be healed.

Once you've excavated happy holiday memories, they become your personal blueprint. "You may not make an exact re-creation of Christmases Past, but the joy of the memories will help shape your plans for the holidays," Judith Blahnik explains. "For example, you might not have time to bake and decorate cookies with your children; even so, you and the children can go to a church bake sale, select cookies and pack some into colorful tins for friends; maybe you do have time for one gingerbread house project; or perhaps this is the year your mother would like to visit and bake cookies with the kids. Right there are three ideas to consider: Pick one and plan it into your holiday."

Pick one. Just as a reminder that Christmas comes but *once* a year and lasts only *one* day.

It goes without saying, but let's say it anyway. When an unpleasant holiday task looms—such as writing out a hundred cards, or organizing the carol sing—you cut the burden out completely or you adapt it. You send out ten cards; you attend a carol sing organized by someone else.

When we consciously honor the reflections from the past, they "can bring heart and energy to your Christmas plans, help them take shape, and make them shimmer with excitement and hope," Judith Blahnik says. A holiday miracle if ever there was one.

Come to Your Senses

A Season to Remember

*I*f it's hard to pinpoint when and where your pleasure took place during Christmas Past, here's a way not only to remember well, but to create a special logbook celebrating your relationships with family, friends, and with the holiday itself. Whether you feel that December whizzes by in a blur of hectic activity, or you find it a lonely time with little impact, recording how many ways it touches you will bring the season into vivid focus, now and in years to come. There's nothing more wonderful than saying, "Ah, yes, I remember it well," with a smile or a laugh.

At a stationer's or bookstore, select a pretty spiral-bound notebook suggestive of the holiday you celebrate (an angel print, red or green velvet for Christmas, blue or silver for Chanukah, bright batik for Kwanza). A good size is eight and a half by eleven inches, and ruled pages will come in handy both for writing and for aligning the recipes, snapshots, or seasonal memorabilia you'll be pasting in. This will become your Holiday Memory Book.

Begin by writing in the year, and a sample (or color photocopy) of the Christmas card(s) you're sending this year, and to whom.

Paste in small swatches of your wraps, ribbons, and tags . . . and write what gifts you gave to whom. Do you feel a little guilty throwing out particularly pretty gift wraps and trimmings once you've unwrapped your own gifts? Although it's perfectly polite to recycle unblemished bows, ribbons, or paper, you can also preserve the memory of the decorated gift by creating a minimontage of your favorite wrappings in your Memory Book. Be sure to note down who had packaged the gift so beautifully.

Save invitations to holiday parties you've enjoyed (including your own). Jot down what you wore or what fantastic outfit some-one *else* wore, what foods were served or were notably delicious, how the party space was decorated. In short, create a record of what was memorable about each occasion. And don't stand on ceremony—this isn't only about big parties. Spontaneously shar-ing a late-night cup of cider in your pajamas with a favorite neigh-bor is something you'll be happy to look back on, too. If something feels like a special occasion, it is a special occasion. (You might decide not to document unmemorable office parties or family reunions, and that's fine. This is a book for happy memories, not for *every* memory.)

When it's time to take down displays of holiday cards, bring out the book again. Paste in the cards you find most beautiful or clever, or the ones with personal messages you'd like to preserve. Have people enclosed photos of themselves, their children, their pets? Into the book they go! (And remember to note the children's or pets' names, for thoughtful mentions in next year's cards.)

Have the words to a particular seasonal song or poem acquired special meaning for you? Record them in the book. Paste in the ticket stub to a holiday film you attended, program notes from a musical event that moved you, the menu from a festive restaurant dinner. Even a small clipping from the schedule listing of a won-derful old Christmas movie you caught on TV, or an hour of early carols you heard on the radio, counts as a valuable sensory memento. When you open your book next year you'll be reminded of what you enjoyed, so that you can make sure you do it again.

Even if you spend this time of year in a fairly solitary fashion, there are so many ways that even fleeting human contact or widely attended seasonal events can make the season a little warmer. Creating keepsakes of these special moments is like cupping an eternal flame of kindness, thoughtfulness, and connectedness between your hands. When you come back to your notes . . . surprise! They're still warm.

What you will have created is a three-dimensional Gratitude Journal for the holidays, and the good that we remember with thanksgiving always grows.

In time, this Holiday Memory Book may become the first thing you turn to as you begin your holiday preparations. Take your time filling up and flipping through the pages. See how often you have brought joy to others, with a greeting or a gift or with your presence on a festive evening. Feel how heavy the book is becoming, how even the smallest touches, given or received, can remind you of the generosity of the human spirit . . . including your own. "Christmas is a bridge. We need bridges as the river of time flows past," Gladys Taber tells us. "Today's Christmas should mean creating happy hours for tomorrow and reliving those of yesterday." And they can, once you start remembering them.

All You Really Want
from Santa, Baby

*You cannot give to people what they are incapable
of receiving.*

—Agatha Christie

I know what you really want from Santa, although I doubt if it's
on your list: a guarantee that you'll make it through the holidays without a relationship meltdown. The reality is that you
long for a little help in spreading the holiday mirth, and the other
you might share your life with doesn't seem willing or able to make
any significant contribution to the common good. Perhaps I can be
of assistance. While working on *A Man's Journey to Simple Abundance* I chanced upon some insider knowledge that could save you
from spending the holidays behind bars or him on the floor of one.
The entire purpose of this book was to bring the sexes closer
together (at least on the page) and I had fifty brilliant men set the
record straight about the *real* differences between men and women.
This included the shocking revelation that men do not actually *hate*
Christmas. What they hate are the holiday-activated mood swings,
and not just yours, but theirs.

You see, the holidays highlight a slew of things men *think*
they're no good at—decorating, cooking, prettifying, relating,
sitting around doing nothing but talking, and thinking of others.
Since men are deeply invested in their own competence, four
weeks of exposing the opposite (real or imaginary) is frankly
unbearable. So they become unbearable as well. Loss of control is
the ultimate male fear.

Then, too, forced intimacy is never an attractive prospect for a
man, and the holidays demand family closeness. That's why he's
running as far as he can from you, the kids, and the holidays. He's

505

so, so nasty. Who'd want to spend time with him? Once upon a time, however, men enjoyed the holidays—when they were children. Since Mr. Big isn't able to access his inner child in the presence of women (not to be confused with *acting out* his inner child, which all men I know do very well), he's actually melancholy during the holidays, and that makes him embarrassed and angry. It just looks and sounds like he's angry at you.

Yes, they have confessed this to me, in strictest confidence.

Another reason for surges in tumultuous testosterone: women are much better shoppers than men. This phenomenon has been studied; results show that the gifts women buy are returned less than half as often as those men buy. Men buy much more impulsively and spend far more money on presents than women do, and the reason is that most men have little tolerance for standing in a store and figuring out what to purchase for someone else. With the exception of sporting goods and tools, do you know a man who's ever shopped his way out of depression? Men want to be in and out in five minutes. Even if a man wants to get you a fabulous present, he has no idea how to, which sets him up for failure. Hence, grumpiness.

What's a woman to do? Give him tasks that he's good at and you don't want to do: heavy lifting; taking care of anything "ready to be assembled"; picking up relatives or guests at the airport or train station; carting packages to the post office; putting up the tree and stringing the lights (indoors and out); bringing in firewood; shoveling snow; and buying last-minute items from a carefully written, *detailed* list, including brand names. He would also greatly appreciate a list of presents you want (as will you), including where to get them and in what *size*.

And the one-size holiday gift any man would adore, appreciate, and never return? I would suggest *A Man's Journey to Simple Abundance* but I'm too modest. Here are some ideas. Season tickets for his favorite local team; an IOU that promises a romantic interlude where and when he chooses (within reason); a gadget that reflects his passions (but nothing practical); a hair transplant; the return of lost youth (e.g., that electric guitar he coveted but never got when he was fifteen, and making out by the lights of the Christmas tree).

There's one gift you'd love from him this minute, if he could give it to you, but he can't. So let me be Santa's helper: it's the certainty that *every* reaction he has during the holidays has *nothing* to do with *you* and *everything* to do with the powerful emotions he's trying to hide.

Come to Your Senses

The Twelve Days of Christmas

*W*omen are great givers and stingy receivers. As you shop for others, are you remembering the most deserving person you know? Probably not. But one magnificent *Just what I always wanted . . . how did you guess?* wrapped bauble should be underneath the tree with your name on it. And we all know how it will get there, don't we?

One of my favorite holiday traditions is honoring the Twelve Days of Christmas with small, pampering gifts intended to remind me that when it comes to self-nurturing, it's not just the thought that counts.

Assemble the goodies in advance, in a large basket, a pretty shopping bag lined with tissue paper, or the biggest stocking you can find. Set your presents in a place where you will see them, to increase your pleasure with the happy anticipation of withdrawing each gift. Start to savor your treats during a half hour stolen from every evening, beginning December 13.

1. Windblown, radiator-dried-out skin needs extra moisturizing. Place in the basket a small bottle of almond oil (available from gourmet markets or health food stores). To use, just dampen your fingertips with the oil, and apply on your face with upward strokes.
2. Don't forget your lips! Prepare for your basket the following: In a small bowl, mix several drops of honey with two tablespoons of petroleum jelly; spoon into a small, clean jar. Dab on to soften dry, chapped lips.
3. Are your fancy soaps reserved for guests? Indulge yourself with a single bar of fine-milled, scented soap in a seasonal fragrance such as the divine combination of frankincense and myrrh. Gift and bath shops often sell these individually wrapped, for just a few dollars apiece. Don't discard the manufacturer's wrapper—tuck it into your lingerie drawer, to subtly scent your undergarments for months to come.
4. A one- or two-bite, wrapped fancy chocolate from an expensive chocolatier won't wreck your diet and will be good for your soul!
5. Counteract the chocolate with the largest, most perfect organic apple you can find in a health food or gourmet shop. Once you discover how tasty it is, you may want to continue giving this kind of gift to yourself well beyond Christmas.
6. Place two oranges, one lime, and a banana in the gift basket. When the banana becomes ripe, treat yourself to a nutritious tropical smoothie: Squeeze the citrus fruits, peel and slice the banana. Combine the juices and banana slices in a blender, along with one-half cup of yogurt or soy milk. Pour into a tall glass, and drink to your health!
7. Make your own scented after-bath powder by placing one cup of cornstarch into a Ziploc bag and adding a few drops of your favorite perfume, rose water, or vanilla

extract. Zip the bag closed and shake well. Pour the powder into a tightly lidded jar. Be sure to include a fluffy puff when you place this goody in your basket.

8. At a health food or herbal shop, purchase small bottles of soy oil and peppermint essential oil. When your legs are tired from a long day of walking or standing, this is the gift to choose: Combine one-half cup of the soy oil with four drops of peppermint essential oil, and use this to massage your legs. Follow with a warm footbath. Pat dry.

9. Buy an inexpensive metal-polishing cloth at a hardware or variety store. Spend a relaxing afternoon or evening polishing all your jewelry. Play dress-up for a while, before putting away all your sparklies!

10. How long have you been using the same old hairbrush? Replace it with a good-quality new one and, at least the first time you use it, give your hair the hundred strokes your grandmother may have enjoyed as a daily ritual.

11. Have your washcloths worn thin to a see-through nubble? Buy a couple of thick Egyptian-cotton washcloths from a luxury bath shop. Set aside some time for a leisurely hot bath . . . and make sure that cloth strokes every inch of your skin, from top to bottom.

12. Settle-Me-Down-Tea will hit the spot after all that Christmas shopping. Purchase as loose tea and mix together two parts dried peppermint leaves with one part chamomile flowers. Store in a jar or tin. To brew, use one teaspoon of the mixture per cup of hot water, and steep at least ten minutes.

You could go on and I usually do, so you might also want to add to your basket a pure linen hankie for your purse (once you get hooked on this indulgence, and you will, look for them in flea markets), a large, gorgeous powder puff and rose-scented talc, or a Christmas-themed mystery to read while you're waiting in line, such as Agatha Christie's *The Adventures of the Christmas Pudding, Holmes for the Holidays* (that's Sherlock), *Hercule Poirot's Christmas,* or Georges Simenon's great French police-detective *Maigret's Christmas.*

December kicks off my annual monthlong Christmas-classic

cinema celebration. Do you have one? Spread the films throughout the season because they're available on video and also frequently shown on cable television. My favorites include Barbara Stanwyck's *Christmas in Connecticut* and *Remember the Night, Holiday Inn, White Christmas, The Bishop's Wife, Miracle on 34th Street, It's a Wonderful Life,* and two helpings each of Charles Dickens's *A Christmas Carol* (the George C. Scott and Muppet versions) and Louisa May Alcott's *Little Women* (1933 with Katharine Hepburn and the 1994 version with Susan Sarandon as the beloved mother, Marmee). An amazing reference is the American Movie Channel's *Great Christmas Movies* by Frank Thompson.

As *Little Women*'s Jo March believed, "Christmas won't be Christmas without any presents," and this includes presents for you.

Christmastide at Newton's Chapel

*I do hope your Christmas has had a little touch of
eternity in among the rush and pitter-patter and all.
It always seems such a mixing of this world and
the next — but that after all is the idea!*

—Evelyn Underhill

My life's new chapter is being written in a hamlet so small that our postal address requires the name of the village next to us, and the name of the town closest to the village. "Earth's crammed with Heaven" here, as Elizabeth Barrett Browning describes it.

Especially during Christmastide at Newton's Chapel.

Because the whole episode seemed, from the start, like folly, I kept insisting that Newton's Chapel was just going to be a writing retreat. Yet with each successive visit over the last five years, my weary soul sank root shoots a little bit deeper into the English countryside until my homing instincts began to take hold, especially during the holidays. As the poet Sallie Tisdale puts it, "Here I stay, a free woman, unable to move."

Although we don't know when the Chapel was originally built, since the thirteenth century it's been recorded as the property of the owners of Woolsthorpe Manor (a deceptive name, as it's really just a large farmhouse). In the sixteenth century, Isaac Newton's great-grandfather purchased the manor, and on Christmas Day, 1642, Isaac Newton arrived on the planet under adverse circumstances. His mother, Hannah, had been widowed suddenly during the pregnancy, and the months between her husband's death and the birth of her first child were racked with uncertainty.

Not surprisingly, Isaac's birth was difficult. He was born prematurely, was sickly, and was not expected to live. His mother said that Isaac was such a wee thing that he could get lost in a cradle, so she kept him in a quart pot, propping up his tiny head and neck with rag bolsters. When Isaac was three, his mother remarried, and her new husband wanted nothing to do with the boy, who was then shuttled among relatives for the next nine years until he went off to study mathematics at Trinity College, Cambridge.

It is impossible for me to ready Newton's Chapel for the holidays without thinking of Isaac's unhappy and lonely childhood. It shaped his private life so profoundly; he never married, and even intimate friendships were fraught with such intensity that they isolated him even further. Certainly he wouldn't have known many happy Christmases, growing up here. So I try to make up for it. Despite my considerable feminine wiles, I probably don't stand a ghost of a chance with Isaac (since he has been dead for 275 years), but we seem happy together for the time being. Have you ever seen the enchanting 1947 British film *The Ghost and Mrs. Muir* starring Gene Tierney and Rex Harrison? It's a romantic fantasy about a young widow who moves with her daughter to an English cottage by the sea, only to fall in love with the ghost of its former owner, Captain Gregg. As Maya Angelou confessed in her memoir, *The Heart of a Woman,* "If one is lucky, a solitary fantasy can totally transform one million realities." Should that be true, I'm a very lucky woman indeed.

When people visit me, the first comment they usually make is how peaceful the Chapel is, how healing the energy feels throughout its small rooms. One friend described it as simultaneously enervating and soothing; other friends have been known to cross the threshold and burst into tears, as if some mysticism has touched a hidden sorrow, and here they have found a refuge from their pain. By the visit's end, no one wants to leave (which is my biggest problem) but their beaming faces, laughter, and renewed enthusiasm announce that they're ready to go.

Sir Isaac Newton's Christmas celebrations (had there been some) would have taken place in the years between Shakespeare's time and the Georgian era of Jane Austen. Elizabethan Christmas celebrations were called *revels,* and they involved great feasting among both the rich and the poor and entertainments such as plays and pantomimes. Both are still very much a part of the British Christmas. Do you remember the old English carol "Here We Come A-Wassailing"? It tells the story of poor child carolers going door-to-door to offer all they are able to give—their song and holiday blessings—to their wealthier neighbors, in return, one hopes, for a bite to eat. The tradition of wassailing (from the Saxon meaning "Good health to you"), with guests partaking of a cup of "good cheer," began during Shakespeare's time and still continues today, especially in the countryside.

I prepare my first seasonal wassail bowl about mid-December when we bring in the Christmas tree and begin decking the Chapel's walls (there are no halls!). The scent of fresh evergreens mingling with that of the wood burning in the fireplace, and the heady aroma of my hot, frothy wassail punch—spiced cider and dark English ale, with nutmeg, sugar, cinnamon, and roasted apples—makes everyone swoon. Quickly, the tree and greens are set down on the floor, and we stand around my Aga cooker, sipping, sighing, and tucking into warm gingerbread.

My tradition of the wassail bowl is a perfect example of keeping the holiday rituals that are meaningful and continue to bring you pleasure, even as your life changes. When I was married, our family used to have an annual open house during the holidays, and

I served wassail, homemade eggnog, and mulled wine. At Newton's Chapel, this wonderful assortment of holiday refreshments (with the recipes refined to trigger unadulterated bliss) continues to bring rosy cheeks and contented smiles to the faces of all my friends celebrating Christmas with me on the other side of the Atlantic. As it will yours.

Newton's Chapel
Cup of Cheer

Charles Dickens wrote about wassailing and imbibing spiced wine at a family holiday gathering, however humble the home setting might be. In *A Christmas Carol,* every member of the Cratchit family—yes, even down to Tiny Tim—toasts the holidays with a hot mixture of gin and lemon. The few glasses they own are passed from person to person. And in *The Pickwick Papers* the entire family "sat down by the huge fire of blazing logs to a substantial supper, and a mighty bowl of wassail, something smaller than an ordinary wash-house copper, in which the hot apples were hissing and bubbling.

"This," said Mr. Pickwick, looking around him, "this is, indeed, comfort."

This recipe serves a crowd; to adapt it, reduce the amount of both ale and cider to one pint. But I'm rarely alone once the wassail starts simmering on the stove.

You will need:

2 quarts apple cider
6 cans dark English ale (I like Bass)
2 cinnamon sticks
A spice ball (cheesecloth or a metal tea ball filled with 1 teaspoon whole cloves and 1 teaspoon whole nutmeg)
1 tablespoon dark brown sugar
One lemon, sliced
6 small lady apples

Put everything into a large saucepan (the biggest you can find; I use a lobster pot) and simmer on the back burner for 20 minutes. Don't let it boil! As your punch evaporates, you may replenish the cider and the ale. It's the ale that makes it frothy.

While the wassail is heating up, place small lady apples (often available seasonally at good green-grocery shops) in a baking tin; sprinkle brown sugar over them and roast them for 15 minutes at 375°. When they're ready, pop them into the punch. For a non-alcoholic version, simply eliminate the ale.

Better than Christmas

"It's better'n a Christmas," they told their mother,
"to get ready for it!"

—Margaret Sidney (1881)
from *The Five Little Peppers*
and How They Grew

Slowly, surely, the season's magic spell takes hold. We start looking forward to the holidays. It seems that Lady Hope has tucked the surly twins Expectation and Experience into bed for a short winter's nap. Or perhaps She served them a cup of wassail. Whatever's going on, there's a festive energy in the air. Today we start decorating.

This past Christmas was the first time I "settled" into Newton's Chapel, and it seems appropriate that the heart of this book was lived, written, completed, and celebrated in this blessed spot. Because here is where I've gently but persuasively been romanced by the ordinary. Love lessons are what they're called around here.

Decorating for the holidays was a surprising lesson. I've always pulled out all the stops when it comes to decking the halls, cramming Christmas into every nook and cranny wherever I happened to live. But less really can be more. When I started preparing the Chapel for Christmas, a certain royal influence, who also shares the space with Sir Isaac and me (affectionately known as Her Ladyship), was specific in her preferences. They were simple, splendid, and, as I would later discover, amusing in their historical accuracy for the twelfth century.

As soon as you walk into Newton's Chapel, she greets you—a massive, gray stone head of an extraordinary woman—Queen Eleanor of Aquitaine, carved near the time of her reign, give or take a century. She was a "gift" to me from both the Great Mother and from her previous owner, who certainly didn't want to part

515

from her. The spring day I found her buried beneath the bushes in his backyard (because in twenty years he hadn't found a suitable spot for her), I knew we were meant to be together.

Well, this prior owner was also passionately in love with her, but he finally and reluctantly agreed that Queen Eleanor deserved more than he could provide, which is how the Lady came home to a familiar setting—a stone niche in a nave.

From the eighth to the twelfth century, as Christianity deepened its hold over the civilized world—particularly Britain, Scotland, and Ireland—shrines that had once honored the Goddess were "re-created" in the image of monarchs or the Virgin Mary. My Eleanor wears a carved crown and wimple (a veil that's folded to cover the head and neck and closely frame a woman's face), but her serene and comforting countenance is a familiar representation of the Great Mother. (Marion Zimmer Bradley's riveting novel *The Mists of Avalon* tells this story beautifully.)

It's possible that at one time Eleanor's presence graced a private medieval chapel. When I gaze up at her, during my meditations, I often wonder, what were the prayers of the women who asked her blessings before me? Probably they were about what really matters—love, children, health, the land, and their animals. Perhaps they lit large ivory candles and placed gifts of flowers and greens before her. I certainly can't look at her and not want to honor and offer boundless thanks to Spirit for her company. During the four seasons, she wears nature's adornments: in the spring and summer, flowers, in the fall, foliage. For Christmas, she wears a crown of holly, ivy, mistletoe, evergreens, and crimson roses. Before her are a few gilded apples. Not surprisingly, apples are a theme at Newton's Chapel, but they became Eleanor's offering when I discovered that, during the Middle Ages, Christmas Eve was also known as Adam and Eve's Day, and the festive plays that were performed told the story of the expulsion from Eden. Throughout the year I gather branches that have broken or fallen from my apple tree and save them, so that during the holidays I can add them to the fire; their fragrance sweetens the air like the scented prayers the ancients offered.

This holiday season, let your senses help in the selection of your decorations. Winter offers a startling array of natural fragrances, which is utterly amazing, as few flowers are growing. But there's pine, yew, larch, spruce, cedar, cypress, fir, juniper, and bay. Find as many different greens as you can and sniff deeply. Let your favorite fragrance determine your tree.

Maybe you think you've looked at holly, ivy, mistletoe, Christmas cactus, and the like, but have you *smelled* them? And have you *seen* them? What shapes are their leaves? How many berries does holly or mistletoe typically have? Touch them gently; feel the velvety softness of poinsettias, the smooth, succulent flesh beneath the cactus's prickles. If you've been decorating your home with synthetic counterparts—scentless, artificially colored—your explorations of living plants should come as a revelation. This year, bring home the real thing. You'll be acquiring the company of the beautiful and living. You'll also spend a healthier holiday surrounded by plants. Living plants or even cut, genuine evergreens—be they wreaths, garlands, sprigs—will literally freshen the air you breathe.

Enjoying winter greenery was a tradition long before plants became incorporated into Christmas imagery. In fact, their pagan associations kept them outside the realm of Christian acceptability for some time. (If you can believe it, mistletoe, which was the most sacred plant to the ancient Celts and grows on apple trees, is still banned from some churches!) But you needn't be a Druid to enjoy the spiritually uplifting qualities of plants. The only ceremony this pleasure requires is to stop and smell the greens!

Go on a few greenery field trips, in the wilds or to florists and tree vendors (who might be happy to give you the clippings left over after they've shaped their Christmas merchandise), to collect samples of lots of kinds of seasonal plants. Create your own miniature evergreen forest on a tabletop or desk. Add as many different kinds of pinecones as you can, along with attractively shaped nonevergreen twigs and branches that you might glean from lawns, sidewalks, or parks. Include touches of seasonal colors such as dark red, raw cranberries, vividly orange clementines, and pale ivory pears, arranged simply on a plate surrounded by magnolia leaves.

Experiment with new ways to display traditional evergreens in your home. Place them where humidity will help to release their scents. Swag the edge of a tablecloth with an evergreen garland, pinning it to the cloth from below. Hang small wreaths on interior doors, not just on your front door or windows. Tuck evergreen fronds above the top edge of hanging picture or mirror frames. Suspend a branch from the top of your shower curtain, to fill the steamy bathroom with its fragrance as you bathe (absolutely, lavishly erotic). Place a tabletop live tree or a bright red poinsettia in your bedroom, to remind you of the season as soon as you awaken and to sweeten your holiday dreams. (But not if you have pets. Please check with your vet first because some plants like poinsettias are toxic to them.) On each headboard, I hang large bunches of mistletoe, in honor of Walter de la Mare's poem "Mistletoe":

> *Tired I was; my head would go*
> *Nodding under the mistletoe*
> *(Pale green, fairy mistletoe),*
> *No footsteps came, no voice, but only,*
> *Just as I sat there, sleepy, lonely,*
> *Stopped in the still and shadowy air*
> *Lips unseen—and kissed me there.*

If you don't believe me, you'll just have to try for yourself, won't you?

Come to Your Senses

It's a Wrap

*H*as gift-wrapping become a chore for you, or do you enjoy it as a way to express your holiday spirit? Be it dreaded or delightful, you can turn gift-wrapping time into your own tradition: a celebration of the paper ephemera associated with the holidays.

Depending on how many items you need to wrap, set aside a day or an afternoon or evening when you won't be disturbed. Let the answering machine take your calls. Put some seasonal music on the stereo. Pour yourself a large mug of eggnog. To make commercially prepared eggnog lighter, blend it with half a glass of skim milk. Top with some nutmeg and enjoy.

Now, stop. When was the last time you truly *looked* at and enjoyed your gift wrappings from a recipient's point of view? Do you take care to fit printed designs to coordinate with the dimensions of their packages, or do you start wrapping with whatever size paper fits? Do you creatively combine the colors and styles of the paper, ribbons, bows, or tags, or do you use the same trimmings for every gift? Think about it. Giving people the same old wrap and ribbons is rather like giving them the same card a second year in a row. What can you do to make this year's gifts unique . . . perhaps so beautiful that people will be reluctant to open them?

If you're all thumbs, don't despair. The primary secret of handsome packages lies in crisp folds. Even butcher paper will look impressive as long as you prefit the paper to each gift. Hold the paper to the item, and pinch gently along each edge to mark the dimensions, then place the paper on a hard surface and fold each edge sharply all the way through. Then wrap for real. The folds will help keep the paper neatly in place as you tape the edges closed. Curved or lumpy items, on the other hand, might best be nestled into tissue paper and tucked into a decorative shopping bag or placed in a box so pretty that you don't have to wrap it; or twist colorful tissue paper or cellophane wrap at each end and secure each twist with a bit of tightly tied ribbon.

Be bold with leftover scraps of paper. Instead of discarding them, use tape or a glue stick to create panels of two or more coordinated papers—for example, a Santa print plus a stripe that picks up its colors. Wrap each side of a large box with a different pattern, or combine two papers at an angle across a small one. (Two different finishes of the same color, such as a dull and a bright gold, are especially elegant.) Cut strips of paper and lattice them together like a piecrust. Use quilt-block shapes to create a patchwork design of papers taped together on the underside.

A spectacular wrapping is a simple jewel-colored tissue paper, covered with colored netting, then pulled together with a simple silk ribbon bow. Pull the tulle and tissue upward for a shot of glamour.

If you're short on ribbon, try using one color on the horizontal and another on the vertical, or combine yarn, velvet, satin, or curling ribbons. Hit your sewing supplies for lace, rickrack, or seam tape. Instead of bows, why not attach miniature cookie cutters, jingle bells, small ornaments meant for wreaths or tabletop trees, pinecones or an evergreen sprig, or an inexpensive holiday pin? (I scour garage sales and flea markets during the year for inexpensive costume-jewelry "baubles.")

There are lots of variations on traditional gift tags, once you start playing. Write with gold or silver ink on a genuine holly leaf, and apply it to the package with double-faced tape. Use cookie cutters to trace holiday shapes onto a brown paper bag, then cut them out to use as tags; buy a white gel marker and your message will look like icing. If you're skillful at origami, use a small folded figure, such as the ever-popular flying crane, as a combination tag and ornament. Fold a paper doily into a lacy gift card; cut white circles of paper into snowflakes; delight a little girl (or a grown one!) with an old-fashioned chain of paper dolls as her present's tag.

"Bright sun shines across the drifts / And bright upon my Christmas gifts," mused the nineteenth-century Canadian poet Marjorie L. C. Pickthall. But not half as bright as the smile on the person who receives your love wrapped up in ribbons and heartstrings.

Out and About

He went to the church, and walked about the streets,
and watched the people hurrying to and fro, and patted children
on the head, and questioned beggars, and looked down
into the kitchens of houses, and up to the windows,
and found that everything could yield him pleasure.
He had never dreamed that any walk — that anything —
could give him so much happiness.

—Charles Dickens

On the morning after his nightmarish time-travel, the enlightened Scrooge discovered exhilaration in the everyday. Dickens was describing the epitome of romancing the ordinary . . . and he was writing in 1843!

Happily, twenty-first-century Christmases may still provide these opportunities to romance the ordinary, and they don't require you to be scared witless first. Honestly, have you taken any time out from the hustle and bustle to soak up the sheer Christmasness of Christmas? Probably not. Let's take a walk.

This year, make finding your own "winter wonderland" a priority, wherever you live or work. Set aside a clear, bright evening for a leisurely stroll. Pick a neighborhood where you feel comfortable spending perhaps an hour or so after dusk. And then, just ramble along.

If you've picked a shopping district, peer into store windows to see how each owner has chosen to commemorate the season. How does the displayed merchandise reflect the holidays? You're window shopping for decorative ideas. Kitchenware all in red and green? Paper products in blue and silver? Party dresses and accessories? Imagine that you are a child, pressing your nose against a toy-shop window as if you're seeing it all for the very first time.

Look at the shoppers on the street beside you. Are they frazzled, tired, burdened with bundles and the feeling that holidays are a chore? Are they unenlightened Ebenezers swiftly passing the displays without seeing them? Forgo such companions for other shoppers, jubilant over their purchases. Do they join you to look at the brightly lit displays? Bask in their goodwill, and try exchanging a word or two about the sights you're sharing, or even about what gifts they may be bearing. Just saying "You look as if you've had fun shopping today!" might create a flash of camaraderie to lighten your way as both of you continue your walk.

One of my favorite rituals is to stroll through a neighborhood looking at all the different ways that people decorate their homes, from small wreaths on the doors or a dusting of snowflakes on the windowpanes, to all-out electrified extravaganzas. Can you see inside the windows? Which homes have proudly opened their drapes to show off a Christmas tree, blazing with colored lights? Don't feel shy about drinking in the sights. They were put there for you, too.

"There is nothing sadder in this world than to awake Christmas morning and not be a child," Erma Bombeck once sighed wistfully. "Time, self-pity, apathy, bitterness, and exhaustion can take the Christmas out of the child, but you cannot take the child out of

Christmas." What would make you feel like a child again . . . or what treat could you give yourself now that you always wanted as a child? When was the last time you wrote and mailed a letter to Santa? When was the last time you actually visited Santa? Hold your inner child by the hand, and join the line waiting to meet him in a department store. Sit on his lap, whisper your wishes, test whether his beard is real. Ask Santa what *he* wants for Christmas. You hold the power to make *his* day memorable, as well as yours. And yes, get a picture of the two of you, then frame and display it on the table where you'll leave Santa's milk and cookies.

You might be surprised come Christmas morning. You've been *very* good this year (probably too good, so at least reap some benefits . . .).

Dress up and take yourself to a performance of *The Nutcracker*. Whether you're a longtime fan or this is your first exposure to the ballet, curb your adult reactions and give yourself over completely to the experience. Notice how often the ballet exalts the magic of Clara's everyday world: toys that come to life; whirling snow; flowers that dance with the dewdrops; the unique personalities of such treats as hot chocolate, sugarplums, and marzipan. Really *listen* to the music as you watch the story unfold. How did Tchaikovsky make the tree *sound* as if it is growing? What makes the snow-scene music so . . . *snowy*? How skillfully does he capture the many moods and activities of a Christmas party that unites young and old? When the curtain is down and the lights are up, pay close attention to the excitement of your fellow pint-size attendees. How can you resist a smile at the little girls dressed so proudly in their holiday finery? Eavesdrop blatantly as they chatter about which ballerina *they* like best and strike balletic poses of their own. Admit it . . . in your heart of hearts, you're doing the same thing.

North Pole, we are making progress on the festive front.

The Believer

What has happened to me has been the very reverse of what appears to be the experience of most of my friends. Instead of dwindling to a point, Santa Claus has grown larger and larger in my life until he fills almost the whole of it. It happened in this way. As a child I was faced with a phenomenon requiring explanation. I hung up at the end of my bed an empty stocking, which in the morning became a full stocking. I had done nothing to produce the things that filled it. I had not worked for them, or made them or helped to make them. I had not even been good—far from it.

And the explanation was that a certain being whom people called Santa Claus was benevolently disposed toward me. . . .

And as I say, I believe it still. I have merely extended the idea. Then I only wondered who put the toys in the stocking; now I wonder who put the stocking by the bed, and the bed in the room, and the room in the house, and the house on the planet, and the great planet in the void. Once I only thanked Santa Claus for a few dolls and crackers, now I thank him for stars and street faces and wine and the great sea. Once I thought it delightful and astonishing to find a present so big that it only went halfway into the stocking. Now I am delighted and astonished every morning to find a present so big that it takes two stockings to hold it, and then leaves a great deal outside; it is the large and preposterous present of myself, as to the origin of which I can offer no suggestion except that Santa Claus gave it to me in a fit of peculiarly fantastic goodwill.

—G. K. Chesterton
The Tablet 2

Come to Your Senses

Trees Telling Tales

Many give Prince Albert credit for originating the ritual of tree decorating in England in the early 1840s. But Victoria's German-born consort was simply bringing to his British hearth a custom well established in his homeland. A widely circulated 1848 engraving of the royal family gathered by their tree launched the notion that you didn't have to be German to trim the branches.

In illustrations of Victorian Christmases, small, unwrapped gifts and edible treats—what we would now deem stocking-stuffers—hang from the boughs of trees, along with garlands of fruits and nuts and wax candles. (*Do not even think of* imitating this custom at home. Their trees were freshly cut and a servant stood by with a bucket of water!) Larger presents, such as rocking horses or dolls, were left unwrapped around the base. The tree was transformed into a glowing, glorious gift basket bearing "fruits" that could be plucked from the branches and enjoyed—not just admired, hands off. Because the tree was decorated on Christmas

Eve, after the children were asleep, their discovery of it the next morning was as big a part of the joy of the holidays as were the gifts. But that kind of surprise is virtually impossible for most women to pull off.

Do you struggle each year to dream up a new decorative "theme" for your tree, even if it means spending a small fortune to make everything match? Or do you prefer the tree of least resistance, hauling out long-familiar trimmings hung from habit or economy? You can break from tradition by rediscovering the pleasures of an *old* ritual. Create a fresh look using all-natural materials—articles and supplies that are already a part of your home—and the presents themselves.

String cranberries, air-popped popcorn, or small balls crumpled from aluminum or colored foils to create lightweight ropes or dangling grapelike clusters. Loop ribbons or lace around fruit and nuts, and hang them from the branches (you don't have to guess my favorite). Hang pinecones or sprigs of other holiday foliage.

Cut extra gift wrap into small strips and loop them into old-fashioned paper chains. Make miniature cascades of curling ribbon. Unfurl a spool of fabric ribbon as a garland, or tie bows onto the branch tips. Fold brightly colored papers and foils into decorative shapes—pleat a square of tissue, then tie it tightly through the center; fold a round paper doily in half and then pleat it into a fan. Hang as tree ornaments the Christmas cards you receive.

If a Christmas tree could be monogrammed with your personality, what would it be? Do you love to bake? Trim the tree with cookie cutters, buffed-to-shining measuring spoons and cups, and holiday-patterned muffin or candy cups. Do you sew? Unfurl your fabric edgings into garlands, and hang your thread spools as individual ornaments. If you crochet, buy a cone or two of white or sparkly cotton, and hand-hook snowflake or flower motifs. Do you love jewelry? Transform necklaces into sparkling garlands . . . hang beaded bracelets from the branches . . . pin on your brooches and earrings. If you collect teacups or demitasse cups, tie their handles to the boughs, along with pretty tea-bag packets or small boxes of tea. Create a scented tree: cut tissue or fabric circles, enclose a spoonful of sachet or peppermint leaves in each, and gather up the edges into fragrant puffs; or stud beribboned citrus fruits with

cloves. If you long for spring, burst your tree into bloom with silk flowers and rosette-trimmed ribbons, or even flower silhouettes clipped from printed fabrics. Create a whimsical "stocking tree" by hanging your sock collection from the branches, with candy canes or other small items poking from their tops.

Do you have a child (or your own sweet tooth) to delight? Ornament the tree Victorian-style with paper or lace mini-cornucopias of candies, string hole-in-the-middle sweets into garlands, or suspend candy canes from their looped tops. Bake gingerbread or other rolled, decorated cookies and hang them on the tree. Individually hang small toy gifts ("pretend" cookware, cars and trucks, dolls or action figures, etc.) instead of wrapping them into a single package and let your child find them on Christmas morning. (This last bit of decorating you *might* be able to pull off the night before.)

Don't forget the area around the tree. Instead of a purchased tree skirt, drape the base with a lace or velvet curtain panel, a holiday-theme tablecloth, a fluffy afghan or quilt; you might even pile colorful throw pillows all around. I love to pick up a few yards of lush upholstery remnants at the fabric store. You could arrange a simple white sheet and loosely loop extra ribbons on it or sprinkle the cloth with glitter. (I wouldn't, however, if you have small children or pets.) Collaborate with your child to create a fanciful scene with her favorite dolls or stuffed animals, a train set, or even brightly colored pull toys . . . or make your own tableau and surprise the child with new, unwrapped gifts. (At our house you could always identify Santa's bounty because his gifts were never wrapped. He didn't have the time and neither do you!)

However you trim your tree, enjoy its company throughout the holiday; sample tidbits from the branches or simply delight in the way its "arms" so readily hold all you have given it of yourself. The poet Ezra Pound asks us to "Learn of the green world what can be thy place / In scaled invention or true artistry." Perhaps he was inspired by the sight of a Christmas tree.

O Holy Night

Christmas Eve is the Ceremonial of Gifts, of gifts that
are given to explain something which the heart cannot say.

—Abbie Graham

This is the night of Madonna and Child, but it's not silent. That's because the child has taken over the kitchen in a baking frenzy, Madonna's feeling like a virgin for the very first time, and the child's mother doesn't know whether to laugh or cry, so she's doing both. Actually, my baby—home from her first semester at college—can play any kind of music she wants tonight. I didn't get around to baking Christmas cookies this year, and if she wants to fill the void, well, bless her little baby big girl heart. But we do have guests coming over for Christmas Eve dinner in less than an hour and I would love to have access to my oven. Okay, no warm wild-mushroom profiteroles with our seasonal drinks. I suppose they'll keep until tomorrow and so will our festive moods, if Mom's willing to improvise. Do you think celery boats with chèvre and walnuts will go nicely with champagne? Hmmmm. The recipe says they need to be refrigerated for several hours in advance. Perhaps that's not *really* necessary. If it is, we'll just pop another cork and open up the olives.

"Little baby big girl" was what I used to call Kate when she was a toddler, during those precious years when she'd run ahead on her own, fearless as long as Mom was still in view when she glanced back. It's impossible not to glance back on Christmas Eve. My happiest Christmas, until tonight, was her first. She was just a few weeks old and I was nursing her by the lights of the Christmas tree. Suddenly, she paused and looked up and straight into the windows of my soul. After the longest stare, she broke into a huge grin. Newborn babies smile instinctively from contentment, but this was her first smile of recognition. *I know you! You're my mother!* Perhaps she was having her first reunion with her past life. I know I was experiencing my future perfect promise. The real Christmas miracle: we birthed each other.

Over the years as she grew in grace and wisdom before Spirit and her astonished mother, the baby I had held that night would help a blind woman see again, restore hearing to my ears with the lilt of her laughter, calm with the touch of her hand the storms of discouragement and discontent raging in my heart. What we call a miracle, Heaven calls Love.

Perhaps because the world frequently requires us to walk on water, women become expert at doing what everyone says can't be done. The oil for one night burns in the temple for eight (or the money stretches till the end of the month), leftovers become a feast, hurts are healed with a kiss, the shoe that cannot be found *anywhere* is recovered, the yearlong science project that *must* be finished in less than twelve hours (and this is the first you've heard of it) goes to school in the morning.

Look, you've done it again. Christmas has arrived and you've survived. What's more, you're ready. Or if you're not, you're as ready as you will be. Or should be. So stop. I bring you glad tidings. They'll never miss the wild-mushroom profiteroles if you're smiling and don't confess. (Celery boats with chèvre and walnuts *do* need to chill for several hours, though, in case you're curious.)

Ponder this. The first Christmas unfolded the way it did because, one ancient night, an exhausted and harried innkeeper's wife *stopped* long enough to be moved by the power of Love. She *improvised* so that a frightened, unmarried teenage girl about to give birth to her first child could be comforted. And in so doing, she midwifed a miracle that would change the world. Forgive me if you must, but may I gently point out that on the first Christmas Eve, God the Father was in Heaven. God the Great Mother was on earth. In my heart, I see the older woman leaving the crowded, rowdy dining room and rushing up the stairs to her bedroom, opening up a trunk, and bringing forth her *best,* making sure that all she *had* would be all the mother and baby would *need.* She gathers in her arms linen and silk, the blankets from her own bed, her favorite shawl.

In my imagination, I can also *see* the young girl's thankful smile, *hear* her sigh of relief, *taste* the salt in her tears. I *smell* not only a barn but the aroma of the broth the older woman helped the younger sip to keep up her strength. As I hug my own daughter, I can *feel* the reassurance both women felt in each other's presence. I *know* that the older woman's sacred gift of generosity and the younger woman's gratitude are not insignificant footnotes to what has been called the Greatest Story Ever Told. It's how the *Wonder* unfolded.

"On Christmas Eve love is clothed with visible vestments, with gifts and written words, with holly-wreaths and flowers and candles. The love that through the year is silenced by busy-ness is expressed in terms of tangible beauty," Abbie Graham wrote in 1928. "As I watch the Christmas candles burn, I see in them a symbol of the Great Love which dipped a lustrous spirit into human form so that the world in its darkness might be illumined and made beautiful."

It's not blasphemy to believe that on that Holy Night, the Lustrous Spirit that helped light the world's darkness wasn't coming only from the Child.

There were also two women in that stable. Tonight two women are in the kitchen.

Come to Your Senses

Blooming Change

"It is winter proper; the cold weather, such as it is, has come to stay. I bloom indoors in the winter like forced forsythia; I come in to come out." So the writer Annie Dillard tells us. "At night I read and write, and things I have never understood become clear; I reap the harvest of the rest of the year's planting."

Change ambushes us so many times, upsetting our comfortable routines. But in January, which will soon be here, change is expected, even invited. We are hopeful for its opportunities and all the possibilities the New Year has to offer. However, by the time most of us feel not just the desire but the motivation to make changes in our life, we're overcome with impatience, even if we intellectually know that lasting change only happens gradually.

One of my favorite new ways to celebrate personal change is to plant a small indoor bulb garden. Different bulbs can be "forced" throughout the year, but in January, I plant paperwhites. Using twigs and small tags, I label each new positive impulse—"Be more adventurous," "Flirt every day with someone new," or "Make bed every day"—and tie it to the shoots of a bulb. This is much more festive than listing one's wavering resolve on paper.

Psychologists tell us that it takes twenty-one days for a new habit to take hold, which is just about the time it takes for most indoor bulbs to bloom. What I love about this ritual is that it keeps reminding me in a fresh way that positive, conscious change brings about unexpected beauty in our daily round.

On some days, nothing much seems to be happening in my bulb garden or in my life, but looking at the slow, steady growth of the bulbs is an encouraging prompt to keep at it. Suddenly overnight there is a growth spurt, inner and outer. "Our consciousness rarely registers the beginning of a growth within us any more than without us," George Eliot wrote in *Silas Marner*. "There have been many circulations of the sap before we detect even the smallest sign of the bud."

What new change would you like to plant this week?

Going One-on-One

If all the year were playing holidays,
To sport would be as tedious as to work.

—William Shakespeare

*P*iano tinkling, glasses clinking, clock ticking. New Year's Eve. Does the thought of parties and blow horns leave you feeling out in the cold, nose pressed against the glass of others' festivities, even if you are in the middle of them? Surely this has to be one of the most pressured "date nights" of the year for those who are alone, right up there with Valentine's Day. But even if you're not alone, the pressure to be jovial is horrendous.

So make a change for the better. Cut loose from the tension by seeking out the real meaning of this night. Out with the old year, in with the new. *Your* year, not that of a crowd screaming a countdown.

Go ahead and dress up, light some candles, place a bottle of champagne on ice. Instead of tuning in to Times Square, put on whatever music or video was your most exciting discovery this past year. While you're at it, set out other items you can admire as evidence of time well spent: recently purchased or renewably beloved books, that wonderful hat you found in a vintage shop . . . the memo your boss sent around announcing your promotion . . . a souvenir from that dreamy cruise you took last summer. . . .

Did you write in the diary you so faithfully promised yourself you would at the beginning of the year? Crack it out, even if you didn't *quite* keep it up. What about a Gratitude Journal? A Wonder Book? Even a written-in datebook will do. Revisit yourself during these last twelve months. Remember. Relive. What were your red-letter days? Red-eyed days? With whom or where did you have the best times?

Think about the people who have mattered to you in this last year, and also about those you perhaps feel a trifle guilty toward for having neglected or lost touch with. Who is *missing* from your datebook of this last year? Who is a special addition to it? Make yourself a list of people with whom you may not exchange holiday cards, but whom it would feel so good to call over the next few weeks just to say, "Now that the Christmas crunch is over, let's find some time to get together," or, "I just wanted to say that I realized, when thinking over this last year, that the office is so much cheerier now that you're on our staff." Or take a pen and paper to honestly write, "I'm sitting here on New Year's Eve and just realized how long it's been since I've heard from you . . ." How many more years will go by if you wait primly for the *other* person to pick up the phone or the pen? If you are thinking of him or her now, go ahead, take the first step toward renewing contacts you wish to continue. Dame Fortune can't change your destiny on her own.

If your aloneness has been pressing upon you, think of one new thing to do in this new year, to place yourself among others who share your interests. Joining a film club or taking a theater subscription, volunteering at a soup kitchen or a museum, or even just placing yourself regularly at a place where familiarity might lead to conversation (why not give yourself Sunday brunch dates at the same café, for example). These are all comfortable methods of mingling, even for the shyest woman in the world, and you're in the company of one now.

That brings us to yet another way to spend New Year's Eve. Why need it be thought of as only a loud-party time or a "date night"? Are you close to (or do you wish you were close to) another person who may, too, be staying home? Why not spend the evening *together,* quietly toasting in the New Year as well as celebrating your mutual good company? Think about it: Wouldn't it be lovely to wait up till midnight, almost as if for Santa Claus, with a favorite child who might indeed need a sitter if his or her parents wish to go out on this night? What about that sweet elderly neighbor? Go ahead, knock on her door bearing sherry and cookies and a big smile. Or why not arrange an exactly midnight phone date with a cherished out-of-town relative or friend?

And even if your eyes are too heavy-lidded to stay up for the New Year's arrival in your time zone, you've plenty of other midnights to choose from. As we realized with particular potency on the night of the second millennium, New Year's Eve strikes twelve at one-hour intervals all around the globe. In fact, you might find so many ways to welcome the New Year that one midnight won't be enough to accomplish it all! But isn't having a choice a delicious dilemma?

Once More with Feeling

There are times when Life surprises one,
and anything may happen, even what one had
hoped for.

—Ellen Glasgow

"Suddenly Old Year jumps up with a burst of energy. Time to be gone. He opens the twelve waiting trunks and in a frenzy tries to pack in all the treasure of the past months to take with him into that unknown place behind the stars," the English writer Phyllis Nicholson wrote in *Country Bouquet,* a memoir of months, published in 1947. It seems hard to believe that just four splendid seasons ago we were given the same gift. If we did not cherish each day when it greeted us, did we even notice its arrival or departure? If we didn't, what did we miss?

Old Year knows, which is why he's not letting one sensory pleasure of this last year escape his grasp. "Yesterday's daffodils, June's rose-embroidered gown, September's frock of sunlit amber. With greedy hands he falls upon the wealth of loveliness about him, fearful to make his long dark journey alone into the emptiness that divides us from eternity. But he cannot take this beauty away. There is too much. How can all Nature be bundled into twelve small boxes? Sprays of lilac, primroses, waxen lilies, green and yellow leaves, bare branches of frosted silver fall behind him. Out tumbles the harvest moon, gleaming like a sovereign in the night. Old Year reaches for the rainbow, but the coloured arc eludes him in his haste. What of the nightingale's song, the scent of hay and mignonette? He cannot steal those, since they are locked for ever in our hearts."

Are they? I wonder.

One last look. One minor chord. One more taste. Just another

535

touch. A final scent to remember. Can you begin to choose? Thank Heavens we don't have to.

"One . . . two . . . midnight strikes over the cold quiet fields," Phyllis Nicholson wrote more than a half century ago. We open the door to let Old Year out "with such spoils as he can carry. But the burden is too heavy." Neither Life nor Love can be hoarded. "He drops it on the threshold, leaving the riches of twelve short months heaped about our feet."

And we gather them up once more. Grateful, days we once called ordinary are now aglow in simple splendor. Finally, we've come to our senses.

Blessed are we among women, and we know it.

Upon Finishing
This Book

*If we had keen vision and feeling for all ordinary
human life, it would be like hearing the grass
grow and the squirrel's heart beat, and we should
die of the roar which lies on the other side of silence.*

—George Eliot

*B*efore I embraced each day as a hopeful romantic, I never
truly appreciated the magic and mysticism of the English
writer George Eliot's observation. However, a week after finishing this book I visited friends in Edinburgh, a city clad in mystery because most of the time it's also misted in fog and rain. In
Scotland one soon learns that pleasures can't be contingent on the
weather, which, actually, is a handy attitude because the sooner
we accept the clammy bits with good humor, the sooner we make
room for the unexpected and unforgettable. As we were roaming
through the Royal Botanical Gardens, drenched to the skin, one
of my friends took a small bag of nuts out of her purse, jangled it,
and told me to get ready for a surprise. Quite frankly, I wasn't
interested in surprises, I just wanted to get into some warm, dry
clothes. But then suddenly, out from beneath the bushes came
two squirrels. They stopped for a moment, looked at us, then at
each other. Next, they slid across the soaking grass with nothing
less than a sense of glee. When they reached our ankles, both fine
fellows sat up on their hind legs and begged for treats. We burst

out laughing. My friend bent down with a handful of nuts, and one of the squirrels began eating out of her hand. The other little guy, still on his haunches, looked up at me, as if to say, "Get on with it, woman." Life was flirting with me.

Now, I'd never seen squirrels tame enough to eat out of your hand and was quite taken aback. Though we have plenty of squirrels in America, they shy away from human contact. While I hesitated, afraid of getting bitten, this little squirrel didn't peel his gaze from me. My friends reassured me that these particular Scottish squirrels were tame, not rabid, and besides, they didn't bite the hands that fed them. Meanwhile the beggar stared my common sense down by cocking his head from side to side with a swagger. Remember Rocky the Flying Squirrel? Well, here he was. But my mind was racing with red flags and caution (which in the States would have been warranted because wild animals do carry rabies, even if they're cute). Nonetheless, I was frozen in fear. But it wasn't fear of rabies as much as it was fear of the unknown. Finally I couldn't resist him, so I slowly bent down with a handful of nuts. He leaned in toward me and rested both tiny paws on my palm for a nanosecond before taking a nut and scurrying a few feet away to nibble it. Both our hearts were pounding, but I couldn't distinguish between them.

"Don't eat so fast," I whispered, but he wasn't listening. And so he came and went for a few minutes, repeating the ritual of politely resting his little hands in mine, then locking his gaze before taking a nut. His paws were so delicate, the pressure so slight, it sent shivers of pleasure up my spine. Recalling this exquisite moment, I remember the sight of raindrops on his head, transparent yet filled with a spectrum of color; the frosty spring air was fragrant with lilacs and dirt. But for my own sighs of wonder, I might even have heard the grass growing. Too soon, the spell was broken, and with his hunger appeased, my dashing, small, squat stranger scampered off, taking my heart with him, but leaving me with no regrets.

There were many other wonderful moments with my friends that glorious weekend, delicious food, sips of vintage champagne, much laughter, and even a few hours of Scottish sunshine, but when I think of how Life and I celebrated finishing this book, it's the memory of my seductive little go-between that makes me smile the most. Not just because of the magic of the encounter, but my receptivity. I've learned a lot through romancing the ordinary. Biggest lesson: Love wears many disguises. What's important is not what Love looks like at any moment, but whether or not Romance knows where to find *you*. Every day. Everywhere. In everything that you do or desire. Especially when you least expect it.

"To the one who knows how to look and feel, every moment of this free wandering life is an enchantment," the nineteenth-century adventuress Alexandra David-Neel reminisced in her memoirs. It's my prayer that as we've journeyed though the year together, you've discovered this sensuous secret in the sights, scents, sounds, tastes, and textures of what the world dismisses—your daily round.

Please go slowly. Give yourself permission to get caught up in the Rapture. Although this book was centered around one year, the living of it took me nearly two decades and its writing over two years. I've deliberately included more sensory pleasures in each chapter than you'll ever be able to dabble in on first go-round. Just pick one or two a month and gradually discover your essensual passions. Romance is more intoxicating when lovers take their time. Don't rush.

So savor, swoon, be swept away.

May your soul never be sated.

May you know the thrill of being ravished by Love in a public park on a cold, wet, ordinary day.

May you feel yourself beloved on the Earth.

—*Sarah Ban Breathnach*

Selected Bibliography

Enough, Friend.
If you want to read on,
Then go, yourself become the book
and its essence.

—Angelus Silesius

My sources for quotes have been many and varied. Collecting the pithy and the profound has been a passion of mine for more than twenty-five years, and I gather and glean from many sources: books, magazine articles, reviews, newspaper features, radio interviews, television broadcasts, plays, and film. However, my favorite collections of quotations are *The New Beacon Book of Quotations by Women,* compiled by Rosalie Maggio (Boston: Beacon Press, 1996); *Bartlett's Familiar Quotations,* 16th ed., edited by Justin Kaplan (Boston: Little, Brown and Company, 1992); *The Columbia Dictionary of Quotations,* compiled by Robert Andrews (New York: Columbia University Press, 1993); *The Oxford Dictionary of Quotations,* 5th ed., edited by Elizabeth Knowles (Oxford, England: Oxford University Press, 1999); *The Oxford Dictionary of Phrase, Saying, and Quotation,* edited by Elizabeth Knowles (Oxford, England: Oxford University Press, 1997); *The Oxford Dictionary of Literary Quotations,* edited by Peter Kemp (Oxford, England: Oxford University Press, 1997); and *Bartlett's Book of Anecdotes,* edited by Clifton Fadiman and Andre Bernard (Boston: Little, Brown and Company, 2000).

Abram, David. *The Spell of the Sensuous: Perception and Language in a More-than-Human World.* New York: Pantheon Books, 1996.
Ackerman, Diane. *Cultivating Delight: A Natural History of My Garden.* New York: HarperCollins Publishers, 2001.
———. *Deep Play.* New York: Random House, 1999.
———. *I Praise My Destroyer.* New York: Vintage Books, 1998.
———. *A Natural History of the Senses.* New York: Vintage Books, 1995.
Aftel, Mandy. *Essence and Alchemy: A Book of Perfume.* New York: North Point Press/Farrar, Straus & Giroux, 2001.
Alexander, Jane. *Spirit of the Home: How to Make Your Home a Sanctuary.* London: Thorsons, HarperCollins Publishers, 1999.
Allende, Isabel. *Aphrodite: A Memoir of the Senses.* New York: HarperFlamingo, 1998.
Anglesey, The Marchioness of. *The Countrywoman's Year.* London: Michael Joseph Ltd., 1960.

Ban Breathnach, Sarah. *The Illustrated Discovery Journal: Creating a Visual Auto-biography of Your Authentic Self.* New York: Warner Books, 1999.

———. *A Man's Journey to Simple Abundance.* Ed. Michael Segall. New York: The Simple Abundance Press/Scribner, 2000.

———. *Sarah Ban Breathnach's Mrs. Sharp's Traditions: Reviving Victorian Family Celebrations of Comfort and Joy.* New York: The Simple Abundance Press/Scribner, 2001.

———. *Simple Abundance: A Day Book of Comfort and Joy.* New York: Warner Books, 1995.

———. *The Simple Abundance Companion: Following Your Authentic Path to Something More.* New York: Warner Books, 2000.

———. *The Simple Abundance Journal of Gratitude.* New York: Warner Books, 1997.

———. *Something More: Excavating Your Authentic Self.* New York: Warner Books, 1998.

Bauch, Nancy, and Michelle Lizieri. *Awaiting a Lover.* New York: Viking Studio, 2000.

Beck, Martha Nibley. *Finding Your Own North Star: Claiming the Life You Were Meant to Live.* New York: Three Rivers Press, 2002.

———. *Real Simple,* "Lies About Love." February 2001.

Bedichek, Roy. *The Sense of Smell.* Garden City, N.Y.: Doubleday & Company, 1960.

Begg, Deike. *Synchronicity: The Promise of Coincidence.* London: Thorsons, HarperCollins Publishers, 2001.

Berger, John. *About Looking.* New York: Vintage International, 1991.

———. *The Sense of Sight.* New York: Vintage International, 1985.

———. *Ways of Seeing.* London: British Broadcasting Corporation and Penguin Books, 1972.

Bernstein, Francis. *Classical Living: Reconnecting with the Rituals of Ancient Rome.* San Francisco: Harper San Francisco, 2000.

Birkitt, Dea. *Spinsters Abroad: Victorian Lady Explorers.* Oxford: Basil Blackwell Ltd., 1989.

Blahnik, Judith. *Checklist for a Perfect Christmas.* New York: Mainstreet Books, Doubleday Publishers, 1996.

Bodine, Echo. *A Still, Small Voice: A Psychic's Guide to Awakening Intuition.* Novato, Calif.: New World Library, 2001.

Bowes, Susan. *Notions and Potions: A Safe, Practical Guide to Creating Magic and Miracles.* New York: Sterling Publishing Co., 1997.

Bradley, Marion Zimmer. *Mists of Avalon.* New York: Ballantine Publishing Group, 1982.

Browning, Dominique. *Around the House and in the Garden: A Memoir of Heart-break, Healing and Home Improvement.* New York: Scribner, 2002.

Browning, Frank. *Apples: The Story of the Fruit of Temptation.* New York: North Point Press/Farrar, Straus & Giroux, 1998.

Brussat, Frederic, and Mary Ann Brussat. *Spiritual Literacy: Reading the Sacred in Everyday Life.* New York: Scribner, 1996.

———. *Spiritual Rx: The Prescriptions for Living a Meaningful Life.* New York: Hyperion, 2000.

Burton, Sir Richard. *The Kama Sutra of Vatsyayana.* London: Benares, 1883.

Calvert, Catherine. "Porch Swings, Old Novels, and Memories of Summer Past." In *The Quiet Center: Women Reflecting on Life's Passages from the Pages of Victoria Magazine*. Ed. Katherine Ball Ross. New York: Hearst Books, 1997.

Cameron, Julia. *The Artist's Way*. New York: Putnam Publishing Group, 1992.

———. *The Vein of Gold: A Journey to Your Creative Heart*. New York: G. P. Putnam's Sons, 1996.

Carlino, Cristina. *The Rainbow Connection: How to Use Color and Energy to Transform Your Life*. New York: Doubleday, 1999.

Carson, Rachel. *A Sense of Wonder*. New York: HarperCollins Publishers, 1988.

Chesterton, G. K. *The Tablet 2*. London: Tablet Publishing Co., 1974.

Chiazzari, Suzy. *The Healing Home: Creating the Perfect Place to Live with Color, Aroma, Light and Other Natural Elements*. London: Ebury Press, 1998.

Close, Barbara. *Well-Being: Rejuvenating Recipes for Body and Soul*. Chronicle Books, San Francisco, 2000.

Colwin, Laurie. "Gingerbread." In *Home Cooking: A Writer in the Kitchen*. New York: HarperPerrenial, 1993.

Conger, Nancy. *Sensuous Living: Expand Your Sensory Awareness*. St. Paul, Minn.: Llewellyn Publications, 1996.

Cooper, David A. *God Is a Verb: Kabbalah and the Practice of Mystical Judaism*. New York: Riverhead Books, 1997.

Cooper, Jilly. *How to Survive Christmas*. London: Bantam Press, 1998.

Coren, Victoria. "War on WILTS—or Women in Leather Trousers." *The Daily Mail*, May 16, 2002, p. 52.

Cox, Janice. *Natural Beauty for all Seasons: 250 Simple Recipes and Gift-Giving Ideas for Year-Round Beauty*. New York: Henry Holt and Company, 1996.

Crawford, Ilse. *The Sensual Home: Liberate Your Senses and Change Your Life*. London: Quadrille Publishing Limited, 1997.

Curott, Phyllis. *Book of Shadows: A Woman's Journey into the Wisdom of Witchcraft and the Magic of the Goddess*. New York: Broadway Books, 1999.

———. *Witch Crafting: A Spiritual Guide to Making Magic*. New York: Broadway Books, 2001.

Daglish, E. Fitch. *Enjoying the Country*. London: Faber and Faber, 1952.

Damon, Bertha. *Green Corners*. London: Michael Joseph Ltd., 1947.

Davis, Alison. *A Sense of Wonder: A Spiritual Guidebook*. Hampton, Conn.: Little River Press, 1984.

Dement, William C. *The Promise of Sleep*. New York: Delacorte Press, 1999.

Dolnick, Barrie. *Simple Spells for Hearth and Home: Ancient Practices for Creating Harmony, Peace, and Abundance*. New York: Harmony, 2000.

———. *Simple Spells for Love: Ancient Practices for Emotional Fulfillment*. New York: Harmony, 1994

———. *Simple Spells for Success: Ancient Practices for Creating Abundance and Prosperity*. New York: Harmony, 1996.

Dolnick, Barrie, Julia Condon, and Donna Limoges. *Sexual Bewitchery and Other Ancient Feminine Wiles*. New York: Avon Books, 1998.

Domar, Alice D., and Henry Dreher. *Self-Nurture: Learning to Care for Yourself as Effectively As You Care for Everyone Else*. New York: Viking Press, 1999.

Dunne, Catherine Bailly. *Interior Designing for All 5 Senses*. New York: Golden Books, 1998.

Edwards, Gill. *Pure Bliss: The Art of Living in Soft Time*. London: Piatkus, 1999.

Ellis, Aytour. *The Essence of Beauty: A History of Perfume and Cosmetics.* London: Secker & Warburg, 1960.

Esquivel, Laura. *Like Water for Chocolate: A Novel in Monthly Installments, with Recipes, Romances, and Home Remedies.* New York: Doubleday, 1992.

Fairbrother, Nan. *The Cheerful Day.* New York: Alfred A. Knopf, 1960.

————. *An English Year.* New York: Alfred A. Knopf, 1954.

Fearon, Ethelind. *Most Happy Husbandman.* London: Macdonald & Co. Publishers Ltd., 1946.

Fisher, M.F.K. *With Bold Knife and Fork.* New York: Smith Mark Publishers, 1996.

Florian, Douglas. *Winter Eyes.* New York: Greenwillow/HarperCollins Publishers, 1999.

Franck, Frederick. *The Zen of Seeing: Seeing/Drawing as Meditation.* New York: Vintage Books, 1973.

Fraser, Kennedy. *Ornament and Silence.* New York: Alfred A. Knopf, 1996.

Gaynor, Mitchell L. *Sounds of Healing: A Physician Reveals the Therapeutic Power of Sound, Voice and Music.* New York: Broadway Books, 1999.

Gillotte, Galen. *Book of Hours: Prayers to the Goddess.* St. Paul, Minn.: Llewellyn Publications, 2001.

Goldstein, Darra. *The Winter Vegetarian: A Warm and Versatile Bounty.* New York: HarperPerennial, 2000.

Graf, Susan Johnston. *W. B. Yeats: Twentieth-Century Magus.* York Beach, Maine: Samuel Weiser, Inc., 2000.

Graham, Abbie. *Ceremonials of Common Days.* New York: The Woman's Press, 1923.

Hamill, Sam, ed. *The Erotic Spirit: An Anthology of Poems of Sensuality, Love and Longing.* London: Shambhala, 1999.

Hardie, Titania. *Enchanted: Titania's Book of White Magic.* London: Quadrille Publishing Limited, 1999.

————. *Witch in the Kitchen.* San Rafael, Calif.: CEDCO Publishing Co., 2001.

Harrison, Barbara Grizzuti. In *Out of the Garden: Women Writers on the Bible.* Ed. Christina Buchmann and Ceilina Spiegel. New York: Fawcett Books, 1994.

Heilbrun, Carolyn G. "Unmet Friends." In *Writing a Woman's Life.* New York: W. W. Norton & Company, 1988.

Henderson, Julie. *The Lover Within: Opening to Energy in Sexual Practice.* Barrytown, N.Y.: Station Hill Press, 1987.

Heuer, Ann Rooney. *Creating the Peaceful Home.* New York: Friedman/Fairfax, 1999.

Hoffman, Donald D. *Visual Intelligence: How We Create What We See.* New York: W. W. Norton & Company, 1998.

Holland, Barbara. *Endangered Pleasures: In Defense of Naps, Bacon, Martinis, Profanity, and Other Indulgences.* Boston: Little, Brown and Co., 1995.

Holmes, Marjorie. *Beauty in Your Own Backyard.* McLean, Va.: EPM Publications, Inc., 1976.

Hopkins, Martha, and Randall Lockride. *Intercourses: An Aphrodisiac Cookbook.* Memphis, Tenn.: Terrace Publishing, 1997.

Housden, Roger. *Soul and Sensuality: Returning the Erotic to Everyday Life.* London: Rider, 1993.

Hunt, Roland. *Fragrant and Radiant Healing Symphony.* Essex, England: C. W. Daniel Company Ltd., 1937.

Hurley, Judith Benn. *Savoring the Day: Recipes and Remedies to Enhance Your Natural Rhythms.* New York: William Morrow & Company, 1997.

544

Irion, Mary Jean. *Yes World*. New York: R. W. Baron, 1970.

Jaffe, Azriela. *Create Your Own Luck: 8 Principles of Attracting Good Fortune in Life, Love and Work*. Avon, Mass.: Adams Media Corporation, 2000.

Johnson, Anna. *Three Black Skirts: All You Need to Survive*. New York: Workman Publishing, 2000.

Keller, Helen. "Three Days to See." *Atlantic Monthly,* January 1933.

Kendall, Elizabeth. *House into Home*. England: J. M. Dent & Sons, 1962.

Koren, Leonard. *Wabi-Sabi for Artists, Designers, Poets & Philosophers*. Berkeley: Stone Bridge Press, 1994.

Kunz, Edith. *Fatale: How French Women Do It*. Phoenix, Ariz.: Bridgewood Press, 2000.

Larmoth, Jeanine. *Victoria: The Romance of Hats*. New York: Hearst Books, 1994.

Lawlor, Anthony. *A Home for the Soul: A Guide for Dwelling with Spirit and Imagination*. New York: Clarkson Potter Publishers, 1997.

Lawrence, Robyn Griggs. "Imperfect Beauty." *Natural Home,* May/June 2001.

Leigh, Michelle Dominique. *The Japanese Way of Beauty: Natural Beauty and Health Secrets*. London: Thorsons, HarperCollins Publishers, 1994.

L'Engle, Madeleine. *Two Part Invention: The Story of a Marriage (The Crosswick's Journal, Book 4)*. New York: Farrar, Straus & Giroux, 1988.

Levy, Naomi. *Talking to God: Personal Prayers for Times of Joy, Sadness, Struggle and Celebration*. New York: Alfred A. Knopf, 2002.

Lindbergh, Anne Morrow. *Gift from the Sea*. New York: Random House, Inc., 1955.

———. *North to the Orient*. New York: Harcourt, Brace & Company, 1935.

Lloyd, Claire. *Sensual Living*. London: Conran Octopus Limited, 1998.

Lovric, Michelle. *How to Write Love Letters*. Knoxville, Tenn.: Shooting Star Press, 1996.

McClanahan, Rebecca. *Word Painting*. Cincinnati, Ohio: Writer's Digest Books, 1999.

McCoy, Edain. *Bewitchments: Love Magick for Modern Romance*. St. Paul, Minn.: Llewellyn Publications, 2001.

———. *Enchantments: 200 Spells for Bath and Beauty*. St. Paul, Minn.: Llewellyn Publications, 2000.

McSweeney, Kerry. *The Language of the Senses*. London: McGill-Queen's University Press, 1998

Mannes, Marya. *But Will It Sell?* Philadelphia/New York: J. P. Lippincott Co., 1964.

Mansfield, Katherine. *Bliss & Other Stories*. Hertfordshire, England: Wordsworth Editions Ltd., 1998.

Matthews, Caitlin. *Celtic Devotional: Daily Prayers and Blessings*. New York: Harmony Books, 1996.

———. *Celtic Love*. New York: Harper San Francisco, 2000.

Maurine, Camille, and Lorin Roche. *Meditation Secrets for Women: Discovering Your Passion and Inner Peace*. San Francisco: Harper San Francisco, 2001.

Mendelson, Cheryl. *Home Comforts: The Art and Science of Keeping House*. New York: Scribner, 1999.

Merker, Hannah. *Listening*. New York: HarperCollins Publishers, 1994.

———. *Listening: Ways of Hearing in a Silent World*. Dallas, Tex.: Southern Methodist University Press, 1992.

Millar, Elisabeth. *The Fragrant Veil*. St. Paul, Minn.: Llewellyn Publications, 2000.

Millay, Edna St. Vincent. "Renascence." *Collected Poems: Edna St. Vincent Millay*. New York: Harper and Row, 1956.

Milne, Lorus, and Margery Milne. *The Senses of Animals and Men.* London: Andre Deutsh Limited, 1963.

Montgomery, L. M. *Anne of Green Gables.* New York: Grammercy, 1998

Moore, Thomas. *The Re-Enchantment of Everyday Life.* New York: HarperCollins Publishers, 1996.

———. *The Soul of Sex: Cultivating Life as an Act of Love.* New York: Harper-Collins Publishers, 1998.

Muller, Wayne. *Sabbath: Restoring the Sacred Rhythm of Rest.* Oxford, England: Lion Publishing Plc., 1999.

Myss, Carolyn. *Sacred Contracts: Awakening Your Divine Potential.* New York: Harmony Books, 2001.

Nicholson, Phyllis. *Country Bouquet.* London: John Murray Publishers, 1947.

Norris, Gunilla. *Being Home.* New York: Bell Tower, 1991.

O'Donohue, John. *Anam Cara: A Book of Celtic Wisdom.* New York: Cliff Street Books, 1997.

Pagram, Beverly. *Folk Wisdom for a Natural Home.* North Pomfret, Vt.: Trafalgar Square, 1997.

Perers, Kristin. *The Seasonal Home: Decorating Ideas Inspired by the Seasons.* London: Ryland, Peters & Small, 1998.

Person, Ethel S. *Dreams of Love and Fateful Encounters.* New York: W. W. Norton and Co., 1988.

Peske, Nancy, and Beverly West. *Cinematherapy: The Girl's Guide to Movies for Every Mood.* New York: Dell, 1999.

Pollan, Michael. *The Botany of Desire: A Plant's Eye View of the World.* London: Bloomsbury Publishing, 2002.

Raine, Kathleen. *Collected Poems.* New York: Random House, 1956.

Ree, Johnathan. *I See a Voice: Deafness, Language and the Senses—a Philosophical History.* New York: Metropolitan Books, H. Holt and Co., 1999.

Reeve, Lindbergh. *No More Words: A Journal of My Mother, Anne Morrow Lindbergh.* New York: Simon & Schuster, 2001.

Rice, Edward. *Captain Sir Richard Francis Burton.* New York: Scribner, 1990.

Ripperger, Henrietta. *A Home of Your Own and How to Run It.* New York: Simon & Schuster, 1940.

Robinson, E. Kay. *The Country Day by Day.* London: Holden & Hardingham Ltd., 1921.

Robinson, Jane. *Unsuitable for Ladies: An Anthology of Women Travellers.* Oxford: Oxford University Press, 1994.

Robinson, Marilynne. *Housekeeping.* New York: Noonday Books, 1997.

Robyn, Kathryn L. *Spiritual Housecleaning: Healing the Space Within by Beautifying the Space Around You.* Oakland, Calif.: New Harbinger Publications, 2001.

Rohde, Eleanour Sinclair. *Rose Recipes from Olden Times.* London: Routledge, 1939.

Rosenzweig, Ilene, and Cynthia Rowley. *Swell: A Girl's Guide to the Good Life.* New York: Warner Books, 1999.

Sark. *Eat Mangoes Naked: Finding Pleasure Everywhere and Dancing with the Pits.* New York: A Fireside Book, Simon & Schuster, 2001.

Sarton, May. *Journal of a Solitude.* New York: W. W. Norton, 1973.

Schaef, Anne Wilson. *Meditations for Living in Balance.* San Francisco: Harper San Francisco, 2000.

Sexson, Lynda. *Ordinary Sacred.* Charlottesville: University Press of Virginia, 1992.

Showers, Paul. *The Listening Walk.* New York: HarperCollins, 1991.

Sinetar, Marsha. *Reel Time: Spiritual Growth Through Film.* Ligouri, Mo.: Triumph Books, 1993.

Slung, Michele. *Living with Cannibals and Other Women's Adventures.* Washington, D.C.: Adventure Press/National Geographic Society, 2000.

Smith, Delia. *One Is Fun.* London: Hodder and Stoughton, 1985.

Smith, Dodie. *I Capture the Castle.* Boston: Little, Brown/An Atlantic Monthly Press Book, 1948.

Snyder, Rachel. *365 Words of Well-Being for Women.* Chicago: Contemporary Books, 1997.

Spaar, Lisa Russ. *Acquainted with the Night: Insomnia Poems.* New York: Columbia University Press, 1999.

Steinbach, Alice. *Without Reservations: The Travels of an Independent Woman.* New York: Random House, 2000.

Steindl-Rast, David. *A Listening Heart: The Spirituality of Sacred Sensuousness.* New York: Crossroad Publishing Co., 1999.

Tapert, Annette. *The Power of Glamour: The Women Who Defined the Magic of Stardom.* New York: Crown Publishing, 1998.

Tapert, Annette, and Diana Edkins. *The Power of Style: The Women Who Defined the Art of Living Well.* New York: Crown Publishers, 1994.

Toth, Susan Allen. *England for All Seasons.* New York: Ballantine Books, 1998.

Tressider, Megan. *The Secret Language of Love.* San Francisco: Chronicle Books, 1997.

Tuttle, Cameron. *The Bad Girl's Guide to Getting What You Want.* San Francisco: Chronicle Books, 2000.

Twain, Mark. *Eve's Diary.* New York: Harper & Brothers Publishers, 1906.

———. *Letters.* Vol. 2, 1896, p. 641.

Vienne, Veronique. *The Art of Doing Nothing: Simple Ways to Make Time for Yourself.* New York: Clarkson N. Potter Publishers, 1998.

———. *The Art of Imperfection: Simple Ways to Make Peace with Yourself.* New York: Clarkson N. Potter Publishers, 1999.

———. *French Style: How to Think, Shop and Dress Like a French Woman.* Columbus, Ohio: Express Publishers, 1993.

von Arnim, Elizabeth. *The Enchanted April.* London: Macmillan and Co. Ltd., 1922.

Wallace, Oliver A. *A Taste for Adventure.* Grand Rapids, Mich.: O-Washtonong Publishing Co., 1962.

Waterhouse, Debra. *Why Women Need Chocolate: Eat What You Crave to Look and Feel Great.* New York: Hyperion, 1995.

Wheeler, Karen. *The Scented Home: Living with Fragrance.* New York: Carlton Books Limited, 2000.

White, Michael. *Isaac Newton: The Last Sorcerer.* Reading, Mass.: Addison-Wesley, 1997.

Whyte, David. *The House of Belonging.* Langley, Wash.: Many Rivers Press, 1999.

Wilson, Frances. *Literary Seductions.* New York: St. Martin's Press, 1999.

Worwood, Valerie Ann. *The Fragrant Heavens: The Spiritual Dimensions of Fragrance and Aromatherapy.* Novato, Calif.: New World Library, 1999.

———. *Fragrant Sensuality: Aromatics and Nature's Essential Oils.* New York: Bantam Books, 1996.

With Thanks and Appreciation

Writing is an act of love. If not, it is merely paperwork.

–Jean Cocteau

I've always thought of my books as love affairs. Usually that's because the rites of courtship for both affairs of the heart and passions on the pages are similar, a roller coaster of emotion: desire, approach, flirtation, wooing, infatuation, lust, love, bliss, rapture, disappointment, adjustment, change, estrangement, reconciliation, reckoning, resolution, relinquishment. *Romancing the Ordinary* has been an ardent suitor for the last twenty years, appearing every so often but always at the wrong time and place, reminding me of Rhett Butler's wry comment to Scarlett O'Hara that he'd like to catch up with her "in between husbands." Well, eventually he does, and Captain Butler's invitation to get married "just once for fun" proves too irresistible for Scarlett to turn down. So it was with this book.

But no woman's romance is experienced (or endured) without the help, support, advice, and wisdom of her friends, and I'm indebted to some extraordinary women, particularly my intimate circle of personal assistants who gracefully cordon off the rest of the world so that I can write: Dawne Winter, Karen Woodard, Rebecca Frankel, and my sister, Maureen Crean, who oversees our Web site. My life's wondrous new chapter at Newton's Chapel could not have begun (or continue) without the enormous gifts and talents of Elaine M. Lees.

For creative brainstorming, always invite Joslyn King, Adina Kalish Neufeld, Wendy Posner, and Roma Halatyn to the party and you'll begin to bask in your own cleverness.

If Iris Bass ever asks you to come out and play, close the day planner and take a leap, especially if you're writing a book. Iris, who is an accomplished editor and writer, was generous enough to help me gather my scattered thoughts and then lose them again in one sensory romp after another. She taught me that if the work's not fun, then the writing's just paperwork, and I'm grateful. I'll look forward to another tutorial.

To my colleagues at Scribner and The Simple Abundance Press, more gratitude than words can say. While there are too many people to list individually, from editorial to production, marketing to publicity, I know your contribution and won't forget it.

As always, the contribution of two extraordinary women—my dear friend, literary agent, and business manager, Chris Tomasino, and my daughter, Kate Sharp—can't even be described. The truth is that every book deserves to be dedicated to them, but modest ladies that they are, they won't have it. Still, I think that by now my readership knows how much they mean to me; I only hope they do, too.

But each book bears the unique blessings of an invisible benefactor which is reflected in my dedication. I agree with W. B. Yeats that there is only true romance, the soul's, and during the long process of writing this book, my beloved confidant, Anne Windsor, gently helped a hopeless romantic become a true believer in the Church of Improbable Happy Endings. You hold this book in your hands, dear Reader, because Anne Windsor held the vision of it in her heart, especially during the rough patches when I believed I would never find love again in life, or on the page.

I only pray that all who helped me bring this special book into full being can read my affection, appreciation, and gratitude between every line.

Boundless blessings to you all.

Dearest love—
Sarah

—Sarah Ban Breathnach

Index

Photograph Credits and Permissions

Sarah Ban Breathnach would like to hear from you. Please write to:

Romancing the Ordinary
P.O. Box 77420
Washington, D.C. 20013

or

Visit her Web site at:

www.simpleabundance.com

To find out about forthcoming books from The Simple Abundance Press, and to register for The Simple Abundance Press e-mail update, please visit its Web site at:

www.simpleabundancepress.com